MICK & KEITH

The Pretenders
Paul McCartney: the Biography
Billy Bragg: Midnights in Moscow
Bob Marley: Songs of Freedom
Jimi Hendrix: the Ultimate Experience
Punk: the Illustrated History of a Music Revolution
Oliver Stone: the Making of His Movies
George Lucas: the Making of His Movies
Firefly: Noël Coward in Jamaica
Rude Boy: Once Upon a Time in Jamaica
Reggae Explosion: the Story of Jamaican Music

MICK & KEITH

Chris Salewicz

ORION

First published in Great Britain in 2002 by Orion
an imprint of Orion Books Ltd
Orion House, 5 Upper St Martin's Lane,
London WC2H 9EA

A CIP catalogue record for this book
is available from the British Library

ISBN 0 75281 858 9

Typeset by Selwood Systems, Midsomer Norton

Printed and bound by
Butler & Tanner Ltd, Frome and London

ER

CONTENTS

To my mother,
Margaret Salewicz

'MEMO FROM TURNER'

The only performance that makes it, that really makes it, that makes it all the way, is the one that achieves madness. Right? Am I right? – Turner

In August 1968, three weeks after his twenty-fifth birthday, Mick Jagger rented an Irish mansion in Tuam, County Galway. For Mick it was paramount that – even at 100 guineas a week, the price of the property – he have time in the peace of the wild Irish countryside, away from the pop music sycophants, police pressures and pot-smoking cosmic spivs of newly psychedelic London. He needed headspace to prepare for his part in a feature film he had signed up to star in, for $100,000 plus seven and a half per cent of the film's net profits. Marianne Faithfull, with whom he had now been in a relationship for almost exactly two years, was pregnant – if the baby was a girl, the couple had decided she would be called Corinna. But Marianne had been warned that there were some potential complications with her pregnancy: when she had last visited her Harley Street obstetrician he had prescribed complete rest.

The film Mick was about to make had first been discussed in 1966, when it was called *The Performers*, the brainchild of Donald Cammell, a painter turned screenwriter; he was part of the Chelsea set of bohemians and aristocrats into which Mick Jagger and Keith Richard, his schoolfriend and songwriting partner, had slid with ease following the success of the Rolling Stones. Cammell had failed to secure the services of Marlon Brando, a close friend, for the lead role in what was now titled *Performance*; but he had persuaded Mick to take it, convincing the Stones' singer that he was essentially typecast for the starring part. With graphic intensity the film's plotline revolved around the fall of Chas, a minor London gangster, a vicious bitplayer in a 'firm' modelled on those of the Kray and Richardson families. On the run from both the police and his own hoodlum associates, Chas finds what he thinks will be a refuge in the house of Turner, a reclusive rock star, whom Mick Jagger was to play. Also cast was James Fox, a

1

British actor of growing stature, as Chas, and Anita Pallenberg, formerly the girlfriend of Brian Jones and now firmly locked into a relationship with Keith Richard, who was to play Pherber, the female lead. Initially that part had been offered to Marianne Faithfull, but her pregnancy had prevented her taking the role.

Every Friday Mick would fly out from London for a long weekend with Marianne and Nicholas, her three-year-old son by John Dunbar, her husband of three years from whom she was separated. Although he had given the script of *Performance* a cursory reading, Mick to begin with had accepted Donald Cammell's vision that all he needed to do was play himself. Returning to Ireland, he quickly saw that his character of Turner ('Old rubber lips. 'E 'ad three number ones, two number twos and a number four,' was how Lorraine, the eight-year-old daughter of Mrs Gibbs, Turner's housekeeper, described him) bore only superficial resemblance to himself. Marianne Faithfull, with some thespian experience herself, suggested a solution – to play Turner as a cross between Brian Jones and Keith Richard: 'Brian with his self-torment and paranoia and Keith with his strength and cool'. Although Mick Jagger accepted his girlfriend's advice, turning Turner into a composite character, undercurrents of his own persona would inevitably leak into the part but not so much that they would cause an imbalance. There was, however, a consequence that had not even crossed Marianne's mind. 'What I hadn't anticipated,' she later realised, 'was that Mick, by playing Brian and Keith, would be playing two people who were extremely attractive to Anita and who were in turn obsessed with her.' As far as the future of the Rolling Stones was concerned, not to mention the relationship between Mick Jagger and Keith Richard, the repercussions of playing Turner would linger for the rest of their careers.

At the time of filming, *Beggars Banquet*, the Rolling Stones' newly completed album, was still awaiting release. When it finally hit the shops four months later in December 1968, the record's pièce de résistance would be the semi-epic, samba-based 'Sympathy For The Devil'. It was a number inspired by the novel *The Master and Margarita*, a satire by the Russian writer Mikhail Bulgakov which concerned an impromptu arrival by the devil, travelling under a number of assumed names, on the streets of Moscow in the aftermath of the Russian Revolution. Marianne Faithfull, ever keen to educate Mick Jagger in literary matters, had turned him on to the book; she herself had been introduced to it by Kenneth Anger, an artist and film-maker who was part of the set of chic London groovers attached to Mick, Marianne, Keith and Anita, and Donald Cammell.

Born in Los Angeles, Anger was the author of the book *Hollywood Babylon*, a notorious account of the salacious scandals that formed the seamy underside of Tinseltown. Yet he was equally well known as an artist, a pioneer of underground film-making who liked to experiment with innovative editing techniques; in the late 1960s Kenneth Anger's films were considered especially hip, drawing capacity crowds to their screenings at venues such as the Arts Lab in London. Much of his work was distinguished by its homoerotic content; this was especially true of *Scorpio Rising*, a celebration of biker culture, in which Anger intercut shots from *The Wild One*, the 1954 motorcycle-gang classic starring Marlon Brando, and images of Jesus Christ, played out to a rock 'n' roll soundtrack. A long-held personal obsession of Anger had been realised in the making of a film to be called *Lucifer Rising*; when it was finally released, retitled *Invocation of My Demon Brother*, on the underground circuit in 1969, a Moog synthesiser soundtrack by Mick Jagger accompanied a segment of the film – it was a consolation prize for the director, as he had tried hard to persuade Mick to take the part of Lucifer. As composer on the Anger film, Mick Jagger was replacing Bobby Beausoleil, also previously cast as Lucifer, a one-time member of the group Love and the lead guitarist and sitar-player for the Magick Powerhouse of Oz, a rock ensemble formed in San Francisco to perform the soundtrack. Beausoleil, who sincerely believed himself to be the devil, soon became a part of the murderous cult led by Charles Manson, and was ultimately sentenced to life imprisonment.

Anger would refer to his films as 'magickal spells', and indeed his reputation rested to some extent on his renown as an occultist and devotee of Aleister Crowley, who in the 1920s had been branded by the *Daily Express* 'the wickedest man in the world'. In Sicily Crowley had established something of a dark precursor of a hippy commune, a temple to strange 'magical' practices, free sex and drug-taking: 'Do what thou wilt shall be the whole of the law', was the conveniently self-justifying philosophy of Crowley's cruelty-streaked universe. Eventually he was kicked out of Italy by edict of the fascist dictator Benito Mussolini. Kenneth Anger visited the Sicilian building in 1955, ignoring the curses of locals – a dead cat was deposited on the doorstep on the day of his arrival – and spent three months attempting to restore it to its former state of inglory. Anger's fascination with Crowley extended to his having tattooed on his forearm the number 666, the mark of 'the Beast' (by which sobriquet Crowley was also known) from Revelation, the final book of the New Testament. It was an allure also felt by Donald Cammell, who admitted that Anger was 'the major influence at the time I made *Performance*'.

As suggested by his painterly credentials, Donald Cammell's background was not that of the usual English technician-director. Within the drug-befuddled atmosphere of the Stones' milieu, increasingly riddled with arcane occult references since the addition of Anita Pallenberg, his background was unimpeachable: his father, an academic at Edinburgh

University, was a close friend and biographer of Aleister Crowley. Crowley's sexual predilections, moreover, seemed to have taken a hold on Cammell: in Paris, where his endlessly social apartment had been a frequent port of call for, among others, Mick Jagger, Keith Richard and Brian Jones, Cammell had most recently lived in a *ménage à trois* with the model Deborah Dixon and sixteen-year-old Michèle Breton, who was cast in *Performance* as the gamine Lucy. Anita Pallenberg, given the part of female lead in *Performance*, also had a two-way fling with Cammell and Deborah Dixon. 'That was Donald's thing, threesomes,' said Marianne Faithfull. Hardly unexpectedly, therefore, the domestic arrangement of Turner, Jagger's character, was a similarly troilistic set-up with Pallenberg and Breton, in a house located at 81 Powis Square in west London's Notting Hill. The district was then a shabby, near-anarchic neighbourhood inhabited in equal parts by down-at-heel working-class Londoners, West Indians and such outsiders as artists, gays and hippies; the Portobello Road antiques market, which bisected the area, was all that would draw bourgeois 'straights' to Notting Hill. The film is littered with in jokes and artistic allusions: the Argentine writer Jorge Luis Borges, proto-rappers the Last Poets, the blues legend Robert Johnson and the celebrated heroin-addict author William Burroughs are all referred to at various times.

Donald Cammell had already secured a screenwriting credit for the film *Duffy*, an undistinguished would-be with-it caper movie. To guarantee his directing credit on *Performance*, Cammell had convinced Warner Brothers, the Hollywood studio producing the film, by telling them he would co-direct with his friend Nic Roeg, Britain's leading cinematographer. Roeg had an impressive track record that included shooting Francois Truffaut's *Fahrenheit 451*, John Schlesinger's *Far from the Madding Crowd* and Richard Lester's *Petulia*. Notwithstanding the portents brought to the film by the assorted assemblage of individuals involved, Cammell had done nothing to disabuse Warner of its delusion that the presence of Mick Jagger ensured it was taking on a wacky musical money-spinner along the lines of the Beatles' *A Hard Day's Night* and *Help!*. Somehow the studio had ignored the clear indications in the screenplay that *Performance* was a psychosexual miasma featuring sadism, buggery, gay sex and the consumption of drugs, which overhung the plot and the after-hours activities of the cast and crew like a narcotic cloud. In a script instruction for Chas, the alter ego of Turner, Donald Cammell had unambiguously spelled out a central philosophical core of the film's tone of sexual ambivalence: 'Perhaps he has realised that these three people are not concerned with the demonic and pathetic problems of gender that rot the human race ... that they don't waste their lives and loves trying to define their sexes.' 'I feel like a man. I'm normal,' says Chas, Fox's character, at one point, shortly

4

before he is obliged to confront the core of such rigid thinking within himself.

Chas was to be played by James Fox, the English actor who had starred in *Duffy*, but whose reputation had been secured by his role as an upper-class Englishman devilishly manipulated by the scheming Dirk Bogarde in Joseph Losey's 1963 film *The Servant*. Fox was already part of the Stones' set: at a gig by the group in Rome two years previously Fox, who had been living in the city, arrived with 'the Gettys' and met 'Mick Jagger, Brian Jones and the rest'. On his return to London, the actor had run into Mick and Marianne Faithfull at a party hosted by Dirk Bogarde at the Connaught Hotel; Fox was with his girlfriend Andrée Cohen, whose androgynous appearance especially appealed to Marianne, who was rarely bothered by social niceties in her lesbian fantasies. 'Faithfull and Jagger, Fox and Cohen – the four quickly became inseparable, whiling away the evenings at Jagger's Cheyne Walk house in a haze of music and mind-altering substances,' wrote Mick Brown in his monograph on *Performance*. 'It was a curious friendship in which the louche pop star would constantly tease the upper-middle-class actor about his accent and manners, but it blossomed, in Donald Cammell's phrase, into "a little romance".'

Fox was the son of Robin Fox, an established theatrical agent, a director of the Royal Court theatre and a stage producer. Having read the script of *Performance*, his father became concerned, even perplexed that his son was considering taking the part, and advised against it: he did not consider it a good career move. By the time the film was in production, Robin Fox was dying from cancer, adding cumulatively to the psychological torment that increasingly afflicted his son as work on the film progressed.

On 3 September 1968 filming commenced on *Performance*. On the first day of shooting Mike Molloy, the camera operator, was observed by the rock-star male lead as he hammered small pieces of wood into the floor as markers for the Rolling Stone's perambulations about the place. 'I don't need those fuckin' things,' snapped Mick. Otherwise, it was the usual cinematic set of illusions and serendipitous half-truths: although the exterior of a house in Powis Square was used, instead of number 81 it was 25, and the interior and garden were actually those of a run-down residence in Lowndes Square off Sloane Street in Knightsbridge. Christopher Gibbs, the antiques dealer and socialite friend of Mick Jagger, had dressed the house in the manner in which he had designed the interior at 48 Cheyne Walk, the new home of the Rolling Stones singer – that gothically gloomy confusion of Moroccan tapestries and mosaics, Indian mirrors, brass-studded furniture and vague nods to modernism that could be defined as rock-star rococo.

As could the house's occupants: with his hair dyed jet-black, and dressed in embroidered satin Chinese chemises, Mick Jagger frequently looks like a transvestite prostitute. Anita Pallenberg, her geometrically cut blond hair falling around the sides of her face, resembles an even more beautiful Brian Jones. Mick Jagger is most 'in character' when he is playing Turner in gangster mode: besuited, hair greased back, transmogrifying into Chas, performing 'Memo From Turner', a brooding, black, masterly song written for the film. Today this sequence seems like the ultimate, most extreme video, made years before such a medium even existed. In other scenes Mick is not always as convincing as the legend of the film would have us believe. The ever-present problem with rock 'n' roll stars attempting to become film actors cannot be suppressed: 'Oh look, there's Mick Jagger,' you clock subconsciously every time he appears on the screen. And as he is playing a composite exaggeration of himself and close friends, he is often exposed in this role: when he reads the passage from the final story in Borges' *Fictions* ('At this point something unforeseeable occurred. From a corner of the old room, the old ecstatic gaucho threw a naked dagger, which landed at his feet. Dalmain bent over to pick it up. "They would not have allowed such things to happen to me in the sanatorium," he thought'), his saliva-strewn enunciations have the exaggerated clarity of a favoured boy acting a lead role in a school play to which he is not altogether suited.

Yet it is easy to give Mick Jagger the benefit of the doubt for his *Performance* performance, and to be overtaken by that myth, the one that just wouldn't go away because it was true: that on the set of *Performance*, during the filming of the sex scenes, Jagger actually fucked Anita Pallenberg, the girl of his best friend. Later an uncut tape of the footage won an award at a festival of pornography in Holland.

Over this Keith Richard, who had fallen deeply in love with Anita, came close to losing his sanity: he would sit for days at a time in his powder-blue Bentley outside the house in Lowndes Square, too cool to barge in on the set to discover what really was going on between Mick and Anita. Accordingly he would despatch either Robert Fraser, his Mayfair art gallery owner friend, or – much worse, as far as Donald Cammell was concerned – 'Spanish Tony' Sanchez, Keith's favoured drug dealer, to find out what was happening. Eventually, Spanish Tony was banned from the set after being suspected of stealing a gun being used as a prop. ('His excuse for coming on the set was to bring me drugs,' said Anita.) Fraser too was declared *persona non grata*: 'I barred Robert Fraser from the set of *Performance*,' said Cammell before he killed himself in 1996, 'because I felt he would cause too much trouble, and Keith was trying to sabotage my movie because he was jealous of Mick with Anita. He didn't want Anita to do the film and wouldn't speak to me for a long time and wouldn't perform on the track of the music; but Anita was having the time of her life. She'd go home to Keith, who'd be terribly jealous when he heard she'd been in bed with Mick. I was also scared of Robert's machinations, and I expected trouble from him because he was so tight with Keith – they were such good friends. I adored Robert, but treachery was an affectionate game with him.'

Keith Richard and Anita Pallenberg were staying at Robert Fraser's flat in Mount Street, Mayfair. Anita had rented Fraser's home from him for a very large amount of money and then been rather surprised when the landlord hadn't moved out, thereby creating another *ménage à trois*. Shortly before filming started, Keith wrote the song 'You've Got The Silver' there for Anita, an expression of his adoration of her. Keith, Anita, Robert Fraser and Marianne Faithfull ('Mick was always out making money and hustling away,' Marianne recalled with distaste) would hang out for days on end, in the inevitable hashish haze, all sprawled together on Robert's enormous and exquisite seventeenth-century four-poster bed, its yellow silk hangings intertwining with their stoned bodies. 'The scenario would always be Keith at the head of the bed, with guitar,' said Marianne, 'Anita looking ravishing, glittering and shining and covered in amazing things; Robert in some extraordinary lime-green or pale pink suit, with his winkle-pickers – and me on the other post. That bed was like the bed of life. We spent hours and hours there, and it was there Keith wrote "You Got The Silver". He wrote it for Anita, with me and Robert there at the birth of the song.'

Anita, however, was going through a different experience: 'That was a funny period. It was very difficult for me. Keith and Robert were both so cynical and sarcastic, slagging off the movie every day. I'd come home from filming and they would be slagging off Jagger, slagging off everything. I got quite confused. ... In that period drugs seemed to be the biggest happening. The bathroom was the most important place. First you'd shoot up, then you'd puke, then you'd feel great. For me though, it always fizzled out because next morning I had to go to work. It just didn't seem real. I don't know what opinion Robert had of Donald Cammell and the film, because Keith thought it was rubbish. Although I think Keith liked the finished film, but we never really talked about it.'

'That film was probably the best work Cammell ever did, except for shooting himself,' said Keith. 'I did kind of like Donald, but I found him a vicious manipulator of people, a selfish bastard. Any redeeming qualities were totally swamped by a very mean streak, which probably in a way came out of an inferiority complex. He was a failed director. He shot himself because he realised who he was.'

At one moment in *Performance* Anita Pallenberg shoots a hypodermic syringe into her rangy, sumptuous buttock, and Turner scolds her: 'You shoot too much of that shit, Pherber.' 'Too much of vitamin B_{12} has never hurt anybody,' she ripostes – slyly, knowingly junkie-hip, a pointing towards imminent dramas and a downfall in what was ostensibly her 'real life'. Keith Richard's response to the confused pain he felt over Anita's 'work' with Mick Jagger was to write several of the songs that appeared on *Let It Bleed* ('I wrote "Gimme Shelter": "I feel a storm a-coming, gimme shelter".'), the Stones' almost flawless masterpiece. He also put such negative energy into the efforts at recording 'Memo To Turner' with the Rolling Stones that the resulting song was, in Cammell's words, 'still and lifeless': finally, it was re-recorded with Steve Winwood and Jim Capaldi from Traffic, and Ry Cooder.

Out of the midst of this psychological and psychic brouhaha, Mick Jagger emerged apparently not only unscathed but even firmer in his sense of destiny. 'Nothing really touched him,' wrote Marianne in her auto-biography, *Faithfull*. 'In the same way that some actors get to keep their wardrobe, Mick came away from *Performance* with his character. This persona was so perfectly tailored to his needs that he'd never have to take it off again.' In fact, he came out of the film with two new characters: an exaggerated version of the shamanic, sexually ambivalent Jumpin' Jack Flash, into whom he was already osmosing, and the Turner-as-gangster figure, the amoral hoodlum for whom anything is justified if it will bring him profit. In many ways, the making of the film was the making of Mick.

But it was the end of a large part of Mick's boyhood friend and song-writing partner. Keith's solution to the excoriating angst and confusion he felt over Mick and Anita's egotistical sexual dishonesty towards him was to anaesthetise himself with heroin. By the time the production of *Performance* wrapped, Keith Richard was a heroin addict.

CHAPTER 1

CROSSFIRE HURRICANE

The parents – Joe and Eva – were surprised by the birth of their first child, having confidently expected it to be a girl. It was two weeks after his birth date of 26 July 1943 that the baby's name was first registered at Dartford Town Hall, on 9 August, the one his mother and father had finally chosen: Michael Philip Jagger. His birth date coincided with those of Aldous Huxley, Bernard Shaw and Carl Jung; he later developed an abiding interest in the latter's theories of the collective unconscious and archetypes, becoming an archetype himself, taking on the heroic role of warrior-magician that he first developed during stage shows in the late 1960s. Blessed with distinctive baby-blue eyes, little Mike very quickly grew a leonine mane of ginger hair.

So was he born in 'a crossfire hurricane', as he later declared, describing the origin of his alter ego Jumpin' Jack Flash? Not exactly, but the early days of the infant Mike Jagger were still times of some stress and strife. The Second World War had begun just twenty-one months previously, and Dartford in Kent, just outside the edge of south-east London, was on the bombing run taken by Germany's Luftwaffe on its way to the working-class East End of the capital. The town had already been decimated by conventional bombing by the Luftwaffe – over eleven thousand local homes had suffered bomb damage. In June 1944, when the baby boy was ten months old, the Nazis began their V1 unmanned flying-bomb raids on London, a partial response to the allied invasion of Europe on the sixth of that month: the very inaccuracy of these early missiles only increased the mood of edginess in the town, which formed part of what became known as Doodlebug (the nickname for the V1) Alley.

On 8 May 1945, however, Dartford town centre resounded to the music of dance and brass bands as a victory party was held: Adolf Hitler had committed suicide and the Third Reich had capitulated. Mike Jagger went to the celebration with his mother, who kept a tight grip on her twenty-one-month-old son: she was obliged to soothe the crying boy when a dog

9

ran over and snapped at the gathering seated around her at a table. Mike's first conscious memory was the sight of his mother tearing down the blackout sheets from their windows. A general election was held on 26 July 1945, the Labour Party being voted into power with its promise of an egalitarian, socialist future. By the time Mike's younger brother Christopher Edward was born, on 19 December 1947, the Jaggers were living a comfortable, middle-class life in the west of Dartford at 39 Denver Road, a crescent of white pebble-dashed houses.

Soon a previously undetected anger surfaced in four-year-old Mike; in retrospect this seemed to be a response to the arrival of his brother, a typical case of sibling rivalry: Mike Jagger realised he was no longer always going to be the centre of attention. Chris Jagger began to be subject to the jealous wrath of his older brother, who for much of his early childhood bullied him as a matter of course. His mother remembered that at the age of four 'he had a phase of hitting people for no reason'. 'Chris was just a punchbag. Mike used to beat him up regularly,' she said. The older boy also recalled using him as a whipping post. 'I used to beat him up, but then that's quite a common thing with brothers.' But this ire wasn't restricted to his brother: on a seaside holiday, Mike kicked down every sandcastle he came across. Such a vicious character trait seemed far removed from the modest determination and physicality of his father. 'If he takes after his father,' said his mother, 'he'll be bald before he's thirty.'

The Jagger family originated in the West Riding of Yorkshire, a county that has always viewed itself almost as an independent nation, and there the family's bloodline could be traced back to the thirteenth century. Later Mick Jagger would romantically attempt to mythologise the surname as a synonym for 'stabber', with all its wild sexual connotations, but this was not the truth: a 'jagger' was an itinerant pedlar (as Mike himself would become on a worldwide scale). During the eighteenth and nineteenth centuries the Jaggers had emigrated to Ireland and the United States, where some family members fought as Federal troops in the Civil War. By the end of the 1800s, some of the remaining Yorkshire branch of the Jaggers had moved almost the length of the country to the 'garden county' of Kent. David Ernest Jagger, the grandfather of Mike, by profession a teacher, then moved north of the Thames to the village school at Wickham Bishops in Essex, just east of Chelmsford.

The First World War broke out the year after his second son Basil was born, on 13 April 1913, and David joined the newly instituted Royal Flying Corps, leaving the two boys to be cared for temporarily by his own two brothers. Although life expectancy in the Royal Flying Corps was at that time only three weeks, David Jagger survived the very dangerous part this service played in a deadly war. Then he moved first to Lower Peever in Cheshire to become a headmaster, and then to Greenfield in adjacent Lancashire, where Basil became one of his father's pupils. Basil showed an early aptitude for sports of all sorts, especially physical education and cricket, at which he was exceptionally gifted. Moreover, his modesty and air of moderate humility ensured he was neither overlooked nor disliked. It seemed in keeping with such a self-effacing approach to life that one day he declared that he would prefer to be known simply by the down-to-earth name of 'Joe', instead of the more pompous-sounding Basil. Attending the grammar school in Oldham, he gained a reputation as an excellent football player. But such superlatives only served to make this balanced, quiet man feel awkward.

After studying first at Manchester University and then King's College, London, Joe Jagger took up a teaching post in Bedford before moving in 1938 to Dartford, Kent, to become head of physical education at East Central, a boys' boarding school; to its 300 boy pupils was added an influx of girls and almost immediately it changed its name to Downs School. By this time Joe had shaken off some of his air of apparent diffidence, becoming a confident and enthusiastic teacher who easily imbued his pupils with his own fondness for sport. He rented accommodation at 147 Brent Lane, in the south-east of Dartford. With the advent of war in September 1939, Joe volunteered as an air-raid warden. Not long afterwards he and a rather striking-looking woman called Eva Scutts were introduced through a mutual friend.

Alfred Charles Scutts was a slight man from Greenhithe, Kent who had emigrated before the First World War to New South Wales in Australia; there, this family was remembered as being rather distant. Just outside Sydney, New South Wales's largest city, Alfred Scutts developed the craft of yacht-building he had begun in Kent. The only girl among his five children was Eva Ensley Scutts, who had been born on 6 April 1913. Although Alfred spoke frequently of returning to England, his wife Gertrude – demonstrating a strength of will that was replicated in her daughter – eventually left Australia without him, taking the children back to England in steerage class on the SS *Rotorua*. The ship set sail from Sydney in January 1917 at the boiling height of the antipodean summer: snow was falling when the ship docked in Liverpool, eight weeks later, the vessel having successfully avoided the deadly German warships and submarines that prowled the European Atlantic seaboard.

Moving back to Kent, the Scutts settled at 233 Lowfield Street, Dartford, south of the town's market. Dartford then had a population of 24,000. Eva, who was now four, was sent to the local Church of England school. Alfred soon followed his family back to England.

Leaving school at sixteen, Eva became an office worker in nearby Bexleyheath. Then she began a career as a hairdresser: now she wore her hair cut diagonally across her distinctive, high forehead, drawing attention to her face and distinctive pair of fat, sensual lips. She enjoyed dancing at Dartford's Glentworth Club and parish halls, and would sing at Holy Trinity Church. An exceptionally neat and tidy woman, Eva dominated the Scutts household. 'It was almost a museum,' said Arthur Key, a neighbour, of the manner in which this pretty, intelligent woman oversaw the family home. In 1940, when she was almost twenty-seven, Eva announced to her parents that she had become engaged to a physical education teacher called Joe Jagger, a man whose shyness was compensated for by his physical approach to life. He had been born seven days after his wife-to-be. When she met Joe Jagger, Eva, who had embarked on a course of self-improvement, pursued him with relentless determination. 'It's now or never,' she is said to have almost threatened the humble PE teacher, in order to finalise the plans to marry that they had discussed. At the end of a grim autumn of German bombing raids, the pair were married on 7 December 1940 at Holy Trinity church, Dartford. Joe's best man was Albert, his brother. A wedding reception was held at the Coneybeare Hall, attended by fifty guests. Afterwards the newly-weds took a typically crowded wartime train to chilly Cheshire for a week's honeymoon. On their return they moved into Joe's rented semi-detached house in Brent Lane. A little over three months after both Eva and Joe's thirtieth birthdays their first son was born, on Monday 26 July 1943.

After the war, Joe became the physical education teacher at the local secondary school. Then in 1954 he moved on to be the lecturer in physical education at Strawberry Hill, Twickenham, a Catholic teacher-training college which taught missionary teachers destined for Africa or Asia. Already in 1947 he had become part of the staff on the Central Council of Physical Recreation, where he was one of the founders of British basketball, launching the Kent County Basketball League the following year. He was seen by Bob Clash, with whom he worked, as 'superbly fit, keen, disciplined – but with a genuine empathy for children. Young Mike was lucky to have him as a father.' As a pioneer of British basketball, Joe wrote the subject's definitive work, published in 1962 by Faber and Faber. He even went to the USA to referee matches.

At home in Dartford, his eldest son Mike became an able mimic. Even when he was a very little boy, Eva would catch him standing in front of the living-room mains wireless, singing along and making up his own words to songs that sailed out of the set. At other times his mother would start to sing to herself, and Mike would immediately join in. Grandma Scutts would take him along to Central Park in Dartford to listen to the Salvation Army brass band, whose oompah music the boy avidly devoured. Even so, his mother considered him 'the least musical of the family'. 'I used to like marching bands,' said Mick 'the military bands of different regiments that I heard on the radio when I was a small child. But I never went to any concerts or dances or plays: the pantomime was the only large show I was ever taken to. I loved it.'

In September 1947, at the age of four, Mike Jagger began his primary education at Maypole Primary Infants School, Dartford. 'He was rapidly acknowledged as bright, energetic and extrovert,' said the writer Christopher Sandford. In the summer of 1950 a teacher photographed Robert Wallis and John Spinks with their arms around their fellow pupil, Michael Jagger. Spinks lived nearby at 25 Heather Drive. He became Mike's closest friend, playing together with him on the waste ground between their houses. He told Sandford that Mike 'possessed tremendous energy ... He was always stamping his foot, tossing his head, screaming and shouting. Anything to let off steam.' But he also insisted that Mike was very much a mother's boy: 'He did everything he was told by Eva.'

Early in September 1950, just over a month after his seventh birthday, Mike began his junior-school education at Wentworth Junior County School, where he was Pupil 112. Stuffed into Mike's brown leather school satchel for some time would be a pocket chemistry set. Always ready to gather up books from desks, he was seen as a pleasant, helpful pupil. A popular boy among his contemporaries, he was liked less by most of the teachers, his habitual morose air a deterrent to close contact. In February 1951 at Wentworth Mike met Keith Richards for the first time. 'Keith and I went to school together ... We lived in the same block. We weren't great friends but we knew each other,' Mick said later.

CHAPTER 2

SCORPIO RISING

Keith Richards was born on 18 December 1943 at Livingstone Hospital, East Hill, Dartford – the same hospital in which Mick Jagger had emerged into the world almost five months previously.

The Richardses lived at 33 Chastilian Road, on a council estate close to the Jaggers' privately owned home. Keith's father, Herbert William Richards, was part of a large working-class family from Walthamstow in north-east London. He had met Doris Maud Lydia Dupree in 1933 while they were both working at clerical jobs in an office in central London. The Duprees were originally Huguenots, who in the seventeenth century had fled religious persecution in France and escaped to the English-ruled Channel Islands, subsequently moving to England. Doris's father, Keith's grandfather, Theodore Augustus (Gus) Dupree, had been gassed in the First World War, forcing him to abandon his saxophone playing. So he turned to the guitar, piano and fiddle, and throughout the 1930s had run dance bands, spending his earnings as though they were pouring out of an open tap. During the 1950s he had worked – as 'Gus Dupree, King of the Country Fiddle' – in a country-swing band that would play the American Air Force bases scattered around the perimeter of London. Gus Dupree, who for a time had also been a baker, became the heroic role model of the young Keith Richards.

As well as being King of the Country Fiddle, Gus had a job as a janitor at Highgate School in north London: the son of Yehudi Menuhin, the acclaimed violinist, was a pupil at the school, and Gus befriended the maestro. 'They'd even have a bit of a scrape together on their violins,' an impressed Keith confided later about his fascinating grandfather, who from an early age showed him that contact with the gifted and famous was not necessarily beyond his reach.

In 1936 Bert Richards and Doris Dupree were married, and moved to Dartford. Bert was working at the local General Electric factory when he was called up in 1942 to serve with the Bedfordshire and Hertfordshire Regiment. While serving in France in 1944 with the D-Day invasion forces, he was wounded in the leg and sent to an orthopaedic hospital in Mansfield, Nottinghamshire. Doris and baby Keith went to join him there, staying until the end of the war, when they moved back to Dartford. Keith once said that his first real memory was of his mother pointing at the skies and declaring, 'It's a Spitfire'.

Now Bert took a job as a supervisor at the Osram light-bulb factory in Hammersmith, on the far side of London from Dartford; every day Keith's father would get up at five in the morning and return home at six in the evening. Accordingly, his son spent most of the time with his mother, who would search the radio set all day long for the kind of American big-band music her father adored.

'With six aunts, he was a bit spoiled,' said his mother. 'It was great being an only child ... didn't have to share my toys!' said Keith. Keith first went to Westhill Infants School at the end of his road. Keith was a loner, and hated school from the very start. He was easily tearful, and more fond of animals than he was of other children. 'Keith was very chubby. He was squat, had fat little legs and wore a little brown hat with little brown boots. He always seemed to have a cold. His nose was always red and his face stark white!' Doris Dupree Richards told Barbara Charone for her 1981 biography of her son.

At Wentworth Junior County School he met Mike Jagger, who was in the year above him. 'I distinctly remember the first conversation I had with Keith,' Mick recalled later of the moment when their destinies were almost magically set in motion. 'I asked him what he wanted to do when he grew up. He said he wanted to be like Roy Rogers and play guitar.' ('I liked the kind of cowboy who carried a guitar instead of a rifle,' Keith remembered. 'I'd meet Mick in the playground – we were only about four or five years old then, and lived very close together – and I'd tell him, "Oh boy, that Roy Rogers! And that palomino, Trigger! Wow, man, they're something else." It never interested me at all, the music he played. It was just the image, the guitar. When you're a kid, cowboys are very intriguing.') Mike noticed that Keith had big ears that stuck out from the sides of his head. Keith was conscious that Mike lived in another, more rarefied world. Keith didn't really know anyone on his council estate. He was aware, however, that he was working-class. On the edge of the Thames were plenty of concrete army 'pillboxes', replete with gun-slits, that had been built in preparation for repelling the German invasion that in the early part of the war was expected any day. In common with children all around the British coast, Keith and his friends played their own war games and made gang headquarters in these exciting, odd reminders of what could have been. Keith's father Bert was a tennis player, and Keith would be his ballboy at Sidcup Civic Tennis Court.

Keith and his mother would regularly travel up to London to see Grandfather Gus. 'Gus had this guitar standing in the corner, and he was always afraid Keith would break it,' said Doris Richards. 'He would go up and strum the strings; he loved the sound and admired Gus enormously.' 'When I used to visit him off the Seven Sisters Road,' said Keith, 'there was an upright piano, and on top was this guitar, but I couldn't reach it. In any case, you couldn't touch it. You wouldn't even dream of it: "That's Grandad's". But what I found out years after he died was that he only put it up there when he knew I was coming. So the son of a bitch had me spotted from when I was this high. Then when I was about ten or eleven I asked him if I could play the guitar, and he said, "If you're going to play the guitar you've got to learn this one thing called 'Malaguena'. If you play that, you can play the guitar." '

No matter how ham-fisted Keith's playing efforts, his grandfather showed active enjoyment in it, encouraging him to play the instrument. Keith would go along with Gus to the instrument repair department at Ivor Mairants' guitar shop on Charing Cross Road in London's West End. 'I knew all the guys who built and repaired guitars. They used to sit me up on a shelf, give me a cup of tea and biscuits, and the glue would be bubbling away. I got introduced to music like that: I'd see broken violins going by and watch the guys fixing them, with that smell of glue. I only knew the back way in. It's been the story of my life ever since – always round the tradesman's entrance.'

Prior to the global creative impact of Elvis Presley in 1956, with his first records on the RCA label, Britain of the 1950s was a distinctly black-and-white place. From the moment the first notes of 'Heartbreak Hotel', Elvis Presley's first RCA release, wailed out of Radio Luxembourg, the country was illumined by the primary-colour world in which Elvis dwelled. Keith Richards was even more taken by the cultural revolution Elvis's music set in place: here was a guitar-playin', truck-drivin' Roy Rogers who simultaneously performed and sounded like both black pimp and rockabilly moonshiner from his home state of Tennessee: 'The world suddenly went Technicolor,' he said. It was the beginning of a lifelong love affair with the work of the young Elvis Presley. Nothing would ever be the same again.

CHAPTER 3

ONE DOZEN BERRIES

Reflecting his father's promotion to Director of Physical Education at Strawberry Hill College, in the summer of 1954 the Jaggers moved to a large, pebble-dashed detached house amid the leafy greenery of the village of Wilmington, just outside Dartford. A signifier of middle-class aspiration, their three-bedroom house, one of a handful of buildings in a private road, possessed its own name: 'Newlands'.

The move to Newlands was a chapter marker in the life of Mike Jagger. Having passed his eleven-plus examination, receiving the results two weeks before his eleventh birthday, he started his secondary education on 15 September 1954 at Dartford Grammar, a school founded in 1576 whose uniform included a gold-trimmed maroon blazer and cap; in order to be accepted at Dartford Grammar, he had also taken and passed the school's separate entrance examination, in which he came 72nd out of 161 candidates.

In all aspects of the Jagger family life there were signs of sophisticated upwardly mobile optimism (they were part of a society about which soon-to-be prime minister Harold Macmillan would proclaim that its constituents had 'never had it so good'). For example, they took holidays abroad, on 'the Continent', as Europe was commonly referred to in Britain in those days. In 1953 they had taken their summer vacation in Spain. Wearing a straw sombrero tilted back on his head, in the manner of a Hollywood Mexican, Mike had posed with a toy guitar for a holiday snap. On this same baking-hot Iberian excursion, Mike bought his first real guitar; as it was a cheap model of undistinguished marque, his father was especially impressed by the sounds his son managed to coax from the instrument. His mother noted that Mike was particularly partial to imitating the Latin sounds of the likes of Edmundo Ros that would be heard on their wireless, her eldest son mimicking the lyrics with cod-Spanish gibberish. The family was not especially musical and of them all, Mike was considered the least so. The house had no record player.

Before such expeditions had become at all commonplace for British families, in 1955 the Jagger family went to St Tropez in the South of France for the summer holidays, pitching a tent on Tahiti Beach. His schoolboy French already coming in handy, the twelve-year-old Mike conversed haltingly with the locals, interpreting for his mother. The two Jagger boys spent most of their time swimming in the warm Mediterranean, which they loved – all his life Mike loved swimming. When Chris wanted to tease his brother, he would call him by his name's more working-class diminutive, 'Mick'; as the older Jagger boy hated its very sound, this was guaranteed to have the desired negative effect.

Just prior to the trip to St Tropez, Mike's father helped his son secure a summer job at a US army base near Dartford; there Mike Jagger coached the children of American servicemen in physical education and athletics. According to Robert Wallis, a Dartford Grammar contemporary of Mike Jagger, who spoke to Christopher Sandford, it was here that a black cook called Jose played him genuine rhythm and blues for the first time. When he returned to Dartford Grammar School in September 1955, friends noted that certain words he pronounced now carried American inflections. His ambition, he said, was to own a red Cadillac.

Was this an endeavour to make himself seem interesting? Some contemporaries at Dartford Grammar thought that Mike was a rather anonymous boy. His brother didn't feel he had many friends, and noted that he was something of a stay-at-home. In his first years at Dartford Grammar, Mike Jagger was unglamorously industrious. 'I was just an ordinary rebellious, studious, hard-working kid. I really did used to work hard at school.' Chris's abiding memory of his brother – when Mike was not busy thumping him – was of a studious boy, always buried in books, showing little interest in music: 'I really think he wanted to be a businessman. I think Mike's main ambition as a boy was to be rich. Money meant a lot to him.' When Roy Carr asked him in an *NME* interview in 1975 if he had had a strict upbringing, it didn't strike a chord – even though the Jagger family would say grace before every meal: 'Not particularly, it wasn't as bad as some of my friends. I never got to have a raving adolescence between the ages of twelve to fifteen because I was concentrating on my studies, but then that's what I wanted to do and I enjoyed it.'

In his first-year exams Mike came fifteenth out of thirty pupils. He was noted for being hard-working. 'A good start,' was the verdict from Dick Allen, his form master, in his school report at the end of his first year. Twelve months later he showed himself to be sticking to the same standards: 'Has worked well'; 'Immaculately well behaved'. He was also a strong athletic all-rounder, frequently absorbed with the cricket stumps, badminton nets and basketball hoop in the back garden at Newlands. 'He went through a Tarzan period when he would swing from tree to tree, giving out loud cries and screams. He used to terrify me,' said Eva. With his father he would even go rock-climbing, and Joe also instructed him in the art of canoeing. However Mike was reluctant to put in the hours of practice necessary for success in athletics, for which he showed a natural gift.

The headmaster of Dartford Grammar was a man called Ronald Loftus 'Lofty' Hudson. Predictably, 'Lofty' Hudson's nickname arose from his extremely slight build. Lofty didn't especially take to the new boy: adults found there was something slightly annoying about Mike's demeanour, his air of sullen other-worldliness. By now, his mother and father remembered, their son Mike had become obsessive about listening to music and imitating vocalists. 'I've never known a youngster with such an analytical approach to things. If he copied a song, he copied it slavishly, every note. He was able to capture the sound exactly, even when he was as young as eleven or twelve,' said Joe Jagger.

In the world of physical education, Joe Jagger was by now showing himself to be something of a high-flier: in 1957, a sign of his status in the field, Joe was made technical adviser on *Seeing Sport*, a half-hour programme on Associated Television, the broadcaster to the London region on the new commercial network. In three programmes, beginning with the one broadcast on 7 May that year, he used Mike, clad in a white singlet and shorts, to demonstrate the techniques he was endeavouring to teach: kicking a football around, climbing into a tent, rock-climbing with his dad. In the first programme, Mike and his father climbed together, the Jagger boy having a rope wrapped around his waist and being hauled up a rock face, all to the running commentary of presenter John Disley. After this he appeared in subsequent programmes. Among his peers at school this brought Mike Jagger tremendous kudos: in those days no one knew anyone who had been on one of the two channels showing on British television at the time. Robert Wallis, a fellow Dartford Grammar pupil, remembers him becoming something of a local personality. The eldest Jagger boy responded by affecting an air of permanent boredom. But he had had a considerable glimpse of celebrity, which he now perceived as a not unattainable possibility, somehow, in some way. The endlessly practical, somewhat pushy Eva Jagger, meanwhile, became a demonstrator of cosmetics.

That year, when he was almost fourteen, Mike's voice broke. Like many of his peers Mike Jagger soon fell prey to the seductive idea of becoming a rebellious teenager. Now, to the chagrin and irritation of his teachers, the previously model pupil began to do the minimum of schoolwork to get by. He started sweeping his hair back, sculpting its unruly curliness into the de rigueur quiff with the assistance of lavish globs of Brylcreem. As far as he could he began to customise his school uniform in the direction of the Teddy boy fashions of the day – he would wear a regulation white shirt, but one with a fashionable cutaway collar that emphasised the tight triangular Windsor knot of his tie, whose V-shaped tongue he cut off so that it resembled the newly fashionable square-ended version; his black Oxford lace-ups were substituted by the kind of moccasins he had first seen being worn by US servicemen on the local base. He seemed to wear a permanent sneer.

From this time on his teachers noticed that Mike Jagger went into an academic decline. As he developed into an archetypal moody teenager, he was no longer interested in the schoolwork that had previously absorbed him. 'With Mike,' said a classmate, Paul Ovenden, 'you had the impression he had to be number one. When he found out he wasn't, he tended to give up.'

Mike's interest in fashion mirrored the arrival of rock 'n' roll in Britain. He was not taken with the avuncular Bill Haley and his anthem 'Rock Around The Clock'; even the extraordinary appearance and sound of Elvis Presley, who had had such an effect on Keith Richards, moved him not at all. It was Little Richard, the outrageously camp black rock 'n' roll hero, who first stirred the blood and fire of Mike Jagger. Dick Taylor, a school-friend, recalled Mike asking his father for the money to buy 'Good Golly, Miss Molly', and Joe's refusing: 'I ain't giving you the money to buy that trash,' Jagger later insisted were his polite father's unlikely words.

His spell at the US army base when he was twelve had fired his imagination: Mike Jagger had become fascinated by what later became known as 'Americana'. His father's affection for basketball had already set him on this path, and Mike Jagger owned a pair of genuine American basketball boots, the type of footwear sported by many of Britain's duck-tailed juvenile delinquents-in-the-making, instead of the black gym shoes worn by most of his schoolmates. Another boy at Dartford Grammar, Peter Holland, noted Jagger's distaste for 'waffly pop'. He was only keen, he said, on 'real' music. America, he would inform those who would listen, was 'where it's at'.

But the natural facility for sport that clearly ran in the family still held some sway within Mike Jagger. Mike remained able at basketball and cricket, from time to time playing for the school's first XI. But his previous enthusiasm for sport began to wane. Joe Jagger felt that his eldest son was uninterested in the constant regimen required for success in that field, also observing Mike's rebellious undertone in distancing himself from such school activities. Immediately after breaking the school record for running the half-mile, Mike disturbed his father by pronouncing running to be 'a drag'. His once immaculate cricket 'whites' were now covered in grass stains. A magnanimous soul, Joe Jagger would wash the car of the grammar-school teacher who gave Chris Jagger extra tuition in mathematics, and even occasionally provided basketball coaching at Dartford Grammar, for which he would also lead canoeing parties.

The one sport in which the somewhat diminutive Mike Jagger was still interested in fully participating was basketball, its Americanness part of the attraction. A fast, exciting and intelligent game, it appealed to Mike Jagger's quick mind and peripheral vision. Soon to be part of a team of his own, the psychology of gamesmanship that Mike learned here was invaluable. He might as well have been sprinting and leaping around a stage. A basketball court is also similar in size to the stadium stages on which, within little more than ten years, he would be bounding and bouncing about in his beloved United States.

Mike Jagger would still attend the school's Army Cadet Force, with its disciplines of rifle marksmanship and square-bashing, although he stopped going as soon as membership was made voluntary – Dartford Grammar was bringing itself in line with the government's abolition of National Service in 1958, a significant date in the development of the entity of the British teenager. He remained a member of the school history society, though the jazz club held much more interest for him. 'There was traditional jazz and skiffle. People tend to forget how enormous that was. I was in loads of skiffle groups. I used to play with Dick Taylor, who was a folk guitarist, and another friend who I went to school with. But these skiffle groups were also playing rock 'n' roll numbers. Nearly every guitarist was a folk player, but they also played whatever was on the charts that week. English rock 'n' roll really started with skiffle groups.'

Although Mike Jagger had first been inspired in the direction of rock 'n' roll by Little Richard, his other inspiration was an artist who could not have been more different: the cerebral-looking Buddy Holly. As it would later be by the Beatles and the Rolling Stones, Britain in 1958 was sharply divided into those who were fans of Elvis Presley and those who took to Buddy Holly: the bespectacled Holly wrote his own songs, which gave him a veneer of academic credibility and seriousness, something that many of his fans seemed themselves to emulate. 'It seemed very easy to sound like him,' remembered Mick. 'And that was the appeal of it: it sounded so home-made.' When Buddy Holly and the Crickets toured Britain for the first and only time, in March 1958, Mike went to their show at the Granada Cinema, Woolwich, with Dick Taylor, his close friend from Dartford Grammar. The compère was one Des O'Connor, soon to be catapulted to television stardom. Tucked away in the middle of Holly's thirty-minute set was a song called 'Not Fade Away', that had a rather different beat to the rest of Holly's largely self-penned material. Going to this show together was a deeply bonding experience for Dick Taylor and Mike Jagger. From then on, Mike was a frequent visitor at Dick's parents' house in Bexleyheath, where he discovered that his friend was a pioneer in musical taste. Here he first heard such urban blues masters as Howlin' Wolf, Jimmy Reed and Muddy Waters. All over suburban Britain teenage boys were listening to black US blues. The music was hard to come by, often necessitating a trip to Dobell's, the specialist jazz shop in Charing Cross Road, to seek out obscure blues records; such visits always took on the aspect of a pilgrimage.

Now Mike Jagger's ambition began to show direction: he tried to become the singer of a group being formed by Mike Turner, another former pupil at Wentworth County Junior School, and David Soames, who lived in Wentworth Drive, Dartford, where the audition was held. But the two other boys thought Mike's singing style too odd for him to become their singer. Later, on the bike ride back to Wilmington, Jagger and Soames talked about Jagger's imminent GCE O-level examinations.

As though they were his birthday present, Mike's O-level passes arrived in July 1959, the week he turned sixteen: after Lofty Hudson had made him knuckle down to work, Mick passed seven Ordinary level GCEs; he fared best in English language, for which he received 66 per cent, in contrast to English literature, for which he scraped his lowest pass mark at 48 per cent; for French he got 61 per cent, whilst history, with 56 per cent, was his third most successful O level. Latin, geography and maths were his other passes.

'His successes owed more to intelligence than effort,' said Christopher Sandford. 'He was by then blatantly coasting. Jagger's report for the year 1958–9 – "too easily distracted" – shows the corner had been turned. All that gang 'were regarded as reprobates,' said a schoolfriend.

That summer Mike went with another boy to Italy on a celebration holiday that Joe Jagger had organised. Back at school for the two-year A-level GCE course, Mike Jagger showed that his growing years had only increased his capacity to irritate adults. On one occasion when he was in the sixth form, he turned up at a school function having swapped his school blazer for a fingertip-length semi-drape jacket, its dark pattern embellished by silver threads. It was the kind of garment in which the most threateningly narcissistic of the local Teddy boys attired themselves, and was inspired by the fashions worn by the likes of James Dean in his 1955 hit film *Rebel Without a Cause* – although Mike himself was never impressed with Dean's acting style. Eva Jagger especially disapproved of this item of clothing, which seemed to suggest that her once ambitious son might grow up to be nothing more than one of Dartford's street-corner louts. While Arthur Page, a Dartford Grammar teacher, perceived that he was 'basically decent', he also felt that when he was with his cronies, Mike Jagger would always be sniggering behind the teacher's back. Mike was developing in other ways, however: in Ann McAulay he had his first steady girlfriend, and she would go round for afternoon tea at the Jagger household. She always found Mike Jagger to be very shy.

Dick Taylor had left Dartford Grammar after his O levels and started a foundation course at Sidcup art college. As the proud owner of an old drum kit, he formed Little Boy Blue and the Blue Boys, a group whose line-up consisted of Alan Etherington, Bob Beckwith and Mike Jagger. Among their repertoire was Dale Hawkins' 'Suzie Q', Howlin' Wolf's 'Smokestack Lightning' and Don and Bob's 'Good Morning Little Schoolgirl'. They attempted to play material by all their heroes, including Jimmy Reed, whom Jagger absolutely loved: Reed's 'Bright Lights, Big City' and 'Honest I Do' would be recorded by the Rolling Stones. Ritchie Valens' 'La Bamba' was the first song on which Taylor remembered Mike singing, coming out with words in his by now customary cod Spanish in a version that lasted a full twenty minutes.

On one of their Saturday-afternoon excursions to Dobell's in 1959, Mike and Dick rounded off the experience by going to the Academy, a celebrated art-house cinema off Oxford Circus, to watch the film *Jazz on a Summer's Day*; this exemplary documentary about the 1958 Newport Jazz Festival, beautifully directed by fashion photographer Bert Stern, featured performances by such jazz giants as Louis Armstrong, Dinah Washington, George Shearing and Thelonious Monk among others. Tucked away in the movie, his patent-leather pompadour and sneering grin permanently giving him the appearance of one of those pimps whose look Elvis Presley had tried so hard to emulate, was Chuck Berry, the black poet of rock 'n' roll sensibility; he was the real reason that Jagger and Taylor had gone to see the film, which because of Berry's performance became something of an epiphany.

Although Little Boy Blue and the Blue Boys played together for two years, they were so convinced that they were the only people in England who liked this kind of music that it never crossed the group's collective mind to try playing before an audience. The only person for whom they ever performed was Taylor's mother – she was always taken with the show put on by Mike. One of the reasons the Blue Boys existed, however, was because a new musical revolution was in the air; you could sense it in the streets every time you passed one of the art-school students who dressed very similarly to Mike – navy-blue donkey jackets on their backs, their hair flopped forward.

The group also would practise at Alan Etherington's house, using his parents' radiogram as guitar amplification. One day Mike turned up at rehearsals in some distress: he had bitten a small piece out of his tongue when he had slipped from a climbing rope during a school PE lesson. He was very worried it would affect the sound of his voice; but if anything, this small accident improved his vocal timbre, as the four musicians heard on Chuck Berry's 'Around And Around', the first song they put down that evening on Taylor's Philips reel-to-reel tape recorder. Jagger was pleased that his voice sounded somehow more slurred, 'blacker' even.

At home, Mike was forced by his father to persist with his physical training. On one occasion Dick Taylor went round to the Jagger house to go out with Mike. As they were leaving the house, Joe Jagger's voice reprimanded his eldest son: 'Michael, your weight-training.' Mike was obliged to spend thirty minutes pumping barbells. Even so, Taylor noted, 'he was chameleon-like . . . incredibly polite to his parents, forever grousing behind their backs'.

Clive Robson had opted for an A-level arts course, studying both history and English in the same classes as Mike Jagger. The English course was taught by one Eric Brandon, who Robson rated as a 'terrible' teacher: tears would come into Brandon's eyes as he read *King Lear*, leading Mike to mimic the wavering squeal of his voice. Only the French and history teachers expressed any interest in this already unconventional boy. But despite the disapproval of Lofty Hudson, the headmaster, he was made a school prefect.

At the end of July 1960, when he was just seventeen, Mike Jagger had a summer-holiday job selling ice creams outside Dartford public library, in front of the town's War Memorial. One day a boy he hadn't seen for a considerable while came along and bought a vanilla cone: it was Keith Richards, and they had a brief conversation. In the Christmas holidays at the beginning of 1961 he earned four pounds ten shillings a week, working as a porter at Bexley Mental Hospital.

As soon as he reached the legal driving age of seventeen, Mike took his driving test, passing on the first attempt. Joe would generously let Mike take the school basketball team to away games in his Dormobile. Despite a tendency to allow his peripheral vision to assess every girl he passed, he was a good, capable driver.

By the time he was in the upper-sixth form Mike Jagger was considered by Lofty Hudson to be the possessor of a distinctly bad attitude, an assessment that for any rebellious teenager would be considered a mark of considerable merit. But unbeknown to his headmaster, the boy was academically pulling himself up by his bootstraps, determined to secure a university place. Eventually even Lofty recognised this: 'In the sixth form,' he wrote in his letter of reference to prospective universities, 'he has applied himself well on the whole and has shown greater intellectual determination than we had expected'. Hudson also commented that 'he is a lad of good general character, though he has been rather slow to mature'. But, he added, 'the pleasing quality which is now emerging is that of persistence when he makes up his mind to tackle something'. By now Mike was secretary of the basketball club, as well as a member of the school's cricket first eleven. He also played rugby for his house. Lofty also wrote, with an unintentional irony that is now immediately apparent, that Jagger was 'interested in camping'. And he noted his fondness for such other extra-curricular activities as climbing, canoeing and music.

By now Mike was fond of quasi-hipster terms like 'drag' and 'gas'. His studied air of rebellion, however, was only superficial: 'Basically he was well behaved,' noted Dick Allen, his form master in the upper sixth. In fact, in order to pass his English literature A level, he tutored himself with a correspondence course in the subject.

On 26 July 1961, Mike Jagger turned eighteen. When that August his A-level results came in, he had passed two subjects with high grades – history and English language – though he had unexpectedly failed French, one of his best subjects. The two passes, however, ensured his place at the London School of Economics, where he was to study economics and political science – Lofty Hudson had secured him a place there, as long as he passed two of his A levels. Mike didn't know what he would do afterwards for a living, and thought about a career in the legal profession or as a historian, or as some form of writer, probably in journalism.

By the middle of the decade the London School of Economics (the LSE, as it was more generally known) had become a hotbed of student protest. Although it was as yet far away from its days of radical ferment, the LSE was already notorious for its left-wing thinking. Among the guest lecturers was Harold Wilson, soon to be Labour prime minister, though he was not thought to be especially iconoclastic: he was really rather conservative. Mike's tutor at the LSE was Walter Stern. He considered Jagger to be shy and polite.

On 17 October 1961, as he waited at Dartford station to travel up to the LSE, again Mike ran into his former primary-school friend Keith Richards, who was waiting for a train to take him to the course he was attending at Sidcup art college. Rather unusually for Keith, he was early that morning. Mike had a pile of records with him, including Chuck Berry's newest LP *One Dozen Berries*, that had just arrived by post from Chess in Chicago, and *The Best of Muddy Waters*. In its own small way this was a great moment in the history of popular music; akin to the moment, just over four years previously, in July 1957, when Paul McCartney had ridden his bicycle over to St Peter's church fête in Liverpool to see a rock 'n' roll group he had heard of called the Quarrymen, and had for the first time met John Lennon. Mick and Keith now renewed their friendship from primary school, discovering they had a mutual friend in Dick Taylor, who was attending Sidcup art college with Keith.

At the LSE Mike discovered the writings and thought of Marx, Engels and Keynes. And, in a shift not as extreme as his father's change of name from Basil to Joe, he became the earthier Mick. His friends were accordingly instructed in how he was now to be addressed. In December 1960 he was accepted for the highly desirable student employment of working on the Christmas post for the Royal Mail in Dartford, a job Clive Robson also took on. Robson remembers Mick in a pub with 'arguably the ugliest girl in England in tow'. Over pints of bitter, Mick would express to Dick Taylor his dilemma as to whether he should continue at the LSE or dedicate himself to music.

CHAPTER 4

A TERRIBLE RACKET

In 1955 Keith Richards moved with his family across Dartford from Morland Avenue to 6 Spielman Road, located on Temple Hill, a new council estate.

As a child, Keith had a beautiful soprano voice. 'Before I could play an instrument, I used to sing. I was a choirboy soloist at school for the choirmaster, Jake Clair. It was a way of getting out of physics and chemistry, because if you gave me a bunsen burner back then, I'd set the school on fire.' Clair diligently rehearsed Keith and the rest of the choir. 'The weirdest thing was that me and the three biggest hoods in school were singing like angels in Westminster Abbey at Christmas. It was me, a guy called Spike and another named Terry. During 1956 and 1957 he would also sing in the annual inter-schools competition at the Albert Hall in South Kensington, and he and his reprobate schoolfriends even performed before the Queen at the newly opened Royal Festival Hall. But when Keith's voice broke, he became surplus to the choir's requirements. 'I think that was when I stopped being a good boy and started to be a yob,' he said later, affirming his assessment of himself as one of the school's 'hoods'.

In September 1956, when he was twelve, Keith began his secondary education at Dartford Technical College, a secondary-modern school designed for those rejects who had failed their eleven-plus examination, with all the attendant social stigma. The next year, in an effort to make his father proud of him, Keith joined the Scouts, which he attended regularly for over two years, managing to fit Baden-Powell's world of short trousers, knot-tying and fire-lighting into his fantasy cowboy world. Within three months he had been made leader of the Beaver Patrol, the name in later life reducing him to ready ironic mirth. ('That was a commando unit, that patrol, compared to what the Scouts were supposed to be about!')

'I was in the Scouts for about two years, and I learned an awful lot about how to live out there in the woods. Certainly, that's what I wanted to learn. But every year they had these huge gatherings of us Scouts from all over the country, like summer camp – a jamboree. And at one of them I smuggled in a coupla bottles of whisky. Soon afterwards there were a couple of fights that went down between us and some Yorkshire guys, and so I was under suspicion. All the fighting was found out after I went to slug one guy – but hit the tent pole instead – and broke a bone in my hand! A few weeks later I had some dummo recruit come in, a kid just offensive to me in every way, and I knocked him out, so I got thrown out! I couldn't imagine going on and on with it anyway, but I learned certain aspects of leadership from that, and I also learned that if you dump me on top of a mountain with just the bare necessities, I'll survive.'

That September of 1957 he was kept down to repeat the previous year's schooling. Keith did not have a conventional approach to his education, however: 'In cross-country I would start off with the main bunch, and as the others raced off into the distance, I would hide myself behind a bush or tree and light up. A quick fag made me feel right as rain. Then it was just a matter of hanging around until the others came back, all exhausted. I'd tack myself onto the last few and accompany them back to school.'

By now Keith Richards had heard rock 'n' roll for the first time, namely 'Rock Around The Clock', which he really liked, as did his musical mother. His personal antennae became attuned to record releases from the United States, particularly those of the rockin' holy triumvirate Elvis Presley, Jerry Lee Lewis and Little Richard. He also loved the galloping New Orleans boogie of Fats Domino. In 1958, after nagging his parents to death, he managed to get them to buy him a 78 r.p.m. gramophone from Dartford Cooperative, so bulky and heavy that Keith nearly tore his arm out carrying it home. 'You had to change needles every six plays, and the needles were like nails. It was murder winding it up,' he said. The first record he bought was a version of 'Never Be Anyone Else But You', a Ricky Nelson song on Embassy, a budget-priced 'covers' label sold for four shillings and sixpence at Woolworths. 'I couldn't afford the real version, and the Woolworths version was cheap. It was just something for me so that I could get the guitar chords down.'

In December 1958, for his fifteenth birthday, Doris bought Keith his first guitar, an acoustic that cost seven pounds. Doris paid for the instrument on hire purchase: she adamantly insisted to Keith that she was only making this rather difficult financial commitment on condition he actually played the instrument. But in hindsight it seemed she never really had to make that deal with her son: 'From that day, playing the guitar has been the most important thing in his life. My father taught him a few chords, but the rest he has taught himself.' Keith soon came to appreciate that the reason the cut-price Embassy records were not as good as the originals was because of the quality of the backing instruments, especially the instrumental playing on the records by the magnificent Elvis Presley. He adored guitarist Scotty Moore's economical haunting solo on Presley's addictively shuffling 'I'm Left, You're Right, She's Gone', considering it the most exciting thing ever recorded, and an abiding influence: 'I could never work out how he played it, and I still can't. It's such a wonderful thing that I almost don't *want* to know ... The Elvis fans were the heavy leather boys, and the Buddy Holly ones all somehow looked like Buddy Holly.'

In Dartford he would hang out at the local snooker hall, with the would-be Teddy boys who patronised it in their ice-blue, skintight jeans, velvet-collared mohair suits, sideburns and sculpted Elvis quiffs. He went along to the local fairground with them, joining in as they smashed each other to pieces on the dodgems, threw up on the waltzer and hung arrogantly off the sidebars on the speedway. Thunderous rock 'n' roll rhythms rollicked all the while out of the rides' speakers, the sound sweetened by the aroma of diesel and the dancing scent of candyfloss: with their ever-present overhang of outlaw danger, fairgrounds were simply the most atmospheric places in Britain to hear the greatest rock 'n' roll.

The following year, when Keith was sixteen, his persistent truancy led to his being asked to leave Dartford Tech. His offences were not sufficiently heinous, however, to prevent his headmaster from helping him move on to a commercial art course at Sidcup art college ('commercial art' was always considered a somewhat demeaning, lesser form of art, suitable for oiks like Richards). English art schools, explained Keith, are where 'they put you if they can't put you anywhere else, if you can't saw wood straight or file metal. It's where they put me to learn graphic design because I happened to be good at drawing apples, or something.

'I did graphic design and life-drawing for three years. But basically I played guitar. I went straight into this art school, and I heard these cats playing, heard they were laying down some Broonzy songs. And I suddenly realised it went back a lot further than just the two years I'd been listenin'. I picked up the nearest guitar and started learnin' from these cats.'

There were a lot of other guitar players at art school. 'Everybody's broke ... and the best thing that's going on is in the bog with the guitars. There's always some cat sneaked out going through his latest Woody Guthrie tune or Jack Elliott. Everybody's into that kind of music as well. So when I went to art school I was thrown into that end of it, too. Before that I was just into Little Richard. I was rockin' away, avoidin' the bicycle chains and the razors in those dance halls.'

Also at Sidcup art college was Dick Taylor, having moved on from Dartford Grammar after O levels. Taylor noted Richards' sartorial attire: a purple shirt, jeans, black winkle-pickers and denim jeans jacket, 'always untidy'. Keith would engage in such traditional student occupations as shoplifting, fighting and getting high on period-pain pills. Like many other students, he smoked packets of five Player's Weights, which cost nine old pennies.

Life for Keith shifted along with meeting Dick Taylor at Sidcup. For Taylor was pursuing the possibilities with the guitar that he had first perceived at school in Dartford. Dick Taylor, Keith Richards and the other art-school musicians would play at lunchtime in a classroom next to the principal's office. 'Dick Taylor was the first guy I played with. We played together on acoustic guitars. Then I got an amplifier, like a little beat-up radio. Another guy at school, Michael Ross, decided to form a country and western band. The first time I got on-stage was at a sports dance at Eltham, near Sidcup, with this amateur country and western band.' In the classroom next to the principal's office where the guitarists would get together to play, Keith swapped a stack of records for a cheap electric guitar. At home in Spielman Road Keith would assiduously practise playing his guitar in front of the mirror in his small bedroom. 'My first gig was with Mike Ross from Sidcup art college. Of course we didn't get paid for it. It was some little school, and we played country songs, just him and me. It must have been bloody awful. All I know is that we spent the night in the bus shelter by a park. There was one bitch who was very nice to us but didn't put out. I was about fourteen or fifteen, and that was my first gig.'

Keith was in his final year at Sidcup art college when the meeting with Mike Jagger at Dartford station took place. His eyes had alighted on Mike's pile of imported R & B records, bought by post from Chicago and New York. He noticed the imported Chuck Berry album, *One Dozen Berries*. 'I was going to art school, and it just so happened that the particular train I had to take was the same one Mick caught to go to the LSE, although we didn't normally catch the same train. I noticed these records he had under his arm – otherwise, we may not have said more than hello to each other. He had a particular Chuck Berry record I'd never seen before, so we got talking.'

Although the train soon arrived at Sidcup, where Keith got off, they spent a few minutes discussing the merits of the mighty Chuck Berry vis-à-vis other contemporary US singers. It was then that Keith learned that Mick had an amazing record collection, and that Dick Taylor was a mutual friend. 'I remember the night Keith came in from art school and told me he'd met Mick at the station that morning,' remembered Doris Richards. 'He was really excited about that meeting. He'd been playing the guitar for ages, but always on his own. He was too shy to join in with anybody else, although Dick Taylor often asked him.' 'Keith asked me if I knew a guy named Mick Jagger,' said Taylor. 'I'd never really cottoned on to the idea of doing anything together until Mick came on the scene. Keith knew me and Mick knew me and we thought, "Why not join forces?" '

In November 1961 Keith Richards came over to Dick Taylor's parents' house, to sit in with Little Boy Blue and the Blue Boys. He brought with him his semi-solid Hofner cutaway guitar, on which he showed that he knew his way around most of Chuck Berry's songs. From then on Keith Richards and Mick Jagger and Dick Taylor played together, at both Dick's home and in Mick's bedroom at Newlands.

Chris Jagger thought they made a 'terrible noise'. His parents, notwithstanding Eva's genuine concern that the racket of their rehearsals would disturb the neighbours, were scrupulously patient. With Keith and Dick both on guitar, Mick eventually stopped playing, taking up vocals and the harmonica. They tried to electrify their set-up with amps made from old radios. Keith thought, 'Oh, it just makes it louder,' without at first appreciating the greater complexity that amplification brings. There was no drummer, 'just two guitars and a little amplifier. Usual back-room stuff. It fell into place very quickly.' Eva Jagger noted how they would stop playing as soon as she entered the room. 'I think Mick was a bit sensitive about his singing. He didn't like being watched or overheard.' Although they were not wealthy, Mr and Mrs Jagger cobbled together enough money to lend them to buy amplifiers and speakers. 'We had to, to keep Mick quiet.'

Then two other musicians begin to come over to Dick's house, swelling the membership of Little Boy Blue and the Blue Boys: guitarist Bob Beckwith, who played his instrument through a tiny six-watt amp, and Alan Etherington, who proved himself capable of shaking a nifty pair of maracas. The five would-be musicians would play along to Chuck Berry and Jimmy Reed records, Taylor having swapped instruments for a drum kit he had inherited from his grandfather. 'Me and my friends used to sit in the next room and crease up with laughter,' recalled Mrs Taylor. 'It was lovely, but so loud. I always heard more of Mick than I saw of him. I didn't dream that they were serious.'

Still the group played only for themselves. Very quickly, however, Mick and Keith became inseparable, as though each could provide the other with what he lacked. Dick Taylor noticed what was to become a regular interchange of identities. 'One day, Mick would become Keith. But then on another day, Keith could go all like Mick. You never knew which way round it would be.

'But from then on, Mick and Keith were together. Whoever else came into the band or left, there'd always be Mick and Keith.'

CHAPTER 5

ROLLIN' STONE BLUES

In March 1962, just four months after they had begun playing together in this line-up, the assorted members of Little Boy Blue and the Blue Boys saw something in the weekly *Jazz News* that seemed right up their street: a news item and advertisement for the Ealing Jazz Club, which featured a weekly programme of blues music. Despite its august title, the Ealing Jazz Club was actually only a basement room on Ealing Broadway. 'Turn left, cross the zebra and go down steps between ABC Teashop and jewellers,' the ad copy ran. The Ealing Jazz Club had opened on 17 March, and its first performance was advertised in the *New Musical Express*.

On 7 April, the first available Saturday, Mick borrowed his father's car for the ninety-minute drive from the furthest extremes of south-east London to Ealing on the fringes of west London suburbia. At the beginning of the 1960s every Saturday all over Britain marquees would be erected and men with ludicrous names wearing bowler hats would put wispy clarinets or rasping saxophones to their mouths in an effort to emulate the tremulous sounds of the revered Acker Bilk or the Temperance Seven. The trad jazz boom, a fad to fill the space between the end of the first flush of rock 'n' roll and the arrival of British 'beat' music, had briefly taken over the country, a more mainstream counterpoint to the sea-shanty-singing folk clubs that proliferated in even the tiniest of towns.

Mick and his friends' love for blues, however, only marked them out as having felt the zeitgeist. For they were not alone: the billed headliners at Ealing that April Saturday night were Alexis Korner's Blues Incorporated. Alexis Korner was born on 19 April 1928, and at the end of the 1950s had joined the nationally popular Chris Barber Band as guitarist. For some eighteen months Alexis and Cyril Davies, who played the most extraordinary harmonica, had led the thirty-minute blues break with which Barber, aware of the way the cultural wind was blowing, punctuated his group's set. In late 1961 Brian Jones had been to see a Barber show at Cheltenham town hall: he spoke to Korner afterwards and got on well with him.

Courtesy of Alexis Korner's Blues Incorporated, the Ealing Jazz Club featured blues and rhythm 'n' blues every Saturday night. It was the first club of its kind in Europe. Playing drums with Blues Incorporated was one Charlie Watts, a designer in advertising who had a formidable knowledge of jazz: by 1961 he had written and drawn an illustrated book dedicated to Charlie 'Bird' Parker, *Ode to a High-flying Bird*, which was eventually published in 1965. Alexis Korner had first met Watts around the beginning of the decade, when he used to drum with a jazz group. 'Eventually I asked Charlie, "If I form a blues band, would you like to come in as drummer?" and Charlie said yes, so that's how, around February '62, Charlie and I got together.' Charlie himself later admitted: 'Cyril [Davies] taught me Chicago blues, but I didn't really understand it until I started to play with Keith Richard.'

But when Mike, Keith and Dick arrived at the venue, the music that sailed up to them as they stepped down into the tiny, smoky club was a tenor-sax solo by Dick Heckstall-Smith; the Blue Boys felt this to be very much in the same vein as the trad jazzers. The gang from south-east London were not unimpressed with Blues Incorporated. Going down the stairs into the club, the first thing Keith Richards recalled hearing was: 'Alexis calling, "Dooji Wooji".' He was sitting playing with Cyril, Keith Scott, Charlie, Andy Hoogenboom and Art [Wood]. What struck me was the beat of the drums: before you saw the band you heard it. And visually there was Alexis, looking very chaotic. The club was packed, which impressed me; we thought we were the only ones into it. There was a bar, lots of girls, and we had a great time and started to go there regularly. The second or third time we went, Alexis said, "There's somebody here who plays slide guitar like Elmore James and his name is Brian Jones." And there's this little blond kid sitting on Alexis' stool playing Alexis' guitar.'

What Alexis Korner actually said as he stepped forward before the jam session with guest artists, with which his group always democratically concluded its set, was, 'This is Elmo Lewis. He's come from Cheltenham to play for you.' And then the group kicked into 'Dust My Broom', the Elmore James classic, on which a flaxen-haired young man took up his Hofner Committee electric guitar to devastating effect. 'They were stunned,' said Dick Taylor, recalling Mick and Keith's response. 'Just when it seemed there was no one else who understood, here was a kid, our own age, playing bar-slide blues. Mick was knocked out.'

The loquacious Mick and the taciturn Keith were immensely impressed by the nineteen-year-old Brian Jones. Keith especially was awestruck by what greeted them on-stage. 'It's fuckin' Elmore James,' he gasped. 'I said, "What? What the fuck? Playing bar-slide guitar." '

'At the beginning,' Alexis Korner noted later, 'Mick and Keith hero-worshipped Brian. He seemed about twenty years older than them.'

On vocals in that performance of 'Dust My Broom' was another pro-spective blues singer called P. P. Pond. Like Brian Jones, Pond would sleep overnight on the kitchen floor at Alexis Korner's home in Bayswater, close by Hyde Park – as, it seemed, did half the American bluesmen when they visited London. P. P. Pond was actually Paul Jones, the singer with a blues group called Thunder Odin's Big Secret. Brian Jones had sat in with the group on a few occasions, and that Saturday at the Ealing Jazz Club Alexis Korner had given them the break of playing as interval group. Although the voice of P. P. Pond and the exciting slide guitar of Elmo Lewis gelled so well, this was the last time they would play together: Paul Jones would later drop out of Oxford University to become the singer with Manfred Mann, another blues-based London group who would go on to have con-siderable success. That evening, however, it was the guitarist they were absolutely taken with, an individual who managed simultaneously to appear slight and stock. After Brian had come off-stage, Mick, Keith and Dick spent some time talking to him. They were enormously impressed by Brian: he already had children of his own, while they were still living at home with their parents.

Lewis Brian Hopkin Jones was born on 28 February 1942. His parents were university-educated professionals, and he had easily gained nine O levels and two A-level GCEs in physics and chemistry. He had refused to go to university to study dentistry, as his parents had wanted. Instead, he moved to London in August 1959 and took a job with an optician, a position he left after only one week. 'Brian was really fantastic, the first person I ever heard playing slide electric guitar,' said Keith. 'Mick and I thought he was incredible. He mentioned he was forming a band. He could easily have joined another group but he wanted to form his own. The Rolling Stones was Brian's baby.' Quickly they discovered that there was a deep empathy between the three of them: like Keith and Mick, Brian had for a time thought he was the only white musician in the world who was into black music.

Inspired by what they heard and saw when Brian Jones played at Ealing, the following Monday Mick and Keith posted a tape of a Blue Boys session to Alexis Korner. On it were several songs, including 'Around And Around', 'Bright Lights, Big City', 'Reelin' And Rockin' ', and the inevitable 'La Bamba' with Mick's pseudo-Spanish lyrics.

When Alexis Korner played the tape to Cyril Davies, he liked the sound of Mick's voice. Cyril Davies was a panel-beater who played and lived hard; his heart had been weakened by an attack of pleurisy, but he continued to drink large amounts. The brusque, almost wilfully difficult Davies was not necessarily easy to work with. 'How do you bend notes on the harmonica?' Mick asked him. 'Get a pair of fuckin' pliers,' came the brusque response. 'I rang Mick and invited him to come and visit me,' said Alexis. 'Mick and Keith came up from Dartford and talked about Chuck Berry and Bo Diddley. I talked about Muddy Waters, Memphis Slim and Robert Johnson. We dug each other. Then Mick and Keith started to come down to gigs. They went everywhere together; you never got Mick without Keith.

'At first you got the impression that Keith was just trailing around, but it didn't take long to realise Keith wasn't trailing around at all. He just happened to be quieter. Keith never appeared without Mick. The first day they came to see me it was Mick and Keith. And it was *always* Mick and Keith. Always. Keith never thought of it as Mick's band. We opened the Marquee in May '62.'

By the end of May 1962 Mick Jagger had become a regular guest vocalist with Blues Incorporated, singing three nights a week with them. This was a position of considerable honour. Competition among singers was intense. The only permanent vocalist up to that point had been John Baldry. Art Wood left early on, while Eric Burdon and Paul Jones were only occasional guests. Others, like Rod Stewart and Eric Clapton, were even more fleeting. The singers would appear during the late-set jam session. Eric Burdon, in his autobiography *I Used to be an Animal, But I'm All Right Now*, recalled that he was eager for a chance: 'I got up enough courage during the interval to walk up to Alexis, who was leaning against the bar, and tell him I had hitch-hiked all the way down from Newcastle to see the band. He was quite pleased at this. I asked if there was a possibility of singing with him. We discussed some songs I could try, and he put his arm around my shoulder then wandered off towards the stage to begin the second set.

'I stood in the front row clutching a beer, anxiously waiting to be beckoned on-stage. Standing next to me was a tall, skinny, short-haired, full-mouthed schoolboy singing along with the music and moving in time with the rhythm. Jam-time came around. We both jumped up on-stage.

'Alexis was diplomatic. "How about you two singing together?" Alexis pushed his glasses back, as the sweat poured down onto the rag tied around his forehead.

' "Do you know, 'I Ain't Got You'?" ' I asked.

' "Sure", said the buck-toothed youngster next to me on the stage. "The Billy Boy Arnold thing? Sure, I know it."

'Alexis nodded. "By the way, meet Mick, Mick Jagger. This is Eric Burdon from Newcastle." '

Mick Jagger won his spurs and his first professional singing job, for which he was paid seventeen shillings and sixpence a show. He performed numbers like Muddy Waters' 'Got My Mojo Working' and 'Ride 'Em On Down', and Billy Boy Arnold's 'Bad Boy' and 'Don't Stay Out All Night'. His first performance with Blues Incorporated was marked by his obvious stage fright and the manner in which he tossed about his mane-like hair. Jagger would rotate vocals with the giant-sized John Baldry, who was already singing with the group. But when Keith Richards joined in on guitar during the encore of Chuck Berry's 'Around And Around', a favourite number, Cyril Davies would become incensed by the heresy of this rock 'n' roller.

'I can remember when Mick and Keith first came down to Ealing,' said John Baldry. 'Mick's repertoire then was all Chuck Berry numbers. The first thing I ever heard him sing was 'Beautiful Delilah'. Keith had some tatty old guitar, pretty primitive, but I don't think anybody had good guitars at that time.'

'When we used to do our little Chuck Berry bit,' Mick recalled, 'Keith would get up and plug his guitar in and we'd go leaping in. I don't think Alexis could keep up with this because after a couple of weeks, just as we got there, he'd go "bap" with his thumb pick on the bottom string and break it on purpose. "You just carry on, cock," he'd say. He did this on a couple of occasions, so we knew it was a fake.'

'Mick was into the club almost from the beginning,' remembered Alexis Korner of Jagger's visits to the Ealing Jazz Club, 'sort of standing around waiting to sing his three songs every night: 'Sweet Honey Bee', Muddy's thing, some VeeJay song, and he used to do the odd Bo Diddley song when Cyril wasn't listening.'

A Blues Incorporated splinter group emerged, which included Korner but mainly featured members of the Blue Boys: Jagger, Richards, Dick Taylor, and even, controversially, Cyril Davies. Brian Jones would sometimes sit in, and occasionally another vocalist was employed, a callow youth nicknamed Plimsolls because of his footwear. Although Plimsolls could hardly play at all, he was known to have a reasonably monied background that allowed him to be the possessor of a new Kay guitar. He had another sobriquet, Eric the Mod, and would soon enjoy greater success when he transferred all his attentions to the guitar and reverted to his full name of Eric Clapton. For now, however, whenever Keith's or Brian's guitar went on the blink, they would talk to Plimsolls and borrow his nice new instrument. On drums would be either Ginger Baker or Charlie Watts, moonlighting from his job in advertising.

But Mick was unhappy about playing with Alexis Korner, according to Ian 'Stu' Stewart, 'because of the jazz end of it. Mick didn't really like jazz, and Mick and this other guitar player didn't get on at all.'

*

In May 1962 Brian Jones placed an ad in *Jazz News*, asking for musicians interested in forming a group with him. Ian 'Stu' Stewart, a shipping clerk, was the first person to respond to the audition that Brian held on the second floor of the Bricklayer's Arms in Berwick Street, Soho. When Mick Jagger, Keith Richards and Dick Taylor turned up at the Bricklayer's, Stu was there, playing piano in leather shorts. Keith stood back and studied him as he performed impeccable 'Pinetop and St Louis Jimmy shit', as rhythmically solid as the great Chicago blues boogie-woogie pianist Albert Ammons: Keith had never heard a white man play like that. Every so often Stu would glance out of the window and, without missing a beat, utter such phrases as, 'Cor, look at that!' as one of the many local strippers would flounce blousily by, heading for her next engagement at the next club. He was also checking to see that his bicycle was still chained to the parking meter he had secured it to. Eventually Stu turned, saw Keith and uttered, 'Oh, you're the Chuck Berry artist.' 'I knew I was under heavy penalties,' thought Keith.

That was the first rehearsal by the mainstay of the group that became the Rolling Stones. 'It seemed like we rehearsed for ages. We didn't do a gig for months. We had a great boogie-woogie piano player and a couple of interesting fledgling guitar players and an enthusiastic singer and harp player. And that was it. You do need a rhythm section, and that was the one thing we were lacking and couldn't afford,' said Keith. For his part, Stu noticed that when Keith turned up, as well as the expected Mick Jagger, 'This Dick Taylor guy came with him. I couldn't figure all this out; they used to walk in with amplifiers and speakers, and I'd never even seen those things before, and I could never understand why Dick's guitar only had four strings.'

Ian Stewart noted the immediate empathy between Brian and Mick, and that this seemed to intimidate Keith. But Stu could also see that despite the relationship that was springing up between Mick and Brian, Mick and Keith were set in stone as a double act. For example, when there would be opportunities for a 'blow' with other musicians, including Brian, at a couple of Soho locations – a pub in Lyle Street, a joint in a Wardour Street alley – Mick always announced, 'I'm not doin' it unless Keith's doin' it.'

He also observed that Mick and Keith seemed to have no money whatsoever. Although Mick ostensibly had his student grant, which amounted to about seven pounds a week, Keith seemed to have no visible means of support. After a time, Stu came to realise that Keith existed on what his mother scraped together for him. 'Keith is the only one who is not naturally middle-class,' Alexis Korner told Barbara Charone. 'Keith is a man of belief and Mick is a man of fear. Mick works on fear, that driving thing:

"What if I fuck up?" It's a lot easier to be like Keith than it is to be like Mick.'

Even then Keith was on his way to becoming some form of archetype. 'We lovingly named Keith Mr Unhealthy,' said Alexis Korner. 'He always looked like the unhealthiest cat in the group. But we knew he was the strongest physically. Keith was always the first to look really devastated. And once he looked devastated, he'd go for weeks looking no more or no less devastated. Meanwhile, the others would slowly deteriorate. But Keith did it rapidly and stayed that way. He really is Mr Unhealthy.'

Tucked away in the news pages of the 19 May 1962 edition of *Disc*, a tabloid music paper, was a small headline: 'Singer Joins Korner'. This was the first mention in the British music press of the name Mick Jagger.

A nineteen-year-old Dartford rhythm and blues singer, Mick Jagger, has joined the Alexis Korner group, Blues Incorporated, and will sing with them regularly on their Saturday dates at Ealing and their Thursday sessions at the Marquee Jazz Club, London.

Jagger, at present completing a course at the London School of Economics, also plays harmonica.

On 7 May 1962, almost two weeks before the story appeared in *Disc*, Mick had a meeting with Walter Stern. He seemed very confused, thought his tutor. Jagger appeared extremely dispirited, and was complaining about his daily journey from Dartford – even though it only took twenty minutes if he caught a fast train. He told Stern he was thinking of moving up to London. But he was clearly conflicted about whether he should continue his studies at the LSE, or leap into the musical void. (He had even asked Korner what he should do.) Perhaps Mick had been preparing Stern for the worst. He didn't fare especially brilliantly in the first-year exams that formed Part One of the finals for his BSc. In all three main subjects (Economics, British Government and Economic History) and in each of the two subsidiaries (Political History and English Legal Institutions) he received an undistinguished C grade.

CHAPTER 6

THE YOUNG ONES

In June 1962 Mick left Alexis Korner to join up with Brian Jones, Ian Stewart and guitarist Geoff Bradford, who had worked with Cyril Davies and was into the ethnic blues of Muddy Waters, John Lee Hooker and Elmore James. ('The idealism of Geoff Bradford was to be a key part in Brian's musical education, and in the policy of the Stones,' said Bill Wyman later.) With him Mick brought Keith Richards and Dick Taylor. Ian Stewart said that Mick was only prepared to sing with them if Keith became part of the group. 'Keith liked the Muddy Waters thing, but he also liked Chuck Berry and Bo Diddley as well.' They would rehearse at the Bricklayer's Arms, and Stu noted that Mick and Keith would be there on time for the seven o'clock start. 'Mick was always very together,' said Stu.

In July 1962 Blues Incorporated were booked to appear on *Jazz Club*, on the BBC's Light Programme radio station. The booking was for the same day as the group's regular night at the Marquee club on Oxford Street. In order to ensure that Korner's group could get their residency back the next week, Mick Jagger agreed to play with Brian, Keith, Stu, Dick Taylor and a drummer called Mick Avory. Harold Pendleton, who ran the Marquee, said he would acquiesce only if John Baldry's new group could top the bill, with the Stones playing support, for which they would be paid a fee of twenty pounds. Mick Jagger immediately agreed, and a small story appeared in the next issue of *Jazz News*: *Mick Jagger, R & B vocalist, is taking a rhythm and blues group into the Marquee tomorrow night while Blues Incorporated does its* Jazz Club *radio broadcast gig.* Despite the emphasis once again on Mick in this news story, it was quite clear that even though he had secured this particular show for them, it was understood within the group that it was Brian's outfit who were playing the gig.

Did Mick pull some kind of stroke to become so prominent in the story? Or was it simply that inevitably the singer always seems more interesting to the outsider, including the news editor of *Jazz News*? Whatever happened, at this stage 'The Rollin' Stones' were very definitely Brian Jones' group. Brian was angry that Mick was billed in this way. 'Brian came up with the name,' recalled Keith. 'It was a phone call – which cost money – and we were down to pennies. We got a gig at last, so we said, "Call up *Disc*. Put in an advert." So Brian gaily dials away, and they say, "Who?" We hadn't got a name, and every second was costing a precious farthing. There's a Muddy Waters record face down – *The Best of Muddy Waters* – and the first song was "Rollin' Stone Blues". Brian had a panicked look on his face – he said, "I don't know ... the Rollin' Stones". That's the reason we're called the Rollin' Stones, because if he didn't open his mouth immediately we were going to strangle him and cut him off. Not a lot of thought went into it, in other words.'

The Marquee date was set for Thursday 12 July 1962, a night steamy with summer heat. 'I hope they don't think we're a rock 'n' roll outfit,' Mick worried before the show. The very first set played by the group under the name of the Rollin' Stones at the Marquee ran as follows: 'Kansas City', 'Honey What's Wrong', 'Confessin' the Blues', 'Bright Lights, Big City', 'Dust My Broom', 'Down The Road Apiece', 'I Want To Love You', 'Bad Boy', 'I Ain't Got You', 'Hush Hush', 'Ride 'Em On Down', 'Back In The USA', 'Up All Night', 'Tell Me That You Love Me' and 'Happy Home' – all within the space of fifty minutes. Mick Jagger wore a crew-neck sweater and elephant cord trousers, a comfortable, casual look not dissimilar to the tracksuits in which his father would kit him out when younger, that was to become virtually an on-stage outfit for the singer. Corduroy, so recently the rugged clothing material of the snooty country set but now the height of Mod fashion, was a fabric Mick would favour for the early years of the group's career. Keith was dressed in a dark suit that showed off the collar and cuffs of his sparkling white shirt.

The show was not without its controversial moments: Dick Taylor's bass guitar caused apoplexy among the purist blues fans; they also hated the group's affinity for Chuck Berry, and considered the name of the group to have those unpleasant rock 'n' roll connotations that Mick had worried about. Still, those representatives of London's new tribal group of Mods who found themselves at the show pricked up their ears: word of mouth on the group began to grow from this first show.

After the set, as the musicians gathered around the club bar, Harold Pendleton, manager of the Marquee, acknowledged that they were 'not bad'. But it went against them with him for further bookings that they didn't have a permanent drummer. From then on the 'trad jazz' people put up what seemed to Keith like 'very bitter opposition' to the Stones – and he lay much of the blame for this on the Marquee's main man.

'He was the kingpin behind all that,' said Keith. 'He owned all these trad clubs and he got a cut from trad bands; he couldn't bear to see them die. He couldn't afford to put us on.' Keith Richards had another reason to bear a grudge towards Pendleton: he had been personally singled out at the Marquee for criticism by him, indicating the group might be better off without this Chuck Berry copyist. Mick laughed off the criticism, remaining immovably loyal to his friend.

In one way Pendleton and Keith were thinking roughly along the same lines. Keith was quite aware that it went against them that the group lacked a regular man behind the drum kit. The Dartford guitarist didn't care at all for Mick Avory; on drums he was often out of time. Keith complained: 'He was terrible. Couldn't find that off beat.' In fact, the only drummer any of them knew who understood the R 'n' B backbeat was Charlie Watts. The whole group was rather in awe of this man, with his neat Mod look, who drummed with both Blues Incorporated and a Soho group called Blues By Six. He and Keith got on very well. Brian had tried to persuade Charlie Watts to quit Korner and join up them, but to no avail. Despite Keith's considerable reservations, Mick Avory continued to sit in with the Rollin' Stones, alternating with Carlo Little, who played with Cyril Davies; although the Stones much preferred Little's drumming, he had more lucrative part-time work as one of the tight-knit Savages, who backed the extravagantly histrionic Screaming Lord Sutch.

All summer long the Rollin' Stones rehearsed assiduously. 'Brian really got into Jimmy Reed,' remembered Keith. 'He would sit around for hours and hours, working out how Reed's sound was put together. He'd work at it and work at it. He'd really get it down. Brian didn't consider Berry to be in the same class, but when we proved to him that he was, he really started to dig him. He'd work with me on Berry things. We really got into that. We were working out the guitar parts and the rhythm, which was four-four swing beat, not a rock beat at all. It was jazz swing beat, except there would be another guitar playing. He was a good guitar player then. He had the touch and was just peaking. He said that we were just amateurs, but we dug to play.' For his part, guitarist Geoff Bradford was a blues purist who considered Chuck Berry, Bo Diddley and Jimmy Reed to be commercial exploiters of the form.

Mick had moved out of his parents' house and found a small flat in Brackley Road, Beckenham, still in south-east London; a girl he brought round to cook for him managed to burn a hole in the ceiling. According to Keith, it was at this time that Mick once went round to Brian's flat when Brian wasn't there, and 'screwed Brian's old lady'. This caused Brian and the girlfriend, Pat Andrews, to split up. Now Brian had nowhere to live, so Mick – his conscience touched – gave him the flat in Beckenham and moved back to his parents. At the end of the summer term Keith left Sidcup art college, his course completed. Now Keith became very close friends with Brian. For the first time, Keith left his parents' home: he went to live with Brian in the flat in Beckenham, an area that over the following decade would acquire something of a reputation for creativity. Keith had decided not to bother with getting a 'real job', although once he took the portfolio he had assembled at art school around to a West End advertising agency, who 'gave me the usual la-di-da: "We'll let you know in a couple of days". I just stuffed it in a corner and forgot about it.'

Keith and Brian would spend all day playing together, 'figuring out Jimmy Reed and stuff', according to Keith. 'This was an intense learning period. We would love to make records, but we weren't in that league. We wanted to sell records for Jimmy Reed and Muddy Waters and John Lee Hooker and Howlin' Wolf. We were missionaries, disciples, Jesuits. We thought, "If we can turn people on to that, then that's enough." That was the total aim ... the original aim. There was no thought of attaining rock 'n' roll stardom.'

In August 1962, at the height of summer, Mick and Keith went away for two weeks to Devon in the West Country, a semi-mythical area with a rich reputation for beatnik eccentricity. Hitch-hiking, carrying their guitars, they played in a local pub as an acoustic duo – as, they were later to discover, John Lennon and Paul McCartney had also done three years previously on a similar brief rite of passage.

When they returned to the capital, Mick at last made the permanent move to central London. Situated on the north bank of the Thames, Chelsea had a reputation for bohemian eccentricity and was therefore considered a highly desirable area in which to live. Edith Grove was so far out on its most westerly reaches that it was only a few hundred yards from the border with Fulham. But although the first-floor flat at number 102, with a rent of sixteen pounds a week, was about all that was affordable in the area, it was also an indication of Mick's aspirations.

Brian moved in with him, having decided that his career took precedence over his rancour at Mick's sexual indiscretion. In fact, for the first week at Edith Grove, Pat Andrews – with whom Brian was briefly reunited – and Brian's new child were also living there. They soon moved on. Brian was at home most of the time: he had been fired from his most recent job, as a shop assistant at Whiteley's department store in Queensway on the other side of Hyde Park, for stealing records.

Soon it was Keith Richards' turn to move up to the Edith Grove flat. 'I never consciously thought about leaving Dartford, but the minute I got out I had pretty strong instincts that I'd never go back ' remembered Keith. 'There was no way I was gonna stay there.' Edith Grove seemed a more fun option. 'I started to crash there sometimes, so as not to have to go home ... Mick went through his first camp period, and started wandering around in a blue linen housecoat. He was into that kick for about six months. Brian and I used to take the piss out of him.' Although couched as a 'send-up' by Mick, it was as though he was consciously taking on the female role in the relationship.

A hundred and two Edith Grove was typical of rented accommodation of the time: one entered a gloomy brown-painted hallway, with linoleum-covered stairs and a communal toilet on the first-floor landing. Brian had taken over the front room with double bed, in which was also installed a mahogany radiogram. In the rear bedroom were three single beds, one Mick's, one Keith's and one for a young music fan who was brought in to share the rent as fourth lodger in the eccentric household. His name was James Phelge, an apprentice lithograph printer who worked near by in Fulham Broadway. Phelge was also a drummer, though he didn't possess a kit; but he did own an electric razor, which everyone in the flat would share. Keith: 'Absolutely the most disgusting human being you ever met, also the most lovable. He was the only one who wasn't part of the band, so he kind of roadied for us a bit and brought our spirits up ... He also created a lot of trouble. He was the sort of guy where you'd open the front door and he'd be standing there, streaked, skid-marked underpants on his head, totally naked. "How ya doin', boys?" A hidden hero.' Keith and Phelge used to like to read Dennis Wheatley's black-magic novels. As far as communications went, there was a phone box on the corner of Edith Grove and Fulham Road.

The flat in Edith Grove stank of grime and the raging hormones of only just post-adolescent boys. A couple lived on the floor above them who seemed vaguely to disapprove of the Stones. Keith, Brian and Phelge found out where they left their key while out at work, and would raid their flat for milk, bread or coffee. Girls lived on the ground floor, including one called Judy who would sometimes tidy up the flat for them. 'I think she probably wants Mick to give her one,' Keith confided to Phelge one day, as he played him Johnny Cash's 'Lonesome Whistle Blow'. Accordingly, Keith rigged up a microphone from their tape recorder in the toilet, playing it back to Judy one day after she had visited the lavatory, and then blasting it out through the entire house at maximum volume. Then he found a more practical application for the microphone: he rigged it up to the electric light flex in the centre of the living room, so that it hung down level with everyone's faces, enabling Keith and Brian to try out Everly Brothers-type harmonies together. While they were working together like this, Phelge noted that Mick seemed somewhat moody when he arrived home from the LSE at the end of the day. 'It's because he's feeling left out,' Brian explained. 'He doesn't like it because I'm doing something with Keith. I knew it would upset him. Don't take any notice.'

'I think Brian's much-talked-about isolation from the band started back in the Edith Grove days,' James Phelge said later. 'His choice to use the lounge as his own bedroom and not share it with the others perhaps became the starting point of his estrangement. When you shared one room you talked to each other till all hours. You could lie awake for a couple of hours talking and joking as Keith, Mick and I would, and that seemed to bring you closer. By missing this, Brian created a gap between himself and the others. It was as if somehow a small piece of his relationship with Mick and Keith was always missing. Despite all that has been said and written about Brian, no one would have wished him harm. When you are with someone sharing the last of your food and money to survive, it creates a bond you never forget.'

In the back bedroom, Mick slept nearest the door, next to a wooden cabinet. In the corner opposite Keith's bed was a wardrobe with a mirrored door. All the walls were painted brown, which approximately matched the colour of the carpet. The windows were utterly filthy, and were never cleaned in the entire time the trio lived there. Mould grew in unwashed cups at the edge of the kitchen sink. Plates encrusted with relics of week-old food welcomed eager families of scurrying mice. The sink was as coated in grease as the used frying-pan that sat on the grimy stove next to a thick metal pan; in this, water would be boiled to make instant coffee in whatever containers had been perfunctorily rinsed out. Knives were scattered about the breadboard, each bearing thick traces of the Stork margarine that had been swiped across pieces of soggy, sliced bread, as white as Keith's complexion, that the guitarist would stuff into his mouth to stave off hunger while practising. He and Brian were getting into it now, stuck alone together at 102 Edith Grove all day while Mick respectably set off each morning for the LSE on the 22 bus; Brian hadn't found another job since being given the sack from Whiteley's, and Keith had no intention of having any sort of 'proper' job.

Keith recalls: 'I went out one morning and came back in the evening and Brian was blowing harp, man. He's got it together. He's standing at the top of the stairs sayin', "Listen to this." *Whooooow. Whooow.* All these blues notes comin' out. "I've learned how to do it. I've figured it out." One day he dropped the guitar. He still dug to play it and was still into it and played very well but the harp became his thing. He'd walk around all the time playing his harp.'

Keith and Brian used to play music all day. Keith says: 'There was a time when Brian and I had decided that this R 'n' B thing was an absolute flop. We weren't getting away with it. Brian and I were gonna do an Everly

Brothers thing, so we spent three or four days in the kitchen, rehearsing these terrible songs.

'I made a few phony attempts at getting jobs. I've done my three years of art school and my dad's working day in, day out and does so until retirement. I've got to go through that too, according to him, so that's the reason I'm in Edith Grove ... I'm going as this very unlikely sort of missionary, but there's nothing I can do about it; that's what Muddy did to me, that's what Chuck and Howlin' Wolf did to me, what they all – Elvis, Buddy, Eddie Cochran, Jerry Lee, Little Richard – all of those cats did to me. They fired me up to the point where it wasn't a matter of conscious decision, it was just, that's what I want to do ... Very selfish. I didn't expect anybody else to think it was that important. When you're that age, you can do that kind of shit, as long as you can survive. But of course, once you start living in a place of your own, no matter how mean it is, it's like, payin' your own rent makes a man out of you. Every day is a battle for sheer existence.'

From the start, Brian would try to play Mick and Keith off against each other. 'Like, when I was zonked out, taking the only pound I had in me pocket ... Or he'd be completely in with me trying to work something against Mick.'

Things were not happening all that fast for the Rollin' Stones. In September, a month after they moved into Edith Grove, they played only two gigs, both at the Ealing Jazz Club, with Tony Chapman on drums. When they had a meeting with Tony to discuss their recruitment of him as drummer, it took place at Mick's parents' house. As a reference point, Mick played the Jimmy Reed *Live at Carnegie Hall* album. Mick told Chapman that this was the sort of music the group played. Dick Taylor, however, left the group to go back to art school. The Stones placed an advertisement in *Melody Maker* for a new bass player; without, at first, much success.

In October 1962, Keith experienced a great shock: all of a sudden his parents split up, his father disappearing – Keith would not see Herbert Richards for another twenty years. It was as though the father had been waiting for his son to leave to allow himself to flee the coop. Although he didn't show it, except for occasional outbursts of anger and a hurt look in his eyes that is discernible even in early publicity pictures of the group, the effect on Keith was immense. His absurdist clowning, a mixture of *Mad* magazine's Alfred E. Neuman and *The Goon Show*, became far more exaggerated. In retrospect, a string of dramatic events may be linked to the departure of his father, and the way it geared along the group's career is acutely evident.

That same month, on 27 October, the Stones travelled in Stu's Rover up to the Curly Clayton Studio in north London to make a demo acetate. With Tony Chapman playing drums and Stu on piano, Mick, Keith and Brian recorded Muddy Waters' 'Soon Forgotten', Jimmy Reed's 'Close Together' and Bo Diddley's 'You Can't Judge A Book By The Cover'. The acetate was sent to EMI and Decca Records – both rejected it out of hand. The Decca A & R man, who had also turned down a Liverpool group called the Beatles who had their first single out that month, commented particularly on the hopelessness of the group's singer.

On 24 November 1962, Keith, ill with tonsillitis, went home to his mum's in Dartford, but insisted on playing a date the following evening at the Piccadilly Jazz Club in Great Windmill Street. As Mick had done rather more conscientiously the previous year, Keith got a job that December on the Christmas post, but treated this generally respected source of cash with typically cavalier disregard: he went in for the first morning and didn't even bother to return in the afternoon after his lunch break.

Keith rarely had money to contribute towards the Edith Grove rent so his mother would come up from Dartford, lugging carrier bags of food, and most weeks she would wash everyone's clothes. Realising what a chore the long journey was up from Dartford on public transport, one week Keith and Phelge decided to help her out by washing their shirts themselves: they stuffed the dirty items into a couple of plastic buckets, filled them with water and left them in the upstairs bathroom. It wasn't until some three weeks later that they remembered where they had left their clothes, which only seemed to have rotted a little from the prolonged soaking.

During the legendarily cold winter of 1962–3, the four occupants of the first-floor flat were so broke they frequently went without food, staying in bed much of the time to conserve energy and to try to stay warm. There were some positive omens, however: the 'Judy' who lived below them at Edith Grove, they discovered, was Judith Credland, a pharmacist; she was also a gifted palm-reader. 'You've got the star of fame! It's all there,' she told Mick that winter, although he might have felt that was hardly likely as he, Keith and Brian tucked into Christmas lunch at their favourite working-men's caff, round the corner on the King's Road. Keith and the others had renamed this establishment 'the Ernie', because the workmen who patronised it would customarily address each other by that name. When relatively flush, the musicians would walk up to the Wimpy Bar next to Earl's Court tube station and devour a cheeseburger or two. Back at Edith Grove they stuffed themselves with blackcurrant and apple pies, made by a Welsh company called Morgan-Morgan ('Anyone fancy a Morgan-Morgan?'), sold for two shillings and sixpence at the dairy shop that was run by their Welsh landlords on the corner of Edith Grove and the King's Road.

A friend of Brian's from Cheltenham was in the Territorial Army. With the eighty pounds he would earn from his annual two-week military stint, he would come up to London to hang out with Brian, who would proceed to extract almost every penny of his pay from him, including the entire purchase price of a new guitar and a set of harmonicas. Out walking in the bitterly cold winter, Brian demanded the 'friend' give Keith his sweater, at the same time as making him walk twenty paces behind them. (So how did Brian treat his enemies? wondered Keith.)

To pass the time during the long, dark days of that freezing winter, they developed a hobby – aiming mouthfuls of gob at the walls. Such behaviour would shock Bill, the new bass player: 'I never understood why they carried on like this. Although Keith came from a working-class family, Brian and Mick were from well-to-do families. It could not have been just the lack of money that caused them to sink. Bohemian angst, more likely.'

Bill Perks had now joined the Rollin' Stones, following an audition on Friday 7 December 1962, after which he had come up with the stage name Bill Wyman. He had based it on that of Lee Whyman, his best friend during his National Service days in the army, even calling himself 'Lee' until he dropped it in the February of the following year. Wyman was a friend of drummer Tony Chapman, a travelling salesman who was often out of London. When Dick Taylor had announced that he was giving up the group to study at the Royal College of Art, Chapman had recommended his friend as bass player.

Bill had been taken with Ian Stewart, when he had met the piano player two days before his audition at the Red Lion pub in Sutton, Surrey, where he had gone to see the Presidents, featuring Glyn Johns. Ian introduced him to Mick Jagger, 'who was quite friendly; I then met Brian Jones and Keith Richards, who were at the bar'. In the manner of many successful applicants for positions in pop groups, Bill impressed the Stones with his equipment; he got the job partially because he was the possessor of not one but two Vox 850 amplifiers. At the audition, in the back room of the Wetherby Arms in South Kensington, a fifteen-minute walk up the Fulham Road from Edith Grove, he suggested to Keith that the guitarist use the second one. 'It was the biggest amp any of us had ever seen,' Keith remembered later. Bill was not sure what he had got himself into. Immediately he felt the tensions between the three main members: there was a kind of quiet desperation about both Brian and Keith. Mick's education meant that he was far less insecure and more relaxed about the future than were Brian and Keith – the Rollin' Stones was all they had, which wasn't the case for Mick. 'Mick, the student of economics and political science, seemed to be the only one with an eye on the future if the Stones collapsed,' said Bill. 'He talked about becoming a lawyer, a journalist or politician.

Keith, a professional Teddy boy, spat in his beer to ensure that nobody else drank it. He had no plans to work.'

At the beginning of January Charlie Watts finally gave in and joined the group, replacing Tony Chapman. 'Brian saw in Charlie what he himself had in abundance and demanded from any musician: commitment and idealism,' said Bill. At this stage Mick Jagger was only the singer. It was still clearly Brian Jones' group, and he and Keith Richards worked out on guitar whichever songs the Stones would play. 'The Stones took its musical stance entirely from Brian's passion for American rural blues music,' remembered Bill of that time. Brian's role as group leader even ran to being in charge of the finances, a situation that would soon create considerable controversy.

'Brian had a presence that was definitely electric,' said Bill Wyman, who became a close ally of the blond Stone. 'Mick did too, in a strange way, but I always felt Mick's personality was more self-consciously constructed: I don't remember him having the same sort of magical aura in those early days. When we were playing blues, I don't think anybody took much notice of Mick. Much more important was what sound Brian was playing on the slide guitar and harmonica. Mick played harmonica too, but Brian was better, more imaginative.'

Phelge was a jazz fan and would travel out to the Bull's Head in Barnes to watch the likes of Mike Hugg and Manfred Mann. Mick and Keith would tell him how boring this was. Phelge, however, found a like-minded soul in Charlie Watts, who shared his passion for jazz. One day they came back from an outing to Whiteley's in Bayswater where Phelge had picked up a copy of Miles Davis' 'Walkin'' – reduced, because it had lost its original sleeve – the card sleeve in which it came had had its details written in by hand by none other than Brian. Keith told them it was 'pseud's' music, a 'load of old bollocks', a critique only emphasised by the fact that the pair were playing the disc at the wrong speed. Once Keith came in and mooned, and tried to fart in Phelge's face: so Phelge bit him on his bare behind. Keith screamed.

By early 1963 Mick's attendance at the LSE had become most erratic. During that part of the year his group were playing regular gigs on Monday nights at the Flamingo (the stools on which the group would sit on-stage were stolen from the club on 28 January that year), Thursday nights at the Marquee, Friday nights at the Red Lion in Sutton, Surrey, and the Ealing Jazz Club on Saturdays.

In February and March, endeavouring to emulate the black vocal trio employed in the new Cyril Davies All Stars, the Stones rehearsed with two black girl singers, mainly on Richie Valens' 'La Bamba', a song that would eventually mutate into 'Twist And Shout'. But the girl singers weren't all that good, and their giggles disrupted rehearsals. Even though Mick was going out with one of them, Cleo Sylvester, the group stopped working with them.

While Mick cavorted with Cleo and other girls, Keith stayed at home, practising his guitar. Brian would show Keith how to live off the deposits on beer, cider and pop bottles. On the floor above them a couple now lived who were training to be teachers, who would regularly throw 'bottle parties': when the revellers had exhausted themselves from dancing to Duke Ellington, Keith and Brian would sneak off with their empty beer and cider bottles and get back the deposits that had been paid on them. When Keith and Brian used to gatecrash Chelsea parties, they'd walk off with all the empty bottles, taking them round to the off-licence or pub to claim back the three pence refundable on each one, or the two and sixpence if they had been lucky enough to filch one of the returnable soda syphons. 'For food we used to hit the supermarkets, a tomato here, a potato there ... and we never got done. I never considered myself an expert shoplifter, but I mean, we did all right,' remembered Keith.

The rent on Edith Grove was four pounds a week each. Mick would pay it as he was the only group member with a bank account, into which he would pay his student grant. One day he wrote out a cheque and gave it to Keith with a grin: *Pay The Rollin' Stones: £1 million.* They could have done with the money at the time: Mick used a Reslo microphone, which seemed to have a short life span, costing twelve pounds a time to replace; he also used a number of harmonicas, in different keys, which cost four shillings and sixpence each. Keith, meanwhile, taking the hint from Bill, had invested in a Harmony amplifier, borrowing the money for it from his mother.

Once, in January, Keith and Phelge, who had had a brief fist fight with a moody Brian, took a bus to the West End. At the end of the evening they found themselves outside the newly opened, state-of-the-art Hilton Hotel on Park Lane. Stepping inside, Keith demanded a room for the night. When the price of the accommodation was quoted to him, he paled: 'We don't want a piece of cheap shit like that,' he snapped, and walked out of the hotel.

Things were moving at a certain pace. Each Saturday night the Rollin' Stones would play at the Ealing club, and Phelge would loyally accompany them. It was Stu who would drive them to gigs, in his old Rover. He recalled how once, when he was driving them home along the Thames Embankment, they started arguing about clothes, Brian hitting Keith, who punched him back. 'I stopped the car and told them to get out and fight it out between them. They did!'

For three weeks in February, during the bitter-cold winter of 1963, the Ealing club decided to book the Stones on Tuesdays as well. Sometimes Eric the Mod, in his customary garb of lambswool sweater and French-cropped hair, would sing a couple of Chuck Berry songs with the group, giving Mick a break. One night that freezing winter Mick lost his voice, and had to call Eric and ask him to sing the entire set. The Marquee on Oxford Street would book them for occasional Thursday-night sessions, as support to Cyril Davies' All Star R 'n' B Group. Davies had Carlo Little on drums and Ricky Brown on bass, from Screaming Lord Sutch's Savages; on piano was Nicky Hopkins and the guitarist was Bernie Watson, a player so skilled and confident he would turn his back on the audience as he took his set pieces; sometimes John Baldry would guest as Davies' vocalist. At the Marquee in particular, the following that the Rollin' Stones soon acquired of clean-cut, neat Mods looked very different to the musicians on-stage.

On Friday nights the group would sometimes play the Ricky Tick club in Windsor. By January 1963 their regular slot at Sutton's Red Lion pub, a venue distinguished by its ordinariness, had been moved to Sunday night. After one show there, a certain Giorgio Gomelsky, who in 1961 had made a documentary film about the Chris Barber jazz band, came down to the show, and set up a gig for them the following week at the Manor House pub, under the auspices of the Haringey Jazz Club. Soon this became a big scene for the group, when it was added in as a regular Thursday-night show. With these gigs almost guaranteed, the group was now earning about eight pounds a week, the wages of an average working man.

A couple of weeks after their first Manor House date, Giorgio found the group a show at short notice on 24 February, a Sunday night, in the back room of the Station Hotel on Kew Road in Richmond, a venue he promoted. He told the Stones that the Dave Hunt R 'n' B Band, who were booked to play the date (and who would soon mutate into the Kinks, with Mick Avory on drums), was elsewhere in the country, stuck in the thick snow that was clogging up Britain – in fact, the group had simply tired of playing at the pub. On the posters that Giorgio had hastily printed up, the group's name was misspelt as 'Rolling Stones'. Again, Eric 'the Mod' Clapton, local to the area, arrived at the show, although there was only a small turnout of about fifty fans. All the same, Gomelsky offered the Rolling Stones a regular slot at the venue. This led to their playing their last date at Ealing, which they decided they could drop as Richmond paid just as much. At that final Ealing Jazz Club show, Linda Lawrence, Brian's new girlfriend, was there, dancing in front of the stage, when Pat Andrews walked in with Brian's baby. From the stage Mick saw what was happening, and started chuckling while still singing; Keith caught the mood, and also began to laugh. Brian's eyes were downcast, however. But in fact neither of the girls knew who the other was, thereby saving Brian's bacon. (Soon afterwards the Asian promoter who put on the shows at the Ealing club paid a visit to Edith Grove, with a couple of heavy-looking friends. He threatened the group that he would finish their career unless they returned to playing in Ealing on Saturdays. 'Fuck off,' said Keith.)

At a previous Ealing show, Keith had dropped to the floor, his body twitching: he was apparently having a fit, and was only revived by the barman pouring brandy down his throat. Whereupon Keith sat bolt upright, emptied the glass and walked out of the club. This was what was considered in the early 1960s as the sort of zany, satirical behaviour you'd see on the television programmes *That Was The Week That Was* (broadcast at peak viewing time on Saturday evenings) and *Candid Camera*. In similar vein, Keith and Phelge once passed part of an evening at Edith Grove firing air-pistol pellets at the neighbouring window of a beautiful girl and her boyfriend who were making love.

By the time the regular Richmond date came along, the Rolling Stones were also contracted to play a two-hour Sunday afternoon set at Studio 51 in Soho. Then, their musicianship suitably warmed up, they would leave for Richmond. Throughout the month, both at the Station Hotel and Studio 51, the number of fans would almost double with each gig they played. By 31 March, there was an audience three hundred strong at the Richmond club. 'We got the message, and we knew we were on the right track – and we weren't even looking for it,' said Keith. 'That wasn't the reason the Stones were put together. We were sort of evangelists. It was a very pure, idealistic drive that did it. The money we needed to live on we didn't give a damn about. That wasn't the point. The point was to spread the music. We had all these kids coming to clubs, and we were doing what we wanted to do. It wasn't to make money. The money was a secondary thing, and we didn't see any for a year or two.' The group's bookings were still handled from the phone box on the corner of Edith Grove and Fulham Road.

The night after the second Richmond gig the Stones had their second recording session, at IBC Studios in Portland Place in the West End. They recorded Jimmy Reed's 'Bright Lights, Big City' and his 'Honey What's Wrong', as well as Bo Diddley's 'Road Runner' and 'Diddley Daddy', and Muddy Waters' 'I Want To Be Loved'. One Friday night the three Stones returning from the Ricky Tick, were greeted by the sight of Phelge, naked except for his underpants which were on his head, gobbing phlegm at them from the next landing. On another occasion, seeking a novel twist to this gag, he pissed on them instead. 'Too fuckin' much,' said Keith, ducking back towards the front door. Two nights later, Keith and Phelge tied a frying-pan to a piece of string and dangled it against the windows of the girls' below, as though it were a ghost. Soon the three musicians took revenge on their flatmate; Phelge returned on a pouring wet day to find Mick, Keith and Brian staring out of the window into the garden below: after a moment, Phelge figured out what was going on – chunks of shellac lay about the lawn where his 78 r.p.m. copies of Perry Como's 'Magic Moments', Ruby Wright's 'Three Stars' and Cliff Richard's 'Travellin' Light' had splintered when hurled from the flat.

It reminded Phelge of the occasion when he and Keith had set fire to their threadbare, torn sheets, tossing them flaming from the window, calling out that the house was burning down. One day Mick discovered on an envelope that dropped through the letter-box that Brian's full name was L. Brian Hopkin Jones; over this the man from Cheltenham was ragged mercilessly. After a neighbour complained about Keith and Phelge sitting on and bending a metal rod that separated 102 Edith Grove from the house next to it, the two friends yanked off the offending piece of ironwork as they returned from a Richmond gig and shoved it clattering through the complainant's letter-box.

On nights off, Keith liked going to the Scene in Ham Yard off Great Windmill Street in Soho, the number-one Mod club, unlicensed but notorious for the amount of pill-popping that took place. Keith, however, was drawn there by the superb R 'n' B that would be played by Guy Stevens, the disc jockey, at the venue: Stevens, already a legendary figure for his knowledge and collection of American R 'n' B, would always have the latest records, direct from the States – it was claimed that the first Chuck Berry releases in Britain, on the Pye International label, were cut not from master tapes but directly off Stevens' personal US imports.

As March 1963 ran its course, and the snow and ice of that grimmest of winters finally began to melt, turning the streets filthy, the crowds at the Station Hotel grew until every Sunday the place was painfully packed. As at the Marquee, the audience was largely made up of fashion-conscious Mods; in other words, this was a very hip group, one alert to every nuance of the zeitgeist.

By the final Sunday of March 1963, the Stones were building up a fantastic head of steam and were hitting new playing peaks; much of the crowd from Studio 51 would follow them from the Soho afternoon gigs out to Richmond. The Shake, a relatively static dance in which participants would wave their arms above their heads, was coming into vogue, and was certainly the only dance possible at the Stones' now crammed shows at the Station Hotel. When a local reporter wanted to know the name of the club at which the group was playing on Sunday nights, Giorgio Gomelsky, thinking on his feet and recalling how the group would always finish their sets with the Bo Diddley tune 'Doing the Crawdaddy', instantly renamed the venue the Crawdaddy.

Accordingly, on 13 April 1963 the first ever newspaper report about the Rolling Stones appeared in the *Richmond and Twickenham Times*, a page-long piece by Barry May under the headline 'Jazz: Nowadays it means the music that goes round and around – or the Rollin' Stones are gathering them in'. Earlier in the month Giorgio Gomelsky had filmed the group at the Crawdaddy for a twenty-minute short. To work on the soundtrack, the group went into the R. G. Jones studio in London, recording 'Pretty Thing' and 'It's All Right Babe'. The songs were never released.

Amid this snowballing activity, life at 102 Edith Grove went on much the same. Mick was out most of the day at the LSE. Phelge was working at a lithographic printer's in Fulham, and would be home by six. The Stones liked him even more because he had refined the pastime of expectorating on the walls by circling the mucus with a pencil and naming especially glorious examples of green or red-tinged gob: Yellow Humphrey or Scarlet Jerkins, for example. Phelge and Keith's method of cleaning the kitchen was to pour hot water over every surface, the intention being to melt down the grease before scraping it off: often, this second part of the cleansing process was somehow forgotten about.

Every few weeks parcels of import records addressed to Mick Jagger would arrive from the United States, the latest Chuck Berry and Bo Diddley albums on Chess, for example. Brian and Keith would go through the new songs, evaluating their potential for inclusion in the Stones' set. A couple of twin girls called Sandy and Sarah started turning up occasionally; Sandy would spend a couple of hours in bed with Mick, and Sarah with Phelge.

Often Mick would not come back until late, at around midnight, if he had been studying in the LSE library, or not at all if he had chosen to pass by Cleo Sylvester. But the lure of Sandy was guaranteed to give him cause for an earlier return. On one occasion when Sandy had come round on her own to spend time with Mick, Keith and Phelge felt the need to get out of the flat, and wandered the twenty-minute walk to the pie stall on Chelsea Bridge, a regular haunt notwithstanding the lascivious glances of the bridge's high-powered motorcycle-riding leather boys. On the thick broad bridge they stood and mused, gazing to the west at the sparkling light show of Albert Bridge reflected in the black Thames. 'I reckon we're gonna be big one day,' Keith mused. 'We might be little 'uns now, but one day I reckon we'll be big 'uns. I can see it. Get a big house in Barbados and a yacht. I reckon we'll make it ... I reckon it's all starting.'

When they returned to 102 Edith Grove, Keith thudded up the stairs, giving a paternal basso profundo to his bellows: 'Sandy, Sandy. What are you doing here? Why aren't you home in bloody bed? Sandy, where the bloody hell are you?' Barging into the bedroom, they found Sandy desperately trying to leap into her clothes. 'Oh, for fuck's sake!' complained Mick.

If further proof was required of the mushrooming chic status of the Rolling Stones, it came on 21 April. A *frisson* ran through the audience that the musicians could feel on-stage as the crowd parted first for John Lennon, then the rest of the Beatles. The Liverpool group, who were at number one with their third single 'From Me To You' less than two months after they had first gone to number one with 'Please Please Me', had been appearing on the television programme *Thank Your Lucky Stars*, which was filmed at studios in neighbouring Twickenham. They stood and watched the set, which the Stones concluded with a lengthy version of 'I'm Moving On'. Afterwards, the Beatles signed a considerable number of autographs and then came back to 102 Edith Grove with the Stones. The personable Liverpudlians were not at all stand-offish, and congratulated the Stones on their music. Mick was amazed to learn how many songs the Beatles had already written, and that they received a royalty on sales: he picked Paul's and then John's brains about the exact amounts that could be earned.

After a long conversation with John, Mick played him Jimmy Reed's 'I'll Change My Style'. This most belligerent of the Beatles, however, was most unimpressed: 'What's this? I think it's crap.' Mick didn't understand why he didn't like it, if he liked other blues music. Keith and Stu stood talking to George. Brian and Paul talked. Although they stayed up until four a.m. with the Beatles, Keith and Brian were out of bed bright and early a few hours later, heading off to meet the group again at their hotel. The Liverpool group invited them to come and see their show at the Royal Albert Hall the following Thursday.

On 24 April 1963, the Stones played Eel Pie Island for the first time. The day after they had had an audition at the BBC, with Ricky Brown and Carlo Little depping for Bill and Charlie who couldn't take time off work, they had scored the booking at Eel Pie Island Hotel, a prestigious, hip venue in the middle of the Thames close to Richmond. The night after the gig they had unloaded all the equipment at Edith Grove, because Stu needed to get the van fixed the following day. Keith and Brian took advantage of the situation by wiring up the radiogram to the PA speakers and blasting Bo Diddley into the surrounding neighbourhood at one in the morning.

Late the following afternoon Mick, Keith and Brian took the 31 bus up to the junction of Kensington Church Street and Kensington High Street, and walked along to the Albert Hall on Kensington Gore. In order to get them into the building, the Beatles' road crew handed the three Stones guitars belonging to John, Paul and George, which they carried in through the back door of the hall: they were mobbed by girls who thought they were the Beatles. Brian loved this: now he wanted to be a star. Back at Edith Grove, Brian considered whether they should get rid of Bill ('Ernie', as he used to call him slightingly, after the workmen in the caff) so that he could take up the bass. He soon seemed to go off the idea, as Brian was so prone to do.

Meeting the Beatles was psychologically important for the Stones. Only a few months previously, Brian and Keith had tuned in at ten a.m. to the Beatles' first radio broadcast on the Light Programme's weekly two-hour-long *Saturday Club*, presented by the avuncular Brian Matthew. They had been seriously troubled by what they heard, as though they had missed their cue. 'They're using a harmonica – they've beaten us to it,' said Keith, as John Lennon's distinctive mouth-organ work – inspired by the way the same instrument was used on Bruce Chanel's 'Hey Baby' – led into 'Love Me Do', the group's first single. Things became even more gloomy at Edith Grove that Saturday morning when the Beatles played 'Roll Over Beethoven', written by Chuck Berry, Keith's musical inspiration. Phelge felt obliged to perk up everyone's downcast spirits with the light relief of dropping the dirty crockery out of the window. On another occasion he and Keith threw all the dirty, mould-encrusted saucepans, as well as the knives and forks, down two flights of stairs into the garden. Coming back a couple of days later, they found them all in the kitchen, sparkling clean – Judith, the clairvoyant girl in the flat below them, had washed them. 'Keith,' she admonished, 'you can't just throw them out of the window if they're dirty. You have to wash them.'

CHAPTER 7

ANDREW'S JIB

The Beatles had not been the only prestigious members of the audience at the Crawdaddy on 21 April. Giorgio Gomelsky had cajoled Peter Jones, a writer with *Record Mirror*, into coming to see the show. Straight away Peter Jones saw who it was who ran the group – Brian Jones, 'the organizer, with this great memory; he would tell you how much material they had and exactly where it came from. It was he who laid down the guiding policies of the band. It was Brian who supervised every single move they made. He talked about Muddy Waters, Jimmy Reed and people like that. But he was in no way super-optimistic.'

When Peter Jones arrived at the Station Hotel, the group were playing a couple of numbers for the benefit of Giorgio Gomelsky's camera, one of them 'Pretty Thing'. He thought it was excellent. But notwithstanding the presence of the Fab Four, both Brian and Mick seemed down in the dumps, noted the *Record Mirror* man: they were complaining about the way in which the 'scene' was divided up into trad jazz and modern jazz, and how rhythm 'n' blues was looked down on. The journalist's enthusiastic response was to tell them how good he thought they were. He persuaded Norman Jopling, another *Record Mirror* writer, to go down to the Station Hotel the following Sunday.

Under the headline 'The Rolling Stones – Genuine R And B', Jopling's review showed how the show had completely inspired him. 'As the trad scene gradually subsides', he wrote,

promoters of all kinds of teen-beat entertainments heave a sigh of relief that they have found something to take its place. It's rhythm and blues, of course – the number of R and B clubs that have suddenly sprung up is nothing short of fantastic.

… at the Station Hotel, Kew Road, the hip kids throw themselves about to the new 'jungle music' like they never did in the more restrained days of trad.

And the combo they writhe and twist to is called the Rolling Stones. Maybe you've never heard of them – if you live far from London the odds are you haven't.

But by gad you will! the Stones are destined to be the biggest group in the R and B scene – if that scene continues to flourish. Three months ago only fifty people turned up to see the group. Now Gomelsky has to close the doors at an early hour – with over four hundred fans crowding the hall.

Those fans quickly lose their inhibitions and contort themselves to truly exciting music. Fact is that, unlike all the other R and B groups worthy of the name, the Rolling Stones have a definite visual appeal. They aren't like the jazzmen who were doing trad a few months ago and who had converted their act to keep up with the times. They are genuine R and B fanatics themselves, and they sing and play in a way that one would have expected from a coloured US group rather than a bunch of wild, exciting white boys who have the fans screaming and listening to them.

... they can also get the sound that Bo Diddley gets – no mean achievement. The group themselves are all red-hot when it comes to US beat discs. They know their R and B numbers inside out and have a repertoire of about eighty songs, most of them ones which the real R and B fans know and love.

But despite the fact that their R and B has a superficial resemblance to rock 'n' roll, fans of the hit parade music would not find any familiar material performed by the Rolling Stones. And the boys do not use original material – only the American stuff. 'After all,' they say, 'can you imagine a British-composed R and B number – it just wouldn't make it.'

That was the kind of thinking a young Soho hustler with ambitions to be a comedian called Andrew Loog Oldham would very quickly attempt to dispel as unprofitable. After Peter Jones had run into him, extolling the praises of the Stones, the nineteen-year-old Oldham, who had worked as unpaid press agent for the Beatles on their 'Please Please Me' single, came along to see the Stones at Richmond the following Sunday, 28 April 1963. With him he brought one Eric Easton, a headmasterly thirty-five-year-old show-business agent; Easton represented, among others, guitarist Bert Weedon, an occasional chart entrant whose play-in-a-day guitar books provided the rudiments for a generation of British guitar players, including Keith Richards and Brian Jones – and Mrs Mills, a middle-aged piano player who had managed to get hit records out of the kind of singalong medleys you might hear any Saturday night in London's East End pubs.

Two days previously at Windsor's Ricky Tick club, Mick had met nineteen-year-old Chrissie Shrimpton. They were to go out over the following three years. But when Andrew Oldham arrived in Richmond, he caught them having their first row, on their first date, by the side of the Station Hotel.

Andrew Loog Oldham notes in *Stoned*, his autobiography, on his first visit to Richmond Station Hotel, at the end of a beautiful late-April day: 'Halfway down the pathway I saw that I was not alone – there were two figures ahead of me, one with back to the wall, the other facing, arms against the wall. I got closer; they weren't discussing, they were arguing. A girl was against the wall and a boy was pressing his point.

'As I passed them I tried to be invisible, looking away from them, but not quite. The three of us acknowledged each other, I by picking up my pace as I passed by, they by pausing. He gave me a look that asked me everything about myself in one moment – as in, 'What are you doing with the rest of my life?' His lips looked at you, seconding that first emotion. He was thin, waistless, giving him the human form of a puma with a gender of its own; the girl was a bridge to reality. They were both very earnest, hurt and similar: pale skins, brown hair and flashing eyes. And both, very attractive in their similarity, in heat; in the shadows of the pathway I wasn't sure who was mommy and who was daddy.

'I edited all such thoughts out of my mental movie and quickly put a coin in my jukebox and walked on. Later I found out that the Romeo and Juliet in my path had been Michael Philip Jagger and Chrissie Shrimpton on their first date, first fight.'

Oldham was knocked out by the performance of the Rolling Stones in Richmond. 'He looked at Mick like Sylvester looks at Tweetie Pie,' said the jazz singer and author George Melly. Oldham and Easton acted immediately. Luckily for them, Giorgio Gomelsky, who had been so loyally guiding the recent career of the group, was conveniently out of the country. On 6 May 1963 the Rolling Stones' management contract with Impact Sound, the business name for the hastily convened partnership of Oldham and Easton, was signed by Brian Jones at Easton's offices off Baker Street, on behalf of the group, for a term of three years. Mick and Keith waited near by in one of London's ubiquitous Lyons corner houses. Before Brian put pen to paper, he nipped across the road to confer with his compadres. Back with Andrew Loog Oldham and Eric Easton, he made a deal on the side that he would be paid five pounds a week more than the other members.

Keith was told by Oldham to drop the 's' from his surname to make it more like that of Cliff Richard, the British rock 'n' roll singer turned sugary all-round family entertainer; as it subconsciously distanced him from his absent father, Keith was happy to do this. More radical changes were mooted by the group's new management team: initially Eric Easton had only become involved in the project because he wanted to drop Mick Jagger as vocalist, and get in a 'proper' singer – one, presumably, with whom Bert Weedon or Mrs Mills would have felt comfortable. At first Brian seemed perfectly amenable to this. According to Bill, there was dark plotting by Brian Jones about this potential change: Stu had overheard Brian telling Easton that Mick's voice was not strong, and that they should be careful if they needed him to sing every night, and that, if necessary, they should get another singer. 'As soon as the group started to become in any way successful, Brian smelled money. He wanted to be a star. He was prepared to do anything that would make that happen and bring in money immediately, whereas Mick and Keith weren't into that.' Andrew Loog Oldham, however, was insistent that Mick remain in the group.

Yet Stu's having overheard this was like a portent of his own doom: Andrew had no doubt who it was who should leave the group. The same night that Brian signed the contract, the Rolling Stones played another live show at Eel Pie Island just down the Thames from the Station Hotel, the second show of a weekly Wednesday-night residency. That evening Andrew Loog Oldham announced to the rest of the group that Stu could no longer be a member of the Stones – the piano player, with his prognathous jaw and paternal air, 'didn't look right', he decreed. Instead, he suggested, Stu should play on the group's records and become their road manager. Stu still did not know about the plot against him. Brian and Keith returned together to Edith Grove from Richmond: Keith told Phelge that they would have to let Stu know that he was no longer a group member.

When Stu finally came round to the flat two days later, he was told how the land lay. He agreed to stay on as road manager. Keith's acquiescence in this shocking move appeared to startle Stu – he gave Keith a look that seemed to say, '*Et tu, Brute?*' All along, Brian had promised Stu that he was part of the group. Stu, Phelge thought, seemed on the verge of tears. According to Bill Wyman, Stu now became extremely bitter towards Brian Jones: 'The tensions between group members began to increase . . . Brian's relationship with Mick blossomed temporarily, but there was an underlying feeling that ruthless determination was replacing idealism,' considered Bill. 'I thought that the "sacking" was a strange way to repay Stu's incredible loyalty.'

'A lot of changes occurred,' said Keith. 'Our sights were raised. We already thought we were the fucking king and his cousins. Andrew and I recognised the connection to art school and how to sell things. We said, "We've got to turn these people on their hands; they're not going to know what's happened to them in the record business, and either we win or we lose – it's heads or tails." The Beatles were out there and doing some shit, had two records out and both had gone to number one – this was a big deal. Andrew said, "If you want to make records you've got to go down that pop path, get in there and be able to manoeuvre a bit", because in those days you made a record and you'd just see guys in brown coats walking around and pointing a microphone saying, "Stand here and do this". So we said, "We'll just do what the Beatles don't!" It was like not wearing a uniform.'

The implacably faithful Stu was still prepared to offer up to the group any contacts of his who might help the Stones. His schoolfriend Glyn Johns – the same Glyn Johns who played in the Presidents – worked at IBC Studios in Portland Place as an engineer, and was allowed to record any new artists he considered as having talent. Accordingly, the Rolling Stones went in to IBC and put four of their stage songs on tape, one of which was the Chuck Berry song 'Come On'.

On Saturday 11 May the Stones played an undistinguished date in Battersea Park Fun Fair, a 'charity gala', like a large-scale church summer fête but with girls in swimsuits, promoted by the *News of the World*, a publication later destined to play a more negative role in the group's career. It was the first booking secured for them by their new managers, Andrew Loog Oldham and Eric Easton.

The next day at the Crawdaddy, Dick Rowe from Decca Records was in the audience, at the invitation of Andrew Loog Oldham. Desperate to rectify his new reputation as The Man Who Turned Down The Beatles – George Harrison had urged him to see the Stones two days previously – by the following Monday Rowe had offered the Rolling Stones a recording contract. On 14 May 1963 a two-year tape-lease agreement was signed between Oldham and Easton and Decca Records. This was the first time in the history of British record companies that such a deal had taken place: having so risibly missed out on the Beatles, Decca were desperate to secure the group, and almost any terms were acceptable. 'When we started there was great joy at getting a recording contract,' said Keith, 'but at the same time this sense of death, because nobody lasted more than two years in the early sixties. It didn't matter how big you were, unless you were Elvis you were supposed to disappear at the height of your career.'

The following morning the Stones went into the Olympic Sound record-ing studio, off Baker Street, which cost five pounds an hour. They decided on Chuck Berry's 'Come On' as their first single. The final result was under two minutes in length; the B-side featured 'I Wanna Be Loved' by Willie Dixon, who was the guiding musical force behind the seminal Chess Records empire in Chicago. Roger Savage engineered the session and was told by Andrew Loog Oldham, 'Look, I'm the producer and this is the first recording session I've ever handled. I don't know a damn thing about recording, or music for that matter.' Decca rejected the finished result, insisting that the numbers be re-recorded at the company's own studio in West Hampstead.

Although 'Come On' was written by the group's adored and revered

Chuck Berry, it was one of his most poppy and insubstantial songs. And when the Stones' even more up-tempo version of the single was released on 7 June 1963 (other Decca releases that day included Karl Denver's 'Indian Love Call' and Clodagh Rogers' 'To Give My Love To You'), the group decided they didn't like it at all, initially refusing to play the number as part of their live set, much to the chagrin of Dick Rowe. After 'Come On' had been in the shops for a month, however, the group got to play it on the television show *Thank Your Lucky Stars*, recording their performance on Saturday 13 July, to be broadcast late the following Sunday afternoon. Despite his vow never to clean his shoes ('What's the point?' he would berate Phelge. 'They'll only get dirty again'), Keith scrupulously polished his Anello and Davide Cuban-heeled boots prior to this first television appearance – the first glimpse most of the country had of the Rolling Stones, who compromised by wearing identical outfits, velvet-collared houndstooth jackets with coordinated trousers and ties.

At the show Eric Easton told the group he had booked them as one of the support acts on a tour being topped by the Everly Brothers that September.

The night of that first *Thank Your Lucky Stars* appearance, the Rolling Stones left the television studio and charged the length of England to play at the Alcove club in Middlesbrough, two hundred and fifty miles north. Headlining the bill in the tough north-eastern city were the Hollies, a group from Manchester they had never previously heard of; the immense harmonic competence of the Hollies unnerved Brian, as he expressed on the Stones' return to Edith Grove, ready for their two regular Sunday shows in London. What Brian didn't appreciate was that all the groups in the north worked out complicated harmony parts: that was what they had heard on the imported discs from US R 'n' B acts that came into the region through the docks at Liverpool – recordings that presaged the stridently heartfelt, up-tempo vocals of what later became known as Northern Soul. Anyway, from now on the Stones worked on their harmonies: hence the additions of the songs 'Fortune Teller' and 'Poison Ivy' to their sets, which Brian found worked well with the group's new singing arrangements.

Despite 'Come On' only hanging around at the bottom end of the charts, such was the by now national buzz on the group that it stayed there for four months, slowly achieving impressive and auspicious sales of 100,000 copies. Its sales had been boosted by three more television appearances: on 23 August, over five weeks after that first *Thank Your Lucky Stars* appearance, the group featured the single on the second broadcast of the show *Ready, Steady, Go!*. The new programme was marketed as the high-paced 'house' programme of British Mods, broadcast in the London region on Friday nights at 6.10 p.m. with the hopeful tagline, 'The Weekend Starts Here!'. Six days later they appeared on *Scene At 6.30*, an influential, mildly hip magazine programme broadcast from Granada's Manchester studios, presented by a youthful Michael Parkinson; and on 14 September, the Stones were given a repeat performance on *Thank Your Lucky Stars*. As the programme was now recorded and broadcast from Birmingham, the Rolling Stones were also able to slot in two gigs at separate venues in Britain's second city on the same day as they performed on the television show.

After the shows, Mick and Keith were the only group members to drive back in Andrew's car. 'Who could realise, at this early stage, that the splitting of the group in that way would mark our future?' reflected Bill Wyman. 'Keith and Mick were quite prepared to go along with anything Andrew said,' said Ian Stewart. 'They fed off each other. We had very little contact with them in those days. Edicts would just be issued from the Oldham office.'

Meanwhile, the recording of *Ready Steady Go!* became a regular social fixture for both Mick and Keith: if they were in London on Fridays, the day the show was broadcast live, the two Dartford boys, invariably accompanied by Andrew Loog Oldham, would be down in the show's green room, the epicentre of the Mod social scene. Inevitably, there was an unfounded rumour that Mick was having an affair with Cathy McGowan, the show's lank-haired presenter, who had been nationally elevated to the status of Queen Mod.

The director of *Ready Steady Go!* was Michael Lindsay-Hogg, son of the actress Geraldine Fitzgerald. In Andrew Loog Oldham's autobiography *Stoned*, Lindsay-Hogg spoke of how managers of the time were often far more interesting than their artists: 'I remember on one occasion Andrew telling some hair-raising story, while Mick and Keith sat opposite him, hanging on every word, like younger brothers in thrall to their daring older brother. In fact, thinking about it, I wonder to what degree Andrew's gangster pose (I suppose that's what it was) and his bravado (you fuck with me at your peril) influenced Mick and Keith as they developed their stage characters, which would then morph with their real selves and vice versa. Not a little.'

In his seminal book, *Awobopaloobop: Pop from the Beginning*, Nik Cohn concurred: 'I quite liked the cut of Andrew's jib, I liked his out-rageousness. I thought he was an interesting person, I liked his power of self-invention and humour. I wouldn't have said any of the Stones as individuals were particularly interesting to talk to, whereas Andrew was. He was a major creative force in image – and music-making.

'Oldham, without doubt, was the most flash personality that British pop has ever had, the most anarchic and obsessive and imaginative hustler of all ... He struck up immediate contact with Mick Jagger, who was greatly impressed by him and became almost his disciple, his dedicated follower in the ways of outrage. The weird thing was, Jagger on-stage wasn't like Jagger off-stage, but he was very much like Andrew Oldham ... he was more of a projection of Oldham than of himself ... When I saw the Stones in the office or in the dressing room they were young, fairly inarticulate lads, lots of in-jokes and so on. It was Andrew who had the articulateness, the sharpness, the flash and above all the outrageousness.'

By now Mick was seriously involved with Chrissie Shrimpton, who was just seventeen. As though it had become a constant of their relationship, they rowed all the time – nothing had changed since Andrew Loog Oldham first saw them outside the Station Hotel. They had met after Chrissie, acting on a dare that showed her spirit, had gone up to Mick and kissed him when the Stones had played at the Ricky Tick in Windsor the week before the Station Hotel show in April 1963.

Her family was affluent, owning a large house and farm in Buckinghamshire, a few miles outside High Wycombe; her father was a well-to-do builder. Mick now moved a few rungs up the social ladder in more ways than one: Jean Shrimpton, Chrissie's infinitely cool and groovy sister, had, as 'The Shrimp', secured the crown of Britain's top model. Through this association, Chrissie and Mick were given access to the portals of glamorous, hip London which at this point in their careers might have been beyond the reach of the Stones; it was a world of fey, arty men and exciting women who wore tights (known in those days to be a sure signifier of sexual looseness) and miniskirts and who daily swallowed the new contraceptive pill. It was a world in which Mick immediately felt at home, secretly pleased with himself at having pulled off this leap.

Like many middle-class English girls who didn't go on to university, Chrissie had been installed by her father in a one-year course at Pitman's secretarial college, at the fashionable central London branch in her case. When Mick was in London, they would meet at lunchtime or at the end of the day in Hyde Park. To Chrissie Shrimpton's surprise and delight Mick had asked her to marry him as soon as he had made a reasonable amount of money; sensibly, Chrissie had responded by saying she would like to wait a while. It would annoy her when Mick would try to pretend she wasn't there if he was approached by fans when they were out, and her friends tried to intimate that there was a homosexual relationship between Mick and Andrew Oldham.

'There were periods when Andrew was very camp,' said Gered Mankowitz, shortly to be inducted into the Stones' camp as official photographer. 'And it could be either very amusing or slightly unpleasant. He was a very frenetic character; his energies were all over the place, and he would suffer from depression because things didn't seem to work out quite how he wanted them to.

'It was hard to maintain a friendship with him, because he could be so difficult. During those times, he was very camp. I actually think he's as heterosexual as they come. But he played on it, and would exploit every nuance.

'There's no doubt that Andrew was way ahead in terms of image and charisma and style. He must have been a role model to Mick. I'm sure Mick was looking for a role model, as part of his finding himself, and I think that's where his campness came from. I think there's something very showbiz about Mick, and there's an infectiousness about that. Andrew would always take advantage of anything the press said: if people said the Stones were like animals and should be caged up, he'd have a picture of them taken inside a zoo cage; if people said that Andrew was gay, he would act as though he was extremely gay, and push it to the limit. I guess that was part of the plan.

'Tony King – who was known as Tony Queen – was around them, and he could be terribly funny. He became a plugger for the Beatles afterwards – eventually he plugged RCA's disco label in the States, and had a card that read 'homo promo'. It was all part of that very camp, very theatrical, very bitchy world. In the Stones' circle, saying things because they were funny, even if they were cruel, was attractive.'

One of the most effective images that Andrew Loog Oldham lodged in the minds of the British public about the Rolling Stones was that they were 'dirty', with all of the early 1960s prurient connotations of the word. But the only thing that was really 'dirty' was the interior of the flat at 102 Edith Grove. Chrissie Shrimpton often went around with a friend called Lizzie. Chrissie had been inside the flat at Edith Grove only once; on all subsequent visits to collect Mick she would be made to wait in the hall by Keith, who confided with working-class chivalry that it was too filthy in the flat for her to come upstairs. 'On the home front, this growing charisma of Mick's, and his obvious enjoyment of it, was giving Chrissie fits, which she vented in outbursts that were both verbal and physical,' wrote Andrew Loog Oldham in his autobiography. 'When Chrissie slammed the door on him, Mick would ring me at my mother's. He'd walk from Edith Grove, we'd meet at a bench on the Embankment and he'd shout and wail at the Thames and me about the confusion of being in love with oneself, one's girl and one's life.' Chrissie shouted at him all the time, Mick would complain.

What was worse was that from time to time she would also hit him, which frightened him.

Brian was going out with Pat Andrews and Linda Lawrence. Keith remained wedded to his guitar. Accordingly, it was only Phelge and Keith who were in at Edith Grove on the Tuesday night they decided to remove the door of the communal toilet with a screwdriver and hide it in their own flat. This caused something of a fuss in the household. Before the landlord arrived in response to the complaints of his other tenants, the pair had secured the door back on its hinges.

However, the days at 102 Edith Grove were virtually over. At the end of September 1963, the twelve-month lease on the rented accommodation ran out. Immediately Mick and Keith moved into a flat in Mapesbury Road, off Shoot Up Hill in Willesden, but sufficiently near the more salubrious-sounding West Hampstead for Mick and Keith to claim that that was the area in which they lived. Brian went to live with Linda Lawrence at her parents' house in Windsor.

Mick and Keith's new flat in Mapesbury Road was on the first floor, at the front of a large house. It had two rooms. The smaller was Mick's bedroom. Keith slept in the lounge, which had an enormous wooden wardrobe jammed into a corner – most of his clothes, however, lay scattered around the room. Next to his ever-unmade bed – one corner propped up by a pile of books – was a record-player, so positioned that he didn't need to get out of bed to change discs. Piles of records spilled around it: blues, the Everly Brothers, even an LP by a new artist called Bob Dylan. In the kitchen was an enormous photograph of the group at a recording session. They were still in the world of communal bathrooms and there was a payphone in the hallway, Mick and Keith constantly scurrying around for the four old pennies that were needed to make their increasing number of daily phone calls.

In the *Melody Maker* poll that September the Rolling Stones were voted sixth best British group; three months later, in the *NME*'s end-of-year poll, the Stones again came sixth in the best British vocal group category. On 27 September, the Stones ended their Sunday-afternoon residency at the Ken Colyer club at Studio 51 with an extraordinary gig: the place was packed, with four hundred screaming fans outside trying to get in and dancing on the pavement. It was Rolling Stones mania. Afterwards, before they headed off for Richmond, where they were also concluding their residency at the Crawdaddy, the group went for a drink at a local showbiz pub, the Salisbury, and were refused service because of their appearance.

CHAPTER 8

AN ANGEL WITH BIG TITS

The move to the new flat in Mapesbury Road was completed only days before the Stones set off on their first full-scale UK tour, which ran from 29 September, when it opened at the New Victoria Theatre in London, returning to the capital for its closing date on 3 November at Hammersmith Odeon. Headlining the tour, onto which Eric Easton had astutely booked the Rolling Stones within days of assuming control of their management, were a trio of heavyweight acts, slightly past their prime but still credible: the Everly Brothers, Bo Diddley – whose custom-built square guitar case entranced Keith – and Little Richard, one of Mick's inspirations, although he did not join the tour until the date at Watford Gaumont on 5 October. Studying his absurdly, endearingly camp hero backstage, Mick learned how to apply actors' make-up; from Little Richard Mick also learned to take off his jacket during the Stones' set and twirl it teasingly on his index finger, like a burlesque dancer.

'I used to spend a lot of time with Little Richard,' said Mick. 'He was very friendly and a great hero. He used to teach me a lot. I would watch him every single night to see how he handled the audience. He was a great audience manipulator, in the best sense of the word. He had a fantastic show-business understanding of the audience and how to get them at it, what numbers to play and when to quit. I probably learned more from him than from anyone else.'

'The first proper tour was late summer of '63,' remembered Keith. 'Little Richard, Bo Diddley, the Everly Brothers and a few other weirdo acts like us thrown in for good measure. What an education – like going to rock 'n' roll university – six weeks working with these guys every night. You want to know anything about rock 'n' roll, you've got the whole spectrum there. They're the best teachers in the world and at the same time we're getting bigger and bigger on this tour, opening the second half of the show, and the kids were rocking, and that's pissing the Everly Brothers off because they're top of the bill . . . We came off that tour not only full of confidence but knowing and learning shit it would take you years to pick up, by watching Don Peake, the Everly Brothers' guitarist, watching how they delivered things, watching how Little Richard would open a show, how he would swing an audience ... even at that age, nineteen or twenty, you'd wake up and slap your face, saying, "You're working with Little Richard and Bo Diddley". Six months before we were thinking, "If only I could hear him one time", and suddenly you're his friend and he goes, "Pop round the pub, get me a drink, man". Bo Diddley's asking me, "Where the hell is Jerome Green?" "I'll go get him, Bo." Suddenly it's a whole different trip.'

Also on the bill with the Stones, who earned forty-two pounds a night and had been outfitted in matching blue leather waistcoats by Eric Easton, was a motley crew consisting of Julie Grant, Mickie Most, the Flintstones, the Rattles and Ray Cameron. Mick started to wear a metal-link identity bracelet, of the kind dangling from the wrist of every star in the magazine *Salut Les Copains*, a French publication and an offshoot from a hugely successful daily teenage youth show on a national radio station that served as an inspirational style guide for the 'continental' look favoured by Mods.

'On the first tour we wore the suits that Andrew wanted us to wear and said, "All right, we'll do it. You know the game. We'll try it out",' said Keith. 'But then the Stones thing started taking over; Charlie would leave his jacket in some dressing room and I'd pull mine out and there'd be whisky all over it, or chocolate pudding. When we'd got rid of these dog-tooth jackets and the Lord John shirts, Andrew suddenly realised we were different and got fully behind it. After that, the press did all the work for us. We only needed to be refused permission to stay in a hotel to set the whole thing rolling again.'

Bill noted, 'The day after the tour opened was another milestone. During the previous six months Charlie, Stu and I had all taken the chance of leaving regular employment and turning professional with the Stones. Mick, always the last person in the band to take any risk, finally wrote a letter to the Kent Education Committee terminating his studies at the London School of Economics. "I have been offered a really excellent opportunity in the entertainment world", he wrote to them with his droll sense of humour.'

Among the tunes the Stones chose to play on the tour were 'Poison Ivy', 'Fortune Teller', 'Money', 'You Better Move On' and 'Down the Road Apiece', and no less than six songs from the catalogue of the great Chuck Berry – the inevitable 'Come On', 'Roll Over Beethoven', 'Memphis Tennessee', 'Talkin 'Bout You', 'Beautiful Delilah' and 'Bye Bye Johnny', which they habitually played as an encore. In the nine to eleven songs they would play twice nightly, there was not a single original number. Still, their engagingly naive interpretations provided a substantial breath of fresh British musical air when set against the polished professionalism of the American stars on the bill. But there was no getting away from it: the Rolling Stones continued to be no more than a classy covers group.

No wonder Andrew was urging Mick and Keith to write their own material. Their co-manager knew he needed a songwriting partnership in the group to push the Stones to the top. He was also aware that Brian Jones, the blues crusader, was too concerned with musical integrity to be bothered about this. 'Andrew knew he had to bring Mick and Keith together. His problem here was in breaking Keith's natural musical partnership with Brian: from the beginning, as the two guitarists, they had interlinked their lines and worked really well together,' explained Bill.

Andrew Loog Oldham had also moved into Mapesbury Road, sharing the front room with Keith. Now he had the Dartford pair under his eye. Andrew's constant physical presence in the lives of Mick and Keith split the Rolling Stones into two factions. The team of Jagger, Richard and Oldham began to ride roughshod over everyone else in the group, Mick and Keith travelling to gigs with Andrew in his car; the rest of the group would be driven by Stu in the van. Cannily, Bill had managed to persuade the group that he suffered from travel sickness and had to sit in the front of the vehicle – it took years before the others discovered that there was no truth in this whatsoever.

At the show in Cardiff on 6 October a bunch of Bo Diddley fans came backstage. After spending time with their hero, they chatted with the Stones. One of them offered the group a joint of grass. The Stones were so shocked they had him thrown out of their dressing room. In the great tradition of jazz musicians, Charlie occasionally smoked marijuana, but out of sight of the others.

While on this Everly Brothers tour, the rest of the group discovered the extra five pounds a week that Brian had negotiated for himself for being leader of the group. He had also expressed a desire to stay in more expensive hotels than his fellow musicians. In small, tight-knit operations like a pop group, such an action is always seen as the most shocking form of betrayal: the repercussions of Brian's greed were enormous. Said Keith: 'He had this arrangement with Easton, that as leader of the band he was entitled to extra payment. Everybody freaked out. That was the beginning of the decline of Brian. We said, "Fuck you".'

The tour was colossally successful for the Stones, climaxing at the Hammersmith Odeon where, playing on home ground, they had a formidable reception. The Everly Brothers had paper cups thrown at them.

A follow-up single to 'Come On' was needed. Initially it had been decided that 'Poison Ivy', a semi-novelty tune written by Lieber and Stoller and released in 1959 by their protégés the Coasters, would be the A-side of the new single coupled with Benny Spellman's witty, up-tempo 'Fortune Teller' for the flip side. Accordingly, both sides were recorded at Decca's studios in West Hampstead. But neither song seemed up to scratch or sufficiently strong. Although the record was set to be released at the end of August, the Stones had courted controversy by pulling it a week before it was due to come out: 'Poison Ivy' had been scrubbed from the Decca release schedule. What should they replace it with?

During a day off for the Stones from the Everly Brothers tour at the beginning of October, Andrew Loog Oldham ran into John Lennon and Paul McCartney in Jermyn Street, travelling in a taxi on their way back from a Variety Club lunch at the Dorchester Hotel. Andrew told them the group was rehearsing in nearby Studio 51, and that they didn't know what to record for their next single release. The two Beatles said they might have something for them, and walked over to the Soho club with Oldham. There they found the Stones looking decidedly low.

But not for long: John took Keith's guitar and Paul took Bill's bass and sang them the number. John then went over the arrangement with Brian and Keith. After about twenty minutes John and Paul left. Lennon and McCartney's 'I Wanna Be Your Man' was to become the Rolling Stones' second single. 'The way Paul and John used to hustle tunes was great,' Mick recalled. 'We thought it sounded pretty commercial . . . But we were surprised that John and Paul would be prepared to give us one of their best numbers.' 'We just hope they'll like it,' said Keith, as proud as any of the Stones to cover a song by the immensely hip Beatles.

On 7 October 1963 the Rolling Stones went into De Lane Lea studio in Holborn to record 'I Wanna Be Your Man'. As Andrew Loog Oldham was temporarily away from London, Eric Easton produced the record. 'Brian *made* that record with that bottleneck,' admitted Keith, who before long would become a severe critic of the founder of the Rolling Stones. For the B-side, they recorded a song called 'Stoned' that they wrote on the spot, a rapid theft of the distinctive chord structure of Booker T's 'Green Onions'. On 'Stoned' all the group members shared songwriting credits, creating a music publishing company called Nanker-Phelge Music Ltd: the name of the publishing imprint was an 'in-joke' that vaguely fitted the satirical mood of the times, and was personified by the adored 'wackiness' of the Beatles. Not that James Phelge ever saw a share of the cut. Released on 1 November, the song got to number 9 in the charts. It later allowed John Lennon to sneer at how the Beatles had even written the Stones' second record for them. On 20 October Andrew travelled back to London from Liverpool with John and Paul in their limousine; the Stones manager had been hanging out on Merseyside with these ultimate groovers, having left the London group the previous night in the grim Yorkshire surroundings of Bradford where they were on tour with the Everly Brothers. From conversation with John and Paul, Andrew discovered what a mint there was to be made if the Stones could write their own hit songs.

Accordingly, one evening on a day off from the Everly Brothers' tour, Andrew made an executive decision: he pushed the two Dartford boys into the kitchen at Mapesbury Road with the hectoring admonition, 'Don't come out without a song.' After a number of false starts, ('I'm saying, "That's not my job",' Keith told American journalist Stanley Boothe. 'Virtually what he did was lock us up in the kitchen for a night'), Mick and Keith turned in their first composition, an affectingly poignant ballad which they titled 'As Time Goes By', later to be renamed 'As Tears Go By'. 'The most unlikely Rolling Stones material,' thought Keith, 'but that's what happens when you write songs, you immediately fly to some other realm. I can't connect it with what I'm doing.' As though by serendipity, Andrew Loog Oldham was shortly to find the right artist to make the record a hit.

There were no songwriting role models in Britain at the time other than Lennon and McCartney; already the extraordinary productivity of its two writers was part of the myth of the Beatles. (Beatle non-believers would insist that seasoned Tin Pan Alley hacks really wrote their tunes for them.) As well as writing their own hits, by now they had had chart successes with 'covers' of their material by other artists: Billy J. Kramer, the Fourmost, and Cilla Black ... and now here came the Rolling Stones.

The first fruits of Mick and Keith's efforts to emulate the Liverpudlian duo were put down at Regent Sound studio on 20 and 21 November. The Stones had recorded demos of six songs written by the pair at Mapesbury Road: 'Will You Be My Lover Tonight', 'It Should Be You', 'Shang A Doo Lang', 'That Girl Belongs To Yesterday', 'Leave Me Alone' and 'So Much In Love'. Tucked in at the end of the sessions was another song, 'Sure I Do', one of two numbers demo'd by the Stones that bore the credit 'B. Jones'. Although no other artist picked up Brian's song, the sessions were by no means unproductive for Mick and Keith: by March the following year Gene Pitney had a Top Ten hit with 'That Girl Belongs To Yesterday', produced by Andrew Loog Oldham. 'We were already writing hit songs but, like, on the side,' remembered Keith, 'no way we would touch these things with a bargepole by ourselves. Trying to get around to writing a song we could record took quite a while, but once we got into realising that, hey, we already had a couple of hits, we thought, "All we got to do is work on it, and we probably will find it". So we started to work towards that end.'

The other tunes failed to chart: 'Shang A Doo Lang' was recorded by Adrienne Posta for her second single; the Mighty Avengers released 'So Much In Love'; and 'It Should Be You', with 'Will You Love Me Tonight' on the B-side, was released by George Bean in December that year, the first recording to boast the credits of 'Jagger–Richards'.

At the end of the first week in December 1963 the group returned to Regent Sound to put down a further four songs written by Mick and Keith: 'Give Me Your Hand (And I'll Hold It Tight)', 'You Must Be The One', 'When A Girl Loves A Boy' and 'I Want You To Know' (on which title Brian shared the credit). 'Give Me Your Hand' had been written specifically for the Beatles, as thanks for the group's giving the Stones 'I Wanna Be Your Man'; the Beatles said they would only record the tune if the Stones cut another song of theirs, 'One After 909', an offer the Stones turned down. (Was there an element of brinkmanship going on here? An alleged, all-consuming rivalry between the Beatles and Rolling Stones – carefully contrived and disseminated by Andrew Loog Oldham – was now a staple theme in the media. As though rather obviously throwing down a challenge, on 5 November 1963, the night the Beatles played the Royal Variety Performance, the Stones were playing on the Beatles' home turf at the Cavern club in Liverpool.) 'You Must Be The One' was recorded some months later by the Greenbeats for Pye, and released in November 1964. According to Bill, 'Mick and Keith, egged on by Andrew, saw the golden chance to break through.'

Unlike Lennon and McCartney, who would switch songwriting roles at will, Keith was always the one who came up with a tune's music and Mick its words; quickly he learned that to attempt to pen lyrics in structured verse form slowed down the writing process. He would put the words down in more or less stream-of-consciousness style, then juggle them around afterwards until they fitted a form of metre. (Initially Mick and Keith seemed better at writing ballads: as they showed with 'As Tears Go By' and Gene Pitney's 'That Girl Belongs To Yesterday'.)

Meanwhile, Mick set about broadening his mind, approaching life with a reading list. Although Chrissie Shrimpton had rented a flat of her own – fresh from secretarial college, she was now working at Decca Records – she was often round at Mapesbury Road, sometimes accompanied by Camilla Wiggin, a close friend of hers. According to Andrew Loog Oldham, who was only reflecting a contemporary pop PR perception, the relationship between Chrissie and Mick Jagger was very definitely not for public consumption. To Chrissie's chagrin, Mick avidly followed this party line, hence his irritating disowning of her when they were out together. Not so ready to accept the party line was Charlie Watts, although at first he obeyed Jagger's dictum that he must not as yet marry Shirley, his girlfriend.

On 8 November 'I Wanna Be Your Man' entered the *NME* singles chart at number thirty, assisted by the front-page advertisement in the previous week's issue, which guaranteed advertisers of new singles a place in the Top Thirty the following week. That night they played the Club-a-Gogo in Newcastle, the coolest venue in the North-East, known for the hippest sounds and also for the consumption of marijuana that went on within it. The group seemed to be permanently on tour. Before Christmas, Mick said: 'We've only had about four hours' kip each night for most of this week. When we get back to London we'd like to do nothing but sleep until it's time to go on the road again. But there's always so much catching-up to do on jobs we can't look after on tour.'

On New Year's Eve 1963, the Stones played a dance at the Drill Hall in Lincoln, staying at the White Hart hotel. Mick and Keith dressed Brian up in a sheet and knocked on Bill's door. Bill was not pleased: 'Go to bed Brian,' moaned Bill, 'and stop messing about!'

On 2 January 1964 the Rolling Stones went into Regent Sound studios, this time not to make a record of their own but to put down the instrumental backing track for the Phil Spector song 'To Know Him Is To Love Him', written by Phil Spector, a smash by the Teddy Bears in 1958. The vocal was by Cleo Sylvester, one of the two black backing singers the Stones had tried out a year previously. Cleo, eighteen years old and very beautiful, had remained an occasional girlfriend of Mick's. The B-side, entitled 'There Are But Five Rolling Stones', was credited to Andrew Loog Oldham and Mike Leander, and was an instrumental featuring the Stones under the *nom de disque* of The Andrew Oldham Orchestra – a method employed to circumvent any contractual difficulties with Decca.

The date with Cleo Sylvester was something of a warm-up session. The next day, 3 January, the group returned to Regent Sound to record five songs for their imminent first album: 'Carol', 'Route 66', 'Mona', 'Walking The Dog' and 'You Can Make It If You Try'.

Three days later on 6 January 1964, the Rolling Stones began another tour, one that ran for almost three weeks until 27 January. This time the Stones were topping the bill. They were supported by the Ronettes, Phil Spector's black, beehived female trio, as exotic as anything Britain had ever seen on its stages. Phil Spector had sent a telegram to Andrew Loog Oldham to keep the Stones away from his girls, one of whom, Ronnie, was his wife. The Stones and the Ronettes have subsequently indicated that his suggestion was not entirely complied with. 'The only time I remember Mick and me in any slight competition was with the Ronettes, when Mick wanted to pull Ronnie,' remembered Keith. According to Ronnie Spector, Mick seemed to have a head start on Keith: 'The girls took to Mick,' she said. 'He was so sexy, provocative and gorgeous on stage.' In those days, Keith seemed another kettle of fish altogether: 'Not so much shy as quiet,' thought Ronnie. 'I could make him laugh but most of the time nothing was funny to him. He was very into himself, in his own room, in his own world; a bit of a softie.'

Also on the bill were, variously, British rockers Marty Wilde and Joe Brown, relics of the era of British pop established on such television shows as *Oh Boy!* and *Wham!*, still hanging on to their careers, defying the changing wind of musical fashion. Then there was the contingent of 'beat groups': Liverpool's Swinging Blue Jeans, Dave Berry (an extraordinary showman who would perform half hidden by the stage curtains), Mancunian novelty act Freddie and the Dreamers, and Bern Elliott and the Fenmen, who had had a minor hit with Barrett Strong's 'Money', a song included in the Stones' set and played by virtually every beat group in the entire country, including the Beatles.

On 7 January, the second date of the tour, the Stones performed at the Adelphi Theatre in Slough. Absolutely famished at one o'clock the following morning on their way back from the gig, they stopped off at nearby Heathrow airport. In the almost empty cafeteria, they were insulted by a bunch of Americans. Mick Jagger stormed over to the main man and challenged him to a fight. The American responded by punching Mick in the face, sending him flying. Adopting his best Dartford Ted street-fighting posture and hurrying over to help his friend, Keith was similarly thumped to the ground.

Three days later, slotting in a recording session before the pair of shows at the Granada in Walthamstow in east London, the Rolling Stones returned to Regent Sound; a trio of songs emerged that made it onto the first album: Willie Dixon's 'I Just Want To Make Love To You', James Moore's 'I'm a King Bee' and Jimmy Reed's 'Honest I Do'. The Stones also recorded a version of a song that Mick had first heard when he had gone to see Buddy Holly with Dick Taylor: 'Not Fade Away', which was shelved.

The tenth of January 1964 was a busy day in the career of the Rolling Stones; in addition to the recording and tour dates, it also saw the release of the group's first EP, simply titled 'The Rolling Stones'. The EP featured four songs, Chuck Berry's 'Bye Bye Johnny', 'Money' (already released the previous month by the Beatles on their second album), Lieber and Stoller's 'Poison Ivy' (which the group had refused to allow Decca to release the previous August), and the record's stand-out song, the beautifully heartfelt version of Arthur Alexander's classic ballad 'You Better Move On'. As though it was an antidote to the pure pop sensibility that bounced out of every groove of 'I Wanna Be Your Man', the EP was promoted as a single, special emphasis being placed on the notion that this was the authentic 'blues' material that the Stones would perform as part of their live set. Appearing to dismiss the substantial sales of their previous two singles, the EP, whose black-and-white picture sleeve featured the whole group, was sold as being the first 'proper' Rolling Stones record. Within three weeks it had reached number fifteen in the singles chart – by now EPs pulled from the Beatles' albums were constant features in the hit parade.

The song selected by Decca for radio play was 'You Better Move On', and its moody lyrics, enhanced by the sensual enunciation of Mick Jagger which seemed to emphasise every syllable, sailed out of British radio sets until well into the spring of that year. The Arthur Alexander tune propelled the sales of the 'Rolling Stones' EP until it outsold both their first two singles, keeping the raw-sounding realistic representation of the group's live set in the charts for much of 1964.

At the end of January, the Stones went back to Regent Sound to try yet again to record 'Not Fade Away'. Armed with glasses of Scotch and Coke, the group transformed the session into a party. Buddy Holly's 'Not Fade Away' had a Bo Diddley-like arrangement – the Stones took it and emphasised the beat, with Keith on acoustic guitar, Brian on harmonica and Stu on piano. Alan Clarke and Graham Nash of the Hollies, whose crafted harmonies had inspired the Stones to import something similar into their own sound, were on back-up vocals and Phil Spector was shaking maracas. With Mick Jagger Spector also came up with 'Little By Little', the B-side, a song they dashed off at the session, which was credited to Phelge–Spector. Spector's presence certainly added to the sharper focus of both songs: although Andrew was nominally at the production helm, the Stones essentially had their third single, a blast of high-end energy, produced by the most visionary pop-music producer of the day. At the same session they recorded two more tunes, 'Andrew's Blues' and 'Spector and Pitney Came Too' – on the latter, Jagger imitated the voice of Edward Lewis, the Decca chairman. These two songs would never be released.

'Not Fade Away' came out on 21 February, the same day they played the Gaumont, Hanley. The third single from the Rolling Stones reached number three in the charts, vying with the EP for sales, each record stimulating interest in the other.

Four days later on 25 February at Regent Sound the Stones recorded three more songs, including 'Good Times, Bad Times', a tune Mick and Keith had written. Brian was visibly disturbed that this was a Jagger–Richard composition; although he was writing at home in Windsor, where he lived with his girlfriend Linda, Brian never showed the rest of the group his material – his inferiority complex was too great. 'It was a pivotal moment at Regent Sound when Mick and Keith presented their first wares for the Stones to record,' said Andrew in *Stoned*.

The Stones were putting together their first LP. At Regent Sound they would record in the afternoons for the album, before charging off up the road to whatever gig they were playing on the tour with the Ronettes. When Andrew suggested they cover Marvin Gaye's 'Can I Get A Witness', Mick admitted he didn't know the lyrics. After Andrew had made a phone call to the music publishers of the song, Mick ran through Soho to the publishers' office on Savile Row, picking up a copy of the lyrics and running back with them, to record the tune at once, still short of breath. The Stones were running out of material for the LP: when they found they didn't have enough songs, they had to add a lengthy instrumental version of the same number.

After just over a week's break (some week off: they had played another four dates during those seven days, each show a small contribution to the Rolling Stones' becoming the hardest-working live act in Britain in 1964 and 1965), the Stones were off on their third UK tour, which began on 8 February 1964 at the Regal, Edmonton, in north London and wound up on 7 March at the Winter Gardens in Morecambe, Lancashire. For this set of dates, which was given the grandiose title of 'All Star '64', the Stones were accompanied by a bunch of artists who seemed entirely from another era, even though only a few months previously they had been high up in the charts: John Leyton, Jet Harris, Mike Berry and Billie Davies. The Swinging Blue Jeans and Bern Elliott and the Fenmen also added their more contemporary sounds, as did the Paramounts, a tough-sounding R 'n' B group from Southend-on-Sea. The live set the Stones were playing at this time ran, essentially, as follows: 'Talking 'Bout You', 'Poison Ivy', 'Walkin' The Dog', 'Pretty Thing', 'Cops And Robbers', 'Jaguar And The Thunderbird', 'Don't Lie To Me', 'I Wanna Be Your Man', 'Roll Over Beethoven', 'You Better Move On', 'Roadrunner', 'Route 66', 'Bye Bye Johnny' and 'Not Fade Away'.

Midway through the dates, with a symbolism that signalled the seizing of power by British pop's second generation, the Stones found themselves topping the bill. 'John Leyton was the headliner,' said Mick, 'and then as the tour went on we were very lucky with "Not Fade Away". We became so popular on the tour that he had to give up being the headliner, which, as you can imagine, was not very nice. But he was very, very gracious about it and very polite.'

Mick told Ray Coleman from *Melody Maker*: 'I still haven't grasped what all this talk of images is about. I don't particularly care whether parents hate us or not. They might grow to like us one day. We don't set out to be grizzly. I can tell you this much – my parents like me. Success hasn't changed us; I'm not a chameleon.' Mick Jagger always was astute at dealing with the press. He portrayed himself as uncaring about how the group was presented in the media, while in reality he was deeply concerned about the growing stardom of the group. In fact, according to Bill, Mick was 'taking to stardom like a fish to water'. At Romford Odeon, on 25 February, a girl rushed him on-stage, mid-set, grabbing for him. Mick casually slung her over his shoulder, carried her back into the wings from which she had emerged, and carried on with his song.

Mick and Keith had another composition out: Adrienne Posta's 'Shang A Doo Lang', produced by Andrew. Like Noël Coward before her and Naomi Campbell afterwards, Adrienne had gone to the Italia Conti stage school in Clapham. After a show at Windsor Ex-Servicemen's Club, the group drove back to London to her sixteenth birthday party at the end of March. Here Mick met Marianne Faithfull for the first time. She was there with John Dunbar, her boyfriend, who had been invited by his friend Peter Asher. Peter's sister Jane was there with her boyfriend, Paul McCartney. Although Mick, Keith and Brian were at the party, along with Andrew Loog Oldham, Marianne was unimpressed: 'At this point the Stones were not much more than yobby schoolboys; they had none of the polish of John Lennon or Paul McCartney, and compared to my John they seemed very crass and boorish indeed. It didn't occur to me at all that they would ever be part of my life. As for Mick Jagger, I wouldn't even have known he was there if he hadn't had a flaming row with his girlfriend, Chrissie Shrimpton. She was crying and shouting at him, and in the heat of the argument her false eyelashes were peeling off.'

Marianne was the child of a Hampstead intellectual father, who had been involved in British wartime espionage with such later notables as the right-wing politician Enoch Powell and the writer Evelyn Waugh, and an impoverished, equally bohemian Austrian baroness. Their marriage was brief; brought up from the age of six by her mother, she was reared on a succession of stories about a world very far removed from that of the provincial Reading that became her home in the early 1950s. In her autobiography Marianne set her life aside from those of her neighbours with one telling sentence about Eva, her mother (a name she shared, in an interesting low-key synchronicity, with the mother of Mick Jagger): 'She was different, she was difficult, she was foreign, she liked to drink wine at lunch.'

Marianne Faithfull was to become *the* British female icon of the 1960s. As models, the likes of Jean Shrimpton and Twiggy may have been archetypal images; but their very functions rendered them one-dimensional. Marianne Faithfull was profoundly three-dimensional, mouth-wateringly sexy, yet wholesomely safe. Although her later interviews revealed her to be as impressively well read as any sixth-former with a Penguin Modern Classic in his back pocket could desire – she had been to the same jazz, folk and blues clubs; she'd seen Fellini's *La Dolce Vita* at the Academy cinema by Oxford Circus – she always gave off a non-threatening air of naivety; and allied to this was a Mona Lisa-like half-smile of knowing satisfaction that made her seem a very interesting person to know. In Marianne were personified most of the cutting-edge moods of the decade. At the beginning of her career, for example, she had no notion whatsoever of feminism – she'd tried to read Simone De Beauvoir's *The Second Sex* when she was fifteen but didn't understand it at all – but by the end of her relationship with Mick Jagger she was thoroughly acquainted with Germaine Greer's *The Female Eunuch*. At the beginning of the 1960s she was getting drunk on cider to Trad Jazz groups at the Beaulieu Jazz Festival; by the end of the decade, having gone through her acid phase, she was regularly banging up heroin or swallowing downers with high society decadents. Yet when she and Mick Jagger became an item they mutually reinforced each other's mystique and magic: they really were like the king and queen of a New Albion of pop music. All that was yet to come, of course.

Marianne was wearing jeans and a shirt that belonged to John Dunbar. Andrew was wearing eyeshadow. He spotted Marianne, seated on a central-heating radiator with her boyfriend: 'I saw an angel with big tits and signed her,' his line later became. In fact, Andrew was initially disbelieving when told of Marianne's surname: 'Marianne Faithfull? Oh do come on, darling. You'll have to do better than that.'

Everyone was very drunk. In order to get to talk to the angel with big tits, Mick 'accidentally' spilled champagne on her shirt. On the spot Andrew promised to make her a star, telling Marianne that Mick and Keith would write her first record. Although, in fact, it was already written: two weeks prior to the party, on 11 March 1964, Mick and Keith, along with session guitarist 'Big' Jim Sullivan and bassist Erik Ford, had gone into De Lane Lea studios and put down two songs they had written – 'As Time Goes By' and 'No One Knows'. In order to finagle recording time for Marianne Faithfull out of Decca, Andrew told the company she would be recording a song by Lionel Bart, whose musicals *Fings ain't What They Used to Be* and *Oliver!* had been enormous hits. When Marianne turned up at Olympic Studios, he gave her the demo of 'As Time Goes By' as a starting-point: before she finally recorded the song Mick and Keith changed its title – which was identical to the classic known from its performance in the celebrated film *Casablanca* – and reworked the lyrics so that it became 'As Tears Go By'. 'As Tears Go By' was intended as the B-side of the

Lionel Bart tune, an atrocity entitled 'I Don't Know How (To Tell You)'.

Also present at the session were Mick and Keith – 'as quiet as mice', as Marianne remembered them. As they left the studio, they gave Marianne and her friend Sally a lift to Paddington Station to catch a train back to Reading, where she still lived with her mother. In the car Mick tried to get Marianne to sit on his lap, but she refused: 'What a cheeky little yob, I thought to myself, so immature ... I'm certainly not shy and never was, but I admired shy. Keith was shy.'

On later reflection, Marianne Faithfull would come to the conclusion that there was an extraordinary serendipity about Andrew's choosing a song for her which had such lyrics as 'As Tears Go By': 'It's an absolutely astonishing thing for a boy of twenty to have written, a song about a woman looking back nostalgically on her life. The uncanny thing is that Mick should have written those words so long before everything happened; it's almost as if our whole relationship was prefigured in that song.'

'As Tears Go By' was a Top Ten hit. Marianne embarked on a tour of Britain with the Hollies, Gerry and the Pacemakers and Freddie and the Dreamers, among others. She noted that Andrew Loog Oldham never came to see her perform on the tour; his choice of her second single, Bob Dylan's 'Blowing In The Wind', showed he was not infallible: the record was a flop. Moreover, she was becoming uncomfortable with Andrew's self-propagated image of Soho showbiz gangster, a man always apparently ready to break the limbs of recalcitrants or hang them out of windows. None of this was true, but in the cowboy world of English pop music it was a useful image to have, and one that was the obverse of the dapper, safe dandy presented in the persona of Beatles manager Brian Epstein. As his absence from her tour dates suggested, he didn't seem to have enough time for her. Accordingly, she left Andrew to be managed by his former partner Tony Calder, who was succeeded by Gerry Bron.

Almost as soon as Mick and Keith had met Marianne Faithfull, the Rolling Stones were off on their fourth tour of the UK, one that ran from 1 April to 31 May 1964. This time they were quite definitively at the top of the bill. Among the motley crew of support acts were Peter and Gordon, who had recently been at number one in both the UK and USA with the Lennon–McCartney song 'World Without Love'; and on two shows in Bristol the Stones played with the magnificent, black-leather-clad Gene Vincent, crippled (ironically, on the way back from a show in Bristol) in the same car crash that killed Eddie Cochran, a master of rock 'n' roll songwriting and performance. In Bristol, Brian missed the first show.

The tour's MC was one Tony Marsh, a loud-mouthed comedian of considerable ego who was prone to whisky-induced aggression; when

Phelge punctuated a story Marsh was telling with a comment of his own, the comedian punched him in the head and attacked him. His guitar still strapped around his neck, Keith immediately leaped into the fray, hitting Marsh back: 'He's our mate, so mind your own fuckin' business ... You touch him again I'll stick this guitar in your fuckin' head.' Marsh apologised, saying he thought Phelge was some gatecrashing stage-door Johnny – not that that was any justification for hitting him.

At the beginning of the tour the Stones played two dates at the arena-sized Wembley Empire Pool. The *Ready Steady Go!* Rave Mad Mod Ball followed on 8 April 1964. During their performance, the group were mobbed by fans leaping onto the stage. A few days later, on 15 April, the group's first album, simply titled *The Rolling Stones* was released: it went straight to number one, with 100,000 advance orders. *Please Please Me*, the Beatles' first album, had sold only 6,000 copies into the shops before it was released. Writing about the LP in the *New Musical Express*, Roy Carr revealed that Mick and Keith were in disagreement over the record: 'Keith insists it was unfinished, some of the tracks being nothing more than demos; Mick argues to the contrary.' 'We did our early records in a room insulated with little egg cartons,' Keith remembered, describing the studios at Regent Sound. 'It was a little demo studio, a tiny little back room, and it was all done on a two-track Revox. Under these primitive conditions it was easy to make the kind of sound we got on our first album and the early singles, but it was hard to make a much better one.'

Whatever the sound quality, the first album by the Rolling Stones was a milestone in British pop, a blast of sensuous energy that perfectly fitted the time: it was a validation of the sense that the very idea of the Stones felt totally right at that moment, as though the nation's pop-music audience had been anxiously anticipating the group even before it existed. On 24 April *The Rolling Stones* entered the album charts at number one, eight days after the album's release date, replacing *With The Beatles*, the Liverpool group's second LP having been in that slot since before Christmas 1963. In its first week on sale the Stones' album sold 110,000 copies.

As part of the promotion for the album, the group finally appeared in the *NME* Lifelines column. Mick and Keith both lied that they were born in 1944. Mick said his favourite colour was 'red, blue, yellow, green, pink, black, white'. His favourite clothes, he said, were 'my father's'. Keith said his parents' names were 'Boris and Dirt' and his favourite actor was Prime Minister Harold Wilson; under miscellaneous dislikes he wrote 'headaches, corns, pimples, gangrene'. With telling prescience, Brian naughtily wrote 'Hashish' as the name of his sister. In person, Brian was by no means so chipper. Visiting the Stones' founder at his new flat at 13 Chester Street in Mayfair, Phelge told him how much he enjoyed the group's first album.

When he asked whether Brian had written anything like 'Little By Little' or 'Tell Me', the response was irritable: 'It wouldn't matter if I did, they wouldn't do it. You have more chance of getting a song recorded than me,' he told Phelge. 'They won't even listen to anything of mine,' he continued. 'They're not interested in anybody else's songs. Everything has to be done by them. If it's not theirs it's no good.'

On 26 April 1964 James Phelge went round again to Mapesbury Road, for another trip to the Empire Pool, this time for the *New Musical Express* Poll Winners' show. At the flat he told Keith that Brian had complained that he and Mick wouldn't consider recording any of his songs. Keith laughed, calling out this news to Mick in the kitchen: 'Fuckin' Jonesey's been moaning to Phelge that we won't record his songs. Fuckin' typical.'

'They're fuckin' crap,' called out Mick.

'Everything he writes ends up sounding like a fuckin' hymn. They're all dirges of doom. You'd need a fuckin' Welsh choir to record 'em,' continued Keith.

After the *NME* show, Keith noted wryly that Brian Poole and the Tremeloes, who they had dinner with, were wearing the same blue leather waistcoats in which the Stones had briefly attired themselves.

For a photo shoot the morning after they had played at the Palace theatre in Manchester on 3 May 1964, the group were provided with the very visual prop of a vintage Mercedes. As soon as the driver hit the open road he put his foot down: as the ancient vehicle shuddered and swayed along the highway, startling fellow travellers, Keith put his right arm in the air in a Nazi salute as he feigned a Hitler moustache with the fingers of his left hand. On the drive back to London that evening, Stu, loyally at the wheel, fell asleep on the M1 as they neared the capital: the group were woken from their exhausted slumbers by the sound of Keith screaming, 'Stu, for fuck's sake! Look out!' as their van careered towards the embankment by the side of the road, Stu slumped fast asleep over the wheel. The drama occurred a year to the day since the group's outdoor appearance at the *News of the World* Battersea Park show: things had come a long way since then.

In May 1964 Keith started going out with Linda Keith, a model. By now showing signs of the great insecurities that were tearing him apart, Brian's response to Keith's first proper relationship was to behave with outrageous pettiness: one night on tour Keith hammered him, blacking his eye, after Brian had eaten Keith's portion of chicken while the guitarist was having sex with Linda and looking forward to a post-coital meal. The group took to calling Brian 'Mr Shampoo', after he announced to *Rave* magazine that he washed his hair twice a day.

Now Mick and Keith moved out of Willesden, to a flat in the much more salubrious and arty surroundings of Hampstead – 10a Holly Hill, to be precise, off Frognal, a few hundred yards towards the heath from the tube station. To create the then fashionable alpine ski-resort effect, the lounge of the ground-floor flat had modern wood panelling covering the walls. There was one bedroom, with fitted wardrobes and – a sign of great sophistication in Britain in those days – a shower.

The Stones' thoughts were focused on their first trip to the United States, where they were being sold as 'England's Newest Hitmakers', the strapline on the US cover of their first album. In its June edition, which hit the newsstands in the middle of May, American *Vogue* ran a full-page photo of Mick taken by David Bailey, a friend he had met through Jean Shrimpton, accompanied by some unambivalent copy: 'To the inner group in London the new spectacular is a solemn young man, Mick Jagger, one of the five Rolling Stones, those singers who will set out to cross America by bandwagon in June. For the British, the Stones have a perverse, unsettling sex appeal, with Jagger out in front of his team-mates. To women, Jagger looks fascinating; to men, a scare.'

On 1 June 1964 the Rolling Stones disembarked at New York's Idlewild airport from BOAC flight 505. Wearing a suede jacket and jeans, Mick was the first to step off the plane. At the airport press conference, he was asked, 'You play the same kind of music as the Beatles?' He had a one-word reply: 'No.' 'Who's the leader?' came another question. 'We are,' responded Mick Jagger, perhaps to Brian's surprise. 'All of us.' That night Mick was at the Peppermint Lounge (already immortalised in Joey Dee and the Starlighters' hit song 'Peppermint Twist'): among the impersonations he watched by the Younger Brothers, a comedy act, was one they did of Mick Jagger.

In contrast to their recent British successes, the Rolling Stones' first American tour was hard and very depressing work. In a fairground in San Antonio, Texas, a venue with a capacity of 20,000, the group performed next to a tank full of trained seals to an audience of only a few hundred. At their first date, in San Bernardino in southern California, however, the group got the kind of adoring, hysterical response they were used to back home. Moving up to Los Angeles, they had a miserable time of it when they appeared on Dean Martin's *Hollywood Palace* television show. Mick was offered a hundred dollars before the show by a producer to buy uniforms for the group – he refused the money. Introducing a trampolinist, Dino's whisky voice slurred, 'That's the father of the Rolling Stones. He's been trying to kill himself ever since.' Martin, said Keith, was 'a right fuckin' offer'.

Backstage in Omaha, the dressing room was visited by a cop who, seeing that the Stones were breaking a local anti-alcohol ordinance by having a bottle of whisky in their dressing room, pulled a gun on Keith. As Keith had only been drinking Coca-Cola, he bought his own .38 revolver the next day, just in case anyone did that to him again; paying scant regard to British customs and firearms laws, he brought the gun back to London in his suitcase. Omaha, Nebraska, Keith later said, was where he had 'never been hated by so many people I've never met ... Everyone looked at you with a look that could kill.' He also admitted, 'We couldn't see it at the time, but all that was really doing us some good. In England, we'd been used to coming on-stage, blasting off four numbers and going. America, that first tour, really made us work. We had to fill up the spaces somehow.'

In Chicago, the Stones did get to record at Chess studios on Michigan Avenue, their spiritual home, which added an indubitable fillip to their credibility in Britain. At first the Stones had a problem: they couldn't make very good records. 'Come On' could almost be by a Liverpool also-ran group like the Dennisons, and was not really good enough to have been made by Southend R 'n' B group the Paramounts. 'Tell Me', Mick and Keith's own composition on the first album, needed arranging better, without that risibly desperate military-sounding build-up to the chorus. All the same, 'Tell Me' was released as a single while they were in the United States, reaching number twenty-four in the charts – hardly the heights already reached by the Beatles who, by the end of March that year, had occupied the top five slots in the US charts. At Chess, the Stones recorded a version of the Valentinos' 'It's All Over Now', and they had discovered a different sound: thicker, more fulfilled, that you could dance to. The jangling introductory chord sequence helped make it become the sound of the summer when the single was released in the UK on 26 June, becoming their first British number one. Ron Malo was the engineer, later to be responsible for some of the best of the Stones' work. Willie Dixon turned up at the studio and complimented Jagger on his vocals. At the Chess studio, Keith discovered 'fuckin' miles' of tapes of audience noise, useful for adding to 'live' albums.

Grim though parts of their first US tour might have been, the Rolling Stones concluded it on 20 June with two eleven-song shows – one in the afternoon, one in the evening – at Carnegie Hall in Manhattan (the esteemed New York DJ Murray the K, latterly 'the fifth Beatle' and now 'the sixth Rolling Stone', compèred the shows).

Mick and Keith made their own arrangements in New York for the few days after the final Manhattan shows: Phil Spector let them sleep in the offices of Philles Records on York Avenue. Several times the two Dartford boys came out to visit him and his wife at their home in Flushing Estates on Long Island. 'My mother was always nice to our rock 'n' roll friends, especially the Rolling Stones, who usually looked like they could use a good meal,' remembered Ronnie Spector. 'Whenever Mick or Keith came around, she would say, "You boys just come on in here and sit down. Would you like me to make some eggs?" Their answer was always the same: "Yes, Mrs Bennett. If it's not too much trouble." Then Aunt Helen or Aunt Susu would come over and help cook for them. They were so far away from home, I guess they just needed to be around a family sometimes. They'd hang around with us all day, playing records or watching TV.'

When the Stones flew back to London it was to return immediately to the real world: a long-standing booking to play the end-of-term ball at Magdalen College, Oxford, for £100, the fee they had commanded at the time the date was put into their schedule. Milking every opportunity to the maximum, Andrew insisted to the press that the group had returned first-class to Britain specifically for the concert, and were returning to the US the following day to conclude their tour: at the time, this sounded impressive, although it was completely untrue.

A month later, on 24 July, promoting the release of 'It's All Over Now' with a string of ballroom dates, mainly in the north of England, the Stones played the Empress Ballroom in Blackpool. Still Britain's leading seaside resort, Blackpool was then enduring 'Scottish week', the seven days each year when Scotland would virtually close down as the country's workers took their annual holiday. Although the Blackpool show was a sell-out, the audience was made up almost entirely of drunken 'hard' Scottish rockers. Almost from the off, they began to spit at the Stones, with Brian 'Mr Shampoo' Jones bearing the brunt of the storm of spittle. Between songs Keith had words with the chief culprit, the ringleader of these hard-case bullies, who was standing at the front of the stage. His response was to send a green lump of phlegm in the direction of the guitarist. Keith crunched his heel down on the back of one hand of the principal expectorator, and then kicked him in the nose, which became like a burst ripe tomato. As Keith put it later, 'I accidentally stuck my boot in his head.' As a consequence, the Stones were chased from the stage by the yobs, who proceeded to trash all their equipment. As the place erupted, Stu bundled Keith off-stage: 'Keith still thought he was God and that he could kick one of these guys and get away with it.' In the ensuing riot, £2,000-worth of gear was kicked off-stage and wrecked. 'It went too far,' Keith said later with considerable understatement. 'I just lost my temper.'

On 8 August the Stones played in the Hague, their first date in Europe. Two days later in Liverpool Mick was fined £32 for speeding and driving without insurance: he had been on 'an errand of mercy' to see two fans injured in a car crash, said his solicitor. Four days after that the group topped the bill at Wimbledon Palais in south London, and released another

EP, 'Five By Five', which included the instrumental '2120 South Michigan Avenue', the address of Chess Records, where the five songs had been recorded. The tune was credited to Nanker–Phelge, as was the song 'Empty Heart'. Otherwise the record consisted of 'If You Need Me' (Pickett, Bateman, Sanders), 'Confessin' the Blues' (McShann, Brown) and Chuck Berry's 'Around And Around', which became a staple of the Stones' live set. The EP, which showed the full extent of the benefits of recording at Chess, had advance orders of 200,000.

That month Decca released 'As Tears Go By' by Marianne Faithfull, which became an almost immediate hit, peaking at number nine on 18 September; the same record company also released 'So Much In Love' by the Mighty Avengers: both songs were credited to Jagger–Richard. Meanwhile, on 25 September, London Records in the USA put out 'Time Is On My Side', a song recorded for the group's forthcoming second album, backed by 'Congratulations', a slightly cheesy Jagger–Richard composition. The single was a Top Twenty hit.

On 2 October, after a date at Colston Hall, Bristol, the Stones were banned from the restaurant in the Strand Hotel over their appearance. Again, Andrew played the incident to the hilt, getting the story everywhere in the popular daily press. Twelve days later, on 14 October, Charlie married Shirley Ann Shepherd in Bradford. Keith was shocked: he saw Charlie's marriage as a form of betrayal of the group – as John Lennon had shown, 'beat group' members were not meant to be married, lest it damage the musicians' career prospects.

On 14 October 1964 the group played at the Paris Olympia. The artist and prospective film director Donald Cammell threw a party to which they were invited; Robert Fraser, an Old Etonian and army officer who had become an art dealer and who was already a friend of the Beatles, was there. Fraser introduced Mick and Keith to the designer Christopher Gibbs, who in turn introduced Jagger to the celebrated society photographer and painter Cecil Beaton. Chrissie Shrimpton had eventually been allowed to join Mick in Paris for the Stones' gig in the French capital, as had Charlie Watts' new wife Shirley; but not until Mick had protested, 'You won't like being there and you'll just get in our way.' Both Chrissie and Shirley shot their arms up in the air: *Heil*, Jagger. There were riots at the Olympia that spilled out into the streets: on-stage Mick had mimed going down on Keith's guitar – or was it on Keith? In a bar in the French capital, the group were berated by a bunch of guys. 'Are you the Supremes?' one asked. Keith punched him in the face. At a plush restaurant on the Isle de Louis, Mick and Keith ended by playing the Marseillaise on spoons and wine glasses. Keith's glass cracked, red wine pouring onto his trousers.

Ten days later, on 24 October, the Rolling Stones began their second US tour at the Academy of Music in New York, with an afternoon and an evening show. The following day they appeared on the Ed Sullivan Show, performing 'Time Is On My Side'. For the second live venue two days later they switched coasts, flying to Sacramento, California's state capital. The third date on this second US tour, however, gave the Stones national television exposure: an appearance on the TAMI (Teenage Awards Music International) show, shot at Santa Monica Civic Auditorium in southern California. Although there was a balance of white acts – The Beach Boys, Jan and Dean, Lesley Gore, and (*all the way from Liverpool, England!*) Gerry and the Pacemakers and Billy J. Kramer and the Dakotas – the Stones found themselves topping the bill with a five-song set over a host of their heroes: Marvin Gaye, Smokey Robinson and the Miracles, Chuck Berry, and – biggest of all – James Brown and the Flames.

During the two days of rehearsals, Brian and Brown built a friendship: although Mick and Keith would later become good friends with Brown, they were too in awe of this musical legend to be able to speak to him. Mick, meanwhile, assiduously studied the foot movements of the Godfather of Soul, quickly practising them before they vanished out of his head. 'Mick Jagger was the biggest James Brown nut I'd ever met,' said Ronnie Spector. 'When we were on tour in England he kept us up half the night asking questions about James Brown. What was he like off-stage? Where did he learn to dance? How much did he rehearse? I finally had to tell Mick, "Enough already. I don't even know James Brown. I'm a Ronette, remember?"'

On 14 November, the day before the group returned to Britain from the United States, Decca released the Stones' next British single, a version of Willie Dixon's 'Little Red Rooster', a poignant, slow blues number loaded with sexual innuendo that was not the most obvious choice for a hit record: in fact, it became the only twelve-bar blues song ever to make number one in the British singles charts. The record was released at the insistence of the Stones, despite huge opposition from both Decca and the group's management, especially Eric Easton. The B-side was the catchy 'Off The Hook', written by Jagger–Richard, their first up-tempo song.

On 27 November, having been back in Britain less than two weeks, Mick was obliged to appear in court at Tettenhall in Staffordshire on a further driving charge: he had been stopped in his Ford Zephyr in Wolverhampton for using the vehicle without insurance and not having his name in its registration book. 'The Duke of Marlborough had longer hair than my client, and he won some famous battles. His hair was powdered, I think, because of fleas. My client has no fleas,' said Dale Parkinson, his solicitor, in what seemed an archly theatrical attempt to ensure his words would be in the following day's tabloid newspapers. Citing the singer's value to the British export effort, Parkinson pleaded successfully that Mick needed to be mobile and should not be banned from driving.

Mick spent the following couple of days after the court case at Chrissie Shrimpton's place. Keith and Phelge returned to the Hampstead flat in the middle of the night from the Ad Lib club, where they had observed the arrival of Judy Garland. Inspired by the alcohol they had imbibed, they decided to take Mick's Ford Zephyr for a drive. Mick had considerately left the car keys in the flat when he took the train up to Tettenhall for the trial on the driving charge; he had expected to be banned from driving. Keith, however, did not even have a driving licence. After the vehicle stalled on them outside Hampstead tube station, they realised they had better fill it with petrol.

They spent the next day driving around London in the Zephyr. Returning again from the Ad Lib that night, Keith drove in a somewhat erratic manner until he stopped by a set of red traffic lights. 'There's some cops behind us,' Keith informed Phelge. When the lights turned to green, he tried to move forwards. But, in his nervousness, he stalled the car, the police car patiently waiting as the lights went through another set of changes. Then it followed them for about a mile, before briefly switching on its siren and flashing light and pulling them over. All the policeman wanted, however, was Keith's autograph for his daughter.

CHAPTER 9

GET OFF MY FORESKIN

On the sleeve of the second LP, released on 30 January 1965, Mick is at the back in the cover shot. The picture was taken by David Bailey, king photographer of the new allegedly classless British fashion world. Bailey said he deliberately positioned Mick so that the other group members wouldn't think he was getting special treatment because he was a friend. *Rolling Stones 2* was made up of the following songs: Solomon Burke's 'Everybody Needs Somebody To Love', Lieber and Stoller's 'Down Home Girl', Chuck Berry's 'You Can't Catch Me', 'Time Is On My Side' (written by Norman Meade), 'What A Shame', 'Grown Up Wrong', 'Down The Road Apiece' (written by Tony Raye, originally recorded by Amos Milburn in 1946, and covered by Chuck Berry in 1960), 'Under The Boardwalk' (a hit for the Drifters, written by Resnick and Young), 'I Can't Be Satisfied' (Morganfield), 'Pain In My Heart' (Neville), Nanker–Phelge's 'Off The Hook' and 'Susie Q'. The following week the album entered the British charts at number one.

A modified version of the record was released in the United States (where it was titled *The Rolling Stones, Now!*) on 20 March, eventually reaching number five in the Billboard album charts. This American version of the Stones' second LP was quite substantially different from the UK release: it omitted 'Time Is On My Side, 'Under The Boardwalk', 'I Can't Be Satisfied' and 'Susie Q', and added 'Little Red Rooster', 'Heart Of Stone' (already a single in the US), 'Mona' (which had been on the first British album), 'Oh Baby (We Got a Good Thing Goin')', and 'Surprise Surprise'. Under the title *Twelve By Five*, an album had already been released in the US the previous October that was a hotchpotch of the 'Five By Five' EP, 'It's All Over Now' and its B-side 'Good Times, Bad Times'; 'Under The Boardwalk', 'Grown Up Wrong', 'Congratulations', 'Susie Q' and 'If You Need Me' were also on that record. Fans in Britain were outraged at the juggling of recorded songs by this supposedly most purist of groups.

A week after the second Rolling Stones album appeared in British shops, the group began a tour of Australia, New Zealand and the Far East. On the way to Australia they stopped in Los Angeles, where time had been booked at RCA Studios in Hollywood; there they recorded two new Mick and Keith songs: 'The Last Time' and 'Play With Fire'.

Among the support acts on the Australasian tour was The Big 'O' himself – Roy Orbison, king of the melodramatic rock 'n' roll ballad, a man whose enormous talent meant that he had managed to outlast the shift in fortunes brought about for so many by the 'beat boom'. In Sydney the Stones played to 35,000 people in seven nights. Although the backing singers in the Rolling Stones had previously been Bill and Brian, Andrew was by now pushing Keith to sing with Mick, wanting to bill them as a double act. At the same time, far from his homeland, Keith seemed to be investing considerable gusto in getting into his part of yobbish Briton abroad. 'Keith was busy dropping whisky glasses from the balcony into the empty car park five storeys below, to see if he could hear them tinkle on the concrete,' Judy Wade wrote in the *New Musical Express* of the group's stay at the Chevron Hilton, Sydney. While rowing on the sea the following day, Brian, Keith, Charlie and Andrew were heckled by a group of schoolboys: 'Go home Rolling Stones.' Keith's response? 'Come over here and say that.' They did: one of the kids dived into the water, rocking the Stones' boat and trying to turn it over. The tough, loutish Rolling Stones were being bullied by a bunch of schoolboys.

On the way back from Surfers' Paradise in Queensland, the group's car was involved in a minor collision with a surfer's vehicle. Keith whacked his head on the windscreen, getting a nasty headache. After shows at Brisbane Town Hall in Western Australia on the other side of the country, Mick said, 'I almost got torn to pieces, and Keith's shirt was torn so much it looks as though he has been living in it on a desert island for two years.' Following a show on 1 February at the Theatre Royal in Christchurch, New Zealand, Mick complained that their hotel had hardly any bathrooms: 'You can't blame us if we smell,' he said, playing up the familiar Stones-are-dirty line.

The week after they returned to London from the other side of the world, 'The Last Time' was released, on 26 February. The A-side was written by Mick Jagger and Keith Richard, the first Stones single written by the pair; while 'Play With Fire', the B-side, was by Nanker–Phelge, which gave all of the group a share of the credits. Chrissie Shrimpton, now working for Decca Records, was meant to provide a much faster version of 'Play With Fire' for the B-side, but she picked up the wrong tape from Andrew's office. Promoting the single on *Ready Steady Go!*, Mick injured his ankle when mobbed by girls: 'I thudded down on the floor and a mass of girls smothered me. I was stamped on by scores of stiletto heels.'

All the same, Mick still managed to be interviewed on the show *Ready Steady Go!* by Queen Mod Cathy McGowan. Cathy put to him the burning question of the day: how many times a week did he wash his hair? 'About twice a week.' He confirmed that Keith usually cut it for him, and that Keith cut his own, with the assistance of a mirror. Mick also revealed that if he was in a hot country he took a bath every day. When Cathy asked Mick if he wondered whether being married would affect his popularity, he answered, 'It might do. I only fancy unmarried people, so why should anyone fancy a married me?'

'The Last Time' entered the charts at number eight, leaping to number one the following week and staying there for a month – the first time the Rolling Stones had topped the charts with a song written by Mick and Keith. (Also in February, The Mighty Avengers – undaunted thus far by commercial failure – had released 'Blue Turns To Grey' on Decca, the very poppy A-side written by Mick and Keith; and the Toggery Five had released 'I'd Much Rather Be With The Boys', a single on Parlophone, written by Andrew Oldham and Keith Richard.)

From 5 to 18 March, the Stones were off on their sixth British tour, supported by Dave Berry and the Cruisers, the Hollies and an American all-girl group called Goldie and the Gingerbreads. As an encore, they performed an elongated version of 'Everybody Needs Somebody To Love', as featured on their second album, Mick seeming to look at a different section of the audience from that at which he was pointing. On the foggy night of 11 March, they played Huddersfield in Yorkshire. The following day, before a show in Sheffield, they appeared on *Scene At 6.30*, the Granada TV show presented in Manchester by Michael Parkinson. 'I reckon there are three reasons why American R 'n' B stars don't click with British teenage fans. One they're old; two, they're black; three, they're ugly,' Keith told him, somewhat surprisingly.

The final date of the tour at Romford ABC was marked by an incident that must have seemed like striking a motherlode for Andrew Loog Oldham: returning from the Essex show to nearby London at 11.30 that night, Mick, Brian and Bill were refused permission to use a toilet in the Francis Service Petrol Station in East Ham. 'Get off my forecourt,' said the attendant. 'Get off my foreskin,' replied Brian. Walking about ten yards up an adjacent side-road, the trio's micturations were splashed up a nearby wall. Three days later, on the outskirts of Birmingham as they left the city after an appearance on *Thank Your Lucky Stars*, Bill, who was always alleged to have the largest bladder in pop music, needed to pee again. As he emptied himself against a fence, a policeman appeared and shone a torch on him, asking him what he was doing, 'which I thought should have been pretty obvious'. The policeman warned Bill not to do it again.

Just over three months later, on 1 July, a private summons was issued against the three members of the Stones, alleging 'insulting behaviour' at the East Ham filling station: at the court hearing, on 22 July, each of them was found guilty of the charge and fined five pounds, with fifteen guineas costs. The following day's *Daily Mirror* reported the case: 'Wyman asked if he could go to the lavatory, but was refused. A mechanic, Mr Charles Keeley, asked Jagger to get the group off the forecourt of the garage. He brushed him aside, saying, "We will piss anywhere, man". This was taken up by the group as a chant as one of them danced. Wyman, Jagger and Jones were seen to urinate against a wall of the garage.' Across the country schoolboys mimicked their chant (*'We'll-piss-where-we-want, we'll-piss-where-we-want!'*) as they urinated in inappropriate locations.

By the time the court case took place, the Rolling Stones had completed two more overseas tours, including their third set of dates in the United States and Canada, which had begun on 22 April. This US tour followed a three-week sprint, from 26 March to 18 April, through Denmark, Sweden and France. On the first day of the European tour, the group played at the Fyns Forum in Odense in Denmark; when Mick accidentally allowed two microphones he was holding to touch each other, an electric shock was set off which knocked him into Brian, who in turn fell into Bill, who was knocked unconscious. After the bass player came to, the group resumed its first date of the tour. The Stones flew back to London on 11 April for the *NME* Poll Winners' show at the Empire Pool, Wembley. They returned to France to play three nights at the Olympia in Paris, the conclusion of the tour. Although the Rolling Stones were fêted in the UK press as the toast of *le tout Paris*, no one thought to mention that the last residence by the Beatles at the Paris Olympia had lasted for nineteen days.

Whilst playing dates in the West Country, Mick and Keith's Hampstead flat was burgled, all of their clothes being stolen, by fans, it was assumed. On the ground floor, the place was simply too easy for fans to break into. The address also seemed to be public knowledge: each weekend around fifty girls would turn up there. Accordingly, they moved out. For a few weeks Mick and Keith stayed at the Hilton hotel on Park Lane, but such accommodation was far too pricey. Keith found a flat in St John's Wood, and Mick went to stay at the Regent's Park house of his close friend, the photographer David Bailey, who had shot several covers for Rolling Stones' LPs. 'If it hadn't been for David Bailey I'd have been homeless,' Mick said then. 'Staying with him was like living in a hotel; his pad is quite big with three bathrooms and as we were never in at the same time we rarely crossed paths.' One day when he returned to the house, however,

Bailey was there with the actress Jacqueline Bisset, whose picture he was taking. 'Put her on your back and let's try it again,' Bailey suggested to Mick. The photo that emerged from the session led to the beginning of Bisset's career.

Across the Atlantic, after their 1 May show at the Academy of Music, the group got into a fight in Central Park with a bunch of guys in a convertible who called the group 'faggots': as he had done with the gobbing Scot in Blackpool the previous July, Keith kicked one of them in the mouth. Why was he so angry? He was living up to the hip young writer Nik Cohn's first-sight description of him: 'Keith Richard wore a t-shirt, and, all the time, he kept winding and unwinding his legs, moving uglily like a crab, and was shut-in, shuffling, the classic fourth-form drop-out. Simply, he spelled Borstal.' Creatively, however, the Dartford boy was having a profitable time: on 6 May on the American tour, at a motel in Clearwater in Florida, where the Stones had performed at the Jack Russell Stadium, Keith first played Mick a tune he was working on, which he conceived at this point as a sort of folk song. It had come into Keith's head in the middle of the night, when he'd suddenly woken with the riff and words in his head, and had immediately switched on his tape recorder. The next morning Keith sang Mick the lyrics: 'The words that go with this are "I Can't Get No Satisfaction"!' 'I've got my guitar, the early Philips cassette player – the first one, the role model – and I just picked up the guitar and *I can't get no satisfaction ... I can't get no satisfaction ...*'

The song, Keith thought, was not strong enough to be a single, reliant as it was on one specific riff. All the same, Mick and Keith began to work on the number in the Clearwater motel. They first recorded it three days later, on 10 May, at Chess Studios in Chicago, along with another original, 'The Under-Assistant West Coast Promotion Man', and covers of Otis Redding's 'That's How Strong My Love Is' and Don Covay's 'Mercy Mercy'. The version of 'Satisfaction' laid down in Chicago was an all-acoustic recording, replete with harmonica solo, and it didn't really work. Arriving in Los Angeles the following day, the group repaired at once to their favourite RCA Studios in Hollywood – where Mick habitually used a microphone Elvis had sung with – and recorded a very different version of the song. Keith: 'I was screaming for more distortion: "This riff's really gotta hang hard and long". We burnt the amps and turned the shit up, and it still wasn't right. And then Ian Stewart went around the corner to Wallach's Music City or something, and came around with a distortion box: "Try this".' Something about the record made Keith feel nervous, giving him butterflies, he said later. There was an other-wordly quality about 'Satisfaction': it so clearly marked a new chapter in the Rolling

Stones' career, making everything they had previously done seem almost lightweight.

'(I Can't Get No) Satisfaction', coupled with 'The Under-Assistant West Coast Promotion Man', was released in the United States on 4 June. To the consternation of British fans, who in the music press would see a Stones record they had never heard of at number one in the United States, the first time the Stones had hit the top spot in America, the single was not released in the UK until 20 August. Did this indicate that the Stones cared more about the record market in the United States than at home? worried some of the group's British supporters. For the release in their home country, 'Satisfaction' was coupled with 'The Spider and The Fly'.

On 14 August, Mick, Keith and Andrew had time to fly to New York for a meeting with Allen Klein, an American manager and accountant with whom they had decided to hold discussions about replacing Eric Easton. In Manhattan Mick declared, 'The whole British music scene is dead boring now. There hasn't been anything new or exciting for ages ... First there was the Beatles, then us, now there's nothing.' The endless touring continued throughout the summer and autumn: Scotland, Norway, Finland, Denmark, Sweden, Ireland, West Germany, and Austria. Keith threw a wobbler at the Hotel Turku in Helsinki. He pointed three times at a menu, demanding soup. But the soup didn't come on any occasion. Instead, Keith each time was brought a meal on a plate. On the last occasion, Keith flung it to the floor and walked out. Later the rest of the group learned that the word 'soup' he kept pointing at was Finnish for 'supper'. On 14 September the group played the Circus Kronebau in Munich, where Brian Jones met an actress and model called Anita Pallenberg. They spent the night together, with Brian in tears for most of the time over the way he claimed he was being treated by Mick and Keith. Just prior to the West German dates, on 10 September, Mick and Andrew had appeared on a *Ready, Steady, Go!* Rolling Stones special, pawing each other's hair as they mimed in a comedy spoof to Sonny and Cher's 'I Got You, Babe'. The minutes of a 20 September 1965 meeting of the Rolling Stones Limited declared that Mr Michael Philip Jagger was appointed chairman of the company in place of Mr E. C. Easton. There was a full-scale British tour from 24 September to 17 October: a disagreement broke out between Oldham and Easton and Robert Stigwood, the co-promoter of the UK dates, over the group's percentage of their box-office takings. Keith Altham, a journalist with the *New Musical Express*, remembered seeing Keith Richard physically attacking Stigwood in a club, knocking him to the ground.

Following up the US number-one single that 'Satisfaction' had given them, the Stones' new album *Out of Our Heads* topped the American album charts on 21 August; again, the record was released in the USA well before it came out in Britain, where it finally hit the shops on 24 September. Although the Stones supported the record's release with their seventh British tour, they were psyched up for a larger event: their first tour of the United States since they had had a number one single and album.

This tour began on 29 October 1965. Accompanying the group was Gered Mankowitz, an eighteen-year-old who had become the Stones' official photographer. After taking some press pictures of Marianne Faithfull the week that 'As Tears Go By' was released, the photographer had met Andrew Loog Oldham. As soon as he learned of Gered's family background, Andrew took to him: Gered's father was Wolf Mankowitz, the playwright who had written the musical *Expresso Bongo*, the story of a Soho agent who turns a nondescript teenage singer into an international star, a salutary tale of the earliest English rock 'n' roll business. Although it was based on the career of the hugely successful Tommy Steele, Bermondsey's blue-jeaned merchant seaman, *Expresso Bongo* was made into a film (with the poster tagline 'Johnny never had it so good – or lost it so fast!') in 1959, starring a youthful Cliff Richard as the singer with the sublime Laurence Harvey playing his agent. 'When Andrew was fourteen he went to see my father's musical, *Expresso Bongo*,' said Gered, 'and it completely changed Andrew's life. He said, "That's what I want to do when I grow up". When he saw my pictures of Marianne he had no idea who I was. It was only when he came to my studio with the Stones that it all started to click. Wolf was a director of my studio, which was in Mason's Yard, between Scotch of St James and Indica Books. And that gave us an immediate bond, though being Andrew he was continuously cruel about it.'

At the end of a dank day in December 1964, Gered Mankowitz dropped in at Oldham's office in Ivor Court, off Baker Street, just to say hello. 'Then we did our first session at the beginning of sixty-five. The Stones and I got on really well: I was younger than everybody, which I think they found a bit appealing. From the first session came the *Out of Our Heads/December's Children* covers. We got on, they liked my approach.

'Andrew was the brains and the energy. In those days Brian had the most formed image, the most evolved, the most groomed image. He was the one who was physically the most confident. Charlie always had an image. But Charlie's was a retro image. He was into fifties, early sixties New York jazz, and wore suits and interesting jackets and slacks and loafers. Mick and Keith were still kids in a way. They were still finding a space, a place. And that's quite apparent in the pictures – it's why Brian appears in the front of the grouping on the *Out of Our Heads* cover. And there's no doubt about it: even from Brian's haircut you can see he really was the most evolved and the most charismatic.'

Brian Jones' studied air of decadent elegance greatly impressed Gered Mankowitz, who clearly saw the group's founder as the archetype of its image. Mick Jagger and Keith Richard, however, seemed more like permanent teenagers. 'There was a studenty thing about them, an art-school thing. That's where the alternative music and energy was coming from, from those early sixties art schools. It was very much art-school: there were other bands like Them and the Pretty Things who had a much grubbier look than the Stones ever did. Mick and Keith's identity came very much from that background, even though Mick had been to the LSE – and Charlie was similar in a way, because Charlie had been to art school ... I think Brian had an element of show-business about him. He was more advanced in that way. That's what I mean by charisma; he had a presence to him, he'd got an image together, he'd made a conscious effort to look the way he did, whereas everybody else was just evolving, Mick and Keith particularly, and shaking off the ordinariness of early 1960s British teenagerhood.'

All the same, Gered Mankowitz could clearly see the chemistry between Mick and Keith, so strong that he could almost touch it. The relationship between the two Dartford boys and Brian, thought the photographer, was 'pretty good'. Travelling with the group in the United States, he was able to observe it more closely. The only different treatment he received from the group was that 'I had to share a room most of the time with a guy called Ronnie Schneider who was Allen Klein's nephew. He was the bagman, and a good bloke. He was with the Stones for a long time.'

The other musicians on the tour were Patti LaBelle and the Blue Belles, the New Vibrations and the Ramrods, a white instrumental group who backed the other two acts. Newly hot Paul Revere and the Raiders played a few shows; Bo Diddley was on a couple of dates. The Stones had no security guards, and only one roadie, the omnipresent Ian 'Stu' Stewart. But they did have their own plane. 'People today have no concept of what touring was like at that time for what was probably the second-biggest band in the world,' said Mankowitz. 'One roadie, virtually no equipment, the backline, their instruments, all went on the plane with us. There'd be a Transit-type van at each airport for Stu to throw the kit into. Mick would sing through the house PA, which was a disaster; and there'd be no lighting.'

Allen Klein had hired the superstar of US record pluggers, one Pete Bennett, to get 'Get Off Of My Cloud', the new single, onto radio-station playlists and into the charts. 'The planning was so perfect that for the whole tour the record was heading up the charts, and it went to number one in the last week of the tour. It was a really fantastic bit of operating.

'The general atmosphere was pretty good. But it was there that Brian began to show serious oddness in his behaviour. He did a few very strange things. I saw him nearly bottle somebody in a club, for no reason other than that the guy was being persistent and an irritating pest, wanting a piece of Brian, and Brian just completely blew his top and smashed a bottle and was stopped from injuring this guy. That was a nasty incident that showed a side and an aggression that came as a bit of a surprise. I think it was in New York because the way the tour was organised, we had no social life anywhere else at all. They used to fly out after the show, and travel through the night, and arrive at places at three or four in the morning. So there were no fans, no groupies, no partying, no fun. It was only in some of the major cities, where perhaps we were based for two or three days, that there was some fun, some sex and drugs and rock 'n' roll going on.

'We were in Nashville for two or three quite good nights. Brian disappeared. He got out of a limousine in a traffic jam and just disappeared. They carried on without him and announced that he was ill. He reappeared two or three nights later. I never really understood what went on. But there was clearly something about Brian that was strange, and he was having a lot of struggles. I don't think I felt the band were judgemental about Brian. They'd find themselves without him and they had to do a show, and this was at a point in their career when everything really counted. If one member of the group is seriously dysfunctional, the impact on everybody else is that he's putting them on the line. I remember Stu grabbing him once in the wings as he came off and lifting him off the ground, telling him that he was letting everybody down, not just himself.'

In Florida the tour broke for a couple of days in the Miami sun. 'Anita Pallenberg joined Brian there, and then left after a couple of days. They could be unpleasantly cliquey together; he'd whisper in front of you – he and Anita would whisper. He loved to have the feeling that he had one over on you, that he knew something you didn't know. And there was something weaselly about him that made him difficult. After she'd gone he invited me up to his room, and said, "I've got two tabs of acid left, and I wonder if you would like to have one." I said, "No, I'm not interested in acid, thank you very much." So he said, "Oh, okay: I'll tell you what, you take both of them and I'll write down everything you say." He was really out there, Brian. He was experimenting, he was ahead of them, he was freaking. In New York he was hanging out with Bob Dylan: that was the tour when there were the famous lost tapes, when they were hanging out in his room. He introduced me to Bob Dylan. And then there was the tremendous New York power failure, and their idea of laying down a few tracks never happened. They just got completely out of it, as everybody did that night. Brian was showing the character faults that he clearly had. He could be very interesting; he was capable of being incredibly charming and incredibly polite, beautifully mannered. But then he'd turn, and he could be incredibly unpleasant.

'However the band seemed to forgive him his transgressions very quickly. When it all gelled, it was so good – and Brian was such a crucial and integral part of that. Brian had this huge fan base, and his fans were more focused. And it made it more important to try to live with his oddness. But the seeds were being sown. I think it's a real myth that Brian was plotted against. I honestly don't believe that's the case. I think that Brian sowed the seeds of his demise, and that he was responsible for it.

'The other thing that happened, which I think caused terrible problems for Brian, was that Mick and Keith were writing, and Brian couldn't. He was an excellent musician, a very versatile musician, a natural and instinctive musician, and a huge and crucial part of the Rolling Stones; but not being able to write was a big problem for him. He must have known that Mick and Keith were writing. Mick singing and Keith basically being the lead guitar meant he couldn't maintain his position of being the leader of the band. And I guess that was really important to him, that status.

'Andrew instinctively knew that Mick and Keith were the soul of the band, although musically Charlie and Bill were the roots. And Brian was marginalised. Brian was this freaky, blond bomber, and he played up to that. Perhaps he was pushed into that role simply by what was going on.'

To all intents and purposes, Brian's life gave him the opportunities to live a more fulfilled existence: 'Brian was already with Anita, and was always out there; Brian always seemed to have things going on. Keith never seemed to have any girls. Mick was with Chrissie. Mick and I did have one conversation about girlfriends. We had a little chat about how much we missed them. It was very ordinary. It was really rather normal. Touring was rather exhausting; a topsy-turvy world that wasn't very luxurious, nor glamorous: horrible dressing rooms, ghastly food and drink, rooms that were decorated by the local chapter of the fan club, who would lovingly provide awful angel-food cakes. But the Stones responded, and did everything with remarkable good faith. Everybody got time, and they were sweet and nice to fans and media, as they gave interviews and handed out prizes.

'Throughout the tour Mick and Keith were writing songs: sessions were booked at RCA Studios in Hollywood for the end of the tour, to record what became the *Aftermath* album. Marijuana was occasionally smoked, but with great trepidation about the serious legal penalties. In Nashville the group visited the hotel at which the Vibrations and Patti LaBelle were staying. Patti LaBelle and the Blue Belles were ruled with a rod of iron by a very pugnacious little ex-boxer manager. The group was going bonkers for Nona Hendryx. She was beautiful, with the most phenomenal body. There was a lot of teenage-like frustration.'

At the end of the tour Gered Mankowitz travelled to the West Coast with the Rolling Stones. In Sacramento on 3 December, he watched as Keith was knocked onto his back by an electric shock, the rubber soles of his Hush Puppies having saved him from death. At RCA in Hollywood he watched them record songs for the album that would become *Aftermath*. Why did they work there so much? Because the studio was a favourite of many esteemed musicians. 'Dave Hassenger, the engineer, liked it, I think. He was a very well-respected engineer. Jack Nitzsche liked it. I think that the people they knew and respected in LA, like those two, seemed to like the place. I'm not sure whether there were that many independent studios at that point. It had a pretty good reputation – Elvis recorded there. Mick's vocal mike was supposedly the one that Elvis liked to use.

'It was exciting. They were all staying at the Beverly Wilshire, which is a pretty fantastic hotel. It was a good atmosphere in the studio. Jack Nitzsche's wife brought in food. Being that much older, and sophisticated American artists, they were already into nutrition and against fast food. Burgers, fries and ketchup was still pretty good fun. But they were into good nutrition, and she'd come in with home-made food for everybody. There was a nice vibe.'

Then the Rolling Stones came home for Christmas.

CHAPTER 10

COULD YOU WALK
ON THE WATER?

At the beginning of 1966 the public face of the Rolling Stones remained that of Brian Jones. Brian's image of smug, flaxen-haired fop dominated photographs of the group, and in live shows held the audience's attention. For all Mick's reindeer-like on-stage prancing, Brian – one minute still and silent, the next a smirking satyr – simply oozed moody charisma, even though his considerable talent seemed to have been reduced to nothing more than an engine for expressing such histrionic glamour. His curiously waddling form notwithstanding, Brian looked fantastic: he was the personification of rebellious, dandified decadence, and therefore the personification of the Rolling Stones. In a group sold as definitively 'longhaired', 'Mr Shampoo' was the only member who really was.

Despite the fact that the group were now utterly dependent on their increasingly original and addictive songs, in the public eye Mick and especially Keith were mere also-rans next to Brian, a fact of which they were only too aware. The majority of the record-buying public had no inkling of the tempestuous internal politics within the Stones and, apart from the vocals and drums, hadn't a clue as to who contributed what to the group's sound and arrangements.

Now in Anita Pallenberg the group's founder had also scored a definitive piece of 'luxury crumpet', a status symbol 'bird' whom Brian was already beginning to discover was at least his match. Half German, half Italian, Anita seemed unutterably exotic to the boy from Cheltenham, as well as to the boys from Dartford. She had worked with the Living Theatre, and had had a long relationship with the painter Mario Schifano. As long as their relationship lasted, Brian Jones and Anita Pallenberg were the Number One Beautiful Couple in Europe. No matter that Brian, asthmatic, unfit and increasingly unhinged by his drug and alcohol intake, had spent his first night with Anita sobbing paranoically over the way that, apparently, he was treated by Mick and Keith: as 'top-notch totty', rather to Mick's chagrin, Anita left Chrissie Shrimpton in the starting-blocks. For his own part, Keith's relationship with Linda Keith, whose surname suggested her to be either the love of his life or an indulgently narcissistic mirror image, was virtually on the rocks: Linda's fondness not only for marijuana, but also for the downer prescription drug Mandrax and now heroin, which Keith had so far resisted, had placed a strain on their relationship that seemed impossible to resolve.

Thanks to the deal with Allen Klein, who had renegotiated their contract with Decca, the Stones had woken up one morning to discover that they were rich: Mick and Keith, of course, who had begun to receive extremely handsome cheques as payment for songwriting royalties, were much richer than the rest of the group. Keith had recently purchased a Bentley Continental, the same model of the marque that James Bond drove in the by now famous Ian Fleming spy novels: he named it the Blue Lena, after the 'torch' singer Lena Horne.

In April 1966 he had paid £17,750 for a dilapidated moated Tudor manor house called Redlands, six miles south of Chichester, outside the village of West Wittering in Sussex, and he would motor down to the house along leafy country lanes in the Bentley. In London, however, he would frequently employ the services of Tom Keylock, a chauffeur-cum-bodyguard, to ferry him around the busy streets of the capital; those close to Keith felt that this was by far the safest option. He had, after all, allegedly acquired his driving licence by getting a friend to take his test for him under his name. (In his circle Keith became legendary for his eccentric driving methods: discovering to his disappointment that a vintage Mercedes German army staff-car he had bought had a manual gearbox rather than an automatic transmission, he would shudderingly start the car off in third gear, keeping it in that position all the time he drove it.)

But most days when he was in London, during the spring and summer months of 1966, Keith would walk the three or so miles from the flat he still maintained in St John's Wood – where he had been pressured by the landlords to ensure the fans made less noise – across Hyde Park to 1 Courtfield Road, behind Gloucester Road tube station, where Anita Pallenberg had bought a flat and into which Brian had moved with her. Keith's problems with Linda Keith had led him to feel very much alone, and now he bonded again with Brian, as they had in the days when the two of them would be left alone in Edith Grove as Mick continued his studies at the LSE. Despite the fact that, for the group's audience, Keith Richard remained almost entirely overshadowed by Brian Jones, the boy from Cheltenham was for now at least seemingly his best friend. The intriguing high-priestess aspect, embodied in her attraction to the occult, of Anita held more than a small attraction for Keith, who, having grown up in a family dominated by women, was used to having them around. For Keith, the closeness of what even from the first was almost a triangular relationship had positive consequences: by osmosis he picked up elements of Brian's amazing dress sense, transforming his own appearance; soon he would also take Brian's girlfriend. And another vicious triangle would erupt: between Keith, Brian and Mick.

Christopher Gibbs, the fashionable Chelsea art and antiques dealer, had insisted to Anita that she buy the flat, which had only one room and a set of stairs leading to a minstrel's gallery that formed a bedroom of sorts. Gibbs had emphasised to her how extraordinary the place could be made to look if money was spent on it; almost inevitably, in this drug-and-ego-befuddled household, the necessary forward planning had never taken place, so the interior of the residence resembled a much more expensive version of the post-adolescent chaos of the flat in nearby Edith Grove. Mick, exhausted from the constant squabbling with Chrissie and the exigencies of his career, hardly ever ventured over to 1 Courtfield Road; the atmosphere of grime and unwashed dishes was something he found distinctly unsavoury, and he could not avoid picking up on a palpably unhealthy sexual tension that seemed to sit thickly in the air along with the fumes of best-quality hashish. For some of those louche aristocrats who loved to hang out with dandy pop stars, 1 Courtfield Road became the epicentre of their world: Tara Browne, the Guinness heir, would often be round at the flat with his girlfriend Suki Poitier, staying up half the night talking with the two Stones and Anita before disappearing home in his Lotus Elan.

Christopher Gibbs was a central figure in a social milieu into which Mick, Keith and Brian had plunged themselves, and which seemed to them to be daringly sophisticated, a world that now included such locations as Mrs Beaton's Tent, a restaurant in Frith Street, Soho, run by an Australian called Michael Stafford, that became a favourite of the set. When out on his own or with friends, Keith, whose fiery anger seemed to have been subdued by a combination of drug-taking and success, favoured La Terrazza, the fashionable Soho Italian trattoria. Mick, meanwhile, would eat at the Casserole, a compact restaurant with a large gay clientele only a few hundred yards along the King's Road to the east of Edith Grove. The arty world into which Mick, Keith and Brian had been drawn was at the least sexually ambivalent, and often outright gay.

Anita had first introduced Brian to Robert Fraser, the gay Old Etonian art dealer, who had been introduced to Mick and Keith by Donald Cammell in Paris, and who was always on the cusp of the newest scenes. Shortly before meeting Brian, Anita had spent six months in New York with Mario Schifano, and considered herself au fait with the Manhattan art world, not to mention that of Europe. Through quasi-underground figures such as John Dunbar, the now heroin-addicted husband of Marianne Faithfull, and

Barry Miles (known simply as Miles), who together ran the distinctly underground Indica gallery and bookshop now in Southampton Row, the Beatles had already fallen under the attractive spell of Fraser. ('He was the best art eye I've ever met,' considered Paul McCartney, always up for spending the odd ten grand to add another Magritte to his collection at the suggestion of the art dealer.) Now it was the turn of the Stones to take on Robert Fraser as their taste guru, although Mick usually claimed not to have the necessary money to buy any of the works Fraser offered him.

There was no doubt about it, Robert Fraser was interesting. For five days in September 1966 he exhibited a psychedelically painted AC Cobra sports car in the window space of his gallery at 69 Duke Street in Mayfair. The year had begun at the Robert Fraser gallery with the Los Angeles *Now* exhibition, which included work by Ed Ruscha and Dennis Hopper; the whole of July was given over to a collection by Andy Warhol, and at other times during the year, the work of Peter Blake and Jim Dine was also put on display, ending in December with an exhibition by Claes Oldenburg. 'The role of the Rolling Stones was to be the bad kids on the block, early punks if you like, and the Beatles were the good guys. They played their roles very well. They came to the openings, and Mick Jagger said awfully nasty things to everybody, and Paul McCartney was very nice, charming,' Oldenburg remembered. 'I used to go to the gallery a lot and sit and look at the paintings, but I didn't go to the openings, these great social events,' recalled Mick Jagger, his memory notoriously imprecise.

Fraser lived in Mount Street, only a few hundred yards from his gallery, to which he would be transported every morning by chauffeur-driven Rolls-Royce. 'Robert owned this apartment where you'd sit around talking, and now and again you'd have a chat, without being really interested that much,' said Keith. 'Then slowly it became more and more of a friendship. Robert was never one to push ... He observed and gathered together the best and brightest around. They kind of flocked to him, the most interesting people. In a way it was a continuation or a revival of the eighteenth-century salon ... He was incredibly funny, incredibly witty ... Jim Dine I've heard of, and there he is, sitting in the flat! Or it could be Allen Ginsberg. He had incredibly diverse connections.'

Robert also introduced Brian and Anita to the cosmic experience of LSD, the first person in London either of them knew who had taken acid. 'I was just used to hash,' said Anita, 'but one night at his place Brian and I took this trip, went home and started to hallucinate.' Soon Keith too was let in on the secret of lysergic acid. Through Robert Fraser, Keith encountered for the first time an Alfa Romeo-driving former croupier who went by the nickname of Spanish Tony. Fraser, said Mick Jagger, 'was the one who invented Spanish Tony, Tony Sanchez. He's a ghastly person.

Why did he invent him? He did provide drugs, but there was more than one drug dealer around. He was a particularly difficult drug dealer. Unpleasant person. I don't know what Robert's relationship with Spanish Tony was. Possibly sexual, but that's just a guess.' Was there an element of jealousy here? Or protectiveness towards a wayward friend?

In fact Spanish Tony had become friends with Robert Fraser after he interceded with Reggie Kray to save Fraser from a beating over a bad gambling debt. In return, Robert Fraser turned Spanish Tony on to marijuana for the first time at his flat in Mount Street, where Tony smoked his first joint with the Moody Blues. With Fraser acting as his mentor, Tony became a photographer, and shot the cover of the Moody Blues' first album. But he had also fallen into a useful sub-career: 'Spanish' fell in love with smoking, and set about discovering where he could obtain grass and hash in sizeable quantities; soon he found where to purchase other, stronger drugs. As a man who could always be relied on to deliver the goods, Tony Sanchez was soon to become an indispensable part of Keith's circle. 'Like me, Keith was young and impressionable, and he had always been content to follow where Brian led,' said Spanish Tony. 'He turned Keith on to acid, and they were drawn together.'

Keith half moved into 1 Courtfield Road, crashing on the couch or the floor, aware of the sensuous and sometimes strange sounds floating down from the gallery above as Brian and Anita made love. As Anita and Robert had done to him, Brian turned his fellow Rolling Stone on to LSD, which drew them together, accentuating the endless musical improvisation in which they indulged. Again the axis shifted in the Stones, as it had done briefly at Edith Grove: Mick was regarded as the 'straight' because he hadn't done acid, and confessed to being frightened of it. To get his goat further, Brian and Keith began to call him by his surname, which had the desired effect of winding Mick up very much indeed. At the same time Brian's natural paranoia, accentuated by his daily ingestion of drugs, made him extremely fearful of the evident affection that was beginning to emerge between Keith and Anita.

On 4 February 1966 a new single had been released by the Rolling Stones. Although '19th Nervous Breakdown' only got to number two in both the UK and the US, it was another epochal record in this Golden Period of Stones' releases that had begun with 'Satisfaction'. Out later that month was an Andrew Loog Oldham conceit, an LP of covers of recent hits entitled *Today's Pop Symphony by the Aranbee* [R 'n' B – geddit?] *Pop Symphony Orchestra*. The record, comprising instrumental, pseudo-classically arranged versions of recent hits, was produced by Keith; among the material it included was the Beatles' 'There's A Place' and 'We Can

Work It Out', the Four Seasons' 'Rag Doll', Wilson Pickett's 'In The Midnight Hour', Dusty Springfield's 'I Don't Want To Go On Without You', Sonny and Cher's 'I Got You Babe' and the Stones' 'Play With Fire', 'Mother's Little Helper', 'Sitting On A Fence' and 'Take It Or Leave It'. 'Anyone who thinks Keith's talents are limited will be forced to think again,' considered the *Record Mirror* review of the record. How curious, though, that such pseudo-classical arrangements should carry the production credit of the man who, within a few short years, would be canonised as 'Mr Rock 'n' Roll', and 'The Human Riff'. In the same way that Paul McCartney had declared his greatest ambition to be 'to write a stage musical', could it be that Keith Richard's musical source material was far more catholic than he would later admit? The guiding hand of show-business hung over the world of popular music in the mid-1960s, and Keith's outlaw swagger, derived from badmen renegades and Long John Silver-like characters in Westerns and pirate films that were then filtered through his art-school understanding of life, always seemed as much a construct by a hammy actor as a natural outgrowth of his soul.

The oddity of *Today's Pop Symphony* was virtually ignored by the record-buying public, their attention consumed by the Stones' latest hit. The effect of '19th Nervous Breakdown' on Chrissie Shrimpton was almost to give her an actual breakdown: Mick's dolly-bird girlfriend was convinced she was the subject of the record. Mired in a fiery, painful relationship, whose stamp had been set by the row they were having on their first date, when Andrew Loog Oldham saw them for the first time outside the Station Hotel in Richmond, the couple might have split up long before but for the fact that they hardly saw each other. From the end of 1964 until almost the middle of 1966, the incessant on-the-road and studio work schedule of the Rolling Stones, desperate to catch up with the status of the Beatles as biggest group in the world, meant that they toured more than any other British act – with the consequence that Mick seemed hardly ever to be in the country, let alone at home. Although Chrissie occasionally accompanied Mick, she didn't enjoy the creepy on-the-road life, with sycophants in every nook and cranny. Mick had promised that they would finally marry when he got back from the group's third US tour, in October 1965.

Mick and Chrissie were always breaking up. While they were living together in Bryanston Mews in the summer of 1965, Chrissie learned of an American girl called Tish, whom Mick saw when he was in the United States and who had now arrived in London. Accordingly, Chrissie went off with P. J. Proby, the American singer of Elvis demos who had transmogrified into a headlining star with marvellously histrionic hits like 'Hold Me' and 'Somewhere', his hyperbolical version of the *West Side Story* classic. After reducing Jagger to tears when he saw a newspaper story about Chrissie and Proby flying to America together, she called him at the Stones' office to confess that the story was one that she had planted in the press, having learned the art of media manipulation from one of its finest practitioners. Then Chrissie demanded that Tish leave the Bryanston Mews flat immediately: she insisted that she stay on the line, listening on an extension, while Mick called the girl and ordered her out of the flat. Later Mick said he'd gone off with the girl because Chrissie 'wouldn't even make me a cup of coffee'.

It became a physically abusive relationship. Mick seemed deliberately to be picking fights but Chrissie began to take the blame herself for the problems between them. One night as she waited for Mick to return, she became more and more depressed. When he came in the door she punched him in the face several times, cutting him and leaving marks that were visible long afterwards. Mick ran off, and when he returned apologetically, Chrissie refused to be mollified; still raging, she tried to tear down the apartment's curtains.

Her insecurities were not helped by the fact that during 1965 her boyfriend was considered among the fashionable elite to be the hippest young man in London, the prize catch at any social event. In August 1965, for example, Mick Jagger had been best man at the wedding of David Bailey, who was by now his closest friend. Mick was said to be friends with Princess Margaret. And there were scurrilous stories of him sitting with her at society parties as she allegedly took tokes on a joint. Certainly at the coming-out ball of Victoria Ormsby-Gore, the daughter of Sir David and Lady Jane Ormsby-Gore, Mick and the sister of the ruling monarch exhibited their friendship, to Chrissie's considerable irritation: the couple were seated at the table next to that of Princess Margaret, who invited Jagger over but not Chrissie. As soon as he returned, Chrissie, furious at this imagined slight, demanded they leave – *that will put that Margaret in her place!* Mick was not pleased. Always a spirited girl, Chrissie had chosen a two-pound dress from Biba in Kensington Church Street after rejecting the expensive dress Jagger had bought her for the occasion.

In the second week of February 1966, the Rolling Stones flew to New York to promote '19th Nervous Breakdown' and to announce an imminent album, *Could You Walk on the Water?* Inevitably, such cod blasphemy resulted in considerable controversy, and Decca – reverting as ever to stuffy, predictable type – refused to release the record under that title. But the album wasn't even ready, as the group had as yet hardly recorded any songs for it. The Stones appeared on the Ed Sullivan Show on 13 February, performing 'Satisfaction', 'As Tears Go By' (on which Mick and Keith duetted) and the new single. Then they spent a couple of days at RCA Hollywood in Los Angeles, recording twenty new songs written by Mick and Keith, before flying to Australia and New Zealand for an Australasian tour.

Now almost all of the songs on the Stones' eleven-song set list had been written by Mick and Keith: 'The Last Time', 'Play With Fire', 'The Spider And The Fly', 'Get Off Of My Cloud', '19th Nervous Breakdown' and 'Satisfaction' were all included. Supporting the Stones were the Searchers and Max Merritt and the Meteors. The Australasian tour lasted until 2 March, Keith receiving a facial cut on 24 February – Brian's birthday – when girls rushed the stage in St Kilda in New Zealand.

After a brief holiday on Fiji, the group returned to Los Angeles for more recording; Brian brought with him the sitar he had bought on the Pacific island. Towards the end of March another Stones' compilation album was released in the USA – *Big Hits (High Tide and Green Grass)*, which used the cover art and photographs from the now abandoned *Could You Walk on the Water?*. Again, the cover shot of the Stones was dominated by Brian Jones who appeared at the front of the group: at the LA sessions for the new album, Brian hardly played any guitar at all, but instead added textures on piano, dulcimer, vibraphone and marimbas. Jack Nitzsche, meanwhile, had contributed harpsichord to two new tunes, 'Lady Jane' and 'I Am Waiting'.

Almost as soon as the group returned to Britain, they were off on another set of European dates, racing through Holland, Belgium, France, Sweden and Denmark, which lasted from 26 March to 5 April. Amid a motley crew of support acts, including Wayne Fontana and the Mindbenders, the Stones were joined on the bill by Chuck Berry for the 30 March concert at the Salle Vallier in Marseilles. The Marseilles show erupted into a riot, with over eighty fans arrested as they tore the joint apart: during 'Satisfaction' Mick was hit just above the eye by a piece of a seat flung at the stage – he was rushed to hospital where six stitches were needed to close the wound just above his left eyebrow. The tour wound up in Copenhagen.

CHAPTER 11

FIRST NERVOUS BREAKDOWN

On 16 April 1966, Keith formally moved in to Redlands, at once setting about turning his new home into some kind of conceptual testament to creative untidiness: as building work was undertaken on the property he would sleep on a mattress in front of the living room's vast fireplace. However, the Sussex property became very much a country retreat, and Keith continued to spend much of his time at 1 Courtfield Road.

The day before the Redlands move, *Aftermath* – the renamed version of *Could You Walk on the Water?* – was released in Britain. Everywhere that spring and summer there could be heard the sunny sound of the album, sailing out of the doors of boutiques and teenagers' bedroom windows. The record was a masterful distillation of the Stones' misogyny and by now customary stance of adolescent sneering at the older generation: in this vein it contained a number of utterly addictive songs, including 'Out Of Time', 'Under My Thumb', 'Stupid Girl' and 'Mother's Little Helper'. The British version of *Aftermath* was a perfectly flowing landmark LP, even better than the Stones' groundbreaking second album, *Rolling Stones No 2*. For the first time Mick and Keith had written all fourteen of the songs on the record. The American version, which was not released until 1 July (so as not to dent the sales of *Big Hits (High Tide and Green Grass)*), was somewhat inferior: it did not include 'Out Of Time', 'Mother's Little Helper', 'Take It Or Leave It', 'V1' or 'What To Do', and added 'Paint It, Black', a new single released in both countries on 13 May. The song 'Lady Jane', another Stones' foray into courtly Elizabethan pastoralism with a similar tone to 'Play With Fire', was assumed (especially by herself) to have been written for Jane Ormsby-Gore, the Ormsby-Gores having become extremely close friends of Mick. Meanwhile Mick disingenuously confided in Chrissie Shrimpton that he had actually written it about her. In fact he had had the idea for the song after reading D. H. Lawrence's controversial novel *Lady Chatterley's Lover*.

Part of the appeal of *Aftermath* was the deeply personal and transparently sincere nature of the lyrics. Mick had learned to trust the instinct of his emotions and put them into lyrical form, expressing his sense of disgust as he sang from his heart about two interrelated themes: the mores of the bourgeoisie and what we now know to have been the final months of his relationship with Chrissie Shrimpton, his venom and hurt about the relationship pouring out: 'There is only one thing in the world that I can't understand, that's a girl', he sang in 'Sad Day'.

On 1 May 1966 the Stones performed as joint headliners with the Beatles at the *NME* Poll Winners' show at the Empire Pool, Wembley, an afternoon show. The release two weeks later of 'Paint It, Black' came as a shock. In a time of landmark releases by the group, this was the highest point; dominated by Brian's sitar, the music thundered along, driven by Charlie's multi-tracked drumming. Bill played organ as a parody of Andrew Loog Oldham's former partner Eric Easton, who had begun his musical career playing in cinemas. A unique work, it took a quantum leap via Mick's lyrics, which seemed to express the profound pessimism and deep pain of a troubled soul in excoriating lyrics about his personal 'darkness': 'Didn't want to see the sun, flying high in the sky/I wanna see it painted, painted, painted black, yeah'. 'It is one of the greatest songs of the twentieth century,' declared Leonard Bernstein, the conductor of the New York Philharmonic Orchestra.

By the time the record, had raced to number one on both sides of the Atlantic – and it was to be the Stones' last number one for over two years – Mick had other things on his mind. At the end of May, Chris Farlowe's version of 'Out Of Time' – featured on *Aftermath*, and one of the best songs written by Mick and Keith – came out as a single, giving the considerably respected 'white soul singer' Farlowe his first Top Ten hit. The record had been produced by Mick, and its lyrics had already shaken Chrissie to the core: 'You're obsolete, my baby, my poor old-fashioned baby'.

It was not a good month for Chrissie: on 24 May, along with Mick, Keith and Anita, she had attended the twenty-first birthday party of Tara Browne at Luggala, one of the Guinness family estates, at Bray in Ireland. There, she and Mick had tripped together for the first time, a rotten experience for her, as she was swept up by waves of paranoia. During the trip Chrissie became the psychological and psychic mess portrayed in '19th Nervous Breakdown', a song reportedly 'inspired' by that hapless effort by Mick to bond cosmically with his girlfriend.

Chrissie Shrimpton had only begun to appreciate the extent of her boyfriend's drug consumption. For most of their relationship, he had urged her to keep away from drugs. When a member of the Stones' management discovered her the previous Christmas sharing a joint at a Christmas party,

Chrissie had implored him not to tell Mick – he'd be so angry with her, she said. 'Oh, don't worry about that,' responded the aide. 'Mick's been stoned all day.'

On 26 May 1966 the Stones shared a box at a Bob Dylan concert. Earlier that evening they had performed 'Paint It, Black' on *Top of the Pops*, which went out on BBC-TV at seven in the evening, before rushing to the Royal Albert Hall for the famous Dylan performance. Legendarily, the concert shocked Dylan's folkie devotees when the already mythical troubador returned for the second half of the show with his backing group the Hawks, soon to become the Band, and launched into the electric phase of his career. Afterwards it was Keith's moment to have a bad experience. Following the show, he and Brian went to Blaise's, a club in a basement a few hundred yards away in nearby Queensgate, where Dylan later arrived. Nervously, Keith approached him. With a sardonic sneer, Dylan looked straight through him: 'I could write "Satisfaction", but you couldn't write "Mr Tambourine Man".' Shy Keith was really quite frightened by this attack from Dylan's famously poisonous tongue. After a few bolstering drinks, though, he came to the conclusion that Dylan's epochal song 'Like A Rolling Stone' was an attack on his group: accordingly, he took a swing at Dylan, and a short mêlée ensued, in which Dylan was ironically saved by Tom Keylock, his minder for the British dates on loan from Keith, who hustled the American musical god back to the Mayfair Hotel. Keylock pretended not to notice that they were followed by Brian and Keith, Brian drunkenly steering his Rolls-Royce, the pair intent on having another pop at Dylan. Dylan, by now out of his head most of the time on smack and speed, affected not to notice the brouhaha. (Brian had purchased a personalised number plate for his luxury transportation: DD 666, as though he were thumbing his nose at the Deity; there were some who viewed such arrogance as the final straw in the ultimate downfall of 'Mr Shampoo', the leader of the Rolling Stones.)

The following day, by the time the Stones performed their new single on *Ready Steady Go!*, 'Paint It, Black' had reached the number-one spot in Britain. To help promote the single, Mick gave an interview to the *Daily Express*: 'When I was sixteen I wanted to be a journalist. But it seemed too much like hard work. When I went to university to study politics and economics, I thought of going into politics. But I believe it is harder initially to get into politics and then get to the top than it is in the pop world. There are parallels one can draw between the two fields. In selling yourself as a politician, like selling records, not so much depends on what you have to say but on how you say it. The last election has proved the selling power of an image on television.'

Had 'Paint It, Black' been a premonition on Mick's part? Shortly after the Dylan Albert Hall show, Mick suffered a minor breakdown; his soul was rebelling against the stress of the relentless forward course of the Stones and the strain of his unsatisfactory relationship. *Le tout Londres*, meanwhile, whispered fallaciously that this nervous collapse had been caused by Mick's recent drug intake. On 3 June Dr Samuel Weinstock examined the singer at his Harley Street practice and pronounced him suffering from nervous exhaustion. Ten days later, Mick went into what the Stones' office described as 'isolation, having been ordered to take a total rest'.The curtains were pulled tight on the fourth floor at 52 Harley House, Mick's new mansion flat on Marylebone Road, where he stayed in bed for ten days.

On 23 June 1966 the Rolling Stones arrived in New York for the start of their fifth US tour. A story was released by the Stones' office to the *Daily Mirror* in London, reporting that the group was to sue fourteen New York hotels for £1,750,000 for refusing to take bookings from the group, alleging 'discrimination on the basis of national origin'. A 'story', however, was all it was, a fiction made up to fuel the Stones' ever-present undercurrent of fashionable controversy. In fact, they spent their first night in New York on Allen Klein's yacht, the SS *Sea Panther*, which was berthed at the 79th Street pier in Manhattan: the group used the yacht as their East Coast headquarters. A press conference and party was held on the boat, to promote the tour as well as the *Aftermath* album and the 'Mother's Little Helper'/'Lady Jane' single: photographer Linda Eastman came along to take pictures, and Mick spent the night with her, which she wrote about in a US fan magazine.

After initial shows in Boston, Washington DC, Baltimore, Buffalo, Hartford and Atlantic City, the group played Forest Hills tennis stadium in the Queens section of New York; all the dates were in arena-sized venues. Now the thirteen songs which made up their set contained only one song – 'Not Fade Away' – that they had not written themselves. Otherwise it was a run of original hit singles, plus additions from the new album. Returning to Manhattan from Forest Hills, the group congregated at the Café Wha? on MacDougal Street in Greenwich Village, to see a new guitarist whom Linda Keith had recommended, and with whom Keith discovered she had some sort of relationship: the musician's name was Jimi Hendrix, and all five of the Stones were immediately in awe of him. After seeing Hendrix's performance Keith was not at all pleased about Linda's new boyfriend: Linda had even loaned him one of Keith's new Stratocasters. Linda Keith in turn was hardly delighted when she discovered she was just one of many women the wild musical genius from Seattle was seeing. Keith was even more concerned when he realised the extent of Linda's fondness for heroin. In New York, Keith and Brian encountered a twenty-seven-year-old Canadian acid dealer called David Schneiderman, aka Acid King David: call by if you're in London they told him.

Heading out to the West Coast, the group played the outdoor Hollywood Bowl in Los Angeles, always a Stones' stronghold, on 25 July 1966 to 17,500 fans; the support act was a hot new local group, Buffalo Springfield. The next day Mick spent part of his twenty-third birthday on a flight from LA to the venue in San Francisco, returning to Century Plaza Hotel in Los Angeles for the night. The tour ended on 28 July at the International Sports Center in Honolulu, where the group – hardly to their displeasure – were stranded in Hawaii for several days due to an airline strike. Then it was back to Los Angeles for further sessions at RCA Studios in Hollywood. From 3 August until the eleventh of the month, the group worked at a prodigious rate, finishing fifteen songs that were eventually released, including 'Have You See Your Mother, Baby, Standing In The Shadow' and 'Let's Spend The Night Together'. Andrew Loog Oldham produced the sessions with, as ever, David Hassenger as engineer and Jack Nitzsche on piano on 'Who's Driving Your Plane?'

After the tour they went on holiday, although for Mick and Keith their joint vacation in Acapulco was business as usual: there, stoned on Mexican weed and buzzing from the pocketfuls of acid they had brought in from Los Angeles, they wrote the group's next album. Meanwhile, at the suggestion of Christopher Gibbs, Brian and Anita headed for Morocco: there, during one of their several fights, Brian broke his hand on a hotel bedroom wall when he took a swing at Anita. Accordingly, when the group had to make a hurried plane ride to New York on 9 September to perform 'Have You Seen Your Mother' on the Ed Sullivan Show, along with 'Paint It, Black' and 'Lady Jane', only Mick's vocals were live, the group miming to pre-recorded backing tracks. Brian, whose bandaged hand was perfectly visible, played the sitar that dominated 'Paint it, Black' and the dulcimer on 'Lady Jane'.

On 12 September, the Stones shot a promotional film in New York for 'Have You Seen Your Mother, Baby', in which the group appeared in drag, dressed like thirty-year-old women in 1940s wartime. The same theme was employed in the publicity for the record: 'Molly' Richard and 'Sarah' Jagger adorned the single's poster, to great controversy. In the same image Brian wears his customary visage of stoned arrogance: might he have appeared more modest if he had been aware that he would never again tour the United States with the Rolling Stones? Keith, meanwhile, had used the September visit to New York to search for furnishings and objets d'art to adorn Redlands: he shipped back a copper garden fountain and a pair of lioness-skin rugs, indicators of the rococo rock-star style that would become the image not only of his new home but also his own image in the coming years.

To promote 'Have You Seen Your Mother', the Stones were featured in a series of interviews in *Disc and Music Echo*. 'At no time have we been scared that he was going to quit and turn solo,' Bill Wyman said of Mick. 'He gets depressed sometimes and we have to bear with it. He's a bit careful with money, not extravagant like Keith. I also think Mick's a romantic, very much so.' In the same series, Mick described Keith: 'I've known him longer than anyone else in the group. I went to school with him. I still don't know what he's thinking at any time and he really is one of my closest friends. From time to time, we've had little arguments ... we disagree quite a lot but we usually come to a compromise. There's never any hard feelings. He's forgetful and so he doesn't remember to bear a grudge. He's very good at his songwriting now, and we've got a relatively efficient way of going about it. He's very good about the group, very optimistic. This cheers me up when I'm feeling low. I think people find it difficult to know Keith. Sometimes he's shy and other times he can't be bothered to take an interest in people.'

In between Acapulco and New York, Mick and Chrissie Shrimpton had been involved in a minor car crash: his new £5,000 midnight-blue Aston Martin DB6 was involved in a collision near Harley House with a Ford Anglia belonging to the Countess of Carlisle. 'I only bought the car three months ago,' moaned Mick. 'The damage is going to cost around two hundred pounds.' Was there some rivalry with Keith in Mick's choice of new car? Keith's Bentley Continental and Mick's Aston Martin DB6 were both cars that were driven by the fictional but fabulously glamorous James Bond. And was the car crash symbolic of the tension between the two occupants of the DB6? When Jagger had returned from the fifth Stones' American tour Chrissie had felt quite unequivocally that Mick was no longer in love with her: she wanted out of the relationship. But how?

Keith, meanwhile, had been to see Linda Keith's parents in Hampstead: their daughter, he told them, was in danger, and he recommended they bring her back to London immediately, which they did. Although Keith saw her when she returned to the capital, he could sense that the link between them was gone for ever.

CHAPTER 12

REPULSION

The end of the summer of 1966 was a pivotal time in the emotional lives of both Mick and Keith. The Dartford boys had been reunited by the time spent together in Acapulco and by their shared drug experiences. To the consternation of Brian, aware that just a few months previously he had seized control of the awkward triangular relationship between himself, Keith and Mick, the Stones' singer now started to hang out at Courtfield Road with Keith, who was beginning to acknowledge that he was smouldering for Anita, a flame that burned steadily within him when he discovered just how Brian had hurt his hand.

But Keith had almost burned his fingers. By now a frequent visitor to the Gloucester Road flat was Marianne Faithfull, seeking a haven from the junkie lifestyle that had come to dominate her existence with John Dunbar, her addict husband. Thought of by many as a dilettante, Marianne Faithfull in fact never stopped working, touring relentlessly halfway down the bill on package tours. She would go off on tour, bring home piles of cash, and then do the housework. Although Marianne would have to sweep aside heroin paraphernalia in her kitchen to find space to fill her baby son's feeding-bottle, her husband would not permit his wife to indulge in so much as a single toke in their home: drug-taking was considered serious men's business. Accordingly, she would slope off to Courtfield Road to put together endless joints from the latest supplies of premium hashish brought over by Spanish Tony – Red or Gold Leb, Nepalese Temple Balls, the finest Afghani, straight off the hippy trail.

Through John Dunbar, Marianne Faithfull had also become part of the Robert Fraser set: it was Fraser who gave Marianne her first cocaine experience, at a party put on to help raise money for the film *Candy*, written by Terry Southern and Mason Hoffenberg, drawn frequently to London by the availability of prescription heroin. That night at his Mount Street flat Fraser offered her one of half a dozen lines he had chopped out on a mantelpiece; Marianne, unaware of the user etiquette of this particular drug, snorted the lot. For her, it was the beginning of a long relationship with the white powder.

Somewhat infatuated with Keith, whose silent shyness she felt masked an inner confidence and strength, one night, after tripping with the guitarist, Brian and Tara Browne Marianne found that, rather to her surprise, she was having sex with him. Falling asleep in his arms, she found herself hoping when she awoke that more might develop between them. As Keith bade her farewell the next day, however, she realised that this was not to be. 'You know who really has it bad for you, don't you?' he said. 'Mick: didn't you know?'

Was there an element of precognition in Chrissie Shrimpton's intuiting that Mick no longer loved her? For he was about to embark on a relationship that would finally sever the bond with his girlfriend.

From 23 September to 9 October 1966 the Rolling Stones were off on their eighth UK tour. This time the promoter had assembled a truly credible bill, more of the sort that Bill Graham was beginning to put together at events in San Francisco than the pop packages on which the Stones had so often embarked on UK tours: the group was supported by Ike and Tina Turner and the Ikettes, the Yardbirds and Long John Baldry, whom they had first met at the Ealing Jazz Club.

When the Rolling Stones played at Colston Hall in Bristol on 7 October 1966, Brian and Keith invited Marianne Faithfull to see the show. She drove down in her new Ford Mustang. Entering the venue's backstage area, she came across Mick in the corridor outside the dressing room being taught to dance the Pony by Tina Turner (any earlier and she might have found the pair having a discreet snog): much to the delight of Keith and Brian, his performance was decidedly pedestrian.

After an extraordinary Stones' show, Marianne and several other girls went back to the group's hotel, the Ship in nearby Bath. In Mick's room a photographer called Michael Cooper, who was part of Robert Fraser's circle, was showing a straight-from-the-cutting-room print of *Repulsion*, the new film by Roman Polanski. Unable to move due to the amount of hash she had smoked, Marianne sat it out in the room until all the other women had left. Then she and Mick spent the night together. Concerned over her persisting feelings for Keith, Marianne went so far as to phone Allen Klein to discuss her dilemma with him. 'But Marianne, if you go with Keith it'll destroy Mick,' Klein summed up the problem. 'But it's also true that the whole time I was with Mick I was in love with Keith,' she later wrote in her autobiography, *Faithfull*. 'And in this way, I too was drawn into the web.'

Almost immediately after she had spent her first night with Mick Jagger,

Marianne Faithfull flew to Italy with her son Nicholas to spend a few weeks in the autumn sun of Positano, where she had rented a house. While there, she received an incessant flurry of phone messages from Mick. The moment she returned to London, he asked her to go shopping with him in Bond Street; she noticed that he took to this with an almost feminine relish, but it was also Marianne's first opportunity to observe that Mick could be a little tight with his money.

Marianne Faithfull's marriage to John Dunbar was not yet formally over. Although she was initially uncertain as to whether she wanted to be drawn into a new relationship, Marianne found Mick's presence reassuring. He and Andrew Loog Oldham had once visited her at her home in Lennox Gardens, and she had observed Mick's visible distress at the dissolute state of disarray in which she was living. Now Mick was a shoulder to lean on, a man who seemed reliable and sympathetic, that clichéd foundation of so many new love affairs. Mick, hopeless romantic that he was, was already in love with her – though Marianne was as yet unaware how easily the heart of this perpetual tomcat-on-the-prowl could be captured.

Not that she was much different. One night when she was round at the Mount Street flat of the apparently resolutely gay Robert Fraser, she discovered to her surprise that, after the inevitable joint or two, she was rolling passionately about the couch's Indian cushions in a pre-coital embrace with the art dealer. Neither realised that the front door had been left open. Suddenly in walked Mick Jagger, wearing a delicately embroidered jacket from Mr Fish. The sight of Marianne and Fraser so startled him that his upper torso seemed to go into a sort of muscular spasm, ripping the beautiful garment. Recovering himself, he stepped towards the door: 'All right, Marianne? Coming?' She got up and left.

What was needed was for Chrissie Shrimpton to be apprised by Mick of his new romance. Yet confronting the reality of fading or finished relationships was something at which Mick was especially hopeless. Instead, he went about the break-up through devious means: in November, for example, the facility by which Chrissie sent bills for payment to the Stones' office was cancelled, Mick initially feigning amazement at this. Mick and Chrissie were still scheduled to fly to Jamaica on 15 December for Christmas, a long-planned break. Instead, Mick went shopping with Marianne at Harrods that day, followed by a long lunch at San Lorenzo in nearby Beauchamp Place. These events led to a cataclysmic row between Mick and Chrissie Shrimpton at Harley House on Sunday 18 December. On the same day that Tara Browne died in a car smash, Chrissie attempted suicide by swallowing a bottle of sleeping tablets: she was rushed to the Greenway Nursing Home, Hampstead, where her stomach was pumped out. When the bill was sent to Mick, he returned it.

Mick made his first solo appearance on the *Ready Steady Go!* Christmas special broadcast on 23 December, performing 'Out Of Time' and 'Satisfaction' with Chris Farlowe. The next day, Christmas Eve, Mick had all Chrissie's belongings packed and removed from his flat.

Certainly Mick seemed to have been going through a period of finding out who he was. Often he was in thrall to the trends of the day: songs like 'Nineteenth Nervous Breakdown', 'Have You Seen Your Mother Baby' and 'Mother's Little Helper' for example, were all about putting down the older generation, driven by Mick Jagger's belief that older people were a 'drag'; a rather fashionable current of thought in the mid-1960s. Like many young men in the middle of that decade, he endlessly expressed his contempt for the 'bourgeoisie'. In this, he was conveniently re-writing his own quintessentially English middle-class upbringing. Mick now rebelled against his parents, having little to do with them, not bothering to get in touch. Whenever there would be any mention of Eva and Joe Jagger it would be with a petulant raising of the eyebrows and an insistence on what a 'drag' they were. This was a somewhat immature notion for someone who was heading towards his mid-twenties, and one that was considerably at odds with some of his peers – Paul McCartney, for example, told him off about this one night that the Beatles and Stones hung out together at the Scotch of St James. Paul liked his dad, he said.

To add to the ambience of emotional confusion, Keith Richard – who by now had realised how attracted he was to Anita, yet at the same time felt he should behave in an honourable way towards the increasingly wretched Brian – stopped spending so much time at Courtfield Road. In early 1967 he would crash at Harley House for a few days at a time. Once, when Mick and Marianne were making love, he started audibly fantasising about licking Keith all over and going down on him. Marianne was amazed, especially since she was only too aware that Keith, in bed next door, could most likely hear everything Mick was saying – which she knew was probably the intention of her lover. 'For Mick, this homoerotic yearning for Keith may not have been something he ever intended to act upon,' wrote Marianne in her autobiography. 'Had Mick consummated these relationships, they no doubt would have ended in revulsion and destruction. Better for it to remain an unfulfilled desire. That was what gave off the alternating current that drove the Stones.' Eventually, she believed, the incestuous relationship between herself, Mick, Keith and Anita must have become 'profoundly troubling' for the guitarist. 'In the end he really couldn't bear it. And nor could I, which is probably one reason why we eventually ended up doing so much smack, just to block it out.'

CHAPTER 13

KNOW YOUR PLACE

It wouldn't have seemed like a new year if the Rolling Stones had not begun 1967 with more of their by now habitual controversy. On Friday 13 January they released a new single. Its title? 'Let's Spend The Night Together' – which seemed a little obvious, immature and humourless in its efforts to create media brouhaha. Although perfectly catchy and addictive, a tiredness also lay at the heart of the tune, with the suggestion that the cod-naughty lyrics had been specially selected to boost its rather uninspired melody and riffs. No doubt precisely as the group hoped they would, various American radio stations immediately banned the song, thereby only enhancing its word-of-mouth reputation. Ed Sullivan refused to allow the group to perform it with its recorded lyrics, insisting that the words 'the night' be altered to the laughably coy 'some time' – Mick's face broke into a sneer every time he uttered the phrase. The B-side was 'Ruby Tuesday', a composition of Keith's about Linda Keith, featuring Brian on flute. In the United States, 'Ruby Tuesday' was widely promoted, until it became a number-one record; 'Let's Spend The Night Together' rose no higher than number fifty-five. In Britain it was still the A-side.

Sunday Night at the London Palladium was an ITV variety show with an enormous mass-market audience that the Beatles had always exploited to the maximum. Each week the show concluded with the assorted acts climbing upon a slowly spinning carousel and waving chirpily as they held up the letters that spelled out the name of the programme. In the great tradition of rock 'n' roll acts shooting themselves in the foot by being rebellious beyond the call of duty, Mick – despite the protests of the other group members – had made a virtue of always refusing to appear on the programme. Was it an acknowledgement of the weakness of 'Let's Spend The Night Together' that led them now to accept a booking on the show broadcast on 22 January?

When they arrived at the Palladium, behind Oxford Circus, things did not kick off especially well. Keith and Brian turned up together, tripping on LSD, and Brian immediately placed a large waterpipe on top of the piano. Such acts were considered revolutionary gestures in those times. Importantly, a compromise was arrived at with the programme's producer, whereby the Stones simply walked off-stage at the end of their set, as the carousel began spinning. 'The only reason we did the show at the Palladium was because it was a good national plug,' Mick told the *NME*. 'Anyone who thought we were changing our image to suit a family audience was mistaken.' But the worm was beginning to turn in the minds of the Establishment: such a symbolic break with tradition as not stepping on to the carousel was considered a national disgrace.

The London Palladium date was not only used to plug the single: two days before the show, the Stones had released another new album, *Between the Buttons*, the fruits of the August sessions in Los Angeles. It was the first album the Stones had recorded with a conceptual approach. In the *NME*, long-standing Stones' supporter Roy Carr gave it a very bad review. There was no getting away from it: it was a weak, tired album, the songs sounding like out-takes from the *Aftermath* sessions, sub-Kinks songs, and a great disappointment after the excellence of its predecessor.

But in America, where it was released on 11 February, it received a largely ecstatic response. At least the cover was great, another picture by Gered Mankowitz, an archetypal shot of the group moodily hunched up in their overcoats against the early-morning chill. Taken on Primrose Hill in north London after an all-night recording session, it seemed to capture perfectly the zeitgeist, the exactitude of the time. 'Looking back on it now,' said Mankowitz, 'it was an extraordinary thing to photograph a band after an all-night recording session. No grooming, that was the great thing about those days; being a celebrity didn't mean you were surrounded by sycophants, a team of idiots. You didn't have fashion stylists or make-up people. Everything about that band was them. And I felt confident enough to introduce this fluid, slightly druggy, slightly ethereal, slightly strange viewpoint. And it just caught the moment. It wasn't conceptual – that was just the time. It really did have an effect on a lot of people. It's great that Andrew recognised it and encouraged it, insisted that it should be unadorned. It was Andrew's idea actually to put the lettering in Charlie's buttons, to feel that that picture could embody everything about the Stones at that moment, and sell them.'

There was another significant factor about that Gered Mankowitz shot: on the cover picture on *Out of Our Heads*, which Mankowitz had also taken, Brian was right up at the front of the group; and sixteen months later, for *Between the Buttons*, he was right at the back, like an afterthought that was fading away.

*

Andrew Loog Oldham had started his own record company, Immediate, in 1965. At the end of January Mick produced two new singles for the independent label: Chris Farlowe's next record, 'My Way Of Giving', written by Steve Marriott of the Small Faces, who also recorded the song, and Nicky Scott's rendition of the Stones' 'Backstreet Girl'. Neither record sold substantially.

On 28 January 1967 Mick Jagger flew to Cannes in the South of France to meet Marianne Faithfull, who was to appear across the border in Italy at the San Remo song festival. In Cannes, Mick – never one to waste a business opportunity – went with Marianne to MIDEM, the annual music-business trade fair: the Rolling Stones had won Best-selling British Act for the previous year, and Mick picked up the award. (Clearly, the relentless push by the group over the previous two years had paid off: the Stones received six gold discs during 1966, as opposed to the five the Beatles had been awarded.) This too was the first public acknowledgement of the relationship between Mick and Marianne, and the MIDEM paparazzi had a field day. How could the couple escape and find some peace together? After all, they were already accompanied by Marianne's baby Nicholas and Diana, his nanny. Mick's solution was to rent a small yacht, with captain and crew, on which the four of them sailed along the French Riviera, sleeping on the boat, dropping in on Nice before docking in Italy.

After her appearance at San Remo, Marianne needed an antidote to the enormous amounts of black Afghani hash she had consumed during her stay. Out one night at a nightclub, she asked a local disc jockey if he had any 'leapers': he sold her a handful of mild amphetamine pills called Stenamina, which were actually anti-travel-sickness tablets. Marianne stuffed them into the pocket of the jacket she was wearing and thought no more of them; she liked that jacket – it was velvet, and belonged to Mick, with his scent on it.

Then she took Mick for a few days to the house in Positano that she was continuing to rent. While there, Mick pressed her to move in with him at Harley House. Although she hung on to her flat in Lennox Gardens as a home for Nicholas and his nanny, Marianne Faithfull moved into Mick's place on their return to London.

Only a few days after the move, on 5 February 1967, the *News of the World* ran an article in which it was alleged that Mick had taken LSD at the London home of the Moody Blues. In the article a pair of reporters described how they had met 'Mick Jagger' at Blaise's nightclub in South Kensington: while there he had taken six benzedrine amphetamine tablets and brandished a lump of hash; he was also said, highly implausibly, to have admitted to having first taken LSD while on the road with Bo Diddley and Little Richard. 'I don't go much on it now the cats [fans] have taken it up. It'll just get a dirty name.'

It wasn't Mick, of course: it was Brian, seeing straight through the reporters and sending them up in his customarily supercilious manner. Which didn't especially help Mick, and proved even more destructive for Brian, for whom the small episode in a nightclub would ultimately have disastrous consequences, both within and outside of the group.

Scheduled to appear that same night on the Eamonn Andrews television show, Mick announced on the programme that he intended to sue the *News of the World* for libel, and found himself being attacked by comedian Terry Scott and singer Susan Maugham when he declared about the Stones' fans that 'I don't believe I have any real moral responsibility to them at all. They will work out their own moral values for themselves.'

The next day a writ was served on the Sunday newspaper, with the consequence that the *News of the World* now put even more reporters onto sleuthing out Mick's drug habits. Matters began to gather a curious pace. Almost immediately after the writ was served on the newspaper, David Schneiderman, the 'Acid King' whom Keith and Brian had met in New York on the Stones' last US tour, arrived in London, straight away – as the two Rolling Stones had suggested – getting in touch with the group through Robert Fraser. He announced that he had brought with him a suitcase full of top-grade LSD. Keith and Brian were out of town: they had flown to Munich to watch Anita filming in Volker Schlondorff's *Mord Und Totschlag* ('A Degree of Murder'), for which Brian had been contracted to provide the soundtrack – the film would be chosen as Germany's entry at that year's Cannes Film Festival. Keith returned on Friday 10 February: as soon as he heard Schneiderman was in town with his bag of goodies, he suggested that a select group retire over the weekend to Redlands to sample the wares; that night with Mick, Marianne and the folk singer Donovan, he went along to a session at Abbey Road for the Beatles' *Sergeant Pepper* album, at which the Liverpool group were also invited to come along that weekend for the Acid Test: in the end, only George Harrison and Patti Boyd were able to make it.

The following day the Stones already had a session of their own booked, at Olympic in Barnes. Afterwards Keith travelled to Redlands in his chauffeur-driven Bentley, while Mick drove down with Marianne in his new Mini-Cooper S. In addition to George and Patti, Michael Cooper, Christopher Gibbs, Nicky Kramer, Robert Fraser, Fraser's Moroccan servant Ali Mohammed and Acid King David Schneiderman all turned up at the country house that evening.

The next morning they were all woken by David Schneiderman with a cup of tea and a tab of acid. After a day spent tripping, wandering around the gardens of Redlands and down to the nearby coast, they started to come down. By the end of the afternoon, a very mellow mood hung over the house and its occupants. After George Harrison and Patti Boyd had eaten couscous cooked by Mohammed, they made their farewells and drove back to London.

At seven-thirty in the evening, almost immediately after the Beatle had left, there was a ring on the doorbell. Keith, floating mildly on the last waves of the acid, went to answer it. Standing there was Chief Inspector Gordon Dinely of the West Sussex constabulary; a posse of eighteen uniformed police hovered behind him. 'Mr Keith Richard,' Dinely announced, 'pursuant to the Dangerous Drugs Act of 1964, we have a warrant to search these premises.'

With perfect synchronicity, Bob Dylan's 'Visions of Johanna' cranked out of Keith's record player at maximum volume as the police poured into the house. The rural police officers were not especially competent, but at least they were suitably deferential to the impeccably accented Christopher Gibbs and Robert Fraser: searching Fraser's jacket pocket, one of them came across a box of twenty-four tablets. 'Oh, they're insulin for my diabetes,' explained the art dealer. 'Right you are, sir: still, I'd better take one just to be sure.' (Until then none of the party had been aware that the reason for Robert Fraser's noticeably laid-back demeanour was the heroin on which he was permanently blocked.) Neither Mick nor Keith were found to have anything on them. When a cop picked up the briefcase belonging to Acid King Dave, he blustered that it was full of film which would be ruined if exposed to light. The case was never opened. In the pocket of Mick's velvet jacket was a small lump of brown Moroccan hash: the policeman who came across it stuffed it back in the jacket – the rubbish with which these unsavoury pop stars cluttered up their lives ... In the other pocket, however, he found a glass bottle containing the last four tablets of the Stenamina Marianne had scored in San Remo. Despite Mick's giving the name of a doctor he said had prescribed them – Dr Dixon Firth of Walton Crescent, Knightsbridge – they were bagged and taken away. (Always the gentleman, Mick refused to let Marianne confess they actually belonged to her: think what it would do to your career, he nobly cajoled her.)

As the police were pouring in, Marianne had been making her way down the stairs: her clothes, body and hair having borne the consequences of a day on the beach and in the undergrowth at Redlands, she had decided to take a bath. Not having a change of clothes, she had then wrapped herself in one of the enormous fur rugs that were draped liberally about Keith's home. This was the origin of a story spread by the police, that was soon rampant all over the country, that when they had burst into the house Mick was eating a Mars bar that protruded from her vagina; intended to cause even greater scandal for the couple, it only succeeded in adding immensely to their kudos.

The police carefully itemised their evidence, which included various ashtrays and pipes, and left the house. As they did so, Keith stuck the stylus down on Dylan's 'Rainy Day Women 12 & 35': *Everybody must get stoned!*

Predictably, it was the *News of the World* that had the exclusive on the story of the bust, gloriously detailed in the newspaper's edition the following Sunday. How could Mick's libel suit against the publication now proceed? Meanwhile, Acid King Dave Schneiderman had disappeared completely, never to be seen again. Had he set them up?

It didn't really matter: it had happened. Now Mick, Keith and Robert Fraser tried to do something to steer the episode away. Used by now to the unorthodox ways of the world, they had a thinking session with Spanish Tony, a man in whom lay a sufficient combination of nefariousness, animal cunning and intelligence perhaps to be able to do something about the extremely worrying black hole into which they seemed to have fallen. 'Spanish' came up with a predictable solution: to pay off the police. He claimed, moreover, to have a contact within the constabulary who would be able to make the evidence vanish. Between them, Mick and Keith came up with £5,000 in cash, and Robert Fraser forked out another £2,000. Spanish Tony handed the money over in a pub in Kilburn in north London, but to no effect whatsoever: the *News of the World* story had made the issue too public. There was no way of getting the money back.

To escape the stress of their predicament, Mick and Keith – who were unable to work in any concentrated manner on the group's new album – decided to leave Britain, whose Establishment, they had all of a sudden become aware, seemed to be out to get them. It was decided that, with Brian, they would head for Morocco. To minimise the opportunity for being hassled by any lurking authorities, they agreed to travel separately. While Mick would fly to Tangiers, Keith decided that he would motor in the Blue Lena through France and Spain, crossing by ferry to Morocco. Travelling with him would be Brian and Anita. Much to the relief of his two companions, Tom Keylock was nominated to share the driving with Keith. At the last minute another traveller appeared: Deborah Dixon, who they were to rendezvous with in Paris, was the American girlfriend of film director Donald Cammell, a man towards whom Keith had never felt that partial, perhaps because he was aware that Anita Pallenberg had had a threesome with him and Deborah. Also along on this Moroccan sojourn would be three of the other misfits from the weekend at Redlands: Michael

Cooper, Christopher Gibbs and Robert Fraser, who would be flying. They would all link up, it was decided, at the El Minzah hotel in Tangiers.

Before they departed for north Africa, Mick and Marianne had managed to involve themselves in another minor scandal: Marianne, who was intent on educating Mick, had taken him on 23 February to the Royal Opera House in Covent Garden to watch Rudolph Nureyev and Margot Fonteyn in the world première of Roland Petit's ballet, *Paradise Lost*. Unable to resist a last joint before they left Harley House, they stumbled into the performance eight minutes late. As the guest of honour was Her Royal Highness Princess Margaret, this was considered a terrible insult – notwithstanding the fact that the Queen's sister and Mick were supposed to be friends.

Attempting to create a smokescreen to conceal their eventual destination, Keith, Brian and Anita flew to Paris, where they checked into the George V hotel and rendezvoused with Deborah Dixon. Tom Keylock took the ferry over from Dover to Calais and drove to the French capital in the Bentley with its black-tinted windows, steering the beautiful vehicle as though it was a getaway car in a 1930s film, his customary mode of driving.

Bombing south through the French countryside, Brian was aware of a psychic bond he could almost touch between his girlfriend and Keith. Attempting to anaesthetise himself to this in the only way he knew how, he passed the first day's journey by pouring copious quantities of French cognac down his throat and chain-smoking joints, each containing enormous amounts of hashish. By the time they were fifty miles from Toulouse, this intake, as well as the sexual vibes that were flying about the car, had caught up with Brian, and he could hardly breathe. Was it an asthma attack? or was it pneumonia? No one seemed to know: whatever it was, he was admitted to the Centre Hospitalier d'Albi outside Toulouse.

At Brian's insistence, the other occupants of the Blue Lena left him there, continuing on their way through the Pyrenees and into Spain. Breaking the journey in Barcelona, a restaurant refused to take Keith's Diner's Club card without his passport and the police were called: Keith and Anita were questioned at police headquarters until six the following morning. As the Bentley drove down through Spain, the relationship between Keith and Anita continued to build. Anita ignored a telegram sent by Brian, asking her to meet him from hospital. In Valencia, Keith and Anita spent the night together, but agreed to treat it as a passing whim. Finally, after Anita had spent four more nights with Keith in Marbella, she flew up to Toulouse to meet Brian, on Sunday 5 March. Five days later the couple flew back to London for Brian to undergo further medical tests.

On 9 March, Marianne flew from Naples to Tangiers to meet up with Mick. In Tangiers the Stones' party had taken the entire tenth floor of the

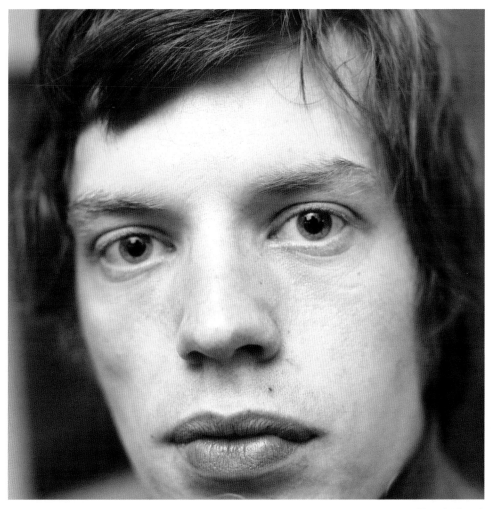

(Pictorial Press)

TOP Keith hadn't yet learned not to smile on television (Pictorial Press)
BOTTOM The winter of 1963. In those days everyone knew that cigarettes were good for you
(Pictorial Press)

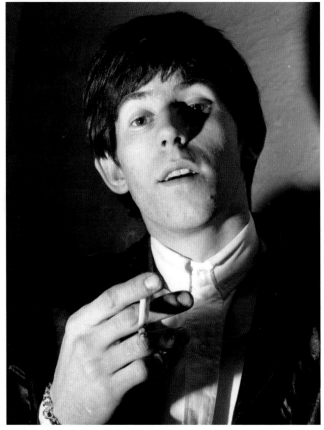

Mick's air of quintessential moroseness brought out the worst in those who were not his fans (private collection); and even in 1963 Keith's pimply jailbird pallor seemed to be setting him on a course for over a decade in which many of his waking hours were spent musing on yet another pending drugs trial (Hulton Archive)

Mick and Keith hit the Big Apple for the first time in June 1964; the city did not immediately fall to them with the readiness they would have liked. A few weeks later they were back on more familiar territory, at the Richmond Jazz Festival, on 6 August (both Hulton Archive)

At the end of December 1965 Mick smiles benignly at Chrissie Shrimpton, the longstanding girlfriend he professed he wanted to marry (Hulton Archive); and sizes up the possibilities in an autograph-hunting fan (London Features International)

Anita Pallenberg with a catatonic-looking Brian Jones at the 1967 Cannes Film Festival: they were about to enter the festival palace to watch Volker Schoendorff's *A Degree of Murder*, in which Anita starred and for which Brian had written the soundtrack. Once Europe's number one Beautiful Couple, they had split up two months previously. Despite Brian's tearful entreaties during the festival, Anita refused to go back to him. Meanwhile, Keith waited patiently in his and Anita's hotel room (Hulton Archive)

Foppish narcissist? Moi? (Hulton Archive)

Mick indicates a rather inappropriate degree of levity as he and Keith appear at Chichester Magistrates Court on 10 May 1967, accused of assorted drugs charges, the consequence of the Redlands bust; the Establishment does not take kindly to such perceived arrogance (Hulton Archive)

Keith: 'Don't worry, Mick. I'll skin up as soon as we get round the corner.' (Hulton Archive)

The morning of 27 June 1967, the first day of the Redlands drug trial: Mick does not seem to appreciate what the judiciary has lying in wait for the pair; Keith wonders where he can get some more of that red leb (Hulton Archive)

Bailed to appeal against their prison sentences, the previous air of naughty arrogance
has vanished from the faces of Mick and Keith (Hulton Archive)

ABOVE Mick and Marianne arrive in May 1968 at the première of *2001: A Space Odyssey*. Now it was their turn to be the number one Beautiful Couple (Hulton Archive)
RIGHT Another day, another court case: Mick and Marianne arrive at Marlborough Street Magistrates Court on 29 May 1969, after being busted for possession of hash the previous day at Mick's Chelsea house (Hulton Archive)

Wearing his Mr Fish shirt-dress, Mick and the rest of the group arrive in an armoured car (top right) at the backstage area for the free concert in Hyde Park on 5 July 1969, which drew an audience of 300,000. Turned into a tribute to the departed Brian Jones, thousands of butterflies were released from cardboard boxes: note their corpses littering the stage (all Hulton Archive)

TOP Mick with James Fox on the set of *Performance* in September 1968; the psychic fallout from the film would severely unhinge the actor (Hulton Archive)
ABOVE In happier times . . . groovily radiant, Anita Pallenberg arrives in July 1968 at the première of *Yellow Submarine* with a preoccupied-looking Keith (Hulton Archive)

El Minzah hotel. Cecil Beaton arrived, and clearly wanted to take Mick's portrait, a shoot that resulted in a famous photograph. The artist Brion Gysin was also in Tangiers, and came by to hang out with them. Keith, Mick and Marianne would spend days with Brion at the Bazaar Petit Port Said, at the premises of a carpet dealer called Ahmed, near the El Minzah hotel; as his ancient transistor radio blared out Radio Cairo, Ahmed would endlessly replenish the bowls of waterpipes with fresh Moroccan hashish as they spent all day discussing the purchase of a rug or a hanging. Ahmed was the best hash maker in Tangiers at the time, and accordingly it was a pleasure doing business with him. Meanwhile, Marianne would be crashed out on a divan in a corner.

On 15 March Brian and Anita finally arrived in Tangiers. That night, after they had been tripping, Brian and Anita yet again began to argue. After Anita had taken sleeping tablets and locked herself in her bedroom, Brian went off and found a pair of tattooed Berber whores. Bringing them back to the hotel, he tried to persuade Anita to have group sex with them, smashing up the room and beating her when she refused. She fled to Keith's room and spent the night with him. The next day Anita sat in a canvas swing by the deep end of the pool, her gaze intertwined with Keith's, who was in the water. 'Keith, Robert and I wandered around the kasbah and on the beach,' said Anita. 'There were these two men walking along the beach in their suits, looking like the Blues Brothers. It was the Kray twins. Robert obviously knew them. He went up to them and said, "What are you doing here?" They said, "Oh, we're on holiday". Me and Keith were sniggering away. "Holiday!" We didn't ask Robert how he knew them. We were too cool to ask that! Sixties nonchalance, you know . . .'

That evening they learned that a plane-load of Fleet Street's finest were on their way to Tangiers to track down the party. Immediately, they made off to Marrakesh.

In Marrakesh, they checked into the Sadi Hotel, again renting an entire floor, demanding that dinner be served at three in the morning. 'We're all in Marrakesh,' Keith said. 'Cecil Beaton's there, Robert Fraser, Brion Gysin, Mick, and the air's like heavy, lots of people are doing acid. I'm feeling guilty.'

'They were a strange group,' wrote Cecil Beaton in his diary. 'The three Stones: Brian Jones and his girlfriend Anita Pallenberg – dirty white face, dirty blackened eyes, dirty canary drops of yellow hair, barbaric jewellery – Keith R. in 18th-century suit, long black velvet coat and tightest pants, and of course, Mick Jagger. He is sexy, but completely sexless. He could nearly be a eunuch. As a model, he is a natural. None of them is willing to talk, except in spasms. No one could make up their minds what to do, or when.'

The next day Brion Gysin was persuaded to take Brian to the Atlas Mountains, to hear the celebrated pipe sounds of the Master Musicians of Joujouka. When he returned to Marrakesh, Keith and Anita had left the hotel, without leaving a forwarding address. As soon as Brian had gone with Gysin, Keith had bundled Anita into his car and they had driven back to Tangiers. Everyone else also left, leaving a shocked, hurt Brian to pay the bill for the entire party. Keith and Anita caught a ferry to Spain. Under the Bentley's petrol-tank flap Keith had hidden a lump of Moroccan hash; it was one of the only places Spanish customs didn't look as they tore the car to pieces. If the drug had been found, the sentence would have been a mandatory eleven years in the Cadiz calaboose.

The couple drove only as far as Madrid, where they took a plane to Heathrow in London. There, Keith and Anita went immediately to the crash pad that Keith still kept in St John's Wood, the scene of his dying relationship with Linda Keith. Brian flew to Paris to stay briefly with Donald Cammell, arriving on his doorstep drunk, his customarily elegant clothes in tatters. Then, in deep pain, he returned to London. He drove over to the flat in St John's Wood and when Keith opened the door, he collapsed on the carpet in front of him, beseeching Anita to return. This was not the last of such occasions. For a long time Brian refused to accept that Anita had left him, just as he had refused to accept that he was no longer 'leader of the Rolling Stones'. 'He never forgave me,' said Keith. 'I don't blame him.'

The day Brian returned from Paris, the *Daily Mirror* reported new developments in Mick and Keith's drug busts:

Two of the Rolling Stones pop group, Mick Jagger and Keith Richard, have been accused of offences against the drug laws. Summonses against the two men, both aged 23, were issued after a police raid on Richard's £20,000 farmhouse at West Wittering, Sussex. The summonses, due to be dealt at Chichester magistrates court on 10 May, are expected to be served next week. Two other men, not yet named, are also to be summonsed.

The summonses were served the following week. Mick was charged with illegal possession of amphetamines, Robert Fraser with possession of heroin and Keith was charged for 'premises', under the catch-all terms of an anomalous, widely abused clause in the 1964 Dangerous Drugs Act, which found the owner or landlord of any property in which there was illegal drug consumption to be as guilty as those partaking of the particular substance.

A week after Brian had finally returned from Morocco on 18 March 1967, the Rolling Stones began a three-week European tour, opening in Malmö in Sweden. Here, they were assiduously searched – sixteen pieces of luggage were rummaged through – in a customs inspection that took over an hour. Mick was body-searched, down to his underclothes, at which point he demanded an independent witness. 'They were looking for pot,' he said afterwards. The following night, 26 March, the group played Helsingborg, and two thousand fans rioted: chairs, bottles and fireworks were chucked at the stage, and truncheon-wielding police stormed into the crowd. 'Why do you have to hit girls on the head with batons?' demanded Mick from the stage.

After Sweden, the group raced through four dates in Germany, in Bremen, Cologne, Dortmund and Hamburg. Anita Pallenberg, whom Brian had met in Germany, was now with Keith, who stood on the other side of Mick Jagger on-stage. So it was with no great ease that Brian embarked with the group on the tour, and Keith was conscious all the time of Brian's bitter resentment. 'Mr Shampoo' was unaware, though, that at this stage Anita, who had gone to Italy to play a part in Roger Vadim's sexual science-fiction fantasy *Barbarella*, had not in fact committed herself to Keith – although she was committed to leaving Brian.

To add to the atmosphere of confusion, despite having won Anita Keith began an affair with a German model called Uschi Obermeier, who accompanied him to the quartet of German shows. This seemed only to rub Brian's face even deeper into the dirt of his depression, a personal shame that would have been magnified a thousand times if he had appreciated that this was the last time he would tour with the Stones. It would not be the last time, however, that Keith would see Uschi Obermeier.

Each time the group crossed a border they were harassed mercilessly by customs. In Italy they played two shows in Milan and Genoa, where Mick met up with Marianne. Then the wet-dream couple flew to London (with further searches at customs), while the rest of the group went to Paris for their next shows. Himself arriving in Paris on 11 April for the show at the Olympia, Mick called a press conference to complain about the treatment being received by the group: 'I feel as if I am being treated as a witch.' After the show in Dortmund, the Olympic long-jump champion Lynn Davies had been quoted in the *Daily Express*, complaining about the group's language at breakfast in the hotel they had shared. 'I felt sick and ashamed to be British,' he said, with an air of smug self-satisfaction. At the press conference in the French capital Mick Jagger retorted: 'We deny that we were badly behaved. We hardly ever used the public rooms at that hotel. They were crammed with athletes, behaving very badly.' In that week's edition of *Melody Maker*, the Redlands bust having propelled him to the forefront of 'underground' figureheads, Mick spoke with some prescience on the subject of drugs: 'There are only about a thousand real addicts in Britain, and nobody is going to make a fortune peddling heroin because the addicts can get it on prescription. But if we stop this, the Mafia will move in and we're going to have the same problem as America.'

At Le Bourget airport as they were leaving France the following day, an extraordinary incident took place. Tom Keylock, now promoted to road manager, had given the immigration officials the group's passports. But the procedure was misunderstood by one of them, who began to scream at the group in French. 'Calm down,' Mick suggested. This appeared to provoke an extraordinary rage within the man, who proceeded to punch first Keith, then Mick. Then he grabbed Keith by the lapels and punched him again in the chest. The group made their excuses and left the country.

Their next stop on the European tour was Warsaw, the capital of Poland. In 1967 Poland was still a distinctly Iron Curtain country, firmly under the autocratic heel of the Soviet Union. The Rolling Stones' two shows on 13 April, at the Palace of Culture, were a reflection of this regime. Almost as soon as the group had entered the three-thousand-seater venue, they learned to their displeasure that tickets for the front rows had been issued to the children of Communist Party apparatchiks. At the end of 'Lady Jane', the set's third number, Keith stepped to the front of the stage, waving to the group to stop playing. 'Oy, you lot,' he barked at the neatly suited audience in the front rows. 'You can fuck off out of here, and let the others come down to the front.' He glared at them with hatred until they shuffled out of the hall. Outside in the street, a riot had erupted as over a thousand teenagers tried to break into the Palace of Culture, partially influenced by a stall from which Stones' employees were handing out free records by the group. Water cannon and tear gas were turned on them until they dispersed, during which time an even larger crowd tried to attack the venue through a side door.

Back at the group's hotel after the show, a Polish teenager managed to make his way up to Mick's room, where, in halting English, he tried to talk to him about the blues. Mick dismissed him offhandedly; he was absorbed in listening, he said, to his current favourite record, the Beach Boys' *Pet Sounds*. 'It was our idea to go to Poland,' Mick said later. 'I wanted the kids there to have the chance to listen to us. I think our records will be on sale in the East in a few years. I'd love to go to Leningrad. We shall never tour America again. It's very hard work and one bring-down after another. You have no idea of how terrible it is unless you've been through it. Every place you go there is a barrage of relentless criticism, and after about the fourth week you just start lashing out.'

In Zurich the following night, as Mick performed on-stage before an audience of twelve thousand, he was flung to the ground by a fan, who then jumped on top of him. 'The youth hoisted himself onto a twenty-foot-high stage, specially built to keep fans at bay, and rushed Jagger from behind,' reported the *Daily Mirror*. 'He grabbed Jagger by the lapels of his floral jacket and flung him to the floor. Then he began jumping on the singer. Detectives rushed to Jagger's rescue but the Stones' road manager, Tom Keylock, yelled at them to stand aside. He waded in with an uppercut at the youth's jaw, and broke his hand.'

The tour concluded on 17 April at the Pathanaikos football stadium in Athens. Keith and Anita flew to Paris, where Keith set about buying an apartment, and then went on to Cannes for the annual film festival. *A Degree of Murder*, which featured Anita, was Germany's official entry that year. As Brian had composed the soundtrack, which had been hailed at the festival as a masterpiece, he also arrived in the South of France, checking into the same hotel as Keith and Anita: the first night he was there, Brian tried to persuade Anita to go back to him, as Keith waited patiently in his room.

Mick had returned to London the day after the Athens show: he wanted to show support for Marianne, who opened that night at the Royal Court Theatre in Chelsea's Sloane Square, playing Irina in Chekhov's *Three Sisters*. On the opening night Glenda Jackson, her co-star, was extremely irritated that, instead of sending the customary bouquet of flowers, Mick had despatched a small orange tree that took up approximately half the space in their tiny shared dressing room. Leaving the theatre after the first performance, Mick was bundled into a waiting car, closely followed by Prince Stanislaus Klossowski de Rola – 'Stash', as he was rather better known, a member of the Swiss aristocracy and a prospective pop star who had become a close member of the Stones' inner circle.

One evening while Marianne was playing her part at the Royal Court, Mick received an unexpected pair of visitors at Chester Square: the American poet Allen Ginsberg, with whom he had become acquainted through the Robert Fraser set, and Tom Driberg, a gay Member of Parliament in Prime Minister Harold Wilson's Labour government. Driberg was god-father to Mick's former fling, Cleo Sylvester, had been an acolyte of Aleister Crowley, was an outspoken advocate of homosexual rights and had signed the pro-marijuana advertisement in *The Times* paid for by George Harrison. He was also a spy, a double agent working for both the KGB and MI5. 'Oh my, Mick. What a big basket you have!' exclaimed Driberg delightedly, putting his hand on his host's thigh, on noticing a cast on the mantelpiece that the famous Plaster Casters of Chicago had made of Mick's penis. Under the influence of the more sensuous lifestyle that now surrounded him, Mick was beginning to discover his sexuality, and that he possessed an unharnessed libido that was aroused by either beauty or intelligence, and preferably a combination of the two. He was also learning that he was not especially partial as to with which sex he exercised his impulses. Allen Ginsberg later talked openly of himself, Driberg and Mick having slept together. Mick and Driberg certainly became close friends after the visit, as though they shared a bond of some kind.

Perhaps Mick felt he needed support from within the government. With his court case coming up, he was engaged in a serious public relations exercise. 'Teenagers are not screaming over pop music any more, they're screaming for much deeper reasons,' this spokesman for a generation told the *Daily Mirror*. 'We are only serving as a means of giving them an outlet. Teenagers the world over are weary of being pushed around by half-witted politicians who attempt to dominate their way of thinking and set a code for their living. They want to be free and have the right of expression; of thinking and living aloud without any petty restrictions. This doesn't mean they want to become alcoholics or drug-takers or to tread down on their parents. This is a protest against the system. I see a lot of trouble coming in the dawn.' Did Mick do his case a colossal amount of good with interviews like that one? At least he revealed himself as being highly intelligent and articulate, and utterly in touch with contemporary culture and a burgeoning underground. But wasn't such thinking almost guaranteed to be perceived as inflammatory, even dangerous, by the Establishment who ruled the judiciary?

Apart from the drug bust, Mick's life seemed awash with problems. On returning to London from the European tour, he had been informed by the Harley House landlords that the other tenants had complained about the constant fan presence, and he was asked to quit the premises as soon as he could. Accordingly, he rented a town house in Chester Square in Mayfair, where he would hold court most nights until the early hours, as most of groovy London passed through its portals. No less a figure than John Lennon decreed that during this period Mick was 'the king of the scene'.

CHAPTER 14

I REALLY AM THE
BLACK QUEEN

On 10 May 1967 a somewhat abashed King Mick and Keith Richard arrived in a red minicab at the court in Chichester, West Sussex. Mick was wearing a green jacket, white shirt and dark grey floral tie; Keith was dressed in a navy-blue jacket and pink tie; Robert Fraser, who was already there, wore a light grey suit. Together the three of them stood at the front of what was usually the jury box. The charges were read out: Keith was accused of allowing Redlands to be used for the smoking of cannabis resin; Mick was charged with possession of amphetamine sulphate and methyl amphetamine hydrochloride; and Robert Fraser with possession of heroin and eight capsules of methyl amphetamine hydrochloride. The charges, stressed Mr Geoffrey Leach, counsel for Jagger and Richard, would be denied most strongly. When the court broke for lunch, Mick and Keith came out into the street where around six hundred screaming and cheering fans were waiting. After electing to be judged by members of a jury, the three defendants were sent for trial at West Sussex Quarter Sessions on 22 June; they were duly released on £100 bail, and smuggled out of the court's back door. With them in court was Les Perrin, a publicist of considerable reputation who had been taken on by the group. As they left court, Perrin actually grasped Mick by the hand at several tense moments.

At four o'clock that same day, around the time they were leaving court, Brian was busted for possession of cannabis, at the flat in Courtfield Road. With him was twenty-four-year-old Prince Stanislaus 'Stash' Klossowski de Rola, the son of the painter Balthus. The pair appeared the following morning at West London Magistrates, and elected for trial by jury. It became obvious that the Establishment had decided to take the Stones down a peg or two; it was time these pop-music whippersnappers were put in their place. Ever a worrier, Brian was literally to be made ill by these events.

Mick Jagger's response, however, was to show that he had grown into his position as defender not only of himself and his group but also of his generation. As pop music's leading intellectual, he clearly demonstrated the advantages of even an uncompleted university education: on 21 May, for example, at the instigation of Les Perrin, he appeared on BBC TV's *Look of the Week*, discussing the relationship between performers and audiences with Professor John Cohen of Manchester University. 'That was a very difficult period,' he said later. 'The drugs, the brawls, the internal squabbling. It's hard to recreate. It was a difficult time in society, you had a lot of people going against you, authority figures. You were supposed to live up to some sort of reputation, always defending it.'

Most issues during the so-called Summer of Love of 1967 seemed rather stressful for Mick and Keith: on 3 June Marianne Faithfull collapsed on-stage at the Royal Court, during a performance of *Three Sisters*. As with Mick's breakdown the previous summer, the rumour abroad was that this was caused by her drug intake; this was correct, Marianne hadn't expected the acid to kick in so strongly that night. But enough of internal trips: it was time for the Stones to take external ones, and they all went on holiday.

'There was a time in sixty-seven when everybody just stopped, every-thing just stopped dead,' said Keith. 'Everybody was trying to work it out, what was going to go on. So many weird things were happening to so many weird people at one time.' On 15 June Mick and Keith added vocals to 'All You Need Is Love', the Beatles' next single; when it was released on 7 July, the B-side – 'Baby You're A Rich Man' – featured Brian playing soprano saxophone. The day after the recording at Abbey Road, Keith and Anita flew to Paris. Mick, Marianne and Marianne's son Nicholas and his nanny went to Tangiers.

Over the weekend of 16 to 18 June, Brian was in northern California, at Monterey Pop, the first of the 'Love Generation' mass festivals. He intro-duced the set by the Jimi Hendrix Experience, which concluded with the guitarist setting his guitar alight by spraying lighter fluid on it during his cataclysmic version of the Troggs' 'Wild Thing'. The event, at which drug consumption was overtly apparent, marked the symbolic inauguration of 'Rock Music' as a creative entity – and as a marketing force.

Such chimes of freedom proved deeply disturbing to the prevailing forces of darkness. On 27 June 1967, Mick, Keith and Robert Fraser were driven in Keith's Bentley to a rendezvous with a police car, which sped ahead of them to the Chichester court for their hearing. Mick and Robert Fraser had spent the previous night at Redlands.

The case of the art dealer came up first: Fraser pleaded guilty to pos-sessing heroin tablets, not guilty to the other charges; he was found guilty of illegally possessing twenty-four heroin tablets, and remanded in custody.

Mick's case took place that afternoon. After six minutes the jury found him guilty of illegal possession of Marianne's amphetamine tablets. Although Mr Havers, Mick's QC, requested leave to appeal, the Stones' singer was sent with Robert Fraser to Lewes Prison, thirty-eight miles away, for the night on remand, prior to sentencing.

Keith, whose case had not yet been heard, was allowed to go home. The following day he brought Mick fresh clothes, a book on Tibetan philosophy and a 184-piece jigsaw puzzle. Mick and Fraser had spent the night in a room in Lewes prison hospital. The singer had felt extremely scared, on the verge of tears. At seven o'clock the following morning the pair were woken and taken back to Chichester Crown Court. In that morning's newspapers, reporters were already questioning whether it had been necessary for them to be handcuffed on their way out of court, another clear attempt by the constabulary to put them in their place.

In the courtroom, which now awaited the trial of Keith Richard, was Marianne, who had arrived in Chichester early that morning. Much of the case against Keith seemed to rest on the fur rug in which Marianne was scandalously said to have been wrapped; though the name of the 'female pop star' was not allowed to be mentioned. There was, moreover, no mention of the consumption of Mars bars. At lunchtime Keith left court in his Bentley. He went to the same town-centre hotel to have lunch as Marianne, who was not allowed to speak to him. Mick and Robert Fraser, meanwhile, were taken downstairs to the court cells, where they were allowed to have lunch brought in for them, chosen from a menu that reeked of mid-1960s English provincial pseudo-sophistication: Mick dined on the inevitable prawn cocktail, roast lamb and strawberries and cream, and shared a bottle of Beaujolais with Robert Fraser. At the end of the day, the case was again adjourned, and Mick and Robert Fraser went back to the prison in Lewes for the night, Keith returning to Redlands.

The next morning, 29 June, Keith took the oath and entered the witness box, where his articulacy and worldly demeanour seemed at odds with an appearance only emphasised by his late-Mod cockerel cut; when asked by Malcolm Morris, the prosecuting counsel, whether he would agree that, 'in the ordinary course of events you would expect a young woman to be embarrassed if she had nothing on but a fur rug in the presence of eight men, two of whom were hangers-on and another a Moroccan servant?'

'Not at all,' responded Keith.

'You regard that, do you, as quite normal?'

'We are not old men. We're not worried about petty morals.'

This response proved a pivotal moment in the public perception of Keith Richard. At this point he came into his own, as though he had bestowed a blessing on an entire generation. Although garlanded with respect for these utterances by his own age group, they only further sealed his fate in the minds of the jury and the judiciary: Judge Block summed up with clear attempts to influence the jury in the direction of a conviction. In that he was satisfied. At 3.45 p.m., after an absence of just over an hour, the jury returned; the foreman declared that they had unanimously found Keith Richard guilty of the charge of allowing his property to be used for the illegal consumption of cannabis.

All three defendants were then recalled to the dock for sentencing. This time, Keith came first. He was given a jail term of twelve months, and ordered to pay £500 towards the costs of the case. The guitarist went pale and raised his eyes skywards. Then it was the turn of Robert Fraser: six months in prison, and £200 costs. The society art dealer and Keith were led off to the cells below the courtroom. Mick Jagger, left alone, looked extremely nervous. As he was sentenced to three months in prison, and ordered to pay costs of £100, he too went pale, almost collapsed, put his hand to his head and began to cry quietly. He walked to the cells from the dock in shock, shaking his head and whistling to himself. All three defendants were given leave to appeal.

In a black trouser suit and wearing dark glasses, Marianne arrived in Keith's Bentley at Chichester Crown Court with characteristic tardiness, twenty minutes after Robert, Keith and Mick had been sentenced. Ushered in by Tom Keylock, Marianne went downstairs to the cells. She saw Mick for twelve minutes and gave him newspapers, magazines, fruit, sixty Benson and Hedges cigarettes, a science-fiction book and a set of draughts. Accompanying her was Michael Cooper, a miniature camera tucked in his jacket which he used to shoot off a roll of frames of Mick behind bars. He was observed, however, by a prison officer who immediately confiscated the film. Marianne emerged from the cells in tears. Two hours later the convicted felons were driven to prison, leaving – as a cunning ruse – by the front entrance of the court. Mick, handcuffed to a cop, was again close to tears. Keith Richard and Robert Fraser were handcuffed together, Keith staring dead ahead. The police seemed to continue to relish this handcuffing process.

Mick was sent to Brixton prison in south London, where he was given a cell to himself, and Keith to Wormwood Scrubs, close to Notting Hill in west London, where he became prisoner 7855. Locked in his cell, he pushed the chair to the tiny, high window and stared at the sky until nightfall. His job in prison, he was told, would be making trees to decorate Christmas cakes. He was offered hash and acid by other prisoners, who advised him that the 'screws' had been awaiting his arrival with eager anticipation. Keith, who always favoured the art-school outlaw point of view, took some consolation from what the experience would teach him about prison. However, neither of the Dartford boys had their hair forcibly cropped, a further ritual debunking which the Establishment seemed to expect would be part of their punishment.

But the following afternoon Keith, already heartened by the cheers that rang out through the prison when 'Paint It, Black' came on the radio, got the word through the prison grapevine. 'You've got bail. You're out, mate.' At the High Court of Criminal Appeal, he and Mick and Robert Fraser had been granted bail of £5,000 each, plus two sureties each of £1,000, contingent on their appeal against conviction.

Les Perrin, Stan Blackbourn and solicitor Peter Howard went to arrange the release from prison of the two Stones. Mick was let out of Brixton at 4.25 p.m.: he wore a beige sports coat and green Paisley tie. Leaving the prison in Keith's powder-blue Bentley, he was driven to Wormwood Scrubs, arriving at 5.08 p.m. He and Keith then went to their counsel's chambers for a briefing about the case. At the instigation of the astute Perrin, afterwards they retired for a drink to the Feathers pub in Fleet Street, in those days still the heart of the British newspaper industry. In the Feathers, a brief interview was conducted with the *Daily Mail*.

Oh, how moderate, sensitive and thoughtful they both sounded: clearly they had been diligently instructed by Les Perrin. 'I just went dead when I was sentenced. I could think of nothing,' said Mick. 'It was just like a James Cagney film except everything went black.' 'I was so stunned at the sentence that I just went limp,' said Keith. 'I thought of nothing. Later I just wept.' He described being given an 'ill-fitting uniform and a sort of lumber-jacket'. 'The other prisoners were great. They even shared their tobacco with me, and tobacco is the scene in there.'

'We do not bear a grudge against anyone for what happened,' said ever-diplomatic Mick. 'We just think the sentences were rather harsh.' He added that he had spent his time in prison 'writing poetry' – actually, the lyrics to '2,000 Light Years From Home', which would feature on the next Stones' album. Graciously, the BBC announced that it had made the decision not to cut the pair out of the *One World* TV show in which the Beatles were to perform 'All You Need Is Love'.

Now it all turned around. Previously anything to do with the Stones had been pilloried by the Establishment, and loathed – to the group's advantage – by Fleet Street. But now the press were on their side. For the following day's edition of *The Times*, dated Saturday 1 July, William Rees-Mogg, the august editor, penned an editorial about the incident under a headline, a quote from Alexander Pope, that became a celebrated ingredient of the mythology of that summer: 'Who Breaks A Butterfly On A Wheel?' 'It is surprising ... that Judge Block should have decided to sentence Mr Jagger to imprisonment, and particularly surprising as Mr Jagger's is about

as mild a drug case as can ever have been brought before the Courts.'
Pointing out the anomalies in the trial, the *Times* editor concluded,

Young people are searching for values and for sincere human relationships,
individual and social, as never before and their destructiveness is directed only
at the falsities and hypocrisies of the older generation. It should be the particular
quality of British justice to ensure that Mr Jagger is treated exactly the same as
anyone else, no better and no worse. There must remain a suspicion in this
case that Mr Jagger received a more severe sentence than would have been
thought proper of any purely anonymous young man.

In an outraged front-page editorial in the *News of the World* the following
day, however, the paper fulminated about the scandalous suggestions that
it had followed Jagger and set up the bust to destroy his libel case.

The appeal was brought forward to 31 July. Mick could sense that the
tide was blowing their way. He knew that Les Perrin had done his best: in
addition to having bent the ear of William Rees-Mogg, thereby securing
that vital *Times* editorial, he had also pulled in word-of-mouth support
from liberal-thinking MPs such as Dick Taverne, Junior Minister at the
Home Office in Harold Wilson's government, and Tom Driberg, the gay
Labour MP who was already part of Jagger's set.

Yet the omens were not especially auspicious. On 22 July, Robert
Fraser's appeal failed and he was returned to Wormwood Scrubs. On 31
July the Stones' appeals were heard in reverse order to that of their trial.
Keith's came up first. That morning he had come down with chicken-pox –
he was kept in a room outside the court, unable to hear the testimony of
his learned counsel. After two hours Lord Chief Justice Parker and the two
fellow appeal judges quashed Keith's conviction and sentence: they ruled
that the prosecution case based around the girl in the rug having been
presumed to have been smoking cannabis failed to prove that the house
had been used for the smoking of the drug; therefore Keith could not be
found guilty of 'knowingly permitting' its use in his premises – there was
no proper evidence, and the girl in the rug was a red herring.

Then it was the turn of Mick, who eight days previously had celebrated
his twenty-fourth birthday; he was given a conditional discharge for one
year. 'You are, whether you like it or not, the idol of a large number of the
young in this country,' Lord Chief Justice Parker told him. 'Being in
that position, you have very grave responsibilities. If you do come to be
punished, it is only natural that those responsibilities should carry higher
penalties.'

Once out of court, Mick was driven directly to Golden Square in Soho, the London offices of Granada television, the production company responsible for the prestigious weekly current affairs programme *World In Action*. Les Perrin had set up a coup: assuming Mick's appeal would be successful, he had arranged for him to be interviewed live in a special edition of the programme, to be transmitted from the grounds of Spain's Hall, close to Ongar in Essex. Mick, wearing a collarless kaftan, and Marianne, in the briefest of miniskirts, were flown by helicopter to the location. Producing the programme was John Birt, later director-general of the BBC. Birt became profoundly embarrassed when, not wishing to miss an opportunity for congress, Mick and Marianne became passionate with each other during the helicopter ride.

Deprived temporarily of the skimpily clad Marianne, Mick was joined on the summery lawn of Spain's Hall by William Rees-Mogg, a fervent Catholic, the former Labour Home Secretary Lord Stow Hill, a Jesuit priest called Father Thomas Corbishley and the Bishop of Woolwich. Although dosed with valium, Mick wasted not a moment of airtime in turning the tables on the forces of darkness that had attempted to imprison him for little more than what they considered to be incorrect thinking: 'In the public sector to do my work, I have responsibilities. But my personal habits are of no consequence to anyone else. Until recently attempted suicide was a crime. Anyone who takes a drug, a very bad drug such as heroin, commits a crime against himself. I cannot see how it is a crime against society.' By espousing such a libertarian attitude, all of a sudden Mick leap-frogged over the Beatles to the top of the counter-culture. Through the bust, he had unilaterally become the number-one spokesman for his generation. Yet at first he didn't appreciate this: in the Ad Lib club after returning to London he complained that, 'It was all of them against me, and I just blew it.'

Keith had flowers sent to his mother, and then caught a plane to Rome where Anita was still working alongside Jane Fonda in *Barbarella*.

In the end, Robert Fraser ended up serving only four of the six months to which he had been sentenced, mainly working in the Wormwood Scrubs prison kitchen. Mick and Keith each wrote sincere, caring letters of support to him: when the chips were down their characters came to the fore in a positive light.

'How are things in? on? the old homestead? range?' wrote Keith. 'Michael [Cooper] told me about your letter and I'm glad that it's not getting you down in there we're all grooving for October 2? Love Keith (formerly 7855)'.

Yet at lunch in Alvaro's one day with Keith and Michael Cooper, Jim Dine was aghast at the coyly hip manner in which his two companions were suggesting that they might send acid trips to Robert in prison on a piece of paper. 'I said, "Please don't do that". They looked at me as if I was crazy. Keith said, "Oh, man, it'd be great to send him a trip". I said, "I don't think it would be great".'

Despite the unpleasantness of having to spend some months in prison, the bust had the advantage for Robert Fraser of considerably adding to his kudos. 'The bust if anything was a bit of a treat because it made him famous too,' thought John Dunbar. 'He was more part of the Stones than he would have been. He was in the papers – it's being "in", isn't it? He got to go to court with Mick and everybody, you know. Honestly, it was almost, you know, a good one.' But there were others who felt that Robert took the rap for Mick Jagger and Keith Richard.

Although the Court of Appeal had utterly absolved Keith of having committed any crime (he'd got away with it, in other words), there was no escaping the fact that, although no custodial sentence was imposed, Mick had been found guilty of the illegal possession of amphetamines. Which threw a large question mark over the international future of the Rolling Stones: under the stringent US drug laws, how would this affect the granting of any sort of visa to the Stones' singer?

Before this could be tested, on 11 August Mick and Marianne flew to a country that had no visa requirements for British citizens: Ireland, where they stayed in Dublin for four days with Desmond Guinness. Six days previously, a press release had announced that Marianne would star in a new film, to be titled *Girl on a Motorcycle*, with the French actor Alain Delon. In an interview in *Disc*, Mick gave his views on the trial: 'It was a strain, I suppose. But easy to beat. We didn't mind being at the centre of everything simply because we're quite used to it now. No, I wasn't really scared about the verdict. It was just that it took up so much time, mentally and physically. I kept thinking all the time what I would have to do if Keith went to jail, or if I went to jail. I don't feel bitter. I was relieved, but I soon got over the feeling of relief. Now I'm trying to forget it. It didn't affect us that much.'

As much as anything, Mick's interview was a plug for a new single by the Stones, released on 18 August 1967. It had been recorded back in May, when the future of the group seemed much more uncertain; the song certainly reflected their preoccupations of the time. Really, 'We Love You' expressed the group's perception of the Redlands bust from a higher (or very high) plane. Driven by Nicky Hopkins' piano riff, which was based on Jerry Lee Lewis' playing on his version of Ray Charles' 'What'd I Say', the tune had John Lennon and Paul McCartney providing falsetto harmonies and Brian on Mellotron, the new electronic instrument that would be a dominant sound of the last part of the decade. The song sneered with all the force of counter-cultural superciliousness at 'straights' (by far the majority of the population at the time), and was one of the group's greatest works.

Just in case Mick and Keith's appeal against their convictions failed, the group had spent the day before their appeal shooting a promotional film – one of the very first of what would become known as videos – which could play the new single as they languished in their cells. Never known to waste a good opportunity, the storyline was based on scenes from the trial of Oscar Wilde: Mick played Wilde, Marianne was Lord Alfred Douglas and Keith transformed himself into the Marquis of Queensberry. But the record got no higher in the British charts than number nine; and when it was released three weeks later in the USA, only made number fifty: but the flipside, 'Dandelion', rose to fourteen. The BBC refused to broadcast the promotional film.

Anita was still in Rome, playing the Black Queen in *Barbarella* and in real life. Keith was staying with her, and Mick and Marianne went to visit them. 'There's that line between put-on and reality, which is never quite clear in these situations,' Marianne wrote in her autobiography. 'That line was crossed by our Anita a great deal. Early afternoon there'd be, "Darling, sometimes when I am at Cinecittà I really do believe I am the Black Queen". As a joke, naturally. Then eight hours later and a lot more stoned: "But you know what? I really am the Black Queen", and then another eight hours later there'd be another level of insanity: "I AM THE QUEEN OF ALL I SURVEY!"'

On Thursday 24 August, at the Hilton Hotel on Park Lane, the Beatles attended an introductory meeting on Transcendental Meditation, given by the founder of the philosophy, the Maharishi Mahesh Yogi. Conferring afterwards with the Maharishi, the group agreed to join him the following day at a teacher-training college in Bangor, North Wales, for a ten-day course of meditation. In the same manner in which the Beatles and Stones would appear on each others' records and share the best drugs, Mick Jagger was telephoned and invited along for the Welsh sojourn, an event that shifted an underground interest in Indian philosophy into the wider consciousness.

Duly arriving in Bangor with Marianne on the same train as the Beatles, Mick and his girlfriend were provided with their personal mantras. The following morning the Beatles held a press conference: in keeping with the teachings of the Maharishi, they renounced the use of drugs. Twenty-four hours later, however, the brief moment of peace the Beatles had attained was brusquely shattered: Brian Epstein was dead, of an overdose of sleeping tablets. 'What the Maharishi told us was something to do with individuality. Some way whereby you could live without other people,' said Marianne Faithfull. 'The strange thing about that was that at the moment they were being given a philosophy in which they could live their lives as individuals, at that very second Brian died, the one who'd wanted them to be a group.'

The projected ten-day sojourn in North Wales was hastily abandoned as the distressed Beatles hurried back to London, again accompanied on their train journey by Mick and Marianne. 'We really miss you here, but I'm sure that you're making it and there's no reason for us to worry,' Mick wrote to Robert Fraser on his return to the capital.

We went to see Maharishi Yogi this weekend who really showed us some nice things, it would be great to go to India when you return. I'm sure we could have a groovy time. We're just doing our album now. We really think of you a lot, and hope that you're happy. Everything will be so much more beautiful when you come back, there will be so many things to do. I'm sure you've thought of a million things, so we'll put them all together.

All my love, Mick xx

('Bloody old con,' Mick complained after some reflection to Keith about the trip to see the Maharishi, having expected something more immediately profound, but apparently unappreciative of the Indian master's simple techniques for quietening the mind.)

Opting instead for a more temporal vacation, the following week Mick and Marianne flew first to Amsterdam and then to Paris, where they stayed at the Hotel Meurice. Important issues connected to the drugs trial still had to be addressed. Accordingly, on 13 September, Keith, Brian Jones, Charlie Watts and Bill Wyman arrived in New York. Keith was taken to one side and questioned for thirty minutes over the drugs trial. Then he was ordered to report to immigration offices in Manhattan the following day. As Brian's case had not yet come to trial in Britain, he sailed through immigration. Mick Jagger, sporting the newly de rigueur mutton-chop sideburns, arrived in New York on a later flight and went through an almost identical experience to Keith. After his luggage had been thoroughly pawed over, he too was told to report to US immigration officers at the same office as Keith.

After being questioned further in Manhattan, the Dartford boys were issued with visas valid for a two-week stay in the USA. US Immigration issued a statement declaring that, even though Keith had managed to be found not guilty, it would make a thorough study of their drug cases before deciding whether they would be again allowed into the US. (Not that Keith seemed to permit his fragile legal status in the United States to affect his lifestyle unduly. On that visit his illegal indulgences had indeed managed to alienate a close friend of the group, Scott Ross, a local disc jockey. Keith and Ross had been hanging out at the Plaza hotel, where the Stones were staying, smoking marijuana all night. As Ross was working on a documentary, *You Are What You Eat*, produced by Peter Yarrow (one third of the Peter, Paul and Mary folk trio), Ross had been obliged to depart the Plaza at dawn, heading for work. Later in the day when he had called Keith, however, the Rolling Stone was angry that he hadn't come back to the hotel to continue getting stoned: clearly Keith was suffering from a bad case of the rock-star disease of being unable to comprehend that those around them need to work to make a living.)

One of the reasons the group had travelled to the USA was to shoot the cover of their new album, which took place at Pictorial Productions in Mount Vernon, in New York State. There they art-directed the set for the photo shoot. Gered Mankowitz was no longer the official photographer with the Rolling Stones. Instead, Michael Cooper's assiduous cultivation of the group had landed him the job. The demotion came as no shock to Mankowitz, who had seen it coming throughout the chaotic sessions at Olympic Studios in Barnes for the album that was now titled *Their Satanic Majesties Request* – Decca had predictably recoiled in horror at the group's first choice, *Her Satanic Majesty Requests*, assuming it to be a reference to Queen Elizabeth II. Mankowitz would turn up at sessions at Olympic with Andrew Loog Oldham during the evening, and then be obliged to wait several hours, until as late as three in the morning, before the group arrived, invariably the worse for wear from drugs or alcohol.

Andrew Loog Oldham had been largely absent during the previous year, running Immediate, his independent record label; this had already enjoyed considerable success with several hits, including songs from the Small Faces, Chris Farlowe and the McCoys' classic 'Hang On Sloopy'. Partially because he feared that if he raised his head above the parapet he might become the next target, Andrew had not shown particular sympathy to the drug busts, or even to the sudden voracious appetite of the three Stones' front-runners for drugs. Part of the reason the group behaved in such an anarchic way on *Satanic Majesties* was to irritate him for his lack of support: Oldham walked out on the project after seven weeks and stopped being their manager, a consequence as much of his internal disquiet as any 'difference over musical policy'. At that point the group had no idea of the deep, clinical depression in which Oldham had been mired during his period of absence: he had been receiving electro-shock treatment once a week. (Still, there had been moments of levity: one day Andrew drove down with Keith to visit his old public school, Wellingborough, crashing his sky-blue Cadillac into a building as he drove out of the grounds.)

'One day,' recalled Mankowitz, 'Mick and Michael Cooper came up to

Andrew while I was there, and basically completely ignored me, and Mick said, "This is what Michael is going to do for the cover". And that was it: that was basically the last time I ever saw them or worked with them in the sixties. Until then Andrew had always coordinated the covers. It was over. I think I felt relieved. I had lots going on, lots of work. Hanging out with Andrew was great fun, but I always had to make sure I got up in the morning. I couldn't really live that lifestyle.

'I couldn't relate to them any more, or to the changes that were overtaking them. There was a session where they propped Brian up with cushions and chairs so he could put the instrument in his mouth and he was then able to play. I don't know how he did it. Then he'd collapse. I saw him fall into his food – I think it was duck *à l'orange*, which was always a favourite at Olympic, brought over by an outfit called Meals On Wheels.'

By thus dismissing Mankowitz as group photographer, and replacing him with Cooper, who had shot the sleeve for the Beatles' *Sergeant Pepper* album, Mick Jagger was imposing something of a *coup d'état* on the Rolling Stones and their organisation. This larger subtext to his own deposition did not go unnoticed by the photographer: 'There have been various theories that Mick and Keith decided they were going to alienate Andrew to the point where Andrew just couldn't deal with it. And I think there might be some truth in that. I sensed and saw Andrew's frustration. He wasn't able to get anything done. I think that was really it.

'The band were not particularly unpleasant to me, or anything like that. But they were on another level, they were on another planet, in another place, that I was never going to be, had no aspirations to be. I was in Andrew's camp – there were no two ways about it. I was doing masses of stuff with Andrew on other projects. We were good, good mates by that time. We really enjoyed each other's company and had a great time.'

Within the group there was a dissenting voice – who would be resolutely ignored. 'Mick and Keith couldn't accept that people had different views or tastes from theirs,' thought Bill. 'If you weren't one of their gang, they thought you were *against* the gang. Childish. Anything they didn't want to do was *wrong*, and if they were in a bad mood, everyone was expected to join in. I came close to leaving on many occasions because of the various frustrations and what I considered to be selfishness.

'Stones' performances were frequently affected by the influence of drugs, and it was a wonder there wasn't a bust at the Olympic studios. At the time they thought they played better, as people do when they have had too much, but when they listened to the playback next day, they realised it was bloody awful.'

All the same, on 14 September a significant meeting took place in

Manhattan with Allen Klein, after which the final split with Andrew Loog Oldham was officially confirmed. (Were the Stones yet again mirroring the manner in which the Beatles had lost their manager? Or was it something in the planets?) Not only would all the group's management affairs now be taken over by Allen Klein, but from now on the Stones – or those appointed by them – would produce their own records. More to the point, from now on Mick involved himself closely in the running of the group; at Marianne's advice, he hired her assistant, Jo Bergman, to run the group's new office in Maddox Street, off Regent Street.

Brian continued to disintegrate. London was awash with rumours that he was about to leave the group. All the same, whatever state he was in he was still working at Olympic with the Stones, before and after the climactic management meeting with Allen Klein in New York. After sessions on 5, 6 and 7 September, he had flown to Marbella in the south of Spain with Suki Poitier, the Portuguese-born former girlfriend of Tara Browne, who had been with the Guinness heir in his fatal car smash the previous December. He returned to the Spanish resort with Suki, a doppelgänger for Anita Pallenberg, on 20 October for several days. Brian needed to rest: his court case was set for the end of that month.

On 30 October 1967 he duly appeared in court, shaky and wan despite his faint tan, a consequence as much as anything of the previous night's excesses with Jimi Hendrix at a Moody Blues concert; his voice trembled as he pleaded guilty to possession of cannabis and to allowing his flat to be used for smoking the drug. After a brief trial, Brian was given a nine-month prison term, an extraordinarily heavy sentence; he was taken off to Wormwood Scrubs, where Keith had briefly been incarcerated. As soon as he arrived at the 'Scrubs', the screws threatened 'Mr Shampoo' with the haircut they said he was about to have. A demonstration in the King's Road by about fifty hippies led to eight arrests, one of whom was Chris Jagger, Mick's brother. After an application for appeal was successfully made the following morning, Brian was released from prison on bail of £750.

As Brian's trial took place, Mick and Keith were on a plane to New York; there they were to work with Glyn Johns on remixing the new album, now tentatively renamed *Cosmic Christmas*, and also to have talks with Allen Klein. Shortly before going to a Hallowe'en party at the Electric Circus in Greenwich Village the following evening, they learned that Brian had been successful in his efforts to appeal at the sentence. All the same, Allen Klein felt obliged to issue a statement: 'There is absolutely no question of bringing in a replacement for Brian.' But there was talk in the press of the Beatles and Stones linking up and buying their own studio or starting a record label together.

Brian's appeal was set for 12 December. Mick attended the court hearing. A trio of psychiatrists described him as 'an extremely frightened young man'; the sentence was set aside, and Brian was given three years' probation and fined the maximum of £1,000. Two days later, still in a state of nervous breakdown, Brian collapsed at his new Belgravia apartment and was taken to the nearby St George's Hospital at Hyde Park Corner. He discharged himself the same night.

Now the undisputed leader of the Stones, Mick called a press conference at Les Perrin's office. 'There's a tour coming up,' he began, although this was news to everyone around the group. 'There are obvious difficulties, one of them is with Brian, who can't leave the country.' Although there were rumours that Jimmy Page would leave the Yardbirds to replace Brian in the Rolling Stones, the group insisted they were without foundation and that they could continue as a four-piece until Brian had sorted out his problems.

At least Brian's appeal served as lateral publicity for the Stones' new album, which was released in the United Kingdom on 8 December. In the United States, where it had been released twelve days previously, *Satanic Majesties* had already sold over two million dollars' worth of copies: it was a huge success. In Britain, however, the long-player was widely dismissed – especially by John Lennon, who considered it yet another Stones' rip-off of the Beatles, of *Sergeant Pepper* in this case. Time has been kinder to the record, which can now be seen as an important transitional work.

With their tails between their legs from the critical trouncing they had received at home, Mick, Keith and Brian quit the country for Christmas: Keith and Anita joined Christopher Gibbs and Robert Fraser – fresh from his prison term – in a Marrakesh villa. Returning from Marrakesh to Paris, Keith decided to buy an apartment there, on the Faubourg-Saint-Honore. Meanwhile, with Stash de Rola along for the ride, Brian headed for Ceylon with his new girlfriend, who was none other than Linda Keith; it was as though he was bound in an inescapable psychic prison with Keith Richard and Anita Pallenberg.

On 17 December Mick sent flowers to Marianne, who was filming in Nice, in the last days before the final wrap on *Girl on a Motorcycle*. Mick's gift was a reaction to a troubling disquiet within him, as he sensed that all was not as it should be in his relationship with Marianne. At first, he suspected she was having an affair with Alain Delon, who had indeed attempted to exercise some kind of *droit de seigneur* over her: when Marianne turned him down, the French film star grew difficult and sulky.

In fact, Marianne had found a lover in Tony Kent, an American photographer based in Paris: wooing her with marijuana and claims of his powers as a magician, the photographer had followed her first to Heidelberg, where filming had begun, and then to Nice. In what seemed to the public-at-large to be a made-in-heaven relationship, neither Mick nor Marianne were strangers to serial unfaithfulness – though it was often Marianne, the more reluctant of the two to commit herself, who took the lead in this. More than once, Mick entered his home to find his girlfriend in bed with another woman. His response to this shock? To pull his clothes off and jump into bed with them both.

All Marianne was really looking for was an intimate tête-à-tête. She had fled life with John Dunbar not only because of the used hypodermics that littered her flat, but also because of the mad social whirl in which her husband was perpetually spinning. There was no peace, no headspace. Now, in the manner in which people habitually repeat patterns in relationships, she found life with Mick to be precisely the same. But it was worse: the Rolling Stone's fame meant that he was perpetually surrounded by all manner of hangers-on and sycophants, and he in turn would come to thrive on social climbing and the theatre of life. Marianne found it all rather boring.

But she had managed to engineer a situation at the end of the year when they would be on their own together. For Christmas Mick, who had adorned himself with a newly fashionable beard, and Marianne, accompanied by her son Nicholas, flew off first to Barbados, where they had vaguely thought they might find a property to buy. Failing to do so, they moved on to Brazil, alighting first in Rio de Janeiro. All the while, their vacation was played out to the sounds of Bob Dylan's *Basement Tapes*, a copy of which had been acquired by Marianne. In the city of Bahia, they attended a *santeria* ceremony. There, all of a sudden, the locals seemed to take against the two white adults. Years later, while his mother was being interviewed by the writer Nik Cohn, Nicholas recalled the incident: 'I remember when you were stoned on the beach in Brazil.' 'Oh darling,' responded Marianne, 'in those days we were always stoned.' 'No,' her son corrected her, 'I mean when the people were throwing stones at you.' That day did have a positive outcome, however: Mick heard the samba rhythm that he soon employed to dramatic effect on an epochal Stones' song, 'Sympathy For The Devil'.

Moving up the coast, they found a small town with a beachside cottage to rent and managed to cope with the hammocks that were provided as sleeping accommodation. As part of her holiday reading matter, Marianne had brought with her a somewhat unsuitable tome, a copy of William Burroughs' *Junkie*. Marianne had been turned on to Burroughs' writing by Anita, who was obsessed with the author; what an exquisitely splendid and desirable lifestyle the book seemed to espouse, she found herself musing. After all, if she was smashed on smack she could withdraw into a world in which she could ignore Mick's insistence on living life as theatre. With his sunburned face Mick discovered that he looked exactly like the Santeria Christ that was the dominant religious image of the era. When they returned to London, in January 1968, Mick became a member of the Country Gentleman's Association.

Was Mick feeling some rivalry with Keith? For life for Keith Richard had become that of an alternative country squire: he had taken the desirable contemporary idyll of 'getting it together in the country' to a logical extreme undreamed of by the likes of Traffic, the new group formed by Steve Winwood, who had established home in a communal cottage in Berkshire. The idyll for Keith included a close relationship at Redlands with a deerhound called Syph, which he used while hunting rabbits and pheasants. When the dog was picked up at Euston station, where it had been sent by its Scottish breeder, its greeting had been to spew up promptly over the interior of Keith's Bentley. 'He looks as though he's got syphilis,' mused Keith, and so the dog received its name. On 3 October 1967, however, the animal disappeared without trace, Keith mouthing vengeance at the rumour that Syph – to whose chasing of local livestock he had turned a blind eye – had been taken out by one of the local farmers.

Keith was living life in his own fantasy. With Mick now nominally in charge of the group, Brian sidelined and Andrew out of the way altogether, Keith was free to exist in a creative fabulousness, overshadowed by the dark obsessions of Anita. While not out traipsing his estate, Keith's exist-ence consisted for much of the time in being, in the parlance of the day, totally wrecked; he would sit around listening to very loud music, playing his guitar and ingesting endless waterpipe bowls of Congolose bush and Lebanese Gold. Occasionally he and Anita would have stoned sex, though neither liked this to interfere with their hobby of consuming as many illegal substances as possible. Keith was, however, quietly eaten up with guilt at having stolen Anita from Brian and – he secretly feared – having pushed him over the edge into the psychological and drug casualty he had become. More transcendental moments occurred for him when he observed UFOs in the skies above Redlands, the south coast being a part of England where such sightings were not uncommon. As a consequence he became friends with John Michell, a writer on such metaphysical subjects, whose expertise had accorded him guru-like status in the counter-culture of the late 1960s.

Mick was involved with more tangible realities. Protests against Ameri-can involvement in the war in Vietnam had now spread from the United States across Europe, convulsing societies and driving rifts between generations as it provided a political focal point for Western youth. On Sunday 17 March 1968 assorted factions of the Vietnam war protest movement, which ranged from hardline lefties to stoned hippies, took part in a march that began in Trafalgar Square and progressed to Grosvenor Square in Mayfair, the location of the American Embassy, a couple of blocks from Hyde Park.

By the time it reached Grosvenor Square the demonstration was some fifty thousand strong, and it became clear to the forces of law and order that the more militant elements on the march were not content with simply waving their North Vietnamese Army Liberation flags in front of the heavily fortified embassy, on whose steps stood armed US Marines: they wanted to take it over and destroy this symbol of imperialism. The police responded with unexpected brutality, waves of mounted coppers charging into the rampaging crowd to crack open heads with their truncheons; the ground shook from the pounding of the horses' hooves. As pieces of broken paving-stone were hurled through the air at the mounted cavalry, the figure of Mick Jagger could occasionally be made out as he joined in the missile-flinging.

Following his appearance on the *World In Action* television programme, Mick – his membership of the Country Gentleman's Association not-withstanding – now suddenly seemed part of the real left-wing intel-ligentsia of Britain, a vital cog in the true machinery of the country. Suddenly he was a Paul McCartney-like new intellectual about London: he had intellectual credibility – the Redlands bust had been worth it. The reading which he had been so assiduously encouraged in by Marianne Faithfull was paying off. As he hefted fragments of concrete at the running-dog lackeys of the Establishment, Mick was as yet unaware that the previous evening, only a few blocks away, Linda Keith had been rushed to hospital after overdosing on Mandrax at Brian's rented apartment in Chesham Place.

Keith's radical activities were largely confined to stoned conversations about the 'revolution'. He hardly stirred from Redlands and 'The Fifth Dimension', the name he had given to the studio he had installed in a cottage in the grounds of his country home. The recording facilities were hardly state of the art, consisting of little more than a Philips cassette recorder Keith had recently purchased and which he used to demo material. This included a song that had the working title of 'Primo Grande' and which, following Mick's description of the events of the afternoon of 17 March, became known as 'Street Fighting Man'. (When, two months later in May 1968, the violent protests and strikes of French students and lefties almost led to the resignation of President Charles de Gaulle, the prescience of this song was duly confirmed.)

Also in March, the Streetfighting Man and Marianne looked at Star-groves, a distinctly run-down sixteenth-century manor house located in forty acres of grounds near Newbury in Berkshire that Oliver Cromwell had used as one of his headquarters. Mick snapped the place up for £25,000; he had vague ideas of turning the outhouses of the property into a recording studio, though these never came to fruition.

At the end of February Jimmy Miller, a stylish New Yorker living in London, had been pulled in to produce the new album, inevitably at Olympic in Barnes, where the Stones worked until June on the record that became *Beggars Banquet*. Miller had worked on producing successful records by Spooky Tooth and Traffic, those doyens of underground rock. 'Mick has contacted me,' he said, 'and said he likes the things I did with Traffic. *He* had been producing the Rolling Stones, but he says he doesn't want to be on two sides of the control-room window now.' (Mick had not only been trying to produce the Stones; in January he had also produced 'Though It Hurts Me Badly' for his friend P. P. Arnold, whom he had first met when she was an Ikette on the Stones' 1966 UK tour, for a release on Immediate.)

From 23 to 29 March, with Miller at the controls, the group knuckled to and finished four completed new songs, 'Parachute Woman', 'Child Of The Moon', 'Jigsaw Puzzle' and 'Jumpin' Jack Flash'. 'Jumpin' Jack Flash' had evolved from a riff that first Bill, then Brian and Charlie had originated as, yet again, they waited for Mick and Keith to turn up. When the inevitably tardy Dartford pair walked in, they insisted that the three other members of the group keep playing and embellishing the structure they had come up with: 'Keep playing that and don't forget it – it sounds great.'

With the addition of Mick's outstanding lyrics, inspired by Jack Dyer, Keith's 'old English yokel' gardener ('I started to fool around, singing "Jumpin' Jack", and Mick says, "*Flash!*" And suddenly we had this wonderful alliterative phrase. So we woke up and knocked it together'), 'Jumpin' Jack Flash' would kick-start the next phase of the Stones' career, putting the group back at the top of the charts. Yet when Bill asked if he, Brian and Charlie could share the songwriting credit, he was simply told how greedy he was being. In fact, according to the bass player, although plenty of the Stones' songs were group efforts, the songwriting credits always ended up as Jagger–Richard. This caused great resentment within the group. Was it to throw a further stoned red herring into the controversy that caused Keith to play the bass part on the actual recording of 'Jumpin' Jack Flash'?

Mick and Keith were keen for the group to open their own rehearsal and recording studios. Worried about their finances, Bill voted against the idea. All the same, the group took a five-year lease on property at 47–9 Bermondsey Street in Southwark. Since removing Andrew Loog Oldham from their orbit and signing with Allen Klein, the Stones had found that they did not seem to be any better off at all. Although Klein had renegotiated their contract with Decca, this had not resulted in the expected leap in the amounts in their bank accounts. Instead, Klein had deposited the new advances won from the record company, doling them out in increments whenever necessary. He did this, he told the group, so that they would not be faced with sudden large new tax demands; although this was in fact standard management practice, the group were suitably disappointed.

In May, however, Mick managed to be sent the £50,000 purchase price from New York for 48 Cheyne Walk, a narrow Queen Anne terrace house overlooking the Thames in Chelsea. The property was embellished with a Regency bed and a Louis XV bath, purchased in Ireland for £900, a small fortune at the time. Mick's friend Christopher Gibbs was pulled in to redecorate the house; in turn he brought in the interior designer David Milinaric. While involved with the house, Gibbs came up with the title of the group's next album, *Beggars Banquet*. Then, one spring evening over a joint with Mick at 48 Cheyne Walk, Gibbs had another really good idea, as a consequence of which the Rolling Stones, following Mick's wishes, did a deal with Christopher Gibbs to write a script entitled *The Green Knight* for a potential Stones film, to be shot in India. Although some test shooting took place, nothing came of it. Already in March, Keith, through Anita's Cinecittà connections, had had meetings with a representative of the film producer Carlo Ponti to discuss a suitably spacey script entitled *Maxigasm*, intended to be shot in Morocco and featuring the usual suspects: Keith, Anita, Mick, Marianne and Brian. As with *The Green Knight*, though, nothing happened.

Yet the idea of a film was high on the group's agenda. The television director Michael Lindsay-Hogg, a close friend of Mick, was hired to make a promotional clip for 'Jumpin' Jack Flash' and B-side 'Child Of The Moon', an ode by Mick to Marianne. And some of the recording of the album that became *Beggars Banquet* was shot by Jean-Luc Godard, doyen of French New Wave cinema directors turned Maoist guerrilla film-maker, as the backdrop for his movie *One Plus One*; in the United States the film was released under the title *Sympathy for the Devil*, appropriately enough as the film featured the development of that song – originally titled 'The Devil Is My Name' – from semi-folk song to its final samba and *santeria* incarnation. Godard's purpose seemed somewhat unclear. 'What I want above all is to destroy the idea of culture,' announced the French exist-entialist in an interview. 'Culture is an alibi of imperialism. There is a

Ministry of War. There is a Ministry of Culture. Therefore, Culture is War.'

As well as capturing the isolation of Brian Jones, strumming a guitar that was unconnected to the control room, Godard also caught on film the evening when – like Yoko Ono elbowing her way into the Beatles' recording sessions through her lover John Lennon – Anita Pallenberg joined Keith, Brian and Suki Poitier chanting the backing vocals to 'Sympathy For The Devil'. In a moment of situationist poetry, Jean-Luc Godard's final night of filming at Olympic concluded when his blazing-hot arc lights set alight the studio ceiling. As Bill and Ian Stewart rushed to save the master tapes from the resulting immolation, the fire brigade arrived, soaking the studio equipment and instruments as they extinguished the blaze.

But how precisely successful, you might ask, was Jean-Luc Godard in trying to use the Rolling Stones to preach a Maoist parable about the white appropriation of black music? Lurking in a corner of the footage's frame was a well-dressed man with a sardonic and sadistic sneer permanently fixed to his upper lip. This was James Fox, an actor friend of Mick; in May it was announced that he had been cast to play opposite the Rolling Stones' singer in a film entitled *Performance*, to be directed by Donald Cammell.

In April the group had gone their separate ways on holiday: Mick and Marianne, had accompanied Christopher Gibbs to Dublin, to stay with Desmond Guinness – while there, Marianne became pregnant. Keith flew to Rome where Anita was appearing in the film of Terry Southern's novel *Candy*: he had heard she was having an affair with Marlon Brando, the movie's star. Although the legendary actor at first resorted to ritualistic sneering at the idea of the Rolling Stones, Keith soon warmed to him to such an extent that the first child he had with Anita was named after the method star.

On 12 May 1968 the group made a surprise showing at the close of the *New Musical Express* Poll Winners' show at Wembley Arena. After appearances by, among others, Cliff Richard, Dusty Springfield, the Tremeloes, the Move and the moody Scott Walker, the Stones came on-stage to perform 'Jumpin' Jack Flash' and 'Satisfaction'. The ten-thousand-strong audience went berserk at the Stones' first stage appearance in Britain in almost two years. Although he was of course unaware of this, the show marked the last live appearance by Brian anywhere.

Life still seemed to be running out of control for the founder of the Rolling Stones: a week later, on 20 May, he was busted yet again, at the third-floor flat he had rented from Lord Eliot at Royal Avenue House on the King's Road. After failing to wake Brian at just after seven in the morning, the police had climbed into the flat through a window to find him on the phone, attempting to contact his solicitor: a small brown lump of what appeared to be hash was found in a drawer. Appearing that morning at Marlborough Street Magistrates Court, Brian was remanded for three weeks on bail of £1,000 while the substance was analysed.

The twenty-seventh of May saw the final release of 'Jumpin' Jack Flash', a record whose superficially naive simplicity turned both in and out on itself until it achieved epic proportions – until the mid-1970s the character of Jumpin' Jack Flash became like an alter ego for Mick Jagger. The Rolling Stones' fourteenth British single, it had sold almost a hundred-thousand copies after three days, going straight to number one, where it stayed for three weeks, the group's first UK number one since 'Paint It, Black' in May 1966. In the USA it was in the top spot for one week.

Also at the end of May 1968 the Byrds, the closest comparable American group to the Beatles or the Stones, played at Middle Earth, the new 'underground' venue in London's Covent Garden. By now the Byrds consisted of Roger McGuinn, Chris Hillman, Kevin Kelley and Gram Parsons, who had replaced David Crosby, initially for his skill on the piano. Gram Parsons was a Harvard-educated, implausibly handsome rich boy from Waycross, Georgia; his family had made millions of dollars as the largest shippers of fresh fruit in the state of Florida. Being heir to an orange-juice fortune had been no deterrent to Parsons' gaining a full understanding of the works of the great Hank Williams and his subsequent influence on country music. After moving to Los Angeles he formed the International Submarine Band; the group's repertoire of country sounds took on a further dimension when their live audiences observed their stage garb, country cowboy wear handcrafted by Nudie's Rodeo Tailors in North Hollywood, often incorporating intricately woven marijuana leaves.

Accordingly, Gram had been headhunted by McGuinn following the departure of Crosby, somewhat hijacking the direction of the Byrds with the material he and Chris Hillman assembled for *Sweetheart of the Rodeo*, the one Byrds album on which he appeared, a masterly work widely attributed to have established the template for country rock. 'Gram was very ambitious and very charming,' said Roger McGuinn. 'And he was a rich kid, which meant that he was already a star before he got to the Byrds – having money does that for people, and they just have an attitude that they can do whatever they want. It was like Mick Jagger joining the Byrds! We just went along with it because he had a way of enticing you into doing things he thought would be cool to do.'

After the Middle Earth show the Byrds drove with Mick and Keith by Rolls-Royce the hundred or so miles to Stonehenge – as one did in those days – where all manner of drugs were produced by the two Stones. Although the Byrds were rather impressed, Parsons found this to be especially good fun. 'Gram was just like a puppy dog with them,' said Hillman.

'It was sort of embarrassing, like bringing your kid brother along on a date.' All the same, Gram Parsons soon proved to be a regular part of the furniture at Mick Jagger's place in Chester Square – the Stones' singer had not yet moved into the house on Cheyne Walk, which was being torn to pieces by builders – as well as a sparring partner in all kinds of narcotic excesses with Keith Richard.

After further English dates and a jaunt around Europe, the Byrds were set to play in South Africa, a location that any politically conscious British musician would not have even considered. Keith spelled out the facts to him. 'He was a lovely, warm, down-to-earth guy,' said Keith. 'He didn't know much about the situation in South Africa, so Anita and I explained it to him in Robert Fraser's apartment. It was quite an intense way to meet a guy. So then he didn't go, and he stayed in London, and he started to show me the difference between, y'know, Nashville and Bakersfield. We just used to sit around the piano and sing and get high.'

Following the Sounds '68 festival at the Royal Albert Hall on 7 July, at which the Byrds played, Parsons told McGuinn and Hillman that he would not be going with them to South Africa and that he was leaving the group. In Britain, some felt that Parsons could hardly not have known that South Africa was a racist state. Americans, though, were peculiarly removed from any knowledge of world affairs.

Whatever the reason for Parsons' decision, it was doubtless true that hanging out and getting stoned with Keith was a lot of fun, and that unlike many people around Mick and Keith – who were always wary of being taken for a financial ride by hangers-on – Gram Parsons was never short of the wherewithal to purchase wholesale quantities of drugs. 'For all those who've suggested that the Stones somehow corrupted the young citrus heir from Florida,' wrote Barney Hoskins in *Mojo*, 'there are as many who will assure you that Gram was a willing voluptuary. "He was ripe for the fall," chuckles the writer Eve Babitz, "but he wanted to find somebody who he thought was worthy of falling off the tree *for*!" That somebody was Keith Richard. For a good two years, his and Gram's was the ultimate rock 'n' roll mutual admiration society, so much so that people thought they were slowly mutating into one other . . . From Keith, Gram acquired the trappings of rock 'n' roll style; from Gram, Keith imbibed the sacred laws of country soul, channelling the results into masterpieces like "Torn And Frayed", "Dead Flowers", "Wild Horses" and "Sweet Virginia".'

CHAPTER 15

YOU CAN ALWAYS GET
WHAT YOU WANT

For Mick Jagger 1968 was a good year, the upswing from the terrible troubles of 1967. 'I wasn't taking so many drugs that it was messing up my creative process. It was a very good period, 1968 – there was a good feeling in the air. It was a very creative period for everyone,' he told *Rolling Stone* in 1995. Mick was extremely happy in his relationship with Marianne, with whom he was still living at Chester Square as work progressed on 48 Cheyne Walk. 'It was a wonderful time,' he said. 'The biggest thing in the air was love.' Mick wanted to marry Marianne as soon as her divorce from John Dunbar was finalised; Marianne – once bitten, twice shy – was not so sure. But Mick was castigated by Mrs Mary Whitehouse, self-appointed spokeswoman for the moral majority, on David Frost's London television show for being so immoral as not to marry his live-in partner, and the two guests had a verbal run-in.

His newly acquired job of intellectual spokesman for the underground led to a surprising offer. At a succession of lunches at Soho's Gay Hussar restaurant, MP Tom Driberg tried to persuade Mick Jagger to stand for Parliament, assuring him he would be given a safe Labour seat. The idea of becoming a Member of Parliament in a government led by Prime Minister Harold Wilson seemed only to mystify Mick, however; he was far more interested in ensuring that the Stones got a good album under their belts.

On 6 June Mick, Marianne and Jimmy Miller flew to Los Angeles to mix *Beggars Banquet* with Glyn Johns. Keith and Charlie Watts followed later. Brian, who had walked out on the sessions before the record was even finished, had vanished to the wilds of Morocco where, in the Atlas Mountains, he would record the Master Musicians of Joujouka.

In Los Angeles, Mick and Keith were on the Strip most nights, frequent visitors to the Palomino club, hanging out with Taj Mahal and Gram Parsons, who by now was forming the Flying Burrito Brothers. Keith liked the scene in LA: he recalled how, in December 1966 he, Brian and Anita would go to Watts to buy drugs ('It was the only place we knew where to score'), getting very out of it. Returning in the summer of 1968, Keith was rather surprised to discover that the woman who owned all the headshops on the Strip was actually a rich businesswoman with a house in Beverly Hills.

The party flew back from Los Angeles on Mick's twenty-fifth birthday on 26 July. He was having a celebration party at the Vesuvio club, a venue on Tottenham Court Road which Keith, in something of an archetypal pop-star conceit, had financed after being pissed off over an especially large bill at the Speakeasy, the fashionable pop-stars' nightclub in Margaret Street, behind Oxford Circus. Spanish Tony had been put in charge of the Vesuvio project. Not surprisingly, all things considered, the club's interior, which Keith and Robert Fraser had helped paint, closely resembled a Marrakesh café, with cushions, discreet cubicles, hubble-bubble pipes and Moroccan tapestries. Excitedly, Mick arrived on his birthday at the Vesuvio with advance pressing number one of *Beggars Banquet*. He wacked the stylus down on the vinyl, and the assembled partygoers went wild – it was Mick's birthday present to himself.

But then celebrity guest Paul McCartney made his entry, handing Spanish Tony a 45 r.p.m. white-label single: 'See what you think of it, Tony. It's our new one.' It was the next single by the Beatles, 'Hey Jude', backed by Revolution. The partygoers went even wilder. 'When it was over,' wrote Sanchez, 'I noticed that Mick looked peeved: the Beatles had upstaged him.' After all the guests had gone there was only Mick, Marianne, Robert Fraser and Spanish Tony left in the Vesuvio. Fraser produced opium, which they all smoked in a pipe. In her opium reverie, Marianne joyously told Spanish Tony that she was pregnant with Mick's child.

Paul McCartney having pipped Mick's ego to the post over the groups' respective new records was the least of the problems over *Beggars Banquet*. Yet again, the Rolling Stones were embroiled in a dispute with their record company. The cover of the new album, Mick and Keith had decided, would be a graffiti-covered toilet cubicle they had discovered while in Los Angeles. No more than mildly controversial at the very most, this image produced the habitual apoplectic response from Decca Records; Decca's chairman Sir Edward Lewis told Mick that it was in 'dubious taste', which seemed rather to miss the entire point about his 'product', the Rolling Stones. Nevertheless, Decca refused to release *Beggars Banquet* with the cover art the Stones desired; perhaps this was to the mutual advantage of everyone concerned, as Les Perrin played the resulting publicity to the maximum, easy at a time when so many members of the 'revolution' were concerned with freedom.

Following the fuss over the titles of both *Aftermath* and *Satanic Majesties*, the group decided to surrender quietly: they didn't want the LP to miss the huge Christmas market over the demands of Decca. An off-white gatefold cover, designed like an invitation, was chosen as a compromise; it bore a distinct resemblance to the Beatles' *White Album* sleeve, also released that autumn. The inner gatefold featured a single shot of the group at a baronial-style feast. Mick took a day off from filming *Performance* for the picture shoot, which was held in a rented house in Hampstead, in a room that had been decorated to look like a medieval hall. On the banqueting table was an entire roasted pig: Keith is leaning across the table with a fork and stuffing an apple into the mouth of Mick, an image into which a measure of sexual symbolism may or may not be read; Brian sprawls in a chair at one end of the table, as an Irish setter leaps up on him.

Having moved out of Redlands, Brian had bought his own house in the country, Cotchford Farm, near Hartfield in Sussex, the former home of A. A. Milne, the writer of the Winnie-the-Pooh books; it boasted a full-size swimming pool in the garden. On 26 September Brian's drug case was heard in court; both Mick and Keith attended, to give him moral support. Although Brian was found guilty, he escaped with a fine and a severe warning. In the period after *Performance* Mick was finally learning how to dextrously play the guitar, with lessons from Eric Clapton: did he imagine there might soon be a position to fill in the Rolling Stones? John Dunbar, the estranged husband of Marianne Faithfull, reported that Mick and Eric Clapton were once found in bed together, and this was an expression of the narcissism of the 'scene', something felt to be rather desirable.

On 12 September Marianne managed to miss the première of *Girl on a Motorcycle*, remaining in Ireland where she had been joined by her mother: the film received lukewarm reviews, but its pervading soft-porn cinematography guaranteed sell-out audiences and made the film a hit.

On 17 November 1968 the Stones recorded a new song, 'You Can't Always Get What You Want', Mick Jagger's classic expression of King's Road life of that era. The American Al Kooper played the moody keyboards that drive the song, which the public would not hear for another year. Perhaps the title of the song was a presentiment: two days later Marianne, who had returned to London, was sent to a nursing home in Avenue Road, St John's Wood. On 22 November, she miscarried – as she and Mick had predicted, the child would have been a girl, but Corinna was never to be. Was it something in the stars? The previous day Yoko Ono had also had a miscarriage, losing John Lennon's child. Marianne and especially Mick were devastated; not uninfluenced by the fact that she had borne a son to her husband John, Mick – who still wanted to make Marianne his wife – had been most anxious to have a child with her; the miscarriage would have bad consequences for their relationship. Loving life as a 'family' with Nicholas, Marianne's son, running around the house, paternal longings had been deeply stirred within Mick Jagger.

The same day that 'You Can't Always Get What You Want' was recorded, Decca had run an advertisement in *Record Retailer*: it included copy about *Beggars Banquet*, and mentioned other records about to be released on the label. Mick was very annoyed about this, especially after the Stones' concession to the record company over the graffitied-toilet LP cover controversy. In his official capacity as administrator of the Rolling Stones, he wrote to Decca on 28 November:

Since the commence of our relationship with Decca Records, we have specifically requested the exclusion of all Rolling Stones' records from your 'Bulk Advertisements'. We are therefore most sorry to see that you have included *Beggars Banquet* along with a number of other Decca LPs in *Record Retailer* on 17 November. Much as we do appreciate your (doubtlessly) well-meant intentions, we do not share the same ideals in 'how to advertise'. This is, in fact, a contravention of a clause in our contract. *Please make sure this will never ever happen again – never ever.*

A week later, on 4 December, a launch party for 120 people was held at the Gore Hotel in Kensington, in the Elizabethan Room, for the release of *Beggars Banquet*. A seven-course Elizabethan banquet was served and the menu included boar's head, and cucumber and artichokes in Canary wine. After the meal, Mick took out a plastic foam custard pie and thrust it into Brian's face; masochistically, Brian seemed to delight in this, as though it meant he was still part of the group. Everyone present had been given similar pies: they hurled them at the Stones. Keith, late as ever, managed to miss this part of the celebrations: he didn't turn up until the party was almost over. Although Decca had paid for the event, the row over the sleeve was the last straw in the Stones' relationship with the label. They were still contractually obliged to deliver two albums to the record company, but from then on, Mick and Keith resolved that yet again they would simply have to take a leaf out of the Beatles' book and start their own label.

Beggars Banquet was very well received critically, especially in the United States, almost with a sigh of relief that the Stones had weathered their various storms and were back on form. The return to their blues and rock roots served them well, as did Jimmy Miller's crisp, juicy production: 'You get someone like Jimmy, who can turn the whole band on, make a nondescript number into something, which is what happened on *Beggars Banquet*. We were just coming out of *Satanic Majesties*. Mick was making movies, everything was on the point of dispersal. I had nicked Brian's old lady. It was a mess. And Jimmy pulled *Beggars Banquet* out of all that,' Keith told *Crawdaddy*, the American music magazine, in 1975.

In fact, several of the ten songs on the album were 'nondescript', and time shows the record to be patchy. However, it contained a number of bonafide classics, notably its opener, the infamous but fantastic 'Sympathy For The Devil', 'Street Fighting Man', inspired by Mick's participation in the Grosvenor Square anti-Vietnam War riot, and the extraordinary 'Stray Cat Blues', almost an ode to paedophilia with its line, 'I don't care that you're fifteen years old'. Brian provided graceful slide guitar on the beautiful slow blues 'No Expectations', his last significant contribution to the group, that was like a reprise of his sound on 'I'm A King Bee'; the cod-country song 'Dear Doctor' was a nod to the influence of Gram Parsons and the new country direction of Bob Dylan; the average blues 'Parachute Woman' was weaker still, and 'Jigsaw Puzzle' was actually rather boring, as were 'Factory Girl' and 'Salt Of The Earth', which featured the first lead vocals from Keith on the first verse, 'Let's drink to the hard-working people/Let's drink to the salt of the earth'. But the Stones' considered cover of the Reverend John Wilkins' country blues tune 'Prodigal Son' more than credibly took them back to the days of the Ealing Jazz Club. However, the spread of material on the long-player, coupled with Miller's experience in producing such great album acts as Traffic and Spooky Tooth, successfully marked *Beggars Banquet* as the Stones' first 'rock' LP. They had made the transition into the next stage of their career.

But there was one more hiccup: eight days later, on 12 December, the group was at Intertel Studios in Wembley, recording *The Rolling Stones' Rock 'n' Roll Circus*, a self-produced television special directed by Michael Lindsay-Hogg that also featured John Lennon and Yoko Ono, the Who, Eric Clapton, Taj Mahal and Jethro Tull. The programme would never be aired: Mick allegedly thought that the performance by the Who far outweighed what the Stones did. Until it was finally released on video in 1996, it remained a lost work.

Down at Redlands Mick's best friend was still shooting water rats and feeding them to his geese. A chill had temporarily fallen upon the relationship between Keith and Anita, fall-out from her sex scenes with Mick during the shooting of *Performance*. Both now sought refuge in heroin, and whole days were spent smacked out. All the same, perhaps as some part of their healing, Anita became pregnant.

On 18 December 1968, Keith Richard's twenty-fifth birthday, Mick and Marianne and Nicholas, Keith and Anita flew to Lima, Peru, to begin an exotic Christmas vacation. Checking into the Crillen Hotel, they were soon kicked out for wandering around shirtless. They then moved to the Hotel Bolivar before renting a jeep, in which they travelled around Peru, stopping for the occasional sampling of coca leaves.

From Lima they travelled to Brazil, where Keith was anxious to consult a practitioner of *santeria*. Already the 8 December edition of the *Sunday Express* had reported that Mick and Keith were flying to Rio de Janeiro to meet a celebrated magician. 'We have become very interested in magic,' Keith told the paper, 'and we are very serious about this trip. We are hoping to see this magician practise both white and black magic. He has a long and difficult name which we cannot pronounce. We just call him "Banana" for short.' While staying on a ranch in the Brazilian state of Bahia, Keith wrote a new song, 'Honky Tonk Woman', inspired by the black cowboys who were such fabulous horsemen.

Mick had brought a synthesiser with him on which – unmoved by the controversies thrown up during its production – he was writing the incidental music for *Performance*. This subtext was possibly deliberate: Mick devoted considerable energy to coming on to Anita, without success, Keith and Marianne so stoned on South American grass that they were virtually oblivious to this. After ten days, however, Nicholas picked up a tropical virus, and Marianne returned to London with her son; she had been searching for a reason to escape, psychically battered as she was by marijuana-induced paranoia, and the insecurities and stresses of being with Mick, Keith and Anita.

Back in London Keith took to wearing make-up, a little kohl around the eyes, even a touch of lipstick. As Yoko Ono had been by the Beatles' circle, Anita was accused by those around her of being a witch ('Look how she's changing him ...'). Not that she did much to disabuse this theory: she and Keith had allegedly considered a pagan marriage ceremony, to be presided over by their friend Kenneth Anger, but had decided against it. She was known to carry a 'magical' pouch, Anita's bag of tricks, said to contain a fragment of human skin; although the bags of half the hippy chicks of London carried, along with red packets of Rizla rolling papers, battered copies of the *I Ching* and packs of tarot cards.

'It's something everybody ought to explore,' Keith ingenuously informed *Rolling Stone* two years later. 'There are possibilities there. Why do people practise voodoo? All these things are bunged under the name of superstition and old wives' tales. I'm not an expert in it, I just try to bring it into the open a little. When we were just innocent kids out for a good time, they were saying, "They're evil, they're evil". Oh, I'm evil, really? So that makes you start thinking about evil.' It did nothing to dampen the pseudo-diabolic image of the Stones when it was revealed early in 1969 that Mick would be writing the soundtrack for Kenneth Anger's film

Invocation of My Demon Brother. For the group, however, it was business as usual: by March they were back at Olympic, working on a new album.

The 'sorting out' of 48 Cheyne Walk was deemed by Mick to be Marianne's project; he wanted her to keep his Chelsea house spotless. Marianne was aware of how impressed Mick was with her titled background. He would almost name-drop her status, as much a success symbol for him as the £6,000, seventeenth-century chandelier she had found in an antique shop in Mayfair, its purchase part of her decision to go along with his wishes about the property when she returned from Brazil. The house was Mick's refuge from the world of being a Rolling Stone – not many people were invited over. Mick had a studio in the garden at Cheyne Walk; one night when he was working in it, Stash left him there, climbed in through a window in the house and had sex with Marianne. She rejected the persistent efforts of Jimi Hendrix ('Come with me now, baby, let's split! What are you doing with this jerk, anyway?'), to pick her up at the Speakeasy in front of Mick, a flagrant example of rock 'n' roll cocksman one-upmanship.

On 22 February 1969 Marianne Faithfull released a new single on Decca, 'Something Better', her first 45 since 'Is This What I Get For Loving You?' that had been released almost two years previously, coupled with 'Sister Morphine', a song credited to Jagger, Richard and Faithfull. Both sides were produced by Mick Jagger, who wheeled in a battery of heavyweight musicians for the Los Angeles session, including Jack Nitzsche, Ry Cooder and Charlie Watts. Mick had written the melody for 'Sister Morphine' in Rome, when he and Marianne had stayed there with Keith and Anita. Influenced by the initial dabblings of Keith and Anita with heroin, Marianne had written the song's lyrics after Anita had begun to bleed while they had all been staying briefly on a boat in Brazil; her pregnant condition notwithstanding, a local doctor had given her a shot of morphine. 'Sister Morphine', however, was destined to OD: two days after its release, by which time the record had no doubt come to the attention of Sir Edward Lewis, the single was withdrawn from sale. This only increased Marianne's lack of self-belief.

All the same, in March 1969, Marianne Faithfull opened as Ophelia in Tony Richardson's production of *Hamlet* at the Roundhouse. During the run of the play, Marianne had an affair with Nicol Williamson, who was cast in the title role. They would have sex in Williamson's dressing room before going on stage. At the same time, Marianne was beginning what would turn out to be a long sexual relationship with Spanish Tony, something of a convoluted reaction to Mick's despair about her increasing reliance on heroin. 'I can't believe I did that,' she wrote in *Faithfull*, her autobiography. 'I wasn't getting enough pocket money from Mick and I didn't have any money of my own, so how else would I have been able to get my own drugs? That was the level of my thinking. Not a pretty picture ... Mick never knew too much about my affair with Spanish Tony. If he had, I imagine he would have found it measured up perfectly to his contempt for women.'

Mick Jagger was in fact very concerned about the extent of Marianne's drug consumption – ironically, as she considered she was doing heroin to get through her relationship with him. And the situation certainly wasn't helped by the new neighbours: in May 1969 Keith and Anita bought a house at 3 Cheyne Walk, about two hundred yards from Mick's home, and moved in. The building was previously owned by Anthony Nutting, a Conservative minister. Keith paid for the house in cash: £55,000. Getting the money out of Allen Klein was not easy, however: Tom Keylock had to be sent to New York to collect the money, with instructions not to return until he had it. Klein was now also absorbed with managing the Beatles, who as ever were eclipsing the Rolling Stones. By now Keith and Anita were thoroughly immersed in a heroin habit, their days broken up by regular telephone calls from Robert Fraser that would always end with a discreet inquiry as to whether anyone had seen 'Spanish'. By the middle of the year, Marianne had begun popping round to borrow a line of smack. On 10 August 1969, Anita gave birth to their son Marlon, in the house into which they had just moved.

In April 1969 Mick and Keith had gone to Positano, south of Naples, to write more songs for the group's new album. It was unseasonably cold in Italy that spring. Scrunched up in draughty, barren rooms heated by vast wood and coal fires, they wrote 'Monkey Man' and 'Midnight Rambler', among others. When American journalist Stanley Booth asked Keith about the almost psychotic nature of the latter song, the story of a serial killer, a clear attempt to replicate the sinister tone and epic atmosphere of 'Sympathy For The Devil', the response came from the cosmic cowboy into whom the Roy Rogers fan had now grown: 'It's just something that's there, that's always been there, some kind of chemistry. Mick and I can really get it on together. It's one way to channel it out. I'd rather play it out than shoot it out.'

On 18 May a press release announced that Mick would play the lead part in Tony Richardson's new film, a reconstruction of the life of Ned Kelly, the Australian outlaw who lived in the late nineteenth century. Marianne, presumably having won her spurs for Richardson as Ophelia, was to star with him. Shooting would begin in Australia in the late summer.

A few days later, Mick was involved in an ominous contretemps with the police: he was stopped in the King's Road in his Rolls-Royce with

Alan Dunn, his chauffeur; when a pair of officers attempted to search Jagger and the vehicle, he refused, claiming they lacked reasonable grounds for a search, and called his solicitor. On 28 May the Chelsea drugs squad took their revenge: he was busted by the same cop who had arrested Brian. Late in the afternoon, the police arrived at 48 Cheyne Walk. Mick and Marianne were charged with possession of cannabis. Mick drove to the police station in his new yellow Morgan to be charged. The pair were in court the next day, walking up the steps arm in arm, eminently photogenic. They were told to reappear in court on 23 June, by which time the 'substance' would have been analysed. As they were both due to begin filming in Australia, their defence lawyer asked for a further remand until 29 September.

On 30 May Mick Taylor, a member of John Mayall's Bluesbreakers, was invited to come to Olympic. The next day he recorded 'Honky Tonk Women' with them, Jimmy Miller adding the cowbell that gave the record its distinctive sound. Brian knew nothing of the recording session.

Early in the morning of Saturday 7 June Keith crashed his Mercedes Gestapo staff car eight miles from Redlands. Although the car was written off on the tree he hit, Keith was unhurt, but Anita broke a collarbone. She was treated in Harley Street, and while she was there a worried Keith took a flat in Park Lane for ten days in order to keep a close watch on his pregnant girlfriend. But the day after the crash, on 8 June, he and Mick, along with Charlie, drove down to the country. Already, at Mick Jagger's request, Alexis Korner had been to Cotchford Farm to let Brian know how worried the group were about him. Now the three Stones themselves went down to see Brian at his new home. They discussed their differences over the direction of the group's music: Brian agreed that he couldn't carry on in the Stones. 'What we were trying to say was a very difficult thing,' Keith admitted to Stanley Booth. 'After all, Brian was the guy that kicked Stu out of the band. In a way it's like the script starts to take shape after this. And the guy that kicked Stu out of the band is the first one to crack.'

Brian was stepping out of the fray, they let it be known, so the group could tour the US; with two drug busts, Brian wouldn't have a chance of getting a US work visa. With this argument Mick was conveniently avoiding the pending drug case hanging over himself, and his own drug conviction; but he was also ignoring that Brian was the most accomplished musician in the Rolling Stones. This was the man who had played marimbas on 'Under My Thumb', mellotron on *Satanic Majesties*, and the Arabic brass riff on 'We Love You'. Through Les Perrin Mick made a formal statement: 'The only solution to our problem is for Brian to leave us. He wants to play music which is more his own rather than always playing ours. We have decided that it is best for him to be free to follow his own inclinations. We have parted on the best of terms. We will continue to be friends, and we're certainly going to meet socially in future. There's no question of us breaking up a friendship. Friendships like ours just don't break up like that.'

Like many children of the age, Marianne was big on throwing the *I Ching*, the ancient Chinese oracle. Concerned about Brian while she was with Mick one night, she threw three coins the requisite six times and came up with the six lines that comprised the hexagram whose meaning was Death by Water. Both she and Mick felt extremely concerned by this prediction. At Mick's urging, she threw the oracle once again, and came up with precisely the same reading. Mick's archly cynical façade fell away; deeply concerned, he phoned Brian, who, touched by this attention, immediately suggested that Mick and Marianne come down to have dinner with him at Redlands, where he was briefly staying as work took place at Cotchford Farm, a generous offer to his former fellow group member that Keith had made largely out of guilt.

In West Wittering they found Brian with Suki Poitier. Mick, however, suddenly switched from being the caring human being he had just revealed himself to be: when the meal that Brian and Suki had cooked was served up, he turned his nose up at it, confiding in Marianne that he couldn't eat 'this shit', demanding to go out to a restaurant and 'mortally offending Brian'. But Brian was in no state to go out, and Mick and Marianne left him and Suki at Redlands while they went out to eat.

On returning, they found Brian in a furious rage at their behaviour. His anger culminated in a physical fight between him and Mick, which climaxed when Brian fell into the moat. Aghast, Mick heroically leaped in after him, intent on saving the life of the founder of the Rolling Stones ... to discover that the water was only three foot deep. At least the stoned absurdity of the situation brought solace to Marianne: 'I thought death by water must be a symbolic message. What a relief!'

CHAPTER 16

DEAD BUTTERFLIES

That spring of 1969 Blind Faith, the 'supergroup' starring Eric Clapton, Ginger Baker, Steve Winwood and Rick Grech, played a free concert in Hyde Park, promoted by Blackhill Enterprises, who had pioneered such events with concerts by the likes of Pink Floyd, who they managed. Mick Jagger had turned up and watched them from the side of the stage: as a tribute to him, Blind Faith had performed 'Under My Thumb'.

The Rolling Stones had not played live since their brief appearance at the *NME* Poll Winners' show in London the previous May. A prestigious date was needed to publicise 'Honky Tonk Women', their new single. Accordingly, at a press conference at the Hyde Park bandstand on 13 June, it was announced that the group would play free in the park on 5 July, and that the occasion would also be used to introduce Mick Taylor as the group's new member.

Rigorous rehearsals were required in order to teach Mick Taylor the Stones' music. Mick booked the studio in the basement of Apple, the Beatles' headquarters in Savile Row. (On 28 June, Apple released a new single 'That's The Way God Planned It' by Billy Preston, on which Keith played guitar.) In the evenings, meanwhile, they would move to Olympic in Barnes, where they were recording *Let It Bleed*.

At Cotchford Farm, his new home, Brian Jones insisted that no one have any drugs with them: this was a new phase of his life and he wanted nothing about the place that might bring the police down on him again. However he substituted his fondness for all manner of narcotics with copious amounts of wine. On the evening of Wednesday 2 July 1969, Brian was at Cotchford Farm with his new Swedish girlfriend, Anna Wohlin. Frank Thorogood, a builder who had been working on the house, was also present, along with his girlfriend Jenny Lawson. Towards midnight Brian and Thorogood, both of whom were quite drunk, decided to take a swim in the outdoor pool. Thorogood, who had had to help Brian onto the diving board, soon gave up swimming, pulled himself out of the pool and returned to the house.

Shortly afterwards, just after midnight, he returned to the pool. Brian was lying on the bottom of the deep end, face down. After he was pulled out, Anna Wohlin, a trained nurse, tried to give him mouth-to-mouth resuscitation; meanwhile, Jenny Lawson called a doctor. By the time he arrived, twenty-seven-year-old Brian Jones was dead. It was a watery end for the Piscean, who for years had been slowly evaporating through the fire of the Leonine Mick Jagger and the Sagittarian Keith Richard. 'There was always something between Brian, Mick and myself that didn't quite make it somewhere,' said Keith. 'Always something. I've often thought about it, tried to figure it out. It was in Brian, somewhere; there was something ... He still felt alone somewhere ... Brian was a very weird cat. He was a little insecure. Maybe it was in the stars. He was a Pisces; I don't know. I'm Sag and Mick's a Leo. Maybe those three can't ever connect completely all together at the same time for very long. There were periods when we had a ball together.'

For years rumours circulated that Brian had been murdered. Except that, as Keith put it to *Rolling Stone* two years later, who would have wanted to? Wasn't it more a case, as he suggested, that no one was really looking after Brian? 'Everyone knew what Brian was like, especially at a party. Maybe he did just go in for a swim and had an asthma attack. I never saw Brian have an attack, although I know he was asthmatic. He was a good swimmer. He was a better swimmer than anybody else around me. He could dive off rocks straight into the sea. He was really easing back from the whole drugs thing. He wasn't hitting them like he had been, he wasn't hitting anything like he had been. Maybe it was the combination of things, it's one of those things I just can't find out. We were completely shocked. He was a goddamn good swimmer and it's just very hard to believe he could have died in a swimming pool.'

The news flabbergasted the Rolling Stones. They simply didn't know what to do. On the evening of 3 July they were booked to appear on *Top of the Pops*, to perform 'Honky Tonk Women'. In a dazed state they appeared on the television programme and afterwards went to their offices in Maddox Street. Tearfully, Charlie suggested they should perform the Hyde Park show as a tribute to Brian.

At around 3 p.m. on 5 July the Rolling Stones made their way by armoured military personnel carrier to the space in front of the Serpentine where the stage had been assembled. By now there were an estimated three hundred thousand people in Hyde Park, the biggest audience that one act had ever drawn. They were in the process of enjoying – or enduring – sets by the new hip group King Crimson, and by Screw, Peter Brown's Battered Ornaments and Alexis Korner's New Church. In an effort to ensure their 'outlaw' status, the Stones had arranged for the policing of the event to be carried out by a chapter of the English Hell's Angels – unlike their Californian counterparts, these were mainly nice, suburban young men with a love of beer-drinking, motorcycles and dressing up in black leather adorned with swastikas.

Finally when the Stones took to the stage, making their way through a jungle of potted palms and African drums, it was just after five o'clock. Although everyone was fascinated by the appearance of Brian's replacement, Mick Taylor was so unassuming that hardly anyone noticed him. Unusually, Mick had stage fright before the show, and was suffering from psychosomatic laryngitis. 'He told friends he was terrified of taking the stage for this concert,' said Bill.

With Brian no longer there to steal his sartorial thunder, however, Mick was certainly the centre of attention, a picture of pure androgyny. Above his white bell-bottoms, he was wearing what appeared to be a white frilly dress, especially designed for the occasion by Mr Fish. Around his neck was a studded black leather choker; his face was made up with rouge, lipstick and eyeshadow, and his jet-black hair was longer even than Marianne's had been (she had hacked off her luxuriant locks just before the concert). Was he a man? Was he a woman? Was he a transvestite? Would you let your son marry a Rolling Stone? Dangling down onto Mick's chest, level with his hair, was a wooden crucifix, a visible talisman of protection for this bisexual shaman, but a symbol that seemed at odds with Mick's first words to the waiting crowd, words so extraordinarily, incongruously banal they were clearly covering a rush of awkwardness and confusion: 'We're gonna have a good time. All right?'

He then addressed the matter of the moment: 'Now listen . . . cool it for a minute. I really would like to say something about Brian. About how we feel about him just goin' when we didn't expect it.' He announced that he was going to read something by Shelley; Mick's slurred enunciation made many of the audience at first believe it was to be a poem by 'Che', the revolutionary leader. Then he proceeded to read first stanza 39 and then stanza 52 from Shelley's *Adonais*:

> Peace, peace! he is not dead, he doth not sleep –
> He hath awakened from the dream of life –
> 'Tis we, who lost in stormy visions, keep
> With phantoms an unprofitable strife,
> And in mad trance strike with our spirit's knife
> Invulnerable nothings. – We decay
> Like corpses in a charnel; fear and grief

Convulse us and consume us day by day,
And cold hopes swarm like worms within our living clay.

And then:

The One remains, the many change and pass;
Heaven's light forever shines, Earth's shadows fly;
Life, like a dome of many-coloured glass,
Stains the white radiance of Eternity,
Until Death tramples it to fragments. – Die,
If thou wouldst be with that which thou dost seek!
Follow where all is fled! – Rome's azure sky,
Flowers, ruins, statues, music, words, are weak
The glory they transfuse with fitting truth to speak.

Before the group could plunge into the opening riff of 'Honky Tonk Women', the contents of several cardboard boxes were emptied into the air: hundreds of white butterflies rose desperately above the stage. Yet it became apparent that, rather fittingly, this tribute to the memory of Brian Jones was somewhat flawed: the long, hot hours imprisoned in the cardboard boxes had led to the deaths of most of the butterflies, and only a relative few escaped their prisons; for the entirety of the set, Mick and the Stones felt the corpses of butterflies scrunching beneath their feet as they moved about the stage. Although Keith, who along with Anita had gone into deep shock over the death of Brian, played as though he would rather be in bed, the muddy sound and awkward timing of most of the songs were irrelevant: only a small percentage of the crowd could see the group. But it was the fact that they were there at all that was the point. Six separate crews from Granada television were filming the event, and there was ample time to tidy up the sound before the transmission date later that summer. The Rolling Stones played their memorial concert to Brian for almost exactly an hour, precisely the time required for the TV broadcast. And they redeemed the unevenness of their set with a stupendous twenty-minute version of 'Sympathy For The Devil', complete with Brazilian dancers and African percussion players.

Backstage at Hyde Park Marianne Faithfull, who was making an attempt to fight a growing addiction to heroin, was covered in spots as her body detoxified; but it was also a physical response to the trauma of her having filed that day for divorce against John Dunbar. (In return John would file back, citing her adultery with Mick.) Also in the guests' enclosure, her skintight white buckskins contrasting with her Afro and dark complexion, was the stunning Marsha Hunt, the American star of the musical *Hair*. 'Marianne Faithfull sat on-stage with the other wives, girlfriends and Stones' entourage. Her long blonde hair had been hacked short, a self-mutilation which indicated to me that she wasn't in a good state,' remembered Marsha Hunt. After the show Mick met up with Marsha, with whom he had already begun an affair.

CHAPTER 17

OFF THE PIGS!

Early in the evening of the following day Mick Jagger and Marianne Faithfull left London for Sydney, to begin shooting *Ned Kelly* with Tony Richardson. They were still ensconced in their first-class seats as the inquest opened on Monday 7 July into the death of Brian Jones at East Grinstead Coroner's Court. The formal verdict was death by misadventure.

On 8 July, Marianne Faithfull came very close to joining Brian. In their Sydney hotel suite Marianne woke up and went and sat at the dressing table. Sipping a cup of room-service hot chocolate, she began to swallow 150 Tuinal sleeping tablets. Marianne was in a coma for six days. Mick remained by her hospital bed for almost the entire time. He had woken soon enough to save her from both death and brain damage.

Marianne had attempted suicide in a state of profound depression, compounded by her copious drug intake and efforts at withdrawal, that had been building steadily since her miscarriage the previous autumn, and that had been exacerbated by the news of Anita's pregnancy and the imminent birth of her child to Keith. 'The worst thing of all about being with Mick,' she said, 'was this rule he laid down that you must never show emotion, in case people realised you weren't cool.' Ironically, although Tony Richardson had first asked her to tour America with *Hamlet*, she had instead asked to play a part in *Ned Kelly*, to try to keep the relationship with Mick together. (Now the *Ned Kelly* role went to Diane Craig, her understudy.) 'I wanted to go because I'd been working three months in *Hamlet*, and Mick was always going on holiday with Keith and Anita without me, and I felt very left out.'

The death of Brian Jones was the final catalyst for Marianne. At this juncture it is easy to forget precisely how young all the major players were in this cast: when he died, Brian Jones was twenty-seven years old; Mick and Keith were twenty five (Mick's twenty-sixth birthday came later that month), and Marianne Faithfull was only twenty-two – although without doubt old before her time, she had had no opportunity to process the extraordinary life experiences she had already had. As Marianne sank nearer to death from her barbiturate overdose, she encountered Brian Jones. 'It was the nicest chat I ever had with him, actually,' she wrote in her autobiography. 'He told me how he had woken up and put out his hand for his bottle of Valium, and about the panic that had seized him when he found nothing there. He said he had been lonely and confused and had brought me to him because he needed to talk to someone he knew ... "Welcome to death!" he said brightly.' She watched as Brian stepped over a cliff, with the question 'Coming?' But Marianne decided not to go with him. Lost in an airport, she found herself answering, 'I'm waiting for Mick to come and get me.' Six days later she woke from her coma.

While Marianne floated in her unconscious netherworld, with Mick almost constantly at her bedside, Brian's funeral took place on 10 July. Of the Rolling Stones, only Bill Wyman and Charlie Watts turned up to mourn his passing. Mick's 'film commitments' had given him a partial excuse for missing Brian's final performance. Yet Keith Richard and Anita Pallenberg had no such excuses, other than a deepening addiction to smack and a growing case of rock-star selfishness, as well as deep guilt. But then neither Andrew Loog Oldham nor Allen Klein, both of whose lives had benefited immensely from their contact with Brian Jones, bothered to grace the funeral of the founder of the Rolling Stones.

As ever, when the chips were down, Mick was up to scratch. But the truth was that, in between his visits to the hospital where Marianne continued to recover, Mick Jagger, bearded and with his long hair cropped as short as Marianne's for the part of Kelly, was having a rotten time. He was profoundly depressed, as though his soul was in torment. All the portents were bad: on 18 August he was slightly wounded in the hand from a gunshot on set, necessitating a few days' recuperation. The script of *Ned Kelly* was a disaster – it seemed only half written. Diane Craig, Marianne's understudy, didn't know her lines. And most of male Australia was outraged that their national outlaw hero was being portrayed by a poofter whingeing Pom.

There was further bad news from filmland: in July a preview screening of *Performance* was held at the Granada Theater in Santa Monica, California. The audience had already sat through *Midnight Cowboy*, starring Dustin Hoffman and Jon Voight. But even that dark slice of New York life hardly prepared them for what they saw. 'Get this off the screen,' screamed sections of the audience during the beating meted out to James Fox by Joey Maddocks; people walked out. As well as most of Warner Brothers' senior executives, also present was Dr Aaron Stern, the head of the ratings board of the Motion Picture Producers' Association. The next day he told Warner that he would be unable to give the film anything other than an X certificate, considered the kiss of death for a film in the United States. Although the studio conceded that *Performance* might be re-edited, it also felt that there was a case for never releasing it. Perhaps films weren't a good idea, and Mick and the Stones should stick to what they knew: at that moment 'Honky Tonk Women' was number one in both Britain and the United States.

After Ned Kelly wrapped, towards the end of September, Mick and Marianne travelled back to England via Indonesia and a holiday that temporarily healed them. But after they arrived back in London, Mick's immense workload meant that there was not much opportunity to attend to his wounded girlfriend. Moreover, there were constant reminders from the new neighbours of the loss they had all undergone: Marianne found Anita Pallenberg consumed with guilt over the death of Brian, as was Keith: 'Keith's way of coping with Brian's death was to become Brian. He took on the very image of the falling-down, stoned junkie perpetually hovering on the edge of death. But Keith, being Keith, was made of different stuff. However much he mimicked Brian's self-destruction, he never actually fell to pieces.'

Besides, Keith and Anita now had something to keep them together and hold them together – their son, Marlon, born on 10 August 1969, a particularly poignant reminder of the adage that death is so often balanced by a new life. Robert Fraser, Marlon's godfather, organised a 'tantric' baptism. Around Marlon's bright red Indian rocking crib, an array of turbaned Indian helpers laid out herbs and rice, creating a beautiful garden all round the baby boy. Then three of the helpers began to chant. 'What a way to get baptised, better than getting dunked under the water,' remembered Keith. 'He was given the full name of Marlon Leon Sundeep by the priests. But the baptism went on and on. Just as we thought it was finished they'd go, "Oh, lah-lah", and there'd be some more stuff.'

Ever since Allen Klein had taken over the management of three-quarters of the Beatles – Paul McCartney had refused to go along with it – it had been even harder for the Rolling Stones to get his attention. The Stones needed to get free of him. Legally, he appeared to have the group locked up: Klein controlled their contracts and copyrights, and they had a contract with him until August 1970. Who could get them out? Mick Jagger, the former London School of Economics student, had always mixed in circles that were removed from the world of rock 'n' roll. In 1969, at a social event in Kensington, he met Prince Rupert Loewenstein, a descendant of Austrian royalty and the managing director of the merchant bankers Leopold Joseph. Loewenstein had done some minor-level work for Mick, and now Mick asked him to check out the Stones' financial affairs. Initially when Loewenstein had been contacted by Mick, the banker thought the Rolling Stone wanted him to invest his surplus funds. He was shocked to discover that the Stones were broke. Loewenstein's advice was that, in order to avoid the country's punitive taxation system, the Stones should leave the UK. Equally crucially, he stressed how imperative it was that they get out of the contract with Allen Klein. Now a US tour was vital to put some cash in the group's kitty.

The Rolling Stones were about to embark on their largest-ever American tour, with the first dates set on the group's stronghold, the West Coast. They were all very nervous about the tour; during the time they had been away from live work, the fripperies of pop music had evolved with the growing seriousness and self-importance of rock, its flower-power apotheosis the Woodstock festival that August. The Hyde Park concert had been a testing of the waters, and their fears were to an extent assuaged by the fact that they seemed to have passed muster. Although they were all aware of how badly they had played, the audience hadn't seemed to notice.

It was a funny year, 1969; it was as though the very date was subconsciously acknowledging the end of a decade that was both self-defining and self-deifying. In the United States each record company, anxious not to appear out of touch with the 'revolution', by now had their obligatory 'head'. Such an individual was no doubt responsible for the Columbia Records advertising campaign that ran a tagline of egregious marketing cynicism, *The Man Can't Bust Our Music*, alongside shots of album sleeves for Bob Dylan, Simon and Garfunkel or Big Brother and The Holding Company. The British division of the company put out a budget-priced 'underground' sampler, *The Rock Machine Turns You On*, which was a chart hit; priced fifteen shillings, it introduced new audiences to the likes of Moby Grape, Leonard Cohen, Spirit and the United States of America. Suddenly even this lesser-division stuff was part of the cultural fabric. With the Beatles on the verge of splitting up, something of which Mick and Keith were secretly aware, the Rolling Stones had become by default the top group in the world; these American concert dates would cement that status.

Before the US tour opened, they were to mix *Let It Bleed* in Los Angeles, where they would also rehearse for the live shows. On 17 October the group flew to LA, Mick and Keith staying at the new home – formerly owned by Monkee Peter Tork – of Stephen Stills, in the fashionable rock sanctuary of Laurel Canyon. Stills was the founder member of Buffalo Springfield, who had opened for the Rolling Stones at their last Hollywood Bowl date at the end of 1966, and was now one quarter of the Crosby, Stills, Nash and Young 'supergroup'. Mick and Keith liked immersing themselves in this world, sussing out the vibe, aware that the centre of gravity of the music scene seemed to be shifting to California.

The atmosphere in the lotus-land canyons of Los Angeles, however, was distinctly edgy. On 7 August 1969, a week after the first moon-landings that Mick had watched on television in Sydney and two weeks before Woodstock, a stiflingly hot and still night on which the only sound was the ever-present distant rumble of traffic blowing up on balmy, carbon-monoxide breezes from Sunset down below, a group of young 'hippy types' had murderously invaded a property at 10050 Cielo Drive in Bene-dict Canyon. The sumptuous residence was rented by a friend of Mick and Keith's, the film director Roman Polanski, maker of, among other films, the occult thriller *Rosemary's Baby*. Polanski was in London, partying at the home of London playboy boss Victor Lownes. But Sharon Tate, his pregnant actress wife, with whom he had starred in the film *The Fearless Vampire Killers*, was in the Benedict Canyon house with four friends. All five of them were slaughtered.

The killers were in thrall to a charismatic, bullying, failed rock star called Charles Manson, a dabbler in 'magic' who had at one point taken the Beach Boys under his spell; having seemingly fallen for the first delusion of the consumer of psychedelic drugs, Manson believed himself to be a messiah figure. He had assembled a coven of dysfunctional acid heads, a quasi-apocalyptic book-burning sect known as The Family, deni-zens of a 'hippy commune' who roamed around the fringes of Los Angeles. Irritated that his disciples had not approached the 7 August murders in a sufficiently disciplined manner, Manson led three of them the following night on a further murder mission. They stabbed to death Leno and Rose-mary LaBianca, an affluent couple seemingly chosen at random, who lived in Silverlake, close to Hollywood. Using the blood of Leno LaBianca, walls of the LaBianca home were daubed with the words 'Piggies' and 'Healter (*sic*) Skelter', references to songs on the Beatles' *White Album*.

Five days before the Rolling Stones arrived in Los Angeles, twenty-seven members of The Family, including Charles Manson, had been arrested for serial car theft; the date of their capture was 12 October, the birthday of Aleister Crowley. Their involvement with what had by now become known as the Tate–La Bianca killings was not yet realised: a 'dope burn' or an orgy that had got out of hand were still considered to be the likeliest causes of the killings at 10050 Cielo Drive. Fear continued to sweep the poolsides of Beverly Hills and Bel Air. In Haight-Ashbury in the north Californian city of San Francisco, the worm had turned; the inner-city district that had been the creative epicentre of the hippy movement had become a haven of sinister hustlers, so dangerous that even Charles Manson warned his followers to stay away. It was a mood on the West Coast that Mick, Keith and the Stones might profitably have heeded. Something had become unhinged: such was the degree of alienated polarisation between 'head' and 'straight' culture in the United States that, until the full extent of his horrific acts was revealed, much of the underground press initially acted as apologists for Manson's efforts to 'off' such representatives of 'Pig Amerika', as successful US capitalists were considered by 'heads'. All the same, the Rolling Stones might have asked themselves a pertinent question: was this a time to be singing songs with subject matter like 'Sympathy For The Devil', or that new number 'Midnight Rambler'?

The suspicion that the group were seriously out of sync with base reality was hardly assuaged by a press conference for the group held at the Beverly Wilshire hotel, where Bill and Mick Taylor were staying. It was the usual panoply of showbiz self-regard masquerading as Rock Music Rebellion; as, for example, when Mick was asked about the rumours that the group were thinking of playing a free concert. 'There has been talk of that. I should think towards the end. We'll have to see how things go. I'm leaving it rather blurry. I'm not committing myself,' flannelled, with his habitual vagueness, the man who disliked making decisions.

The high price of tickets for shows on this American tour had caused the charge of greed to be levelled at the group: the most expensive seats at, for example, the Forum in Los Angeles were to cost $8.50; recent concerts at the venue for Blind Faith and the Doors had cost $7.50 and $6.60 respectively. In the *San Francisco Chronicle* Ralph J. Gleason, the respected writer and co-founder of *Rolling Stone*, had written a diatribe, in an article that was very much of its time, against the prices the group were charging:

Paying five, six and seven dollars for a Stones concert at the Oakland Coliseum for, say, an hour of the Stones seen a quarter of a mile away because the artists demand such outrageous fees that they can only be obtained under such circumstances, says a very bad thing to me about the artists' attitude towards the public. It says they despise their own audience.

At the press conference Mick's response was characteristically equivocal: 'We were offered a lot of money to do some very good dates: money in front, in Europe, before we left. Really a lot of bread. We didn't accept because we thought they'd be too expensive on the basis of the money we'd get. We didn't say that unless we walk out of America with X dollars, we ain't gonna come. We're really not into that sort of economic scene. Either you're gonna sing and all that crap, or you're gonna be a fuckin' economist. I really don't know whether this is more expensive than recent tours by local bands. I don't know how much people can afford. I've no idea. Is that a lot? You'll have to tell me.' What a performance from the spokesman for the 'underground', who seemed to have forgotten that he had trained to be a 'fuckin' economist'.

Disingenuously, perhaps with a dig at the Beatles, Mick also denied that the Stones were considering setting up their own record company: 'I don't want to become a weird pseudo-capitalist. The only reason for doing that sort of thing is to change the line of distribution, right? And if you don't change the line of distribution, there's no point. All you've got is a little holding company, and the record company is still releasing your records. So unless you've got a fleet of lorries and sell records for half price, there'd be no point in doing it.'

Not surprisingly, there were those present who felt that the only honest and sensible words spoken at the entire press conference were in the question, laughed off by Mick, put by Rona Barrett, a television gossip columnist much derided by 'alternative' society: 'Are you really an anti-Establishment group, or is it all a put-on?'

When tickets went on sale on 1 November, every one of the twenty-two shows at thirteen separate venues sold out within hours: the controversial 8 November sell-out concert at the LA Forum had gross takings of $230,000; another date was hastily slotted in for twelve days later, and a total of four shows were booked in New York at Madison Square Garden. The tour, which opened in Fort Collins, Colorado on 7 November 1969, would bring in a total of over two million dollars by the time it closed on 5 December at the International Raceway in Palm Beach, Florida, before an audience of 55,000. Supporting the Stones were the very credible Ike and Tina Turner, the R 'n' B duo who had been on the bill of the group's last UK tour in 1966, and B. B. King, the urban blues legend.

As soon as he arrived in Los Angeles, Keith hooked up with Gram Parsons. The guitarist could not help but notice that this seemed to bring out a possessiveness in his schoolboy friend from Dartford; Mick seemed very jealous of their relationship, almost paranoid about it. 'I noticed that there was some weird thing that anybody who was a friend of mine, it didn't matter whether he wanted to be their friend, it was: "You can't have him",' observed Keith. This was despite the fact that Keith had long ago acknowledged, appreciated even, that it was distinctly positive for their relationship, both socially and in working terms, that he and Mick did not spend an inordinate amount of time together. 'One of the ways we've been able to work together for so long is that we have always been able to accept the fact that we have different tastes in the way we want to live.'

What Keith felt was that Mick's nose was put out of joint because, in Gram Parsons, he had encountered someone who had a larger, more evolved view of life than himself: 'Mick had met a bigger gentleman. The biggest gent that I have ever known. Gram got the picture right away. We used to talk about it: "Are you and I going to be friends, or are we going to let somebody else dictate whether we can know each other?" And Gram would say, "But for you it's important. This cat, you work with him, you know ..." He saw it all straight away.' Keith had accepted that part of the creative chemistry between himself and Mick was that, paradoxically, the longer they knew each other – which could be interpreted as the more they knew about each other – the harder their relationship became. Yet Mick's possessiveness, which could leap into outright jealousy, was a problem for Keith; and it also pointed to the loneliness of his musical partner: 'I just wish that he had found a few guys that he got along with.'

In the spirit of the legendary psychedelic artwork produced for Bill Graham's Fillmore Auditoriums, the artwork for the tour poster was in the art nouveau style. Preparing for their shows, the Stones rehearsed daily on a soundstage at the Warner Brothers lot, as well as in Stephen Stills' basement. They were in Los Angeles for almost three weeks before their first show; one night they went to the Ash Grove to watch Taj Mahal and Arthur 'Big Boy' Crudup. Mick had pulled in Peter Rudge, a Cambridge graduate (his induction into the music business had begun with the booking of May balls) who had worked with the Who, as the manager of their on-the-road operation.

On this tour they would be the first of countless subsequent impostors who would be introduced over the PA at the beginning of their set as 'the greatest rock 'n' roll band in the world'. To reflect their regal status, the Rolling Stones established a new set of rules, enshrined in a forty-page contract that included the later much-abused 'rider' about the mandatory provenance of their backstage repast: 'The white wine had to be from *here*, the cheese and fruit had to come from *there*'. This got right up the nose of Bill Graham, who was promoting the show at the Oakland Coliseum, having first pitched for the entire tour and losing it to the William Morris Agency. 'I pride myself on the way I feed performers, especially ones I know come to put on the best show they can for the people. To have Ronnie Schneider and Sam Cutler tell me in such detail what I had to give the Stones to eat and drink got me going right away.' For their shows at the Oakland Coliseum he gave them hot dogs and hamburgers. 'I spread it all out in the dressing room for them to eat. They wanted catered? I gave them catered. I just didn't go to the caterer they would have liked me to.'

In the midst of all this, Mick was beset by a personal crisis that was singularly unforeseen. When the Stones were playing in Dallas on 13 November, British newspaper reports came in that Marianne had left Mick for one Mario Schifano. Indeed, Marianne always partially suspected that

Anita had instigated the affair, calling her and suggesting he 'crash' at 48 Cheyne Walk; part of the attraction was their mutual fondness for cocaine. Within days she had run off to Rome with Schifano and Nicholas – she described him as her 'Prince Charming'. Mick got on the phone to her in Rome, desperate to have her back.

Mick was distraught: this notwithstanding the fact that he had been having an affair with Marsha Hunt, who had appeared so fetchingly at the Hyde Park show in her white leather hotpants suit. Moreover, Marianne's affair was taking place in the full glare of the media spotlight. Each night, bedecked in scarves with a Stars and Stripes top hat (a satirical symbol that showed Mick was philosophically at one with the underground) perched on his head, he had to step out on-stage to dance, on a stage seemingly constructed of broken glass, to the orders of his acolytes: Jumpin' Jack Flash at a Satanic May Ball of the College of Carnal Knowledge and Revolution.

Still, there were always the pleasures of the road, like those of Miss Pamela of the GTOs (later Pamela Des Barres), who introduced Mick to such headshop delights as strawberry douches. Miss Pamela's diary entry for 25 November 1969 reads, 'I am extremely happy. I slept with Mr Jagger last night, and we got along *so* well; honesty, freedom and joy. Genuine. I helped him pack his seven suitcases, and he gave me some lovely clothes ... The sexual experience was quite a joy.' Quietly pining for Marianne Faithfull, perpetually checking the time difference before the next fractious phone call with her in Rome, in the midst of his hour of the dark soul Mick gained a consolation prize: he discovered himself to be a beneficiary of another by-product of the 'revolution' – that he had somehow become mythologised as the Holy Grail of the Quest of the Great American Groupie.

At a press conference at the top of the Rockefeller Center in New York on 26 November, Mick Jagger promised that even after the tour officially ended in Florida three days later (a freezing-cold day, ironically), there would be further opportunities for such shenanigans: 'We are going to do a free concert,' said Mick. 'It's going to be on December sixth in San Francisco.' The show, Mick declared, would be 'a microcosmic society which sets an example to the rest of America as to how one can behave in large gatherings.' The concert was scheduled for the day on which *Let It Bleed*, the Stones' new album, was to be released. After the tour had officially finished, the group spent a couple of days at Muscle Shoals Sound Studio in Alabama, where they recorded a trio of new songs: 'You Got To Move', a version of a blues number by Mississippi Fred McDowell, 'Brown Sugar' (originally titled 'Black Pussy' when it was written while Mick was filming in Australia), inspired by Marsha Hunt, and 'Wild

Horses', a song composed by Keith as a declaration of his love for Anita, with new words penned by Mick about his love for Marianne, his graceless lady, sliding through his hands.

The free concert in San Francisco had been a problem ever since it was first mooted at the end of October. Mick had assumed the group could use the Golden Gate Park in the city, only to discover it was not available without a four-million-dollar insurance bond. A potential venue was then found at the Sears Point Raceway, which was offered free of charge by Craig Murray, its owner. The site had to be rejected by the group, however, when it was learned that its owners were a company called Filmways, a Los Angeles film company who demanded exclusive distribution rights to any film shot at the Raceway. Such a contractual clause would seriously impede Mick's plans. Angry that, at a time when a documentary of the Woodstock festival was being edited for major theatrical release, the film of the Stones' Hyde Park concert had only received one late-evening television broadcast in the United Kingdom, Mick had hired the Maysles brothers – Albert and David (makers of a film about the Beatles first tour of the United States) – to film much of the tour. It transpired that Filmways was affiliated to Concert Associates, who had promoted the Stones' LA shows. Concert Associates were in dispute with the group, accusing them of acting in a financially high-handed manner and of not honouring a promise to play a further Forum show. Just over twenty-four hours before the show was to kick off, the Stones office was phoned by one Dick Carter, who owned the Altamont Raceway near Livermore, thirty miles south of San Francisco. The Altamont Raceway was a stock-car race track on eighty acres of ground.

The support acts were to include such venerable veterans of the San Francisco scene as the Grateful Dead and Jefferson Airplane, as well as Crosby, Stills, Nash and Young, the hot new local act Santana and the Flying Burrito Brothers, the just-born group formed by Gram Parsons. Yet there was certainly a mood of cynicism about the event: at the rehearsal studio that the Grateful Dead were using for their Altamont performance, someone had wittily headed the noticeboard: 'First Annual Charlie Manson Death Festival'. 'Before it happened,' said Jerry Garcia, 'it was in the air that it was not a good time to do something. There were too many divisive elements. It was too weird. And that place, God. It was like hell.'

But it was the Dead who had suggested that the local chapter of the Hell's Angels take the role of 'security' at the event. Here, of course, there was an element of hubris, or perhaps simply horrendous naivety: for Californian Angels weren't like the more benign, 'fashion' version of the motorcycle hellraisers who had policed the free concert in Hyde Park.

These guys were the real thing, psychotic postmodern mountain men who, under the nominal suzerainty of chapter honcho Sonny Barger, obeyed no one's laws but their own. Hiring the Hell's Angels as a security force was simply not a cool conceit.

By six o'clock on the evening of Friday 5 December the first crowds had started arriving at Altamont. At three a.m. the following morning the Stones arrived by limousine – which promptly ran out of petrol – from the Huntingdon Hotel in San Francisco. Mick swanned around, accepting a joint offered by a fellow head. Keith liked the vibes so much he hung out for the rest of the night, finally falling asleep on the grass, before moving into a backstage trailer to sleep the rest of the night. The moon that day was in Scorpio, a reflection of Keith's personal darkness; in his astrological chart he had been born with Scorpio on the ascendant, a portent of an excessive lifestyle.

By midday on Saturday 6 December, 300,000 people had gathered at the speedway track. Traffic was backed up for ten miles, and the only way in to this free festival was either on foot or by helicopter.

It was early in the afternoon when the Rolling Stones arrived. The usually punctual Bill Wyman wasn't with the group; he had missed the flight as he had been busy shopping with his girlfriend when the rest of the group departed for the show. Jefferson Airplane was still on-stage. As soon as he climbed out of the helicopter, Mick Jagger was punched in the face by a teenage boy out of it on bad acid. 'I hate you, you fucker. I want to kill you,' he snarled. A shaken Mick insisted nothing happen to the boy. He retreated into the Stones' backstage trailer where he found Keith sitting with Gram Parsons; the three of them passed the afternoon there, smoking grass and singing country songs while they waited for the unusually tardy Bill.

Although there were stories of the Angels perpetrating violence on the crowd, they were unable to see anything or to find out any more positive information. They didn't know that even during the performance by Santana, the first act up on a stage that was only four foot high, fist – and knife-fights had broken out; when the pretty boys in the Flying Burrito Brothers appeared on-stage and the crowd surged forward, Angels had responded by beating them with pool cues. On hearing what was happening, as soon as their helicopter landed, the Grateful Dead made an instant decision: they climbed back in their chopper and left the site. Jefferson Airplane started their set: when singer Marty Balin tried to stop an Angel from beating a black man, he was himself knocked out with a fearsome punch; complaining as he came to, he was knocked out again.

Part of the established myth of Altamont is that the Stones came on so late because Mick Jagger wanted total darkness in order for his stage entrance to have maximum effect. But in fact it was because Bill had only just arrived from his shopping spree. When the Rolling Stones finally took to the stage, it was seven o'clock. Mick was wearing a black and orange satin suit, the trouser pants stuffed into high-heeled velvet boots. He went straight into 'Jumpin' Jack Flash'. As soon as the Stones had taken the stage, Mick was penned in by Hell's Angels, restricting his movement as they danced around. Even during 'Carol', the second number, pool cues started swinging down, exploding with colossal force on people's heads during the third song, 'Sympathy For The Devil'. There was a small explosion as a motorcycle engine blew up. Although the rest of the group stopped playing at that point, looking on aghast as Angels appeared to be kicking someone to death, Keith carried on – finally Mick's calls to him to stop had their effect. Then the singer addressed the audience: 'Hey, people, sisters and brothers. Come on now – will you cool out, everybody.' But as soon as the Stones started playing again, the violence returned. 'I mean, like people, who's fighting and what for? Why are we fighting? Every other scene has been cool ... We've gotta stop them right now, you know ... there's no point ...'

Keith stepped up to his mike: 'Either those cats cool it, or we don't play. I mean, there's not that many of them.' As Sonny Barger scowled at Keith, the Stones' personal security – moonlighting New York cops – closed in around the group. 'That guy there, if he doesn't stop it ...' screamed Keith, not too threatening in his lace shirt and fitted red leather jacket, singling out a biker at the right-hand side of the stage. Barger scowled at him some more. An enormous Angel seized the mike: 'You don't cool it, you ain't gonna hear no more music! You wanna all go home, or what?'

'Let's have some cool-out music,' suggested Keith, and the Stones were into 'Sun Is Shining', a slow Jimmy Reed blues song, before doing 'Stray Cat Blues', Mick's lascivious ode to under-age sex: but as 'Stray Cat Blues' began, pool cues pummelled down, crushing and crashing heads. Yet after the beautiful 'Love In Vain', it seemed a modicum of balance had been restored to the event: after the song Mick Jagger tried to persuade the crowd to sit down.

Then the group sprang into their classic from 1966, 'Under My Thumb'. As the tune's lilting rhythm lifted the vibe, parts of the audience even began to dance. On the left side of the stage Meredith 'Murdock' Hunter, an eighteen-year-old black guy, conspicuous with his lime-green suit, black hat and blond girlfriend, moved to the beat. He had been there for the entire set, pointedly ignoring the psychotic antics of the Hell's Angels, who did not take kindly to such disrespect. Suddenly he was being grabbed by the throat by one of them. Tugging a nickel-plated revolver out of his pants, Hunter pointed it at the Angel who was attacking him. Then he seemed briefly to point it towards the stage. At this point an Angel stabbed him in the head, and then twice in the back. Meredith Hunter fell to the ground, where over a dozen Angels kicked him to death, carrying him by the force of the attack out of sight of the stage behind a mountain of speakers. 'I wasn't going to shoot you,' were his last reported words.

Again, the Stones stopped playing. Keith was shouting at the Angels, but stopped when he heard they had taken a gun off someone at the front of the stage. At this point no one knew that someone had been killed in front of the group. The Rolling Stones started into the world première of 'Brown Sugar', the song they had recorded that week.

Then, although 'Midnight Rambler' was given a notably brief rendition, it was the rest of the tour set, concluding with 'Street Fighting Man'. As they played their last notes, the group were already edging towards the side of the stage, into their waiting helicopter and back to their hotel in San Francisco, where they finally learned about the murder that had taken place, the sacrifice of a man from the race whose music had inspired them to take up instruments in the first place.

The 1960s were over.

Let them bleed.

CHAPTER 18

ROCK 'N' ROLL BABYLON

In the early hours of 7 December, in Keith's hotel suite in San Francisco, immediately after the group had returned from Altamont, everything seemed even more exaggerated than usual. Despite the blizzard of cocaine and the acrid stench of bourbon and tequila around various members of the entourage, Mick seemed to be in familiar mode, suggesting to Michelle Phillips, latterly of the Mamas and Papas, and Miss Pamela of the GTOs that they adjourn to his suite for a threesome. This considerably pissed off Gram Parsons – like Keith now daubed with eyeshadow, his nails painted – who had been under the impression that Michelle had come to the show with him; but the nervous aura around Mick Jagger was hardly an inducement to the two women to engage in sexual activity with the singer. Was Mick's amorous front merely a cover for his extreme paranoia? Privately he was proclaiming that he suspected someone had tried to assassinate him: should he give up the group altogether, he wondered?

Keith was the first of the group to head out of San Francisco, still buzzing on whisky and coke, and onto a plane to London. Arriving at Heathrow airport, he was met by Anita Pallenberg, holding aloft the four-month-old Marlon. 'Keith, they're throwing me out of the country!' she cried. Quizzed about this by waiting reporters, Keith adopted his by now customary manner of rock 'n' roll prince of insouciance (permanently stoned on one substance or another, this came easily to him): 'It's a drag that you are forced into marriage by bureaucracy. I refuse to get married because some bureaucrat says we must. Rather than do that, I would leave Britain and live abroad. But if I want to continue to live in England, and that's the only way Anita can stay, we'll get married.'

The full extent of the débâcle at the Altamont Raceway had yet to filter through to the British media; asked about the Californian free concert, Keith's response was circumspect, to say the least: the event, he told a UPI reporter, had been 'basically well organised, but people were tired and a few tempers got frayed'. This view was in distinct contrast to David Crosby's: 'I think the major mistake was taking what was essentially a party,' said the member of Crosby, Stills, Nash and Young, renowned for his forthright opinions, 'and turning it into an ego game, a star trip of the Rolling Stones, who are on a star trip and who qualify in my book as snobs. I think they're on a grotesque, negative ego trip, essentially, especially the two leaders.'

Kenneth Anger suggested a magic marriage ceremony for Keith and Anita, but it was felt that in the eyes of the Home Office, who oversaw visa applications for residence in the British isles, this would not be considered with any special regard. ('Kenneth Anger told me I was his right-hand man. It's just what you feel. Whether you've gotten that good and evil thing together. Left-hand path, right-hand path, how far do you want to go down? Once you start, there's no going back. Where they lead to is another thing ... A lot of people have played on it, and it's inside everybody.') Eventually, a subtle media campaign by the ever skilful and astute Les Perrin removed the threat of deportation from Anita. All the same, although there was no formal ceremony, Keith was now to all intents and purposes a happily married family man.

Since his relationship with Chrissie Shrimpton had begun almost seven years previously, Mick had eagerly sought what Keith seemed simply to have stumbled upon. But with Marianne, the impressive successor to Chrissie, he seemed further than ever from such a domestic idyll: not only had she apparently left him for Mario Schifano, but was having an unswerving and growing affair with both heroin and cocaine. That her relationship with these drugs was an anaesthetic to dull the dissatisfaction she felt at so many aspects of her situation with Mick was neither here nor there, for, despite his considerable concern about Marianne's drug intake, he had little or no inkling of the depression that was overtaking her. Such a mood in Marianne was hardly mollified by the awareness that it was now almost public knowledge in London that Mick had acquired a mistress in the beautiful Marsha Hunt.

As Keith was being met by Anita at Heathrow airport, Mick was still asleep in his first-class seat on an overnight flight from San Francisco to Geneva in Switzerland, accompanied by the money that the Stones had earned on the tour, something in the region of 1.2 million dollars. Arriving in Switzerland, his body cavities were searched by the stringent Swiss customs officials. Having deposited the funds in a numbered account, he flew to the South of France on an expedition to find a property to move into, in response to Prince Rupert Loewenstein's suggestion that the only way for the Stones to survive financially was for them to go into tax exile from the United Kingdom. Prince Rupert, who had a reputation for honesty, had by now calculated that in their seven years of existence the Stones had earned a gross income of around two hundred million dollars. Yet they owed so much in tax that they were almost bankrupt.

On 6 December, the day of Altamont, Marsha Hunt was in Lyngby, a pleasant wooded suburb of the Danish capital Copenhagen. She had been acting in *Welcome to the Club*, a film about a black trio performing on a white US services base. When she heard about the disaster at the festival, she noted that this was the third tragedy Mick had had to deal with since she had known him. Mick had asked Marsha if he could send a private plane for her on 10 December to take her with him to Nice in the South of France on his property hunt. But Marsha didn't want that, didn't want to become a public appendage of Mick Jagger. 'Our friendship relied on our being straight with each other. His traits were obvious and were linked to his ambition: his goodness and badness, his obsequious interest in the upper classes, his penchant for Melangina [black] girls, his temptations, his strength and vulnerability. His interest in me was that I offered him unconditional love ... and why not? Must we treat love as some kind of barter?'

Although his trip to the French Mediterranean coastal plain afforded him some idea of the properties on offer, Mick had a rather more pressing engagement awaiting him in London. On 19 December 1969, his case for cannabis possession was due to be heard in London. The occasion marked a reunion of sorts with Marianne, who had been obliged to return with Nicholas from Italy for the trial. The case was over in a matter of hours. He was found guilty, and fined £200 for possession. Marianne was acquitted. (A worrying side-effect of the conviction was that Mick received an eighteen-month ban on travelling to the USA, an irony considering that Brian's difficulties with overseas visas were cited only half a year earlier as one of the reasons for his being sacked from the group.)

Considering the circumstances of their estrangement, Mick pointed out to Marianne, who had been accompanied back to London not only by Nicholas but also by Mario Schifano, that it would not be appropriate for her to return to 48 Cheyne Walk. Besides, Mick had failed to add that Marsha Hunt was staying with him in the eighteenth-century riverside house. The American woman had the impression that Mick missed family life – Nicholas, and the dog – more than he missed Marianne herself, even though Marsha realised he was still in love with his broken-winged angel. Marsha had never intended to move into Mick's home, however: just before Christmas she found a new place of her own, a flat in St John's Wood that she took over from Roger Daltrey, the singer with the Who, paying a rent of fourteen pounds a week. Marsha gave Chris Jagger a job decorating the place.

On 21 December the Rolling Stones presented London with its very own Christmas gift, two shows at the Lyceum, off the Strand in Covent Garden, at five and eight o'clock in the evening. It was a slight but more auspicious coda to the end of the 1960s in Britain than had been provided for the United States by Altamont. As they arrived audiences were sprinkled with fake snow, a piece of seasonal jollity that doubled as a coy drug reference for those who considered themselves truly hip.

For Christmas itself Marianne, Nicholas and Mario Schifano went down to Berkshire to the cottage that Mick had bought for Marianne's mother to live in (Mick always retained the title deeds to the property: when Marianne's mother passed on, he reclaimed it, refusing to let Marianne take it over). Early in the evening of Christmas Day Mick arrived, with a present for Marianne, a small antique silver box packed with cocaine. He spent the night with Marianne, Schifano sleeping on the sofa. The next morning the painter left for Italy. 'Mick,' said Marianne, 'was very pleased with himself.' Mick had spent the rest of the Christmas holiday at Keith's house. As a present Marsha Hunt bought her lover a puppy; she had felt disenchanted, though, when she had gone over to Keith and Anita's with him: 'After one visit to their house, I decided to keep my distance. I didn't find their being into hard drugs cute or adventurous ... Mick doted on Keith, and I didn't voice any opinion but I avoided contact.'

Marianne moved back into 48 Cheyne Walk. Yet Mick continued to see Marsha Hunt. Just after Christmas Mick held Marsha in his arms and told her that he loved her. She was 'deeply touched'. A few days later, as they sat at their table at Mr Chow's in Knightsbridge, Mick told her she would be a good mother and that they should have a child together. Marsha was even more deeply touched. She made an appointment to have her coil removed.

The Stones, who had had a mobile studio created in the back of a truck, started recording at Stargroves; these sessions at his country home afforded Mick ample opportunity for liaisons with Marsha Hunt and other females to whom he found himself momentarily attracted (the opening of the M4 motorway meant girls could be whisked down to him from London in around an hour). Back in London Marianne Faithfull chipped at heroin, smoking the fumes through the card centre of a toilet roll, chasing the dragon.

On 31 January 1970 British newspaper reports stated that the Rolling Stones had begun a law suit against Sears Point International Raceway for breach of contract and fraud, claiming £4,500,000 damages. The suit alleged that owing to the actions of the Raceway, the group had had to move the then projected 6 December 1969 concert to Altamont. But Les Perrin denied that these legal proceedings emanated from the Stones: 'The festival promoters may be suing, but the Rolling Stones are not involved,' he stated.

Yet the group was deeply involved with other elements of the residue of the American tour. In all-night sessions at the beginning of February 1970, Mick and Keith locked themselves away in Trident Studios off Wardour Street in Soho, mixing the ten songs from the live album they had recorded at Madison Square Garden in New York the previous November. 'The album's better than the bootleg record,' pronounced Mick, declaring part of the *raison d'être* for the LP that would be titled *Get Your Ya-Yas Out*. In the United States, the Stones had received the underground honour of being the third group of artists, after Bob Dylan with his *Great White Wonder* 'basement' tapes, and the Beatles with the original version of *Let It Be*, to be featured on a bootleg album. Entitled *Liver Than You'll Ever Be*, this unauthorised LP had been recorded, apparently directly off the mixing desk, at the Oakland Coliseum US concert and was widely considered so far to be the best representation of the group on stage. Packaged in a plain white card sleeve, the title rubber-stamped on one side, *Liver Than You'll Ever Be* was available in London for the princely sum of fifty shillings from such radical outlets as Compendium Books in Camden Town.

The sessions at Trident were filmed by the Maysles brothers for their as yet untitled tour documentary. 'Call the film *Old Glory*,' suggested Mick. 'I don't know a thing about America. It's just the title of a song we wrote a year ago, so I'm suggesting it ... *Love In Vain*. Maybe we should call it that. Pictures of nude chicks. They loved in vain. Naked as they came.' Keith had his own suggestion, one of a schoolboy-like prurience: *Naughty Ladies*. Down at Trident Keith took to wearing a scarlet t-shirt bearing an image of Marilyn Monroe. He would drink steadily from imported bottles of Old Granddad bourbon, for him a sign of the times. Alcohol of course was the least of his current addictions: he would nod out after his habitual trips to the men's room to skin-pop heroin – he had yet to graduate to mainlining the drug.

At the beginning of 1970 Bill Wyman had stopped talking to Keith, his dependency on drugs having made the bass player feel he could no longer be communicated with. Bill's despondency about Keith's psychological state was only exacerbated by the knowledge that the guitarist was now in a worse state than Brian Jones had ever been, of whom Bill had always been very fond. The silence between Bill and Keith continued for much of the next decade.

*

As they walked through Hyde Park a few weeks later, Mick on his way to a meeting at the Dorchester Hotel in Park Lane with Ahmet Ertegun, the charismatic, socialite owner of Atlantic Records, Marsha told Mick that she was three weeks pregnant. They were both very happy. In the lift at the Dorchester they bumped into Stephen Stills: a few nights previously he, Mick, Billy Preston and two of the Edwin Hawkins singers had come over to Marsha's new flat late at night for an impromptu jam session. A handful of Mick's employees were told about the pregnancy, but were sworn to secrecy. However, Mick and Marsha had their first argument over Mick's desire to send the son he was convinced she was expecting to Eton, and his wish to give the boy the hippy name Midnight Dream.

To the wall of his Cheyne Walk kitchen, in which Keith's favourite meal of eggs and bacon with brown sauce was cooked, was fixed a letter from his solicitor, a reminder to him to keep away from drugs of all kinds. The extent to which this was an irony can be judged from the fact that 'Spanish' Tony Sanchez had now moved into Keith's house at 3 Cheyne Walk. Although his job description was 'bodyguard', for which he was paid £150 a week, he was really there as Keith's in-house drug dealer. Number 3 Cheyne Walk was a rather different scene from the ordered life down the street in the narrow Queen Anne house at number 48. It saw an endless procession of people come through its doors, for whom Keith and Anita hardly bothered to dress. Stanley Booth, the American journalist, had accompanied Keith back to London after the US tour. Whenever Booth left Keith's house on foot, he would be stopped and searched by waiting police. 'This kind of attention inspired Keith to do things like go into the tiny garden behind the house and set off industrial-strength fireworks. When the cops came, Keith said there must have been some mistake, we'd been indoors all evening.'

Apart from Marlon, on whom he doted, Keith's principal relationship was now with heroin: although Keith would later claim a working knowledge of the *Kama Sutra*, the drug dulled his sexual feelings, and he and Anita rarely had sex, each blaming the other for this state of affairs. In early 1970, Keith's habit was by no means as extreme as Anita's. (He would soon catch up with her.) One of Keith's justifications for doing heroin was that he said it helped him come down after tours, when the ceaselessly coursing adrenalin generated by back-to-back live shows needed to be quenched. Yet Keith also claimed that the reason for his heroin consumption was never 'recreation'. 'It was about getting the job done,' he said, about putting himself in that artistic space in which he could write songs. Indubitably, wherever the impetus came from, Keith was experiencing a creative peak in 1970 and 1971. He also immersed himself in metaphysical literature, acquainting himself thoroughly with the rudiments of the Buddhist and Hindu religions.

On *Let It Bleed* the Rolling Stones' sound was augmented not only by Mick Taylor but also by the horn section of Jim Price and Bobby Keys – born on the same day, in the same year, as Keith – on 'Live With Me'. Latterly, Keys and Price had been playing with Derek and the Dominos, the group formed by Eric Clapton that, with prescient irony, had disintegrated on the rock of Clapton's heroin addiction. Stranded in London, Keys had run into Mick in the Speakeasy; the Stones' singer had suggested the pair drive out to Stargroves to see what happened. Soon Keys was howling his horn on new songs like 'Brown Sugar' and 'Can't You Hear Me Knocking', and joining up with Price to drive the new song 'Bitch'.

Unsurprisingly to those with any interest in astrology was the fact that Bobby Keys was a co-conspirator in drug consumption with Keith Richard. At least this did not seem to affect his punctuality as much as it did his more famous friend. For, in the manner of Brian, who had been fired for this reason, Keith began not to show up for recording sessions: he had missed the date for 'Moonlight Mile', composed by Mick Jagger and Mick Taylor. Like many heroin users, he became obsessive and secretive about concealing his stash, sometimes in a manner that suggested he might have purchased a Junior Secret Agent kit from a child's comic. For example, he would carry a fountain-pen that had been converted to hold two grams of whichever was the current favourite powder, and while crossing international borders his toiletries bag would contain a shaving-cream canister packed with drugs. After the Lyceum shows, said Stanley Booth, 'we all seemed to sink into a torpor. Anita was already addicted. At Cheyne Walk, and at the thatch-roofed house behind the moat at Redlands, Keith and I talked, listened to music, did drugs.'

Accordingly, many of the details of the Rolling Stones' business in 1970 rather passed Keith by. He only half registered the news, announced on 14 March, that the group were imminently to embark on a European tour, to start in The Hague on 8 May, ending in Helsinki on 7 June after fourteen shows in seven countries. With recording duties overhanging them, the tour was soon pushed back to later in the year.

Mick Jagger's life at 48 Cheyne Walk had become depressing. By the time Marianne Faithfull and Mick finally split in the spring of 1970, she was a serious heroin user. The final straw in their relationship was a heinous example of rock 'n' roll Babylon, the kind of expedient pragmatism about loyalty to one's nearest and dearest that could have been part of the plot in a shopping 'n' fucking soap opera. About to descend the stairs of the Chelsea house, Marianne overheard her name being invoked by Ahmet Ertegun, the head of Atlantic Records; if Atlantic was about to give the Stones a label deal for thirty million dollars, Ertegun was saying, they would want some guarantee that the deal would not be blown by Marianne's increasingly embarrassing behaviour. (Recently, at a dinner with the Earl of Warwick at Warwick Castle, she had fallen face down into her soup, after the five Mandrax she had ingested finally kicked in.) She would need to be dispensed with: and Mick was readily agreeing to this contractual proviso. 'Sitting at the top of those stairs like a child listening to her parents, the precariousness of my situation hit me full force,' she wrote in her autobiography. 'This was writing on the wall that even a junkie could read.'

'That's true,' Marianne said later. 'I'd never told anyone that. That was quite an experience. That was exactly what I did. I heard that – and bolted. Within the next couple of days I was out of there. No wonder, really. I can't say I blame myself for that. I would have had to be very grown-up to be able to walk in and sit down and say, "Were you talking about me, dear?" Nowadays I would, of course.'

Much to the trepidation of Mick Jagger, *Ned Kelly*, the film he had made in Australia with director Tony Richardson the previous summer, was to receive its première on 24 June 1970 at the Pavilion cinema in London. The film was a disaster, as much for the scrappy screenplay as for Mick's seeming almost wilfully miscast. When he had watched a preview with Donald Cammell, the co-director of *Performance*, he had been so depressed by the unmitigated dreadfulness of the film that he had burst into tears. Even before any reviews appeared, this obstinately unlikeable movie had already been slated by word of mouth.

It was a blow for Mick: even though *Performance* had not been seen publicly, he knew its quality; how nice to have transcended the usual woeful limitations of the pop star who turns to acting. And the idea of *Ned Kelly* had seemed so sound: an archetypal western about an outlaw hero, its Australian setting looked likely to give it a unique edge. Instead, cinema audiences' first perceptions of Mick Jagger as an actor was of someone with wooden lines, a fake London accent and a sort of tin-can suit of armour. Thoughts of the film brought up memories for him of the débâcle and despair of filming it, with Marianne close to death: he couldn't help wondering if he might have performed better had he himself not started making the film in a state of shock. On the soundtrack Mick sang a song entitled 'Wild Colonial Boy'.

'That was a load of shit,' Mick commented about the film. 'I only

The personification of late-sixties hipness, Mick, Keith and Anita swan through Heathrow Airport on their way to South America, where they spend Christmas 1968. Although also accompanied on this trip by Marianne and her son Nicholas, Mick never lost an opportunity to come on to Anita (Hulton Archive)

Mick in a portrait shot taken by society photographer and painter Cecil Beaton in Morocco in March 1967; Keith was also photographed by Beaton in the same location, the El Minzah hotel in Tangiers. 'Keith R. in 18th-century suit, long black velvet coat and tightest pants, and of course, Mick Jagger. He is sexy but completely sexless. He could nearly be a eunuch,' wrote Beaton
(both courtesy of Sotheby's London)

Anita with Marlon at Marseilles Airport in August 1970, her face already
altered by excessive living (Hulton Archive)

Mick and Bianca on tour in the United States (London Features International)

Keith, in the suit he had bought at Granny Takes A Trip for court appearances, arrives with Anita at Marlborough Street on 24 October 1973. Despite having been charged with possession of heroin, hash and guns, he escaped with a £200 fine. The picture of this damned pair seems overhung with an aura of near madness (Hulton Archive)

Life was simpler for Mick, going along to watch the final Test between England and Australia at the Oval on 10 August 1972. What did Bianca make of cricket? (Hulton Archive)

Mick and Keith (with Billy Preston in the background) at Dynamic Sound in Kingston, Jamaica, in December 1972, where they were recording *Goat's Head Soup*, an album that didn't seem to carry a trace of its recording location in a single note (both Adrian Boot)

TOP Keith at Dynamic Sound
ABOVE Mick guests in the video shoot for 'Don't Look Back', the first Peter Tosh single released on Rolling Stone Records. Filmed at Strawberry Hill, high in the Jamaican Blue Mountains, the event was an auspicious start to a business relationship that would end in tears (both Adrian Boot)

Keith in the Kingston kitchen of bass supremo Robbie Shakespeare . . .

... and with the Minister of Herb himself, Peter Tosh (both Adrian Boot)

Wembley, September 1973 (both Adrian Boot)

On 11 January 1977, Keith arrives at court in Aylesbury, Buckinghamshire, where he will be found guilty of possession of cocaine. Mick, there to offer moral support, seems as strained as his old Dartford schoolfriend. Soon, in Toronto, Canada, Keith's drug habit will land him in even bigger trouble (both Hulton Archive)

(Adrian Boot)

made it because I had nothing else to do. I knew Tony Richardson was a reasonable director, and I thought he'd make a reasonable film. The thing is,' he concluded, characteristically equivocal, 'you never know until you do it whether a film will turn out to be a load of shit, and if it does all you can say is, "Well, that was a load of shit", and try to make sure you don't do anything like it again.' Much of the vicious criticism for *Ned Kelly* that should have gone the way of Tony Richardson was directed at Mick Jagger personally. Six years previously, Richardson had won four Academy Awards for the film *Tom Jones*. So what had this fine director been doing, working with such a bad script?

Mick gave the excuse that he was preparing with the Stones for a European tour, for his non-attendance at the première of *Ned Kelly*. Marsha was given a ticket, however, and in her long maternity dress sat close to his parents, who were oblivious to the nearby unborn presence of their first grandchild. Marsha, Joe and Eva had met when they had come round to Cheyne Walk one day. Four days after the première, Mick's parked Bentley was broken into near his Chelsea home: a guitar, clothes and a notebook were taken. The same day, Marsha modelled a Thea Porter maternity dress at a charity fashion event at the Hilton. Unable any longer to avoid the issue, Marsha came out to the press at the event about her pregnancy. A media favourite for her combination of exotic beauty, intelligence and genuine honesty, Marsha received not a hint of criticism. But she refused to name the father. Although Mick, quietly proud, was perfectly happy for the world to know that Marsha was carrying his child, Marsha wanted to keep it hidden, threatening to sue a reporter who worked out who the father was. The inimitable Les Perrin threw in a red herring by giving the papers a picture of another girl who it was rumoured Mick was seeing, the actress Patti D'Arbanville.

By now Mick had moved not one but two lovers into 48 Cheyne Walk. Janice Kenner, a tall blond Californian, was on a summer trip to London, staying with her friends Glyn Johns and his wife and baby when Mick announced he needed some help around the house. The inevitable had happened and they had fallen into bed. The self-possessed Janice, however, retained her individuality, refusing to become infatuated with Mick, preferring the role of temporary housekeeper, confidante and occasional lover. Soon there was the arrival of another Californian called Catherine, a top-level groupie as beautiful as she was reputedly brainless. Luckily, Janice was sufficiently perceptive to see that Mick would have been most pleased to find the two women fighting over him in his own home, and steered clear of any such pitfalls. Catherine, however, appeared smitten by Mick Jagger.

On 30 July 1970 Allen Klein was told that the Rolling Stones no longer required his services, and they at once began legal proceedings against him. Neither he, ABKCO Industries Inc., nor any other associated company had the authority any longer to negotiate recording contracts on the Stones' behalf. The timing was carefully planned: the following day the Stones' contract with Decca expired. The mixed tapes of the group's last Madison Square Garden show had been delivered, the handing-over to Decca of the live album the final obstacle needing to be overcome before the Rolling Stones were at last fully in charge of their own recording career. Naturally, Decca had refused to consider a double album made up of one-half Stones, one-half the iconic support acts Chuck Berry, B. B. King and Ike and Tina Turner. The group, never likely to let up in their efforts to get one over on the despised Decca, had their revenge: still liable to present the label with one final studio song, the group's response was to turn in the tapes of a tune with a title not destined for the main playlist on Radio One, 'Cock-sucker Blues'. Each warring party as predictable as the other, the label was so outraged by the lyrics (*'Where can I get my cock sucked/Where can I get my ass fucked'*, ran one rhyming couplet) that it was never released.

On 15 August 1970 the group announced the formation of Rolling Stones Records and, with Prince Rupert Loewenstein handling the negotiations, set about securing the best possible distribution deal with an established record company. Rolling Stones Records was to be run by Marshall Chess, the son of the owner of Chess Records, who had been such a big influence on the Stones in the early days, and who were therefore hopefully a means of staying in touch with their musical soul. 'We want to release the odd blues record, and Charlie Watts wants to do some jazz,' Mick downplayed, with characteristic vagueness, a project that was as much his as anybody's. 'What we're not interested in is bubblegum material. We want to control prices to stop the price of records going up. I'd like to find new ways of distribution. I don't want to do any production.'

The thirtieth of July 1970 saw another significant cultural milestone: the film *Performance* was finally given its world première in New York. The Rolling Stones label had been pushed into existence by the Kinney Group's takeover of Warner Brothers, which had thereby guaranteed its subsidiary of Atlantic Records the fund to sign the group. And it had also provided the wherewithal to re-edit the film substantially and to recoup on its initial investment. The footage had been reassembled as an almost stream-of-consciousness narrative in which a linear time structure was virtually dispensed with. At first, co-director and director of photography Nic Roeg was so outraged by this treatment of the material that he considered taking his name off the film. His later work proved to be reliant on such an effective stylistic device. The film opened in New York to extraordinarily mixed reviews: 'The most loathsome film of all,' wrote John Simon in the stuffy *New York Times*, while the *Village Voice*'s Andrew Sarris declared it 'the most deliberately decadent film I have ever seen'.

On 29 August the Stones flew to the Finnish capital of Helsinki, pausing en route in Copenhagen in Denmark for a press conference. On 2 September the group's European tour opened at Olympic Stadium, Helsinki. The tour incorporated a brand-new set that included its own proscenium arch, with six rows of curtains and several banks of lights.

The next day, when the group played in Malmö in Sweden, Marianne was counter-sued for divorce by John Dunbar, Mick cited as co-respondent in the breakdown of the relationship. On 4 September the stage was stormed by hundreds of fans at the Royal Tennis Hall, Stockholm. Two days later the *Get Yer Ya-Yas Out!* album was released, on Decca in Europe and on the London label in the US, the last album under the contract; those in the know felt that it was not as strong as the infinitely hipper *Liver Than You'll Ever Be*. Shows followed in Aarhus and Copenhagen in Denmark, Hamburg, Berlin and Cologne in Germany. On 19 September the sound-track of *Performance* was released by Warner Brothers: as well as Mick's haunting, staggering 'Memo From Turner', it included tracks by Ry Cooder, Randy Newman and Buffy St Marie. After a date the following day in Stuttgart, the group moved on to a show at the Olympia in Paris on 22 September, which was followed by a party at the Georges Cinq hotel.

At this event, while Keith had an encounter with the finest heroin with which the dealers of Marseilles could supply the French capital, Donald Cammell introduced Mick to a strikingly beautiful woman called Bianca Pérez Morena de Macías. Until it was pointed out to him by onlookers, Mick was unaware that, with her thick lips and high cheekbones, she resembled him uncannily. She spoke little English, and Mick conversed with her almost entirely in French, a tribute to his well-rounded education at Dartford Grammar School.

Born in the politically troubled Central American state of Nicaragua, Bianca was from a distinctly needy background; her mother was separated from her 'businessman' father and ran a drinks stand in downtown Managua. At the age of seventeen Bianca had won a scholarship to study at the Institute of Political Science in Paris. She gave her present age as twenty-one, but seemed to have had rather too much life experience for this to be the case; when a member of the Stones' entourage took a glimpse at her passport she discovered that Bianca was in fact twenty-six years old.

During her time in Paris she had become involved with the actor Michael Caine, and was now in a relationship with the French record boss Eddie Barclay, who told Mick that she was his fiancée. Getting Barclay out of the way, Mick made a pass at Bianca, to which – wisely, as this only further whetted Mick's appetite – she refused to succumb. In repeated phone calls in Paris Mick pestered Bianca to spend time with him: on each occasion she would decline, saying she had an appointment with her hairdresser. After two further shows in Paris at the Palais des Sports, the Stones moved on to play the Stadthalle in Vienna. While in Austria, Mick called Bianca: he told her that a ticket was waiting for her at Paris's Orly airport to take her to Rome, where the group were arriving the following day. As a sign of his respect, and to the consternation of the rest of the group, Mick had booked and paid for a room for Bianca at the hotel in which the Stones were staying.

After he had fractiously punched a reporter in the Italian capital for the crime of 'asking stupid questions', Mick linked up with Bianca, in every sense of the word. A closely guarded secret, she remained with Mick for the rest of the tour. She was there not only at the dates in Rome, but at the Palazzo dello Sport in Milan, where tear gas was fired by the police as 2,000 fans tried to rampage into the sold-out venue. She was present at shows in Lyons, Frankfurt, Essen, Amsterdam and Munich. On 12 October Mick returned to London with Bianca Pérez. At the end of that month John Dunbar was granted a decree nisi from Marianne; as co-respondent, Mick Jagger was ordered to pay costs of £200. Les Perrin countered the potentially negative publicity by issuing a press release stating that the Stones had recorded eight new songs at Olympic.

The tangled love affairs of the Rolling Stones' singer was pushing itself to centre-stage in his life. Everything was coming to the surface: Marsha Hunt was almost ready to give birth. During the group's European tour Marsha noticed that Mick's calls became less frequent, especially after he told her, with surprising ingenuousness, that he'd met an interesting woman in Paris called Bianca. Shortly before she had her baby, Marsha discovered that this Bianca had returned to the UK with Mick, and was staying at Stargroves. Unable to work and therefore broke and in the last days of pregnancy, Marsha had to ask Mick for some money. He sent her £200 and a note that included the phrase, 'I know I haven't been right by you'. The envelope containing the note also included a ring that Mick said he had always worn, which Marsha decided to put on her finger when she went into labour. On 3 November 1970, Marsha arrived at St Mary's Hospital, Paddington – her waters had broken. Initially she was sent home, as there was no National Health bed available for her. When she returned a few hours later, she checked in as Mrs Ratledge. From the payphone in the corridor outside the ward, Marsha Hunt called Mick at Stargroves to tell him that he had a daughter, who she had decided to name Karis.

Two days after giving birth, she climbed into the limousine that Mick had sent to the hospital to pick up Marsha and her daughter and take them home. Mick came round to her flat the same day; Marsha left him alone with his daughter. 'Something was missing when Mick dropped by that day, and maybe that says it: he dropped by,' she remembered. 'He was cordial and charming and in a hurry to be somewhere else. I smiled when he rushed off.'

Ten days later he returned for an equally brief visit. Marsha took him upstairs and dealt out harsh words over his lack of communication with her. 'I hadn't expected him to stab back. He said that he never loved me and that I was mad to think he had. The pain in me burst forth in stupid girl-tears, but he saved me from a shamefaced emotional display by saying that he could take her away from me if he chose. In a measured, sober tone I heard myself saying that I'd blow his brains out if he dared.' Within days Marsha was asked to take a role in *Catch My Soul*, the director Jack Good's rock musical version of *Othello*. With suitable irony, Marsha was to play the part of Bianca. In press interviews Marsha adroitly fielded all questions about the name of the father of her baby.

Donald Cammell, who had something of a mentor-like hold over Mick in matters of film, had persuaded him to release *Gimme Shelter*, the title that had finally been given to the Maysles brothers' documentary of the Stones' latest US tour. Cammell, to whom Mick had shown the film, said it was a masterpiece and Mick was keen on being seen as an artist. Despite the fact that he hardly came over in a favourable light in the film, the thoughtful, intelligent side of Mick could see that showing himself as a flawed human being could only enhance the public's perception of him. Besides, he had invested \$30,000 in the Maysles brothers' film, and wanted to make his money back. *Gimme Shelter* had its première at the Plaza Theater in New York, on 6 December, to exceptional reviews. At the time Mick was in Nassau in the Bahamas, where he had flown on 24 November for a two-week vacation.

On 18 December, Keith celebrated his twenty-seventh birthday with a party at Olympic Studios. George Harrison, Eric Clapton, Al Kooper and Bobby Keys were among the guests; at the end of the party all but the former Beatle played on a stunning rendition of 'Brown Sugar', so powerful that it almost became the official version on the imminent *Sticky Fingers* album.

Cinematic matters were riding high in Mick's life. On 4 January 1971 the British première of *Performance* was held at the Warner West End in aid of Release, the legal-aid charity for those busted for drug possession. Keith Richard, who still felt he had a personal axe to grind about the film, was in the audience. The underground newspaper *International Times* recommended that it was inadvisable to see the film on acid; and despite the studio's anxiety to recoup its costs, Warner Brothers never gave the film a full UK general release. In the 7 January 1971 edition of the US music-business trade magazine *Billboard*, the Rolling Stones were listed as the third best-selling artists in the USA for the previous decade: clearly, Mick should not yet give up his day job.

The enormity of the tax problems faced by the Rolling Stones – they already had tax bills of £100,000 each – meant that there was only one solution: to leave the country at the end of that tax year to avoid Britain's punitive taxation of the rich, thereby becoming Britain's first rock 'n' roll tax exiles. Mick's recent marijuana conviction meant that the United States was out of the question. The only option appeared to be the South of France, for its nearness to Britain and the opportunities it held for a legendary sybaritic and chic lifestyle. But before they left the British Isles, the Rolling Stones were booked on a tour around the country they weren't sure they'd ever be coming back to. On 6 February 1971, the group announced that the concerts would begin on 4 March at Newcastle City Hall, and that after the series of dates they would move to France.

The March tour followed the show in the Tyneside city with a sprint around Britain: Manchester, Coventry, Glasgow, Bristol, Brighton, Liverpool and Leeds, before climaxing on 14 March with two shows at the Roundhouse in Chalk Farm. Bianca accompanied Mick to each show, the pair conversing almost entirely in French; it was clear to all onlookers that they were in love.

Anita Pallenberg, however, did not take kindly to this intruder into the Stones' camp. In front of his new girlfriend, she would attempt to flirt brazenly with Mick; Spanish Tony caught her tickling Mick and squeezing his bottom. Claiming that her own trunk of clothes had been mislaid during the tour, she asked an unsuspecting Bianca if she could borrow garments from her; exquisite, costly dresses were returned crumpled up and stained. In druggy, slurred tones, Anita would fire character assassinations at Bianca: insisting Mick's new girlfriend was a man who had had a sex-change operation, Anita told Spanish Tony she had put a curse on her.

Both worldly-wise and curiously innocent, Bianca evidently viewed life with the Rolling Stones with a curious mixture of open warmth and the icy disdain of aristocratic hauteur – except that there was an occasional glimpse of barely disguised fear in her eyes. On the tour bus, she won $10,000 from Marshall Chess in an apparently casual game of gin rummy. Mired in his own miasma of narcotic creativity, Keith missed most of what was going on around him. 'Bianca's a groovy chick. We all dig her,' he muttered backstage at Green's Playhouse in Glasgow, to the irritation of Anita.

For much of the tour Keith Richard played badly. He travelled separately from the rest of the group, in the company of Anita and Marlon, Gram Parsons and his new wife Gretchen and Bobby Keys. They were always accompanied by Boogie, Keith's dog. After the Glasgow show, Keith attempted to smuggle Boogie onto the plane with him. Inevitably the deception was discovered: in the ensuing fracas with airport officials, Keith called for the assistance of the local police, seemingly oblivious that the contents of his pockets made him a walking illegal pharmacy. After he had turned the knack of missing planes and trains into something of an art form, it became anyone's guess at what time the Rolling Stones would hit the stage for their performances: at the date in Liverpool the show began five hours after the scheduled kick-off.

For most of the following decade the potentially erratic nature of Stones' live performances became part of their myth, one almost entirely dependent on how much heroin, cocaine or alcohol Keith had ingested – something that was quite public knowledge. Ever forgiving, the group's audience was obliged to consider such arrogant dysfunction an expression of Keith's irrepressible rock 'n' roll spirit.

Long before it became a staple accessory for fashion-conscious young men, Keith Richard was a pioneer of the single earring, wearing a piece of bone costume jewellery he had bought on the trip to Peru at the end of 1968. Keith's right earlobe had been pierced in London in a mass session with various members of the Living Theatre. The hole in his lobe was effected by a jeweller friend who, Keith claimed, had ingested a con- siderable quantity of Mandrax as preparation for his task: a sewing needle was employed to drill through his ear, along with a lump of ice to freeze the lobe. The jeweller also pierced Anita's ear on the same occasion. Inspired by such backyard craftsmanship, Keith made his first bottleneck the same night. A needle through the earlobe is sometimes used by acupuncturists as a cure for addictions, but Keith's metabolism was clearly resolutely resistant to the procedure. Those around him were more concerned, especially as it was feared that the guitarist's heroin habit might have an adverse impact on the group's eligibility to take up overseas residence.

Mick had been having abortive talks with William Burroughs at the writer's apartment in Duke Street in Mayfair about the possibility of filming his classic novel *The Naked Lunch*. He discovered that Burroughs, whose profligate use of heroin was legendary, had come off the drug through a process employed by a Dr John Dent, a renowned British addictions specialist. Dent's treatment did not seem especially revolutionary: small tablets of morphine were administered orally, the dose gradually being diminished. By now Dent had died, but his nursing assistant, Miss Smith, a redoubtable former hospital matron, had performed the same cure on

Robert Fraser and assorted Chelsea beautiful people. After the British tour had ended at the Roundhouse, Spanish Tony drove Keith down to Redlands, where he was to be closeted away to come off smack. After four days Keith was pronounced by 'Smithy' to be cured of his heroin addiction. But she had not bargained on the arrival of Michael Cooper three days later, with several grams of the finest Turkish scag. After another week or so Gram Parsons turned up with further supplies of both heroin and cocaine. Keith was hooked again. Back in London at Cheyne Walk, he repeated the cure, in the company of Gram Parsons.

The police in Chelsea were thoroughly aware of Keith's extra-curricular interests. Three weeks before he left Cheyne Walk for France, he was stepping out of his front door when a squad car pulled up, its occupants, as he remembered, demanding he roll up his sleeves: 'Hello, Keith. Let's have a look at your veins. Not on the heavy stuff, are ya? How's Anita and the baby?' Two days after Gram and Gretchen Parsons had come to stay at 3 Cheyne Walk, the trio were driven off by Keith's chauffeur, only for the Bentley to be pulled over almost immediately by a police squad car and all occupants of the vehicle rigorously searched. On 26 March the Stones recorded two television specials for overseas broadcast at the Marquee club. True to form, Keith arrived very late, and immediately fell out with Harold Pendleton, the long-time manager of the Marquee, the leader of the jazz crowd who had tried to hold back the Stones in 1962, something Keith never forgave him for. Behind the Stones' stage set was a sign for the Marquee club. Keith wanted it removed. When Pendleton refused, Keith swung his guitar at him. Luckily, it failed to connect.

Despite the knowledge that Keith had been completely unsuccessful in his efforts to clean up from narcotics, Anita was sent to Bowden House at Harrow-on-the-Hill in north London, a clinic which specialised in addictive behaviour, to try a further remedy: she was to be given a 'sleep' cure, during which time, it was claimed, she would lose her craving for heroin. But the sleeping tablets she was administered were nothing more than common-or-garden Mogadon, hardly strong enough for someone whose body had built up the tolerance that Anita's had to all manner of drugs. Yet Keith managed to persuade his girlfriend to remain at Bowden House, after he had agreed to Anita's stipulation that Spanish Tony would come up to see her twice a day by limousine to administer a medicinal snort of coke.

While driving to visit her in the Bentley one morning with Michael Cooper, Keith nodded out from his latest shot of heroin, driving straight across a roundabout, which he demolished along with his car. The Blue Lena had by now been resprayed pink, presumably on the principle that a luxury vehicle of that colour that was being driven by a wasted-looking rock 'n' roll star would be quite inconspicuous. In something of a state of shock at having been awoken so rudely, Keith leaped out of the car with his stash of junk and disappeared over a garden wall before the police arrived. In the garden behind the wall, seeking a hole in which to bury a handful of Tuinol barbiturates he had found in his pocket, he discovered frequent Stones session pianist Nicky Hopkins, who was making his way down his garden to investigate the sound of the car smash outside his house. Hopkins invited Keith in for a cup of tea. Keith later explained to the police that the crash had occurred after he had been cut up by a Ferrari with Yugoslav number plates.

The group threw their official farewell party on 30 March at Skindles Hotel in Maidenhead, thirty miles out of London. Fellow frolickers included John Lennon and Yoko Ono, Eric Clapton, Stephen Stills and the Faces, a group on the cusp of huge popularity which featured not only the flamboyant singer Rod Stewart but also Ron Wood, a guitarist for whom the phrase 'diamond geezer' might almost have been invented. When, in the small hours of the morning, the hotel owner pulled the plug on the music in response to complaints from neighbours, Mick threw a table through a window. Was Mick feeling a measure of inner tension? Before he left London he asked Marsha Hunt if Maria, her nanny, could bring Karis over to see him.

CHAPTER 19

EXILE IN NELLCÔTE

Preparing Keith for the move to France was not the easiest of tasks for those around him: he simply refused to acknowledge that he was leaving London. On 5 April 1971, the day of departure, a team from the Rolling Stones office arrived at 3 Cheyne Walk, picked up everything around him, packed it in cardboard boxes and shipped it to St Jean Cap Ferrat, to Keith's new home, Nellcôte in Villefranche, built in 1899. He was renting the mock-Roman luxury seafront villa for £1,000 a week, with an option to buy it for two million francs from the present owners, descendants of the Russian writer Leo Tolstoy. Shaded by reassuring, mysterious palm trees and fringed by the flashing colour of its unkempt, tropical jungle of flowers, the Mediterranean heat tempered by a mild sea breeze, Nellcôte seemed like paradise, so far from Keith's origins in faintly down-at-heel Dartford. The view over Villefranche harbour was one of the most beautiful in the world, and there was a magical grotto perfect for smoking a chill-out joint. It was by far the largest and grandest of the various homes occupied by the Stones on the French Riviera. Within a few weeks, the interior of this princely residence would come to resemble that of Mick, Keith and Brian's flat in Edith Grove. Still ensconced in Bowden House, Anita – who spoke French fluently – didn't see her new home until the end of April; Marlon was looked after by Shirley Arnold, an assistant to the group.

After first trying to live up in the mountains above the coastal plain, Mick Jagger took a villa in St Tropez, close to that of Pablo Picasso, where he devoured the huge collection of blues records he had brought to France: when *Performance* producer Sandy Lieberson visited, he joked about linking up all the albums' titles to create lyrics for the new Stones' long-player. Lieberson was discussing a film he wanted to produce, to be directed by Donald Cammell, based on the hip hit play *The Beard* by Michael McClure, a sensual work about the fictional relationship between Wild West legend Billy the Kid and Jean Harlow, the film siren; Mick had tentatively agreed to star in the film. Charlie Watts had moved into a villa on the other side of Marseilles, Bill was in Grasse, close to Keith and Mick Taylor had rented a far less palatial home between the bass player and the guitarist.

On 6 April 1971, the first day of the Stones' official residence in France, the group threw a party at the Canto Club House in St Tropez. Here it was announced that the Rolling Stones label would be distributed through Atlantic Records. Ahmet Ertegun was at the party, along with Stephen Stills, who was now residing in Surrey in England. In addition to promising a new Stones' single by the summer and an album in the autumn, Mick declared that he intended to write a book about the group. The logo of the group's new label was revealed – a tongue widely assumed to be that of Mick Jagger engaged in the practice of cunnilingus; in fact, it was inspired by Kali, the Hindu goddess.

Just over a week later, on 15 April, Don Short, writing in the *Daily Mirror*, reported: 'A familiar sight in the French Riviera is Rolling Stone Mick Jagger dining out in uncommonly conventional style with society girl Bianca Pérez Morena de Macías. All the signs are that the couple plan to marry very soon. Twenty-six-year-old Jagger meanwhile is saying little. At the Byblos Hotel, trendiest place in town, he admitted yesterday: "It's quite true that I have been seeing this girl for some time. But I'm not the sort of bloke who would make a big fuss of announcing a date, am I?" ' Mick also spoke to the *Mirror* about his group: 'The band is not retiring just because we're going away. We'll remain a functioning group, a touring group, and a happy group. We're not going to stay in the South of France for a whole year, we're going on the road. I couldn't live in France for a whole year.'

The interview with Mick was part of the publicity to promote the first single on the Stones' new label, 'Brown Sugar', coupled with 'Bitch'. Far from being released in 'the summer', the record was to be released the following day. The album, *Sticky Fingers*, with a sleeve designed by Andy Warhol, with whom Mick had become friends, would be in the shops a week later. Both the single and album became the iconic records of the summer, international number ones that could be heard playing every-where.

Circumstances provided an additional barrage of publicity. On 2 May, Bianca's birthday, Mick threw a dinner party for her in Paris, presenting his girlfriend with a £4,000 diamond bracelet. Five days later, the *Daily Mirror* dropped a bombshell: 'Pop star Mick Jagger and his beautiful South American (*sic*) girlfriend are planning a secret wedding in France. They have applied for a special dispensation to marry without having the banns posted – which would allow the ceremony to go ahead without anyone but local officials knowing. Jagger called on a senior magistrate yesterday at Draguignan in southern France to make his application. Only two days ago

Bianca said: "There's not going to be a wedding this week, next week or ever. Mick and I are very happy together. We don't need to get married. Why should we?" '

By now Mick had called his parents in Dartford, telling them that on 12 May he would be marrying a woman they had never met. 'Keep it quiet,' Eva Jagger heard her son tell her. 'I don't want it to turn into a circus.' Eva went into Dartford town centre to find a new hat to wear, and took the train up to London's West End to buy a suitable dress. On 11 May she and Joe Jagger took the plane that Mick had chartered for his wedding guests from Gatwick airport to Nice. Once in the air, Eva couldn't help reflecting on how well her son had done in his short life. Accompanying them on the flight were many of London's brightest luminaries, and even she knew who some of her seventy or so co-passengers were, many of whom, despite their wealth, smoked hand-rolled cigarettes during the flight: Paul and Linda McCartney, Ringo and Maureen Starr, Keith Moon, Ossie Clark, Lord Lichfield, Donald Cammell, John Walker of the Walker Brothers, Jimmy Miller, Ahmet Ertegun, Marshall Chess, Ronnie Wood, Ian McLagen, Ronnie Lane, Kenny Jones and the by now inevitable Stephen Stills. Mick put his guests up at the Hotel Byblos, a beautiful, relaxed village complex on the beach.

Mick had received four weeks of Catholic instruction to prepare him for the wedding from Abbé Lucien Baud, pastor of the fisherman's chapel of St Anne. 'It's not a question of his becoming a Roman Catholic, just having an understanding of our faith. He is a very serious, intelligent man. He is an Anglican, of course, and I don't think a practising one. He has a great sense of religion, that boy. He really has a feeling for it,' the Abbé told reporters.

What few of the wedding guests were aware of was that Bianca was already four months pregnant. And she had not really wanted to get married at all – it was Mick who desired that state, as he had with Chrissie Shrimpton and Marianne Faithfull. Yet on the morning of the wedding a considerable controversy arose. Under French law, the putative married couple may opt for one of two marriage contracts: either joint ownership of all worldly goods, or a distinct separation of the two. It was not hard to guess which Mick opted for. This came as a sudden shock to Bianca. As Mayor Marius Estezan and the guests waited in the St Tropez council chamber, furious negotiations were taking place between the legal representatives of both parties to resolve this potential contract breaker. Eventually Bianca was browbeaten into accepting Mick's terms, by which time the atmosphere inside the council chamber was becoming surreal. Members of the general public are legally welcome at the civil marriage ceremony on which, in addition to any religious ceremony, the state in

France is insistent. Accordingly, the place was packed with international photographers and fans. And local officialdom refused to relax this edict for such a momentous occasion.

Moreover, with the momentum of proceedings interrupted by the morning's legal wranglings, Mick suddenly developed marriage fright, initially refusing to go ahead with the ceremony. Eventually, fifty minutes late, the marriage was performed, after Mick Jagger had stormed up to the marriage deck, swearing under his breath about the jockeying photographers, accompanied by an extremely frightened-looking, crying Bianca. In order to prepare himself for the ordeal of the wedding, Mick had fuelled himself on cocaine brought down to St Tropez by Spanish Tony as his wedding present. Behind them, Keith Richard, Mick's best man and the only one of the Rolling Stones to be invited to the ceremony, was having an audible argument with Anita Pallenberg (Marlon cried throughout the ritual). Keith and Anita had gone to considerable lengths to attempt to intercept Spanish Tony's gift before it arrived with its intended recipient.

By the time of the wedding, only just over a month after moving to France, Keith was already starting to tire of his new Gallic existence, and for this he blamed the socialite lifestyle that Mick and Bianca allegedly craved. As though responding to the spirit of this fractious event French radicals, no doubt still fired by the student riots of May '68, kicked in the side of Mick's Bentley as the newly married couple left the town hall.

For the church ceremony to which they then fled, Mick and Bianca were obliged to pound on the door of the building to be admitted, as autograph-seekers swarmed about them. At Bianca's request, and to Mick's embarrassment, the theme from the movie *Love Story* played in the small church. When his bride was led down the aisle by Lord Patrick Lichfield, groovy cousin to Queen Elizabeth II, it was to the visible consternation of Abbé Lucien Baud, astonished that Bianca's rouged nipples were visible in her plunging white St Laurent suit. 'You have told me you believe that youth seeks happiness and a certain ideal and faith. I think you are seeking it too, and I hope it arrives today with your marriage,' he told the couple in his marriage sermon, adding wryly: 'But when you are a personality like Mick Jagger, it is too much to hope for privacy for your marriage.'

The day before the wedding, Mick had telephoned the other members of the group and asked them to the reception. Held in a small rather run-down theatre, part of the prestigious Café des Arts in St Tropez, the party lasted until dawn of 13 May. The groom jammed with Stephen Stills, Doris Troy, P. P. Arnold, Bobby Keys, Nicky Hopkins and Santana's Michael Shrieve and Davis Brown. Still not in the best of tempers, Keith – by now clad in the uniform of a Nazi officer – hurled an ashtray through a window before passing out, thereby stymying Mick's desire for the Stones to perform a brief set. Bianca left early, at about the same time as Joe and Eva Jagger, who had still not found an occasion to present their famous son with his wedding gift. That day Mick and Bianca drove to Cannes, where they boarded a yacht chartered at a cost of £3,000 for their honeymoon, heading for a chateau on the remote Italian island of Micinaggio. The tone of the marriage had been somewhat set for Bianca when Keith ('The Loon') Moon climbed through the window of the bridal suite at the Hotel Byblos. 'My marriage ended on my wedding day,' Bianca said later.

'What more could Mick do for a chick if he digs her?' considered Keith that year. 'I mean, there's nothing more he could do to prove he really digs the chick. Mick always said that marriage is an outdated institution. So his getting married really means that he digs the chick. And that's cool. She's a groovy chick. We all dig her.'

While Mick and Bianca were on honeymoon, Keith relaxed. He was on holiday; although he would often spend half an hour waterskiing, he was also looking after and playing with Marlon in the mornings, with Anita taking over their child after lunch. There were coffee and pastries in cafés in Villefranche Square; walks in the hills with Oakie, Keith's labrador (who would vanish for days at a time, returning covered in blood and mud); 'Simple family pleasures,' remembered Anita. Keith, who in one part of himself had never lost a child's innocent view of the world, was known for how good he was with children. He had quickly ordered in a selection of records from a shop in St Tropez: Gene Vincent, Jerry Lee Lewis, Eddie Cochran, Fats Domino, Little Richard and the Shirelles, which played nonstop. When Dominique Tarle, a young French photographer staying at the house, produced a copy of Van Morrison's *Astral Weeks*, widely hailed as a modern masterpiece, Keith flew it like a frisbee into the swimming pool. He simply laughed scornfully on the occasion when, forgetting where he was, the American writer Robert Greenfield put James Taylor's hot new album *Mud Slide Slim* on the deck.

Thirteen days after the wedding, a fight broke out between Keith and the Beaulieu-sur-Mer harbourmaster; he had tried to stop the Stone attacking an Italian tourist following a minor collision with the scarlet soft-top E-type Jaguar with which Keith had replaced his Bentley (he also bought a 1950s Citroën, a restoration project, and a vintage soft-top Pontiac in Villefranche from a rich Arab; one day it broke down and was never seen again). Still in his fantasy Roy Rogers world, his fiery temper sparked by the raging sun, Keith pulled a toy pistol belonging to Marlon on the harbourmaster and was nearly shot dead by the official's real gun. The police were summoned, obliging Keith to ditch his stash of smack immediately before being charged with assault; he then continued on to his destination, the Cannes Film Festival, where *Gimme Shelter* was being shown. (When the case finally came to court, Keith pleaded self-defence and the charges were dropped.) Already Keith was covering up his boredom with regular large scores of heroin, bought direct from the Marseilles French Connection underworld. Now, for the first time, he and Anita had started mainlining.

Using the mobile studio set up at Keith's house, the group began sessions at the beginning of June in the basement of Nellcôte, in what became known as Keith's Coffee House, for the album that would become *Exile on Main Street*; for now, it had the working title of *Tropical Disease*. The location came about largely because the other group members appreciated that they would never get Keith out of the house to the other properties they had viewed as potential studios. The fact that the basement was said to have been used as a place of 'interrogation' by the Gestapo, who had requisitioned the house during the Second World War, only added to the mythology of the music being created there: the heating vents in the floors were adorned with Nazi swastikas. In fact, there were three levels to the basement, each with half a dozen rooms – one, the original kitchen, had been turned into a washroom, and 'Sweet Virginia' and 'Sweet Black Angel' were recorded there as the washing-up was being done.

Stifling hot in the bowels of the house, the group would record stripped to their waists; Bobby Keys and Jim Gordon were often stuck away down desperately humid corridors, the better to get the requisite horn sound. Although upstairs lay an especially surreal simulacrum of nirvana, the assorted players often felt – perhaps understandably, considering the property's past – that they were recording in a prison cell. Everything was played at ear-shredding volume: 'You could hear the music on the other side of the bay,' said Anita. Although recording officially started at six p.m., it would not really get under way until somewhere between eleven in the evening and four in the morning, depending on Keith's arrival from his bedroom. Fearful that the heavy power demands of the Stones' mobile studio would cause havoc with Nellcôte's ancient electrical wiring system, the road crew ran a cable down to the nearby train track and stole electricity from the French national rail company's circuit.

It was a very difficult time to be around the Stones because everyone was dabbling in hard drugs; Keith and Anita, Jimmy Miller, Bobby Keys and Gram Parsons, who arrived early in July. Through a combination of musical interests and geographical location, Keith's best friend in the Stones became Mick Taylor ('Keith did his best to make Mick comfortable,' said Dominique Tarle), with inevitable consequences for a young and impressionable man anxious to stake his claim in the group: soon he was dabbling with powders.

Even Mick Jagger – who Taylor was disturbed to find was coming on to Rose, his wife – was not immune to the pervading narcotic atmosphere, snorting the occasional line of heroin, which he and Keith would refer to, with coy pseudo-hipness, as 'horse'. Unlike Keith, however, Mick was always in control of his drug intake, able to take it or leave it. Bill Wyman, previously immune to the attractions of illegal stimulants, went through a period of considerable consumption of marijuana. Only Charlie Watts restricted himself to the produce of the area's vineyards.

In July Mick invited Marsha Hunt to the South of France, on the condition that she bring Karis with her. When they were picked up at Nice airport by Mick's driver, Alan Dunn, he told her they would be staying at Mick Taylor's house in Grasse. That evening Dunn took Marsha and Karis over to Mick and Bianca's home. At dinner the newly married couple spoke to each other in French, billing and cooing, almost ignoring Marsha and the baby. The following day, Marsha again went over to Mick's house, when he spent an hour on his own with Karis. At the end of the visit Marsha borrowed £200 from him, and noticed that he hadn't looked her in the eyes during the entire visit.

The prevailing druggy atmosphere of what Bianca described as the 'Nazi state' of the Stones in exile meant that these were not desirable surroundings in which to be pregnant. 'Being a Rolling Stone's wife wasn't her favourite occupation. She was much more comfortable being out of the way. So that situation was difficult for Mick – a bit demanding,' said one visitor Georgia Bergman. This did not seem overly to concern Anita, who also became pregnant during the late summer, and continued to inject herself with heroin three times a day. In view of the way in which Anita would publicly berate Keith for constantly being too out of it to have sex with her – which didn't seem to faze Keith in the least – it seemed almost a miracle that she should be expecting a child at all. During one such argument, Keith accidentally stepped on his guitar, which seemed far more of a cause for concern for him than the increasingly hapless state of his relationship. On another occasion, both having nodded out on their bed, they awoke to find it on fire. ('Nazi vibes,' decided Keith, also his assess- ment of the fire accidentally started in the basement kitchen by Fat Jack, the cook, who existed on the fringe of a local gang of ne'er-do-wells known as the Cowboys, who gradually installed themselves at Nellcôte, taking on liaison duties with Marseilles heroin dealers.)

No doubt following the desire of many junkies to turn all those around them onto a heroin habit, thereby justifying their own addiction, Anita would try to persuade visitors to shoot up – much to the anger of Keith, who personally intervened to save Stash Klossowski, who stayed for most of the summer, from such a fate: 'I don't want him to do it.' ('Although he himself was on it at the time,' said Stash, 'he saved me because I would have been very vulnerable to it. I credit him absolutely with saving my life because I had a moment of depression over an affair with a bad girl. Poor thing, it wasn't really her fault.') Anita's behaviour troubled Keith, reflecting as it did an amplified and exaggerated version of his own vivacious and exciting mother. He would think of his father – the tenth anniversary of the last time he spoke to him was coming up. He'd often wondered exactly why his father had left his mother. As things became clearer, the mystery grew darker, and he'd bang up another armful of smack. Then, after the ritual of nodding out, he'd go down to the studio and work on the album, work really hard, as his father had done.

At Nellcote, the relationship between Keith and Anita began to fall apart. Aware that Mick's marriage to her had resulted in considerable tensions between himself and Keith, Bianca moved back to Paris to await the birth of her child, which was officially announced at the end of July. Although Keith seemed to believe that it was perfectly acceptable to absent himself from recording for several hours at a time to put Marlon to bed, he would lapse into apoplexy over Mick's weekend plane flights to Paris to visit his pregnant wife. Every time the group would get onto a creative roll, he felt, Mick seemed to disappear suddenly for several days. 'Mick spent most of the time on *Exile* away because Bianca was pregnant . . . you know, royalty is having a baby,' he explained to Barbara Charone. (Mick was also busy shopping for a property, settling on a castle, the Château du Roi, near Grasse.)

Apart from occasionally stumbling down to Nellcôte's private beach clutching his beloved Marlon to paddle in the warm ocean, Keith rarely left the house. Why should he? It was like permanent party-time there, often with thirty or so guests for dinner, endless bottles of Blanc de Blancs wine; exquisite platters of shrimp and lobster would be placed on the table – and Keith would suddenly demand bacon and eggs. He ran up a weekly bill of £6,000 for food, alcohol and drugs during the time the Stones lived in the South of France; some of the costs were recovered from the £250 a week he would charge the rest of the Stones for staying there while they worked on the new album.

Keith's endless procession of visitors, including Eric Clapton, who only wanted to watch football on television, stayed for free, however; as did Gram Parsons and his wife Gretchen who stayed at Nellcôte for three months, acting as a musical sounding-board for Keith who sometimes admitted to feeling stifled by the enclosed musical world of his group. ('Vy is it no one ever says goodbye?' wondered Anita, puzzled.) Donald Cammell stayed for a fortnight, working on a screenplay revision of *The Beard*; Michael Cooper turned up for a couple of days, openly taking nips from a bottle of green methadone he carried everywhere with him, the last time Keith saw him; rabbits would be found wandering among the guitars in the living room. One afternoon John Lennon arrived, fresh from visiting an art exhibition in Nice with Yoko Ono; he went up to Keith's bedroom with him, stayed for forty-five minutes and threw up on the carpet as he left the house.

From time to time they would set sail from Nellcôte's private jetty, skimming across the sparkling azure water on *Mandrax*, the motorboat Keith had bought and drove like a racing car, and which on several occasions had to be towed back to the private beach after running out of fuel. Keith would take it for a spin around the ships in the naval basin in Marseilles, intent on discovering whether any sailors had drugs to sell. On 31 July, however, taking advantage of the ninety days he was allowed to spend in his native country every year, Keith returned to London with Anita to attend the première of *Gimme Shelter*, which was received with considerable acclaim.

On 21 October 1971 at the Rue de Belvedere Nursing Home in Paris, Bianca gave birth to a daughter, who was named Jade ('because she's very precious and quite, quite perfect', said her doting father) Sheena Jezebel. Mick was knocked out with his child. He promptly declared to Keith that he would not be returning to the South of France for the following month. A halt was called to recording. With the house almost empty of musicians and hangers-on, Nellcôte was burgled: as well as furniture and objets d'art, eleven of Keith's treasured guitars were stolen, never to be recovered. Keith cried at the loss, believed to have been instigated by the Cowboys. His state of mind was not improved by the knowledge that he had just had to eject Gram Parsons from Nellcôte after he had become utterly dependent on heroin. This was the end of Parsons' membership of the Stones' inner circle, which plunged him into deep depression.

Suddenly the vibes were bad: at Nellcôte the daughter of the chef had started shooting up smack, under the influence of Anita. When the chef found out, he demanded damages of £30,000, otherwise he would go to the police. The very next day, however, the local police arrived at the property. Certain known unsavoury Corsicans had been observed entering the residence, they said. All of the Rolling Stones were now under suspicion of serious drug abuse. Their idyll was shattered.

Contrary to Keith's suspicions – and in fact as he well knew – the time spent by Mick in Paris had not all been part of some indolent jet-set existence. That would have been out of character for the industrious Mick Jagger. As part of his role running the Rolling Stones, he had been having lengthy talks about touring the United States during 1972. At first he had resisted the obvious route of playing similar arena-sized venues to the

1969 tour. At meetings with John Morris, an American promoter who had been involved with Woodstock, he expressed a desire to play venues like the Rainbow theatre in north London, which Morris had recently opened: 'I'd much rather play a three-thousand-seat house on the next American tour than a ten or twenty thousand-seater. Places like the Forum or the Garden are really too big to get something cooking between the band and the audience.'

After hours of discussion, no conclusions were arrived at. The fact was, in the mind of Mick Jagger such vast amphitheatres were indelibly linked with the grim spectre of Altamont, something to be avoided at all costs. However, the prospect of an American tour, along with further recording work in Los Angeles on the twenty songs so far recorded at Nellcôte, gave Keith and Anita the excuse they needed to leave France, and they duly departed at the end of November. But first they had to strike a deal with the French police: that they would continue to pay the rent of £1,000 pounds a week for Nellcôte, as though it was their permanent residence.

On 30 November, Keith and Anita took a flight to Nashville, where Keith intended to replace his stolen guitars; this marked the end of their French sojourn, one that had lasted a little less than eight months. On the same day Mick, Bianca and Jade flew directly to Los Angeles. Even this trip was not without its measure of controversy: when Mick was asked by a Pan Am steward to change to his designated first-class seat, he refused and allegedly swore at the flight attendant. 'I asked him not to use bad language. Then I turned around and started to walk away. He came up behind me and grabbed me by the arm and swung me roughly around,' said Pauline Lough. 'I'd like to give her a good slap in the face because she deserves it,' was the somewhat Neanderthal response from Mick, a man on whom the newly prevailing mood of feminism clearly had made little or no impression, as he denied Lough's accusation.

On 14 December, armed with a warrant, French police entered and tore apart Nellcôte, turning up large quantities of heroin, cocaine and cannabis: they had arrested a Marseilles heroin ring that led them directly to Keith. The French judiciary system awaited the return of Keith Richard to send him to prison.

Yet the drugs had indeed had the effect for Keith of 'getting the job done'. Anaesthetised to outside influences, rolling out of bed and straight into the studio, the communal existence of Nellcôte had inspired him to harness his creative powers in an untrammelled manner that he would never recover. The raw, punky power and sensitive balance of the record that would be called *Exile on Main Street* was so pure that it would rightly be applauded as a masterpiece.

By 4 December all the Rolling Stones were in Los Angeles, working on their new album at Sunset Sound studio. With a customary surly dismissal, Mick was eventually quite contemptuous of the time spent in the South of France: 'I didn't enjoy it at all, fucking drag it was. Everyone else liked it. But it was too hot.' Contrary to their fears when they had left France, the eighteen recorded songs really seemed to work. And the group continued to add to them: Mac 'Dr John' Rebennack was brought in with his Creole percussionists and four female singers – Tammi Lynn, Clydie King, Vanetta Lee and Shirley Goodman – to add vocal texture. In the inevitable all-night sessions, the group honed and tightened the tracks until they flowed like a line of uncut Peruvian flake.

Now that his child had been born, Mick's focus was undiluted; if only to himself, Keith had to acknowledge the work his long-standing songwriting partner had been doing, not only on the songs for the new record, but also on securing the future of the group through the impending tour. Mick busied himself setting up the pre-publicity for the coming US shows, taking on the public relations firm of Gibson and Stromberg, the most celebrated music publicists in the United States; he hired film-maker Robert Franks, a veteran of the Beat era, to shoot a further documentary of the Stones on the road. Mick and Bianca were looking for a house in southern California – almost inevitably, for such obviously prestigious settings mattered to Mick – in Beverly Hills. They found a suitable residence, the former mansion of Marion Davies, one-time mistress of Randolph Hearst, a house with a swimming pool enormous even by LA standards, a boon for Mick's love of swimming. Mick announced that he intended to remain in LA until the US tour began the following spring.

Suddenly he had become a dutiful father and husband, spending almost all his time with his new family when not working. Finally, it seemed, he had achieved the state he had so eagerly sought, first with Chrissie Shrimpton, then with Marianne Faithfull. There was some gossip, however, concerning Bianca's prima donna-like attitudes and an alleged fiery temper; as Michael Caine had warned, Mick's wife did like a good argument – all the time, it seemed.

There was even once again a sense of camaraderie about the Rolling Stones. On 20 December the whole group went to watch B. B. King play in Las Vegas. Eight days later Mick went to a party at which the Who were presented with a gold album for their *Who's Next* LP. At the end of January 1972, Mick, Keith and Mac 'Dr John' Rebennack joined Chuck Berry on-stage at the Hollywood Palladium, Keith plugging in and playing along on 'Sweet Little Sixteen'. Although the audience went crazy at this unexpected treat, the legendarily eccentric Berry, prime inspiration to Keith Richard, kicked them off-stage when the song had finished, complaining variously that Keith was playing too loud, or that he had no idea as to the identity of his on-stage visitors.

Keith may well have been playing too loud. His heroin addiction had taken utter control of him, and he was unable to attend the final sessions for the new album. Mick had Keith and Anita put on a plane to Montreux in Switzerland, where he entered a detoxification clinic. Keith was addicted not only to heroin, but also to cocaine and alcohol. 'He's always been incredibly honest,' said Bill Wyman in his autobiography, 'and admits now that he screwed the band up for that period and beyond; it became extremely difficult to tour because of his and Mick's drug convictions. In March 1972 Keith was in such bad condition . . . in Los Angeles that he had to be flown to Switzerland to undergo a drug cure at a clinic. And the pressure on him from the police was relentless.'

On 14 April 'Tumbling Dice', backed with 'Sweet Black Angel', was released, the first single off the new album, an amyl nitrate blast. Three days later, on 17 April, Anita gave birth in Geneva to Keith's first daughter, Dandelion, also known as Belle Starr; the baby was born with a cleft palate, and there was speculation that this was a consequence of Anita's having continued to abuse her body with drugs during the pregnancy. In his worry Keith couldn't help but muse stonedly on the possible connection between the birth defect of his newborn daughter and Anita's drug usage throughout the gestation period, something that had driven him crazy. Then he'd make the link between Anita's heroin consumption and his own during the months before she gave birth: how could she have stopped, if their home was full of his works? Even though he knew that her internal defences against addiction were almost non-existent, the self-loathing was still intense. And so he'd do some more smack to even himself out.

On 24 April Mick joined the rest of the group in London, their year of tax exile now over. Three weeks later he was back in LA, lunching with Rudolph Nureyev at Sardi's, and joining John Lennon and Yoko Ono recording at the Record Plant. By 17 May, all the Rolling Stones had moved to rehearse in Montreux, where Keith had temporarily taken up residence. Six days later, on 23 May, the entire group went personally to the US Embassy in Grosvenor Square, London – in front of which Mick had demonstrated against the Vietnam War just over four years previously – to pick up their work permits for the American tour. Three days later *Exile on Main Street* was released, with a cover designed by Robert Frank. The record was a number-one hit on both sides of the Atlantic.

Those who closely scrutinised the small print of the credits on *Exile* could detect a significant development. Mick Jagger's co-songwriter was credited as Keith Richard until the final track, track 18, 'Soul Survivor', where he suddenly became Keith Richard*s*. Was Keith going back to being who he really was? Whatever: it was around now that he was once again to be known as Keith Richards. Some people thought Keith Richard sounded better, punkier.

In the United States, which has always worshipped celebrity, the aura of reverence around the Rolling Stones ('the *Stones*, man . . .') was end-lessly self-perpetuating. The myth of the group was taking a quantum leap. Gibson and Stromberg's press campaign involved a blitz on the most prestigious magazines, publications that, with the exception of *Rolling Stone*, ordinarily did not cover popular music. By getting the Stones onto the covers of *Time*, *Newsweek*, *Life* and *Esquire*, with pieces written by 'serious' writers (in other words, ones who did not know anything about rock 'n' roll, which showed in their resulting articles), they ensured that the group was now being thought of as a social phenomenon, an inescapable cultural current.

Almost predictably, the paper that fell for this angle hook, line and sinker was the one whose base audience *were* music fans. *Rolling Stone*, anxious to associate itself with this upgrading of rock from 'underground' to mainstream, sent out on the tour Truman Capote, the author whose faction novel *In Cold Blood* allegedly made him one of the originators of the then currently fashionable style of New Journalism, of which *Rolling Stone* was considered to be in the vanguard. In so employing Capote, *Stone* was committing a terrible act of treachery, for its own writer Robert Greenfield was thereby demoted from his commission to cover the group. In a satisfying act of karmic retribution, Capote never filed a word of copy, and Greenfield's book *A Journey through America with the Rolling Stones*, was considered a classic of early rock writing. Accompanying the wizened, elf-like figure of Capote was Princess Lee Radziwill ('Princess Radish', as Keith would address her), the sister of Jackie Onassis: hence the Rolling Stones were also guaranteed space on the society pages of the world's most influential publications. Jimmy Page, the leader of Led Zeppelin, who were also touring America at the same time, playing to far larger audiences and selling many more records than the Stones, was extremely miffed.

The group rehearsed on a soundstage at Warner Brothers in Burbank in the San Fernando Valley. Then, on 3 June, the Rolling Stones' seventh North American tour opened at Vancouver's Pacific Coliseum. The group were excited: Mick and Keith were observed running hand in hand, almost skipping along, from their private plane, like excited Dartford schoolboys rushing into the sea at Margate on an English bank holiday – except that they were running towards the limousines that would haul them into Vancouver after Keith had fuelled his nose sufficiently for the short journey. Mick was trying to put to the back of his mind the knowledge that only a few days previously an attempted assassination on George Wallace, the firebrand racist governor of Alabama, had paralysed the poll-sweeping presidential candidate; and that the Hell's Angels were supposedly demanding retribution for the débâcle of Altamont. For the entire tour, Mick and Keith each packed .38 revolvers, something they both thoroughly enjoyed. On-stage at the second date in Seattle, Mick preceded the performance of 'Sweet Black Angel', a new song from *Exile on Main Street*, with the announcement that the song's subject, the black militant Angela Davis, had been found not guilty of the murder charges she was facing ('Who got free today? Angela Davis got free today. Fuckin' great . . .'). No one in the audience seemed to know who he was talking about.

Later, Mick complained, concerned about the seemingly erased consciousness of the group's American audience. Was this an effect of the currently fashionable drug, the quaalude, a downer whose hypnotic effect was amplified to a brain-cell-shredding degree when washed down with several gallons of cheap, chemically enhanced wine? Whereas once the youth of America had smoked pot and questioned the state, now they seemed only to want to obliterate themselves into an unquestioning state of mind. (On the other hand, marijuana was now legal in Michigan.) So was Keith's perpetually chemically enhanced existence only a reflection of the collective mood? Was he simply, in his role of cultural archetype, merely the personification of a spirit of existential despair? Whatever he was, the antique black-leather doctor's bag that Keith carried with him everywhere contained every possible pharmaceutical aid he might require to maintain such an outsider mood. To ensure he attracted no attention that might arouse the suspicions of law-enforcement officers, Keith now wore a vivid, beautiful turquoise necklace, and – like every hip King's Road groover – a flash of golden dye down the left side of his hair.

After Seattle, the San Francisco shows at Winterland, on 6 and 8 June, passed without any contact with the Hell's Angels. As the group seated themselves on their plane for the flight to Los Angeles, however, a hot-panted beauty was permitted up the steps to collect an autograph 'for my daughter'. Moving directly to Mick, she asked sweetly, 'Are you Mick Jagger?' and attempted to serve him with several subpoenas related to Altamont. A furious Keith responded the only way he knew how in such an emergency: the woman was summarily ejected from the plane, and her legal papers hurled into the wind. 'He hit me, he hit me,' the woman screamed as she slid down the steps to the tarmac.

In Keith's room there was a permanent party. The party continued on buses, on the plane, in motor vehicles rented to provide sightseeing relief from the ennui of the group's travel arrangements. After a canter through the south-west, the tour hit Chicago on 19 June. Here Keith encountered an even more dedicated thrower of parties: Hugh Hefner, owner and inspiration of the *Playboy* empire. For three days the Stones stayed at the Playboy mansion and a Nero-style orgy took place – Mick displayed a not especially rigorous commitment to his marriage vows; Keith, meanwhile, found more affection in his doctor's bag.

Ironically, the only threats to the Rolling Stones came not in the pistol-packing United States of America, but in the more European-feeling country of Canada. To draw attention to their cause, French Canadian separatists blew up the Stones' equipment truck outside the Forum in Montreal when it arrived for their 17 July concert. During the show, Mick Jagger was struck by a lobbed bottle. When fog forced the group's plane, en route to Boston, to land in Warwick, Rhode Island the following day, a pair of local photographers seized their picture opportunity. Two members of the group's party pushed them away. As a consequence, Keith Richards was charged by the police with assault, and Mick Jagger, Marshall Chess, and film-maker Robert Frank were charged with obstructing a police officer. The Boston Garden show began two hours late: Stevie Wonder, the support act throughout the tour, tried to fill in with a long set – after Boston mayor Kevin White arranged the quartet's speedy release from police custody. After the second Boston show, the following day, T-Bone Walker had a meeting with Mick, Keith and Marshall Chess to discuss his signing to Rolling Stone Records. He didn't sign.

On 24 July, the Stones hit New York; on the plane in from Philadelphia, members of the road crew staged a gang-bang for the benefit of Robert Frank's camera: a girl was eaten out to the orgasmic clapping of Mick, Keith and Bill, who had sent his son up to the front of the plane. There were to be four shows in Manhattan at Madison Square Garden – one that day, two shows on the twenty-fifth, and one on 26 July, Mick's twenty-ninth birthday. During the concert he was given a cake and a giant panda. At the end of the show he pushed custard pies into the faces of members of the group. Afterwards there was a party thrown by Ahmet Ertegun, boss of Atlantic, at the swanky, old money St Regis hotel on 55th Street. Party music was provided by Muddy Waters, from whose song 'Rolling Stone Blues' the group had taken their name, and Count Basie; among the guests were Bob Dylan ('It's encompassing ... it's the beginning of cosmic consciousness', was his opinion of the event to the *New York Times*), Carly Simon, Andy Warhol, Truman Capote, Princess Lee Radziwill, Dick Cavett and countless others. Inevitably, a stripper emerged from a fake birthday cake.

By now, at the end of the tour, Keith was falling apart. He feared that the excesses of making *Exile on Main Street* had drained the last drops of creativity from him. But his almost suicidal dysfunction was being turned into a virtue by the media. Impressionable young music writers read his internal struggle instead as the essence of outlaw rebellion, the quintessence of the rock 'n' roll spirit; Mr Rock 'n' Roll and the Human Riff were just two of the adoring sobriquets garlanded about the World's Most Elegantly Wasted Human Being, as the *NME* began to call him. To a generation of rock 'n' roll fans he became, simply, 'Keef'. If people thought it was so great, and they'd come and cheer you even more when they could tell you were visibly out of it, you might as well shoot up some more smack, open another bottle of Jack Daniel's, smoke another ten cigarettes at once, haul down a couple more lungfuls of hash smoke and hoover up some more Charlie. And Keith would.

For his part, Mick appeared to have a far more circumspect view of life. On 5 August he declared, 'When I'm thirty-three, I'll quit. That's the time when a man has to do something else. I can't say what it will definitely be. It's still in the back of my head, but it won't be in show-business. I don't want to be a rock star all my life. I couldn't bear to end up like Elvis Presley and sing in Las Vegas with all those housewives and old ladies coming in with their handbags. It's really sick.'

CHAPTER 20

IRIE

On 9 August Keith, Anita and the two children moved to a relatively modest house in Montreux in Switzerland, a country that could seem to have been specifically created to cater to the whims of rich tax exiles. Would this not also be a fitting home for a rock 'n' roll aristocrat? Soon every dealer in the country was heading for it, and hanging out for days as they scarfed up what they had just sold Keith.

As he had done in the South of France, Keith sequestered himself away in his new home, trying to write music. It was not easy. Not only had *Exile on Main Street* drained him creatively, but the subsequent US tour had wiped him out physically. His artistic lull was reflected in what he saw around him: Keith felt little empathy with contemporary music, abhorring the glam-rock that David Bowie, Roxy Music and lesser mortals were successfully peddling in the charts. The fact that glam had merely locked into one of the currents within the Rolling Stones passed him by: even before Mick Jagger had first unveiled an exaggeration of his already marketable androgyny by wearing that shirt-dress at the Hyde Park show, Keith had been outlining his eyes with kohl. The shamanic flaunting of the feminine sides of Mick and Keith's personae – the jewellery, the hair highlights, the soft velvety fabrics – in their stage shows was partially responsible for the allure of the Rolling Stones as the Greatest Rock 'n' Roll Group in the World.

But Keith did find some music on which he really got off. Although ska had been a favourite of British Mods in the mid-1960s, Jamaican music in the latter part of that decade had become, paradoxically, the property of racist skinheads, a tribal subdivision that evolved from one Mod strand. *The Harder They Come*, a film set in Jamaica directed by Perry Henzell, began to change that when it was released in the summer of 1972. Shot with the pace and themes of one of the spaghetti westerns adored by Jamaicans, the film was edited with a nod towards early Godard. Henzell cast Jimmy Cliff, a charismatic Jamaican singer who had enjoyed a number of British hits, as the lead character Ivan Rhygin, a Robin Hood of the ghetto who had come to a tragic end in a shoot-out with police in 1948. Adding an extra element to the Rhygin story by turning the gunman into a ghetto youth desperate to 'mek a try' in the cut-throat Kingston music business, Henzell had created a rough-hewn classic that became a staple of late-night cinema, then in vogue.

Part of the film's attraction was that *The Harder They Come* had one of the best soundtrack albums ever released. As a primer for anyone wanting to find out about new music, it was invaluable. As well as Jimmy Cliff's great title song, it contained four more songs by him, all exquisitely poetic yet totally streetwise. There was the rougher sound of the Maytals, and Scotty; and really great tunes from the Melodians and the Slickers. It was an eye-opener for Keith: he thought it was fantastic, he really felt it. He started looking for more Jamaican music, quickly finding the Maytals' fabulous *Funky Kingston* set and the Upsetters' *Double Seven* LP, an introduction to the work of Lee Perry, Jamaica's Picasso of production. As soon as the first snows hit Switzerland, Keith began to rebuild his depleted physical condition by taking up skiing. By now he had a copy of the film *The Harder They Come*; ignoring the various crashed-out bodies around him, Keith would gaze in his habitual stoned state at the lush scenery in the movie and the gated and guarded studios and the piles of ganja: he couldn't help thinking that it seemed a groovier option than beautiful but chilly Switzerland.

On 25 November the Rolling Stones arrived in Kingston, Jamaica. They had booked four weeks at Dynamic Sound, where Jimmy Cliff's sumptuous 'Wonderful World, Beautiful People' record had been made. On Oxford Road in uptown Kingston the Stones checked into the Terra Nova hotel, a building that had formerly been the family home of Chris Blackwell, whose Island Records had released the soundtrack of *The Harder They Come*. The modern Wild West of Jamaica, with its gunmen, tub-thumping spirituality, swirl of action and quiet throb of absolute peace perfectly fitted Keith Richards. He instinctively felt an affinity with the roots-and-culture Rastas he met who seemed to understand something ... *different*. He had sensed that he was at home on the island, with its extremely agreeable pace of life, as soon as he had stepped off the plane; it was comfortable being a pirate once again. Keith loved the island's music and the way it was recorded, in that anarchic manner so characteristic of Jamaica, a land where rules exist only to be broken. 'They realise that the mixing desk is just another instrument, and play it like that,' he said with relish. The Wailers had just released *Catch A Fire*, the other-wordly statement of intent that was their first album on Island Records, and Keith had met up with

Bob Marley, Peter Tosh and Bunny Livingston, the three members of the group, smoking 'herb' with them and 'reasoning'. His own natural rhythm coalesced with that of the island and its music.

However, it wasn't always absolute peace at the Terra Nova. There were the same old hassles: after more of the usual friction between Bianca and Anita, Keith immediately rented and moved into a bungalow overlooking Cutlass Bay in the north-coast resort of Ocho Rios, a hair-raising two-hour drive across the mountains from Kingston. With a twisted appropriateness, the property was owned by the early British rock 'n' roller Tommy Steele, whose story had been fictionalised in *Expresso Bongo*, so inspirational to Andrew Loog Oldham. As the whitecaps sparkled in the bay below, 'John Crow' vultures floated in the air, eddying on the breeze, and local dreads fired up chalices on the terrace, Anita announced that she wanted to spend the rest of her life there. Keith thought it didn't seem a bad idea either. After a group finances meeting in Jamaica, Mick and Keith discovered they were each making about a million pounds a year: they had individually earned around £150,000 from the last US tour. (Due to their songwriting earnings, the two of them picked up about nineteen pence an album, as opposed to the rest of the group's four pence.) Although theoretically Keith was rich, he spent money as though the floodgates were permanently open: over the previous five years enormous amounts had been blown on drugs and legal fees. All the same, the day after the financial meeting Keith bought Tommy Steele's Jamaican house for £75,000 in cash.

The photographer Adrian Boot was then living in Port Antonio, sixty miles away from Kingston in the north-east corner of the island. He received a call from Atlantic Records in New York, who had been turned on to him by the writer Robert Greenfield; they were looking for a photographer to take stills pictures of the sessions. 'So I arrived at the Terra Nova around ten in the morning and then sat around all day, waiting for something to happen. They'd stroll out one by one towards lunchtime. They all seemed to be enjoying Jamaica – it was all very exotic and very cool. Jagger already had that attitude towards everyone which is very charming and professional, which makes you feel at ease. Billy Preston was there. Keith didn't seem to be in the studio much. There was no entourage. They travelled around in beat-up local taxis and ate ackee and saltfish and drank coconut water and adapted very well. I was a bit disappointed because I thought it would be Jagger surrounded by managers, groupies and mirrors. But it was all quite work-a-day.'

It was also good for the Rolling Stones to be out of Europe. On 2 December 1972 warrants were issued in France against Keith and Anita for drug offences, including using their house for dealing heroin; the rest of the group were to be prosecuted for the lesser charge of using drugs.

All the Stones, except for Keith, flew back to Nice for a court case on 4 December: they had been charged with the use of heroin and hashish at Keith's house. However, in court assorted witnesses confessed they had been forced by the police to sign false statements. The four Stones were freed, and headed back to Jamaica. Keith decided to stay away from France. Five days later Carly Simon released 'You're So Vain', a clever paean to narcissism allegedly inspired by Mick Jagger, who sang backing vocals on the song by the woman who had briefly become his lover; Warren Beatty was also suggested as being the subject of the song. The guessing-game as to who the lyrics were about brought 'You're So Vain' huge publicity, and it was deservedly a big international hit.

Dynamic Sound was owned by Byron Lee, a record producer who was also leader of the Dragonaires, a roadshow group whose music was a compilation of Jamaican influences. Curiously, *Goat's Head Soup*, the album that resulted from the Dynamic sessions, seemed utterly oblivious to the music being made all around it in Jamaica. There is not a hint of reggae rhythms on the album. 'Winter' was the first song recorded on the island. In the first month there, the group also taped 'Angie', 'Star Star', and 'Coming Down Again' as well as 'Waiting On a Friend', which finally appeared on the *Tattoo You* album in 1981. (There was some speculation about the subject of 'Angie', the first shot fired in Mick Jagger's astute drive to turn the Rolling Stones into a ballad hits group; initially the song was said to be about Angie Bowie, the wife of Mick's new close friend David Bowie. Bebe Buell, an American model with whom Mick was to have an affair, claimed the song was not about Angie but about David Bowie himself, with whom Mick also had a relationship; and there are those who insist the song was actually Keith's love song to Anita Pallenberg.)

Goat's Head Soup was to be the last Stones album produced by Jimmy Miller, who had become addicted to the lifestyle and drugs of his employers. 'Jimmy went in a lion and came out a lamb,' Keith later told *Crawdaddy* magazine, of just another of the trail of casualties the Rolling Stones was leaving in its wake. Also by now addicted to heroin was another member of the record production crew, Andy Johns the engineer, brother of Glyn Johns. The Jamaican sessions were truncated when Johns learned that his father was dying of cancer. 'Mick put his arms around me and he says, "We'll just stop now, you go home and see your dad".' The group returned to Jamaica for further sessions in February.

Seemingly oblivious to the idea that it might be best to cool it and keep a low profile in a land she didn't entirely understand, Anita Pallenberg continued to flaunt herself in Jamaica, wandering around half naked, sprawling over pretty dreads, her arms flung about them. In a deeply macho country like Jamaica, this was not a good idea; such behaviour seriously contravened the unwritten codes of the island and did no good for Keith's status around 'Ochie', which he sensed. He really loved Anita still, and had hoped that this new, idyllic location would help heal their relationship. But both parties would have had to enter into an unconscious pact over any such fresh start, and, as ever, Anita was making it difficult. Keith flew back to London, hurt and feeling degraded as ever, leaving her in Ochos Rios to her fun. It was more smack for Keith.

While in Jamaica Mick had been vaguely troubled by a communication he received from an occultist in California; the letter explained how the names of those who had succumbed in a recent wave of rock-stars deaths all contained the letters I and J: Brian Jones, Janis Joplin, Jimi Hendrix and Jim Morrison. The occultist came to the conclusion that Mick Jagger might well be next. Mick had also been studying the work of Carl Jung, feeling a resonance from the great writer's theories of archetypes and the collective unconscious; couldn't this warning he had received accord well with Jung's views of synchronicity and synergy? Standing by the pool of the Terra Nova, spliff in hand, gazing at Keith and Marlon splashing in the water, a *frisson* of fear ran through Mick; his edginess, of course, was hardly ameliorated by the powerful Jamaican ganja's ability to unleash waves of paranoia. In fact, there was no life-threatening experience for the Jagger family while he, Bianca and Jade were in Jamaica.

But as soon as the Jaggers returned to London, Bianca's mother almost became a victim. On 23 December 1972, an earthquake devastated Managua, the shabby, sprawling capital of Nicaragua, Bianca's home. Over six thousand people perished in the tremors. At first it was feared Bianca's mother was one of the victims; Mick and Bianca chartered a plane and flew down to Nicaragua with medical supplies, including all the anti-typhoid serum Mick could purchase. In the Central American country Mick was briefly a normal, ordinary person – no one knew who he was. At one point Mick and Bianca were even reported missing in Managua. Mick was also afforded hitherto unrecognised glimpses of the genuinely caring individual into whom the fiery Bianca was growing. On 18 January 1973, the Stones played a charity show at the Forum in Los Angeles for victims of the Nicaraguan earthquake, raising £250,000, breaking George Harrison's 1971 concert for Bangladesh record as the highest-grossing charity rock concert. Pragmatically, Mick himself had suggested the location for the concert, knowing this could do the group nothing but good with the US authorities with regard to their visa status.

The Forum date also served as a useful warm-up show, for the Stones then span off to Honolulu, Hong Kong and Australasia for a tour. Mick's 1969 cannabis conviction had caused him to be refused an entry visa to

Japan, leading to the abandonment of several potentially lucrative dates – precisely the reason Brian Jones had been fired from the group. Mick had had his hair cut, until it only just touched the top of his ears. 'I had begun to feel like an old tart with long hair,' he said.

There were always plenty of rumours around Mick and Keith. In Brisbane on 13 February, Mick was asked about one of the latest ones: was it true that Bianca would star in a film directed by her close friend Andy Warhol? 'Andy Warhol?' asked Mick. 'We work well together. When girls get together there's always talk, but they never get anything done.'

The Stones flew from Australia back to Jamaica in late February 1973, for more work on the new record at Dynamic Sound. There Keith discovered that Anita's behaviour with the local Rastas and ragamuffins was causing something of a furore in the selected monied environs in which he had purchased Point of View, as his Ocho Rios residence was named; the upper-class Jamaicans, terrible snobs, like the English had been twenty years previously, advised Keith to keep an eye on her. But he knew his true love was a complete number, and finding that Anita was perpetually surrounded by local dreads and badmen, Keith flew back to London in March, humiliated.

Mick Jagger had enjoyed a more measured relationship with Jamaica. In Kingston he would disappear for days at a time, driving down to Sabina Park to watch cricket matches. During the stint at Dynamic Sound, however, there had been an incident whose ominous portents should perhaps have been heeded, one that showed how Jamaica could be both heaven and hell. One night at the Terra Nova, a local rude boy had broken into Bill Wyman's bedroom; brandishing a machete, he had forced Bill under the bed while he raped Astrid Lundstrom, the bass player's long-term girlfriend.

Unfortunately Anita refused to let such an incident moderate her behaviour. One evening she and half a dozen or so dreads cruised down from Point of View to the beachside Hilton hotel. Anita wanted to go out drinking, and thought for once that the bar of the Hilton presented a more sophisticated option to the funkier local rum bars she had become used to frequenting. She had not reckoned on the antipathy in Jamaica felt by those who have moved a few notches up the social scale, her lack of awareness springing from a combination of dangerous naivety and supreme arrogance. After a suitably unruly and publicly visible argument as Anita was asked to leave her 'boys' outside the hotel, she and her dread friends were kicked out of the Hilton, Anita rebelliously lighting up a spliff in the car park as she left the hotel's grounds.

Anita had not bargained on the wrath of the Establishment on an island where – despite appearances to the contrary – behaviour and mores are based on deeply conservative foundations. The following day the police arrived at Point of View, quickly unearthing a kilo of marijuana, of which Anita always maintained she had no knowledge. While Marlon and Dandelion were left in the care of one of the housemaids, Anita was slung into the grim, dingy lock-up at Ochos Rios police station; for three days she was repeatedly raped and beaten by both prisoners and police. As soon as Keith received a phone call from Jamaica telling him what had happened, he thought of getting on a plane to the island and personally rescuing Anita: when he realised that, as the owner of the property, he might also be charged with possession of the kilo of marijuana, he thought better of this strategy. Employing the services of an upper-crust Jamaican, Keith learned that the charges could be dropped, but this would cost £12,000. He immediately arranged for the bribe to be paid through this Jamaican connection.

Anita was on the next flight back to London from Montego Bay. When Keith and Spanish Tony met her at Heathrow airport, they were horrified: covered in bruises, she looked as though she had been beaten to within an inch of her life. She ran into Keith's arms, 'sobbing like a lost little girl', remembered Spanish Tony.

Now Anita could tell Keith what had really happened. Keith's upper-crust Jamaican friend, she insisted, had been the person behind her incarceration: he had summoned the police, and had taken the lion's share of the £12,000. The man was due to arrive in London within days, and Keith thought of having him killed. Instead, he decided to put the past behind him, and 'Spanish' was despatched to the Dorchester Hotel to pay him off, and that was the end of that. Interestingly, the horrific incident did not put either Keith or Anita off the idea of visiting Jamaica, or staying at Point of View; Keith learned instead whose palms needed to be greased in order to assure him of an arrest-free existence while on the island. But the trauma of the experience only plunged Keith and especially Anita into an even deeper dependency on the anaesthetic powers of heroin. Friends noticed that after Anita's rape in Jamaica, both of them became more mistrustful, withdrawing into smack.

The tensions of life at home had the consequence of making Keith take on an entirely new persona – that of extrovert rock 'n' roll party animal. He rented a yellow Ferrari Dino and started hanging out at Tramp in Jermyn Street, behind Piccadilly Circus. It was an interesting location, as Tramp was really a straight person's idea of a hip club – hardly rock 'n' roll; but it was where the seriously monied and the beautiful could gather in force, like-minded souls secure in each other's company. (Was Keith completely comfortable with his new, racy playboy image? He thought that Mick's philandering was absurd, and saw through it to the insecurities it masked: 'He's got a few problems with women,' he would comment. Keith Richards is really a one-woman man, the faithful partner, in a way that Mick is not. When Keith acted out his tough-guy hipster role, he was trying to be what he thought Anita wanted.)

Money was similarly also all around Mick Jagger at the beginning of 1973. On 2 May a portrait of him painted by Cecil Beaton sold for £220 at Sotheby's in London. A week later he added £150,000 of his own money to the £350,000 raised by the Rolling Stones concert in January in aid of the Nicaraguan earthquake victims. A thoroughly magnanimous gesture inspired by the terrible plight he had seen in Nicaragua, it secured him the friendship and support of a number of eminent US politicians. Such an act of charity, moreover, flew in the face of a prevalent view of Mick as the personification of meanness. On 17 May he was with Bianca at a party at the Ritz for the launch of GM Records, the label started up by Billy Gaff, manager of the Faces; Mick's brother Chris had signed to the label as a solo artist, and Mick went along to lend familial support.

Mick was running frantically around, trying to keep the whole Rolling Stones operation going. He could barely find time to write lyrics. He was supposed to be a poet: it was driving him nuts. He'd get home to 48 Cheyne Walk, wanting some headspace to get on with his writing, and there'd be the family thing to deal with. On top of that, he was as worried to hell about the state Keith was falling into. Only the previous day he'd dropped in at number 3, needing to talk to Keith about a detail of the European tour he was putting together for the autumn; Anita had told him Keith had just gone to the bathroom. After ninety minutes Keith had still failed to appear, and Mick had left and mooched home along rain-splashed Cheyne Walk, deeply troubled. Would the tour ever happen? This might mean the end of the group. What if he could get someone as a sort of stand-in for Keith, someone who looked a bit like him, even thought a bit like him, a sort of junior version?

That night at the GM Records launch, Mick told Honest Ron Wood, the Faces' guitarist, he'd come out to his house in Richmond, only a few hundred yards from where the Stones had got their first break at the Station Hotel, and have a jam with him.

Despite the terrible experience Anita had endured, the influence of Jamaica on Keith lingered – the place had got into his soul. Jamaica is a country where the dividing line between reality and the spaghetti western seems to have become dramatically blurred, and unfortunately this confusion had developed in Keith to a chronic degree: guns and knives had become for him requisite accessories. At Tramp, Keith would play the Jamaican 'don', adopting the cavalier attitude displayed by such individuals towards the opposite sex. One night, while 'Spanish' had disappeared to the bathroom, the Rolling Stone's table was suddenly surrounded by a bunch of smoothly dressed Sicilians, putting the make on Keith's several women friends: it was a serious and deliberate insult, a test reeking of testosterone. Keith's fiery response was to whip out the Jamaican ratchet-knife that accompanied him everywhere, swinging its hinged blade open; crouching down like the Jimmy Cliff character in the knife-fight in *The Harder They Come*, he lashed out at the intruders. Keith was not really the hardman rock 'n' roll outlaw he imagined himself to be: one of the Sicilians kicked him in the balls as another smashed a chair over his head. Once he had recovered, Keith showed he had not really learned from this experience: Spanish Tony was instructed to have the attackers severely beaten. Instead, 'Spanish' paid the Sicilians to keep away from Tramp for a while. 'See? Anyone messes with me, they're dead,' Keith told Ronnie Wood when he remarked in Tramp that the assailants no longer frequented the nightspot.

Rumours were sweeping the music business and the media that Keith was about to leave the Rolling Stones, to be replaced by Wood. Mick denied this to the *NME*: 'The report has no basis in fact whatsoever, it's absolutely untrue.' In fact, Ronnie Wood had become a close friend of Keith's. One night at Tramp Keith had tried to pull Chrissie Wood, his wife: she ended up taking him back to The Wick, her husband's Georgian mansion in Richmond, the former home of the Mills acting family. After she had given Keith a tour of the house, and he was readying himself to make a move on her, he was a little startled that she should suggest it was time to meet Ron. Keith was even more startled to discover Ronnie Wood working in his home studio with Mick Jagger, immersed in a song they were writing together. Concerned that Keith might never again be eligible for a US visa, Mick had been checking out Ron Wood: could he possibly fit into the Stones as a touring replacement for Keith? More to the point, he had been trying to write with the Face. And when Keith walked in, they were running through the first fruits of this partnership, a little ditty called 'It's Only Rock'n'Roll'.

Tired of the attention of the police at 3 Cheyne Walk, Keith moved in to Honest Ron's Richmond residence, setting up home in a cottage in the grounds. A particular attraction of The Wick was that Woody was one of the first people in Britain to have a VCR, at the time the ultimate rock-star toy. Visitors would watch endless reruns of *Monty Python's Flying Circus* and *The Benny Hill Show*, and Sergio Leone westerns, as well as the film that was still Keith Richards' favourite, *The Harder They Come*. There Keith resumed his affair with the blond German model, Ushi Obermeier, whom he had first slept with at the beginning of his relationship with Anita, on the 1967 European tour. (A gossipy dealer friend spilled the beans about Keith's affair to Anita: when faced with Anita's wrath, Keith invited the guy over to 3 Cheyne Walk and threatened him with a sword that he kept on the wall.)

Keith was not unaware of the work Mick Jagger was having to do to keep the Stones functioning. 'I was devoting most of my time to scoring and taking dope. I was completely out of it, and Mick had to cover for me. He took over completely. I feel I owe Mick. I've always admired him very much for that. He did exactly what a friend should do,' Keith Richards later admitted. In 1987 he spoke of Mick in rather different terms, to the American writer Kurt Loder: 'Throughout most of the seventies, I was living in another world from him. I didn't blame him – he'd earned the right to do whatever he wanted. It was just that I couldn't relate to that. It kind of got up my nose a bit, that jet-set shit and, like, the flaunting of it. But he's a lonely guy, too. He's got his own problems, you know.'

On 25 June 1973, backstage at the Queen Elizabeth Hall on the South Bank, Mick had sympathetically held the hand of a nervous Mike Oldfield before the live debut of his work *Tubular Bells*, a worldwide hit. 'There's so much good music being played at the moment. I'd really like to do a concert like this one,' said Mick after the concert. The next time Mick met Mike Oldfield, he didn't seem to remember who he was.

Keith, meanwhile, was having a hard time remembering who anyone was. It came almost as no surprise to read the front-page headline in the 26 June edition of the London *Evening Standard*: ROLLING STONE RICHARD – GUN, DRUGS CHARGES. Ten members of the Chelsea Drugs Squad, under Detective Inspector Charles O'Hanlon, had burst into the house at Cheyne Walk at around seven in the morning, marching straight up to Keith and Anita's bedroom, where the couple were sound asleep. As the bust occurred, all that was on Keith's mind was how to get into the bathroom alone so that he could shoot up a relaxing armful of smack, the better to deal with his present predicament: the police insisted, however, that the bathroom door remain open. Meanwhile, Anita dropped her stash of cocaine on the carpet and succeeded in grinding it into the fabric. Not only was Keith charged with possession of a minute amount of heroin, a lump of hash and some Mandrax tablets, but with illegally holding a .38 Smith and Wesson revolver, a shotgun and 110 rounds of ammunition. Anita was also charged with possession of drugs, as was 'Stash' Klossowski, who had had the misfortune to crash at 3 Cheyne Walk for the night. The following day Keith Richards was remanded on £1,000 bail; his passport was returned by the court so that he might fulfil overseas commitments.

The police had missed the house supply of heroin, concealed in a secret compartment built into the antique four-poster bed. Undaunted, Anita went along with her own overseas commitment, a plan by which an Italian dealer called Mario would bring over eight ounces of heroin from Switzerland in a hollowed-out photographer's tripod. Unfortunately for Anita and Keith, when it arrived the drug turned out to be diamorphine – a kind of industrial form of the narcotic that was useless, unless Keith wanted to become a large-scale heroin pharmacist. After irritable, petulant arguments with Mario, the dealer was paid off with £3,500, half the agreed fee. Increasingly paranoid that he was being watched by the police, Keith decided he had to get the diamorphine out of the house. He drove it down to Ron Wood's house in Richmond in his new Rolls-Royce Silver Shadow. At The Wick, he buried the drugs in a derelict stable block, and was never able to find them again. So great was Keith's not unreasonable paranoia about a further police bust that he now decided to move his whole family into the guest cottage at The Wick. While waiting for it to be readied for their occupation, he took Anita, Marlon and Dandelion down to Redlands for a few days.

Mick had had a far less eventful year than his songwriting partner; the only real drama had occurred on 10 May: while Mick and Bianca were watching the newly fashionable J. Geils Band on-stage at the Academy of Music in Manhattan, fire had broken out at Stargroves, Mick's Berkshire country retreat. Keith returned to Chelsea on 26 July for the thirtieth birthday party Mick was throwing at the Tithe Street home of David Milinaric, his interior-designer friend. Among the guests was Rod Stewart, busy chatting up Britt Ekland, to the visible annoyance of Dee Harrington, his long-standing girlfriend. For the party Keith wore the brown pinstriped suit he'd bought for court appearances at *Granny Takes a Trip*, the hip rock-star couturier whose premises at World's End on the King's Road was notorious as a source of heroin. Anita turned up in a scarlet ballgown, looking decidedly out of place. She and Keith stayed at the party until their supply of coke had gone and then drove back to Redlands. Mick continued his birthday celebrations by going to the Oval to watch the Test Match.

Five days later Keith's gorgeous sixteenth-century country house went up in flames, the consequence of a smouldering roach carelessly tossed into a waste-paper basket. Spanish Tony, who was staying in a guest cottage, helped a bedraggled, distraught Keith save some antiques and get his Ferrari out of the garage before it was reduced to charred metal. It was not a good summer for Keith Richards: Michael Cooper, who had floated in and out of his life on a haze of junk, died; he was in a wheelchair by now, his body seemingly having seized up from the abuse he had wrought upon it; Gus Dupree, the grandfather who had acted as his musical mentor, passed away; again, for Keith it brought up thoughts of his father, absent from his life and unable to share in Keith's success, as his son wished. The terrible sadness in Keith's eyes, the source of all his addictions, was visibly growing. Yet this only had the effect of bringing more supplicants to kneel before his feet in hero-worship: as is the case with many artists, it was Keith's partially glimpsed yet perpetual suffering that paradoxically drew people to him, sensing a kindred spirit.

On 16 July 1973 an affiliation order was filed against Mick Jagger by Marsha Hunt at Marylebone Crown Court. The extent of his denial about being the father of Karis baffled her to such a degree that Marsha suffered a psychosomatic illness from the resulting strain when the story hit the media. When Mick was asked to make a statement for the press, he retreated into characteristic flannel mode, reminding reporters that Marsha was about to have a new record released – as though this was a publicity stunt. 'His wife Bianca was quoted as saying she didn't give a damn,' remembered Marsha. A hearing was to be held that month.

Marsha couldn't help but feel she'd done her best to resolve these difficulties amicably. The previous summer Marsha had consulted a lawyer as to the best way to obtain regular maintenance money for her daughter from Mick. As they had never married, Karis had no formal legal rights. Marsha was told that a paternity suit was the only option. She contacted Mick, and he invited her to lunch. He made a bad joke about not having sent money for a recent hospital visit by Karis, saying that Marsha probably would have spent the cash on shoes. Naturally, this infuriated Marsha. Afterwards she called Michael Siefert, her lawyer, to agree to his suggestion that there was no alternative but to launch a paternity suit against Mick.

Marsha met Mick again, this time at the Albert Memorial on the edge of Kensington Gardens. She sat on top of the forty steps and watched as the father of her daughter climbed up towards her; and as a small, bespectacled, besuited man suddenly appeared at Mick's side to hand him a writ. Marsha took Mick by the arm and walked down the steps and through the park in an effort to explain to him why she was doing this, that it was over his responsibilities to his daughter. She explained that if he put £25,000 into a trust this would be sufficient to care for Karis. They walked to a pub in Knightsbridge; over a pint of bitter Mick agreed to a trust of £20,000. By the time their solicitors spoke later that day, Mick had reduced the amount to £17,000. But even so, nothing happened, no money was handed over. Thus was issued the affiliation order which demanded, on a day he conveniently left the country for an Italian vacation with Bianca and Jade, blood tests from Mick. On 21 January 1975 Marsha received her first payment of £41.67.

Not that everything was necessarily cosy *chez* Jagger; there were persistent reports of trouble in the Jagger marriage. 'You wouldn't take your wife to the office, would you?' riposted Mick when asked why, as it had been reported, Bianca would not be accompanying him on a forthcoming tour of Europe. With her silver-topped cane and exquisite dress sense, Bianca was a feature at London's hip social events. Reacquainting herself with some of her own Jamaican experience, she had been stunned into reverent silence along with the rest of the audience at the first London concert by the Wailers at the Speakeasy club behind Oxford Circus. Keith had also gone along to the show.

A month after Redlands had burned down, necessitating rebuilding that would take most of the decade, the new album *Goat's Head Soup* was released. Even if it had not been cast in the shadow of the magnificent *Exile on Main Street*, the record could not have failed to be revealed as something of a stinker. From the opening song, 'Dancing With Mr D.', a clear but mediocre endeavour to capture the golden era of Jumpin' Jack Flash's 'Sympathy For The Devil' and even 'Midnight Rambler', it sounded tired and lacklustre. There were a few moments: '100 Years Ago' was the kind of slurred semi-blues at which the group excelled, replete with excellent lyrics from Mick; 'Coming Down Again', a lament for the state in which he found himself most mornings, was sung by Keith, employing the current model of those Dartford choirboy tones; 'Star Star' was the acceptable title for a song actually called 'Starfucker', a Chuck Berry-riffed rocker that resembled a similar hackneyed effort at con- troversy to 'Let's Spend The Night Together': it conjured up little more than a stifled yawn and a sense of oh-they-would-wouldn't-they? 'Can You Hear The Music' was a plain bore.

The production of the record felt leaden; you could taste Jimmy Miller's heroin habit. 'Angie', the first hit single off the album, was a distinct surprise, a maudlin, treacly ballad with a melody capable of being whistled by the most non-musical of building-site workers. Though Rolling Stones diehards were appalled, 'Angie' was a hugely commercial song, and pointed towards the semi-anthemic ballads with which the group would expand its audience as the decade progressed. In a similar shift in mar- keting, the front cover was a simple David Bailey headshot of Mick, his features mildly distorted by stretch nylon, as though this was some kind of pastiche of the stocking masks favoured by bank robbers of the era; Keith's head was similarly adorned on the LP's back cover. So it was clear: there were but two Rolling Stones.

The European tour began the day after the record was released, with a 1 September show before 16,000 fans in the Austrian capital of Vienna's Stadthalle. After dates in Mannheim, in what was then West Germany, and

Cologne, the group flew back to play at the Wembley Empire Pool in London on 7 September, their first UK dates in two and a half years; they had missed Britain out on the *Exile* tour, which only seemed to have increased the group's legend in their home country. In the first-night audience were David Bailey, Donald Sutherland, Elliott Gould, Ryan O'Neal, all three members of supergroup Beck, Bogert and Appice, and Peter Frampton. Ryan O'Neal and Bianca Jagger were seen deep in conversation.

The show received distinctly mixed reviews; the group seemed off form – hardly surprisingly, considering the brouhaha that had taken place the previous day. On 6 September, having hired Blenheim Castle, the birthplace of Sir Winston Churchill, Mick threw a promotional party for the launch of *Goat's Head Soup*. At the event Anita arrived smacked out, wearing only jeans and a t-shirt: when she got there and saw all the beautiful, gorgeously garbed people, she refused to come in, announcing she would remain in the black Daimler limousine in which she, Keith and Marlon had been transported from The Wick. After a few minutes, however, a very out-of-it Anita stumblingly stormed into the party, audibly cursing a sociable Bianca, who was the picture of pleasantness. Above the sound of the new album could be heard Anita's voice, screaming at Keith to leave the party with her. Quietly aghast at more problems from the troublesome neighbours, Mick discreetly suggested to Keith that he get Anita out of there. On the journey back to London this difficult couple periodically attacked each other, fists raining down, as a mystified Marlon tried to ignore his childish parents. The stress and strain of being together were sending both Keith and Anita to the edge of insanity.

After the London dates the Rolling Stones moved north for a show in Manchester. That night, as Keith sat in the dressing-room bathroom in the middle of his habitual pre-show fix, Bobby Keys came knocking on the door. It was bad news: Gram Parsons had overdosed and died, alone in a Los Angeles motel room; his body had been stolen and cremated by Phil Kaufmann, his road manager, in the Californian desert at Joshua Tree. Somewhat unrealistically, a concerned Keith felt that Parsons would not have come to this sorry end had he continued to be under the care and protection of the Rolling Stones. Keith himself was in a terrible state throughout the beginning of the tour, shrouded in all manner of junkie denial and self-mythologising: a good line of his was the one that he told Anita, that if he did heroin while touring his addiction would in fact be lessened, as he'd sweat out all the smack while on-stage.

The news of Gram Parsons' death, however, seemed to have a jolt-like effect on Keith. After further English dates in Newcastle, Glasgow and Birmingham, Keith Richards and Marshall Chess checked into a Swiss clinic where their blood was cleaned of toxins. As soon as Keith left the clinic, allegedly no longer a junkie, he accepted Bobby Keys' offer of a line of cocaine. After a few more dates Keys was dumped off the tour, considered to have lost the plot: mired in a world of drink, heroin and sex, he had made the cardinal error of assuming that he had become one of the Rolling Stones, and found himself pushed into a taxi that was despatched to the nearest airport. The absence of dates in France from the touring itinerary was noticeable. A trot around Germany, Sweden, Denmark, Holland and Belgium ended on 19 October at the Deutschlandhalle in Berlin.

For much of the tour Keith was accompanied by Uschi Obermeier; Mick Jagger, ever anxious to prove his status as group stud (though he was of course a mere also-ran when compared with Bill Wyman) had tried to muscle in on her before Keith could make contact, until the guitarist delivered a curt, 'Jagger, you cunt, leave!' Permanently wired for sound via his early model ghetto-blaster, Keith marched through airports and hotel lobbies blasting out the soundtrack to Jimmy Cliff's *The Harder They Come*. The decadence of the party in Berlin on the last night of the 1973 European tour became mythical: naked girls cavorted on the dance floor of the nightclub in which it was held; dwarves proferred bowls of cocaine.

The first half of the 1970s was indeed a decadent time, and the reputed South of France lifestyle of the Rolling Stones was the template for this. In the maroon, patchouli-scented world of Biba's Rainbow Room on Kensington High Street, cocaine and Mandrax were the norm for a certain androgynous set, and heroin was dabbled with by many others apart from Keith Richards and his cronies. At restaurants like the camp Casserole, the World's End stand-by that had long been a favourite of Jagger's (it was just around the corner from Edith Grove), you might observe discreet post-prandial pinches of cocaine. And everything was overhung by the spirit of Keith Richards, the archetypal art-school outlaw, a not especially desirable role model for an entire generation of similarly disaffected, lonely young men.

None of this went unnoticed by those in positions of power. On 15 October 1973, a day that the Stones were performing a concert in Antwerp, Belgium, Keith and Anita were tried in their absence in a Nice court for the offences at Nellcôte. They were found guilty of the use, supply and trafficking of cannabis, for which they each received a one-year suspended prison sentence; for the charge of heroin use, Keith was fined 5,000 francs. 'Keith invariably emerged from his crises with incredible luck,' thought Bill Wyman. Both Keith and Anita were banned from returning to France for the next two years.

But the sentences were relatively minor compared with what they might have got. And that luck was to hold. Nine days later in London, on 24 October 1973, Keith pleaded guilty to possession at 3 Cheyne Walk of cannabis, heroin and Mandrax, as well as a revolver, a shotgun and ammunition. The defence rested on the grounds that Keith was hardly ever in London, and that a large number of individuals passed through the Chelsea house. Although Keith was technically guilty, as the contraband items had been found in his home, anyone could have left them there. 'The cops even tried to string in this old Belgian shotgun that was built in – ah – 1899 or something,' said Keith after the case. 'The police tried their damnedest to tell this 'ere magistrate that this weapon was a sawn-off shotgun. From that moment the magistrate saw what was 'appenin'.'

Keith was fined a total of £205; Anita received a one-year conditional discharge on charges relating to the Mandrax. At a celebratory party afterwards at the Londonderry hotel on Park Lane, Keith jacked up and then nodded out, setting a bed on fire with his burning cigarette. Several children were playing in the room where the fire started, though no one was hurt. Keith, born under the fire sign of Sagittarius, had begun to attribute the seemingly endless succession of blazes that burned after him like a bushfire to spontaneous combustion; all the same, the Londonderry announced that it would no longer accept bookings from the Rolling Stones, for whom it had been the London hotel of choice since 1969. Soon Keith found himself present at a tragedy in which, seemingly for once, there was no suggestion at all that he might have been involved: on the grim night when the musician Robert Wyatt fell from an upstairs window at a party in Maida Vale, becoming paralysed as a result of the fall. As soon as the accident occurred, and he knew that not only an ambulance but also the police were on their way, Keith was out of there, running off to his Mercedes, which was double-parked on nearby Edgware Road.

While the rest of the group would be exhausted at the end of a tour, Keith would only just be getting started, buzzing on the energy of playing live, his creative juices at their purest and most potent. This was his preferred time for going into the recording studio, now a matter of extreme urgency: for redemption was required for the ghastly mess that was *Goat's Head Soup*. On 13 November the Stones flew to Munich to Musicland Studios, the fiefdom of celebrated disco producer Giorgio Moroder; for this record, however, Mick and Keith would produce the group themselves. With Jimmy Miller no longer on board for production, Mick and Keith decided that for the foreseeable future, they would become the sole producers of records by the Rolling Stones, thereby controlling not only the group's material but also its sound. The production unit the pair of them were forming, they decreed, would be known as The Glimmer Twins. After eleven days in the studio, they returned to London.

*

For much of early 1974, Mick was in serious socialite mode. On 26 January, however, in his capacity of co-director of Rolling Stones Records, he had gone along to check out the New York Dolls when they played at Imperial College in South Kensington, a student venue with an ambitious booking policy. The first visible manifestation of the coming furore of punk rock, the Dolls boasted cartoon simulacra of Mick and Keith in singer David Johansen and guitarist Johnny Thunders. As his reputation – which seemed increasingly dependent on his rumoured nearness to death – reached godlike status in the United States, getting a Keith lookalike became important for new US groups; the newly successful American group Aerosmith, for example, who as well as Joe Perry, a rat-haired, out-of-it guitarist, also had a Mick clone in singer Steven Tyler, became huge. 'We were almost going to sign them at one point,' Mick said of the Dolls. 'I didn't think much of them at all. I think all this posing stuff is going to be tolerated until, oh, the middle of 1974, and then it'll be dead.' (When Keith was asked what he thought of the Dolls, he hardly seemed to have heard of them. 'Didn't one of them die?' he asked.)

On 10 February, Mick was in the Trinidadian capital of Port of Spain, taking time out from the riotous, wildly hedonistic three-day carnival to go along to watch the England versus West Indies Test Match. Five days later, he was at the opening of a new club, the Bottom Line, in Manhattan; the day before, Gerald Ford, the vice-president of the United States, claimed during an interview that he had never heard of Mick Jagger. Ten days later Mick was hanging out with David Bowie at his London recording sessions.

On 13 September 1973 Mick had invited Bowie to the Stones' show in Newcastle, on the *Goat's Head Soup* tour. Bowie had arrived with his friend Scott. After the show, which David Bowie hated, thinking it was desperately dated, Mick and Bianca followed the glam-rock avatar back to his hotel suite; there they found David and Scott in bed together, fully dressed. They went out for the night, gambling. Back in London, Mick went to Tramp and gay films with David Bowie; each was trying to learn as much as they could from the other, each using the other; Mick was photographed with his head in David's lap in a hotel room. Once Angie Bowie, his wife, returned to the house they were sharing in Oakley Street to find her husband and Mick Jagger ('Michael', as Bowie always referred to him) in bed together. 'Mick and David were sexually obsessed with each other. They became very close and practically lived together for several months,' said Ava Cherry, a singer who also lived at the Oakley Street address.

Two weeks after those David Bowie sessions Mick was attending the Academy Awards in Los Angeles with John Lennon; along with the ex-

Beatle, Harry Nilsson, Jesse Ed David and even the unmentionable Bobby Keys, Mick cut some new songs at the Record Plant.

The greater to avail himself of the facilities for superlative skiing, Keith had retreated to Switzerland for the winter and much of the early spring. By 18 May he was back in London, going along with Ron Wood to watch the Who play a stadium-like date at Charlton football ground in south-east London. Keeping his head down in order to avoid further drug busts, Keith Richards had moved back into the cottage at Wood's Richmond home.

Ron Wood was rehearsing and recording for a solo album he was making, and for which Mick Jagger had come up with a title, *I've got My Own Album to Do*, a comment on Faces' singer Rod Stewart's endless excuses when it came to recording with his group. On one tune, 'I Can Feel The Fire', Mick co-wrote the song with Ron Wood and played guitar; together Mick and Keith wrote two songs for Wood's album, 'Sure The One You Need' and 'Act Together'; elsewhere, Keith contributed his customary Dartford vocals and habitual rhythm guitar. Non-original songs on the sessions included James Rae's 'If You Gotta Make A Fool Of Somebody'; Freddie Scott's 'Am I Groovin' You' and Ann Peebles' 'I Can't Stand The Rain'.

Keith enjoyed working with 'Ronnie': 'I've never thought of doing anything on my own. As far as I'm concerned, it's just no fun if you're there by yourself – just you and your ego and of course, your ego always comes out on top every time. You need somebody to bounce ideas off, to have a laugh with. Two people can deflate each other nicely – that's how it works with Mick, and it's happening at the moment with Ronnie. It feels good because it's tight and also it's being done the right way for the right reasons. The only other person I've ever thought about working with in that context was Gram Parsons. That could have been good, but if I was to do something on my own, it would be just ridiculous because it would only sound like the Rolling Stones but without Mick singing.'

Keith Richards played two shows with Ron Wood on 13 and 14 July 1974 at the Kilburn State in north-west London, backed by Willie Weeks, Andy Newmark and Ian McLagan. Although it was widely expected that Mick Jagger would join them on-stage, he was in fact in New York, watching Eric Clapton's Madison Square Garden concert.

Like many rock 'n' roll wives, the quietly strait-laced Bianca Jagger discovered, rather to her surprise, that she was not happy: the rock 'n' roll lifestyle, especially at the rarefied level of her husband's, rendered that state of affairs almost an inevitability. Overshadowed by her parents' divorce, yet brought up in a culture where the family is everything, she had almost desperately desired a conventional loving relationship.

Although she and Mick now had legendary reputations as world-trekking jet-setters, few observers appreciated the precise necessity of this peripatetic existence: Mick would never stay in one territory long enough to be considered a resident liable for taxation. On one occasion when they had been in Britain 'illegally', Bianca had even been reduced to ducking down every time she passed a window at 48 Cheyne Walk. Every time the doorbell rang she would cringe, more concerned that it might herald a visit from Keith and Anita, whose lifestyle she abhorred, than from a spy from the tax office. Latin in temperament, she was prone to fits of either moodiness or extreme anger, to which she was easily moved by Mick's controlling wilfulness, traits that had emerged as he sought to direct the career of a group in which Keith seemed incapable of participating. There would be no tour in 1974, largely because Mick feared the ignominy, and long-term reverberations, of Keith being refused a US work visa.

The new single and album, however, would hopefully tide the group over until alternative arrangements, of one sort or another, could be made. On 9 July 1974 the rather weak 'It's Only Rock And Roll (But I Like It)' 45 hit the shops. It was not an enormous hit, merely making it to number ten in the UK and rising no higher than number eighteen in the US. The Stones made a curious video for the single, directed by Michael Lindsay-Hogg; dressed in white US sailors' uniforms, the group were covered in soap bubbles as they played the song. Publicity stills were taken at the same session: sitting to the right of a pouting, supremely confident Mick, the only group member displaying sergeant's stripes on his navy duds, a dwarf-like Keith looks like a corpse being propped up, his rotting incisors fully on display. The aberration of Keith's appearance notwithstanding, the video and photographs were as tackily camp as anything that might have been dreamed up by the Sweet: was this Keith's concession to glam-rock? Or was it the influence of David Bowie on Mick? Whatever, the pictures and promo film marked a distinct softening of the group's bad-boy image.

In the *NME* dated 31 August 1974, Keith Richards, the personification of that bad-boy image, was interviewed by the journalist Pete Erskine. Erskine asked him about the rumour that he had had several complete blood transfusions. 'That's beautiful,' replied Keith. 'I love that. I've heard about that thing and I'd love to do it just because I'm sure that eating motorway food for ten years has done my blood no good at all. The only time I've ever been to Switzerland is to ski. I gave up drugs when the doctor told me I had six months to live. If you're gonna get wasted, get wasted elegantly.'

Erskine was a talented writer on the *NME* who had fallen hook, line and sinker for the 'outlaw chic' image and approach to life purportedly led by Keith Richards. Shortly afterwards, Erskine added a heroin habit to his panoply of hipness; his first snort of the drug had taken place at 3 Cheyne Walk after that interview. His description back at the *NME* office of that drug-taking session with Richards suggested a macho emphasis on one's status being dependent on the quantity of drugs that had been absorbed, not far removed from being a ten-pints-a-night man. Pete Erskine did not live very many more years. Another writer on the same paper, Nick Kent, was similarly smitten by all things 'Keef'. He already had a bad heroin habit, and his friendship with Keith Richards would lead to a deterioration of his once impressive creative powers.

Everywhere they went the Stones seemed to leave a trail of casualties. Being a junkie wasn't a problem if you had a seemingly endless supply of money; but when those around Keith who were not as well-heeled found themselves similarly addicted to narcotics, their lives suffered even more damage than that experienced by the rich musician. For Keith there would always be someone to put him to bed if he collapsed from smack use. Even Keith's nodding out was often not quite what it seemed. As conversations continued around the crashed-out figure, at a pertinent point he would suddenly open his eyes for a moment: 'No, you're completely wrong!' he would interject, and then fall back to sleep again. Around the offices of the *NME*, Nick Kent would recount the story of how one day out at The Wick Keith denied to him that he ever injected heroin. Almost immediately he picked up a box of tissues, and – as though this was a moment of absolute instant karma – out of it dropped a hypodermic syringe. 'Oh,' Keith blustered. 'Well, I might use one if I have flu.' Moments later, he slumped over, turning a worrying shade of blue. Keith remained in this condition for some minutes, as Kent considered calling an ambulance. Then, as though nothing had happened, Keith opened his eyes and continued their conversation. Soon Kent was behaving in similar ways himself, seemingly having absorbed into his very being every one of Keith Richards' effete, fey mannerisms.

The vogue for heroin around the British music business could be directly attributed to and was personified by Keith Richards. Keith appeared on the BBC2 music series *The Old Grey Whistle Test* on 1 October 1974, interviewed by the show's presenter 'Whispering' Bob Harris. As both interviewee and anchorman smoked cigarettes on the studio set, Keith's tone was hushed, confident, fey, a low voice used to getting what it wanted without needing to be raised; it was the quietly authoritative, almost whispered speech of a man with no experience of anyone ever questioning even his most absurd whim. There was no trace whatsoever of Dartford left in his inflections, which seemed now to come from the self-styled upper-class yet classless Chelsea set. It was the accent of the rock aristocracy: you might have heard Jimmy Page or Marc Bolan using precisely the same mannerisms, both vocal and physical: the little-girlish flicks of the hair, the almost camp angling of the neck and head, the sense of being deeply, glamorously stoned.

Watching that interview, you were concerned that at any moment Keith might nod out on live television – and, of course, he did so for a moment, his eyes rolling up into his head as Keith Richards had a small mini-second snooze in the nation's living rooms. The interview itself was relatively work-a-day. How had the new album come to be recorded? asked a reverential Bob Harris. 'The band was very hot, coming off the road, and we cut half the album with Billy Preston in two weeks. Then we went back for Christmas and gorged. We returned to the studios in February with Nicky Hopkins. After that we left it until April, and Mick and I did the vocals in London, and the mixing, which is the really hard work – that took about six weeks to two months.' There was the usual stuff about wanting to play smaller gigs, and a mention of staying at Ron Wood's house while working with him: 'I lived there for a month, and didn't see daylight.'

Keith also declared an intention to record in Jamaica: 'I've got one thing I want to do in Jamaica with some Rastafarians, who are heavy, happy dudes. They play with drums and chant, and they roped me in to play guitar. So I got my reggae chops together.' (That album, *Wingless Angels*, a record of nyabinghi chants, was eventually made and released in 1996, twenty-two years later.)

On that *Old Grey Whistle Test* broadcast Keith also displayed a heroic state of dental decay, his gnashers gnarled and blackened like waste matter found in the inside of a furnace. Although still fey and pretty in his scarlet, white polka-dotted jacket from 'Granny's', when Keith opened his mouth he looked like an old gypsy witch. Again in the *NME* offices, Pete Erskine had described Keith's fiddling with a tooth that fell apart in his fingers, the fragments casually flicked away. In the first week of November, Keith returned to Switzerland where he underwent an extensive course of dental repair. 'I'm changing my image. I've arranged for a whole series of dental appointments in Switzerland ... I only ever get ill when I gave up drugs,' Keith had announced the previous week. When he returned to London, the interior of Keith Richards' mouth had been given a complete refit, his capped teeth sparkling white and polished, a perfect new set of Hollywood-style incisors in place.

His new appearance did not prevent the incessant rumours that Keith Richards was near death; on his second solo album, *Cry Tough*, the celebrated Young Turk rock 'n' roller Nils Lofgren included an affecting tune entitled 'Keith Don't Go'.

*

Mick and Bianca spent much of the summer of 1974 with Jade at Andy Warhol's house, an unassuming but sizeable grey clapboard building with its own tennis court set in twenty-five acres of land in the tiny, vaguely bohemian town of Montauk, the farthest point on the most easterly tip of Long Island, overlooking the rolling Atlantic ocean. The Jaggers had rented the artist's home for $5,000 a month. A neighbour was Dick Cavett, the American talk-show host, with whom they became friends. Visitors to the residence included Jacqueline Onassis, with whom Mick would ride horses along the beach, John Lennon and Yoko Ono, David Bowie, Eric Clapton, Jack Nicholson, Warren Beatty and John Phillips. Neighbours were scandalised by the pungent aroma of marijuana drifting down the beach, and by the varied sexual antics in the sand dunes.

By October, however, Mick was in Paris, and there were rumours of an affair with the actress Nathalie Delon. Nathalie was by no means the only other woman in Mick Jagger's life. Bebe Buell was an international model who was married to the musician Todd Rundgren, part-genius, part-cosmic buffoon. Rundgren's serial infidelities led Bebe into several affairs, all of which seemed to involve iconic rock stars: Iggy Pop, Jimmy Page, Rod Stewart and – inevitably – Mick Jagger. Like half of his generation, Jimmy Page was a student of the arcane and occult; after casting Bebe's astrological chart, he found that she had a powerfully aspected Mars–Venus connection with Mick, his great rival in the rock-star bedroom stakes.

In September and October 1974, this harmonious alignment of Venus, the planet of love and fiery, energetic Mars was clear: Bebe and Mick saw each other frequently in New York; they suddenly became very close in an emotionally energising, artistically stimulating relationship that seemed to give expression to both their creative talents. Although Mick always liked to stay at the Plaza, he once took Bebe over to the nearby Sherry-Netherland hotel to visit David Bowie. Bowie was in residence in his suite with Dana Gillespie, a beautiful, dark-haired English singer who was signed to MainMan, the company belonging to Tony DeFries, Bowie's manager. When Bowie and Gillespie produced a set of Japanese ben-wa balls, designed to vibrate in the vagina, and suggested they all have sex together, Bebe was utterly shocked. Mick mildly chastised the pair for their suggestion, and he and Bebe made their excuses and left.

Soon after, Bebe was pleasantly surprised when out of the blue Mick declared his love for her when she dropped in at the Plaza hotel on a passing visit. In the same way that he had professed his love for Chrissie Shrimpton, Marianne and Marsha Hunt, he obviously meant it – though one might feel Mick was often in love with the idea of being in love. The twenty-one-year-old Bebe Buell was not naive, however, aware that there were at least four other women, including Bianca, with whom he was presently involved (his affair with Apollonia von Ravenstein, a German model whom he referred to as 'Apples', was the talk of Manhattan; he also had a relationship with Barbara Allen, a New York socialite, and with good-hearted Sabrina Guinness, of the Guinness family), and never felt that she was in love with him. All the same, Bebe Buell found Mick Jagger extremely comfortable to be with, 'brilliant, articulate and very sane – in control of his mind and body and extremely charismatic and powerful', notwithstanding the fact that she was two inches taller than him. She liked the way that his feet were his favoured mode of transportation in Manhattan, as well as his arcane chat-up lines; once he dropped by her apartment on Horatio Street at four in the morning, calling up, 'I've got some yoghurt.'

As with his other girlfriends, Mick would be extremely finicky over Bebe's choice of clothes whenever she was accompanying him; it was not unknown for him to send her back to change her outfit, several of which he had bought for her personally as gifts. Though women usually had a love–hate relationship with his tomcat nature, Mick Jagger's girly side appealed to them. 'He always knew what creams to use, and he often shared his beauty products with me. He'd say, "Let me look at that, Bebe", and then he'd produce a jar and start massaging the contents into my skin. He told me how to steam my face, what herbs to use. No woman on earth knows more about cosmetics than Mick does.' She also observed the peculiar chemistry of his relationship with Bianca; at social events, Bianca would come and sit next to her, making reference to her as 'Mick's little friend', thereby indicating how much she held herself above Mick's philandering.

The eighteenth of October 1974 saw the release of the *It's Only Rock And Roll* album. Although it was to make number one in the United States, it rose no higher than number four in the UK. '*Goat's Head Soup*, to me, was a marking-time album,' said Keith. 'I like it in many ways but I don't think it has the freshness that this one has . . . Rock 'n' roll can't be planned or prepared. You can have a few basic structures, though. I'm not the sort of person who sits down at home with a guitar, writes a song and says, "That's how I hear it", because I play in a band and leave it up to them to tell me how it should go for them.'

Stronger than the staggeringly weak *Goat's Head Soup*, there was still an element of treading water about the long-player. The title track ('Inspiration by Ronnie Wood' read the credit, though no doubt he would have preferred the royalties) had a catchy riff and inane lyrics; 'If You Can't Rock Me', the album opener, had the pile-driving aggression of an *Exile on Main Street* out-take; 'Till The Next Goodbye' and the cod-epic

'Time Waits For No One' were a pair of commercial ballads of the sort that the Stones had successfully pushed up the US charts since 'Time Is On My Side'; 'Luxury' was the group's first reggae tune, a pointed tale of the oppression of Jamaican labour by US corporations; a chipper cover of The Temptations' 'If You Can't Rock Me' seemed rather obvious, as though the Stones were taking the lead from the Faces' celebrated version of the same Motown group's 'Losing You'; 'If You Really Want To Be My Friend' was a soul original; 'Short And Curlies' had Keith on lead vocals, contemptuously baiting someone for being under the thumb of his missus; the funk of 'Dance Little Sister' and 'Fingerprint File', the final tune on the album, was not only a testament to the disco energies that palpably pervaded Moroder's studio, but also a pointer to the direction of the Stones' following album. All the same, there was a very definite sense about the *It's Only Rock And Roll* album of more marking time for the Rolling Stones.

At the end of 1974 the Jaggers moved back into 48 Cheyne Walk. Jade was installed as a pupil at Garden House School off Sloane Square: she was noted for her imperious behaviour towards other children, and for the manner in which she seemed to need maternal behaviour from her teachers. She would frequently be ferried out to spend time with Mick's parents at the house in Westgate-on-Sea to which they had moved.

One night in November 1974 Keith insisted on driving Mick, Ron Wood, Bebe Buell, who was visiting from the United States, and a French girl called Beatrice (with whom Mick was having a fling) to a party for Eric Clapton that was being thrown at the house of the guitar superhero's manager, Robert Stigwood, whom Keith had attacked years before. Bebe Buell never had any worries about Keith's driving; she thought him 'a bit flippant with the one-finger steering and the knee driving, but he inspired trust'. As the Bentley purred out of the driveway at The Wick and headed towards Stigwood's home, Keith decided to drive around a roundabout several times. Within moments the flashing blue light of a police car was behind them, and they were pulled over: Beatrice suddenly found that the illegal contents of the various parties' pockets were dumped on her by the assorted male gallants in the car, men used to others taking the rap for them. When the driver of the police car approached the Bentley, instantly recognising its male occupants, Keith claimed the cause of his circular course was to point out various 'important locations' to the two women in his vehicle. Why hadn't he simply stopped? 'That's not really in my nature. I like to keep moving,' came Keith's reply. Could it be that he had been abusing substances? suggested the policeman. 'Of course not. I wouldn't be driving if I had,' was the guitarist's practised response, before he was ushered on his way.

Patti Boyd, former wife of George Harrison and present lover of Eric Clapton, was at the party. Her presence always hit an uncomfortable nerve in Mick Jagger, who was unable to comprehend that she would sleep with Harrison, Clapton and even Ronnie Wood, but always resolutely refused his own advances. But that night Mick Jagger had other things on his mind: Mick Taylor announced to him at the party that evening that he was leaving the Rolling Stones. Somewhat flummoxed by this news, the Stones' singer retired to Keith's Bentley to cogitate upon the matter over a joint with Ron Wood. 'If he really does go,' Mick asked Woody, 'would you take his place?' It might be difficult, was the response of the guitarist with the Faces, as he was already in a group.

CHAPTER 21

'KEITH'S STRAIGHT, INNEE?'

On 7 December 1974 the Stones started work at Musicland Studios in Munich once again. Nicky Hopkins was with them, but Mick Taylor was not. On 12 December 1974 Mick Taylor officially left a group of which many fans had never considered him fully a member. 'Thank you for the past five years – it's been a pleasure working with you,' wrote Keith in the telegram he sent him. A reason for Mick Taylor's departure from the Rolling Stones was one with which Bill Wyman, Charlie Watts and Brian Jones had become extremely familiar: Mick and Keith's roughshod control of the group meant that his material and input was never translated into songwriting credits and the resulting income from composing. The druggy ambience of the Stones meant that Taylor had succumbed to heroin addiction, and his cocaine habit was so extreme that he had had a plastic septum inserted into his nose. And just to cap the entire unfortunate experience of his years with the group, he knew that Mick Jagger had been to bed with his wife, an unseemly example of egotistical behaviour and sexual manipulation. There was even more than a slight suggestion that the two Micks had got it on together: Marianne and Spanish Tony had once returned to Cheyne Walk to find the pair asleep in bed together.

Taylor proclaimed that he would be forming a group with former Cream star Jack Bruce, but nothing significant came of this collaboration, and the celebrated guitarist never made any further meaningful contribution to popular music. But the more pressing causes of the guitarist's resignation from the group were a mixture of pragmatism – he thought the Stones were dying on their feet and wanted to get out while he still had a good reputation – and self-preservation: the endless circus of drugs and decadence finally had got to this quiet, shy young man, a vegetarian teetotaller when he joined the Rolling Stones in 1969. Mick Taylor wanted to make sure that he didn't keel over before the group did.

In December 1974, back in London, Keith Richards, Steve Marriott and Peter Frampton were all briefly working together on Alexis Korner's second solo album, oddly entitled *Get Off My Cloud*; the irrepressibly chirpy Marriott, whose hard-rock group Humble Pie was close to disintegrating, spent much of the session trying to impress on Keith what a great successor he could be to Mick Taylor. It was also rumoured that as Keith was playing with Alexis, perhaps it was the British blues pioneer who would get the job with the Stones – although Mick and Keith always denied this was ever the case.

The hunt for a new Rolling Stones guitarist began in earnest in January 1975 and was not finally resolved until the beginning of April. Several stellar names tried out with the Stones, including Jeff Beck, already a significant guitar hero in his own right; the names of Beck's fellow Yardbirds guitar players, the deified Eric Clapton and even Led Zeppelin guitar hero Jimmy Page, the quintessential rock superstar, were also mentioned as potential replacements for Mick Taylor. Ry Cooder, Rory Gallagher, Peter Frampton, session ace Chris Spedding and Bowie sideman Mick Ronson were likewise in the running. One by one they checked into the Munich Hilton. But an unexpected outsider outpaced all of the contenders: Wayne Perkins, an American session guitarist. Perkins' credibility was extremely cool as far as Keith Richards was concerned: he had added touches of rock guitar to the Wailers' celebrated *Catch A Fire* album, helping lift it a level or two into the masterpiece it was already recognised as being. Wayne Perkins had been playing with the Stones for a month when Ron Wood arrived in Munich; his wife Chrissie was having an affair with Jimmy Page, and Honest Ron needed to get away from London.

Woody's lead and slide guitar turned out to be the exact counterpoint Keith's rhythm licks required within the context of the Rolling Stones; he could also play choppy rhythm in a double act with Keith. Ron Wood was also a songwriter, having co-written much of the Faces' material with Rod Stewart; he had played bass in the Jeff Beck group and he blew a competent harmonica. His distinctive jangling Zemaitis guitar had defined how many a rocking Faces' song would sound long before Rod Stewart's voice kicked in. What was more, he looked fantastic, a Mod stylist ten years on who seemed to have taken Keith's own idea of himself, added it to his own natural élan and transcended the both of them. (The Faces' sense of androgyny incorporated a 'Likely Lad' terrace football supporter mood of ambivalence.) With his spiky, jet-black rooster crop and supersized cigarette permanently inserted between his lips, a glass of Courvoisier and Coke never far from his hand, Woody moved across the stage in a kind of music-hall version of Chuck Berry's renowned duck walk. He also had a very large nose, which was useful when part of the job description required the ability to ingest nasally enormous amounts of cocaine. In some ways it was unfortunate that Ron Wood had always been a huge fan of the

Rolling Stones, and he remained one while a member of the group, his natural exuberance sustaining him through various tragedies of Shakespearean proportions. When it was clear to all and sundry that he had become a sort of cartoon version of Keith Richards, Junior Keef, in the process seeming to lose his own individuality in a way that subsumed and sidelined his talent, the idea of being a Rolling Stone was enough for him, another art-school boy surrendering to the act of turning himself into living art as Keith rather had done (although, in his case, the word 'living' might have been only relative). But everyone always loved the engaging Ronnie Wood, always up for a *larf*, and it was the same in the Rolling Stones: his uncanny ability always to find the right joke to crack at any given moment diluted the endless stresses in the group, in the studio and on the road. What was more, as a friend of both Mick Jagger and Keith Richards, Ron Wood could draw the two of them together and allow the pair to communicate; Mick felt that if they had Woody in the group, he would again have a conduit to Keith, whose various addictions horrified and frightened the singer. Anyway, it had been the life ambition of Ron Wood, the younger brother of Art Wood, who had played with Mick, Keith and Brian in Blues Incorporated, to join the Rolling Stones. The chemistry of the group was about to alter in a way that, whatever personal tragedies were still to unfold for all parties, was largely extremely positive.

There was only one problem: Ron Wood was still a member of the Faces. On 14 April 1975, it was announced to the press that Woody would be loaned out to the Stones for their next US tour. He would receive a quarter of a million dollars, an enormous amount of money at the time – though not so much when compared to the $450,000 that the other members of the group stood to make. The considerable publicity over Ron Wood's joining up with the Rolling Stones mentioned that Keith and the Face had become such good friends that they had been staying together at Wood's Richmond home. Like a warning to Woody about what he was getting himself into, The Wick was duly raided by the police a week later: Woody was still in Munich, recording with the Stones. The police discovered a smidgen of cocaine and cannabis, and Chrissie Wood, Ron's partially estranged wife, in bed with Audrey Burgon, a close friend. 'I think it was me and Anita the police were after,' commented Keith. 'Before they went to Woody's home they broke into a little cottage at the end of his garden where I sometimes stay when I'm in Britain. I was out of the country at the time but it looks as though they were hoping to pin something on Woody and me in one go.'

At the subsequent trial a year later at Kensington Crown Court, the police evidence – in an apparent rerun of the woman-in-a-fur-rug saga that had overhung the Redlands trial – made much play of the sleeping arrangements of the two beautiful women. Both were acquitted, but Ron Wood had to pay legal fees of £2,000, the equivalent at the time of a working man's annual income.

At the end of April the Rolling Stones transported themselves to the United States. For one particular member of the group, this was not the mere formality it might have been: Keith Richards' drug convictions meant that the issuing of a visa by the US Embassy in London was almost out of the question. Accordingly, Mick went to work in his role of unofficial group manager. Working on the connections he had developed through the charity concert the Stones had played for victims of the Nicaraguan earthquake, he found himself speaking to Walter Annenberg, the American ambassador in London. Off the record, Annenberg told Mick Jagger that if Keith was examined by the embassy doctor and found to be free of drugs, a visa would be granted. So for Keith it was back to the clinic in Switzerland, where once again his blood was cleaned out. As soon as the process had been completed, he took a plane back to London and drove straight to the US Embassy. After the appropriate medical examination, a visa was approved, and Keith was able to reacquaint himself with his drug of choice.

Even here there seemed to be a sinister degree of official collusion: as soon as Keith arrived in New York, a pair of FBI agents visited him in his hotel suite. Expecting a bust or a shakedown, their arrival made him extremely nervous and uncomfortable. The pair of G-men seemed to be operating in an official capacity, however: they told Keith that they were aware that General Motors, in an effort to attract the youth market, was sponsoring the tour. Speaking candidly, the two FBI agents informed Keith that they knew of his heroin habit and that they were most concerned about any adverse publicity that might befall the venerable American institution of General Motors if he were to be busted. Accordingly, they announced, arrangements had been made for Keith to be supplied by them with the finest-quality heroin throughout the coming tour. For the next three months they did exactly that. (Unbeknown to the Stones, this was not the first time the FBI had become interested in the group: Mick Jagger, especially his androgynous appearance, moved J. Edgar Hoover to fits of near-apoplexy, touching raw nerves deep within the secretly homosexual Director of the FBI. As though echoing Hoover's thoughts, the *Star*, a scandal-sheet sold largely at American supermarket checkouts, fired a xenophobic editorial salvo of the sort that might have greeted the Stones in the United States ten years previously: 'Mick Jagger should come to America more often because it does us good, really good to look at ourselves squarely in the eye and see where we have failed. Where have we failed that this simple-faced disciple of dirt is a hero, a rootin', tootin' hero to our teenager kids?

We have this pale-faced foreigner, this Englishman, getting $10 a seat from our kids to see him perform . . .' Must we fling this filth at our pop kids?

On 1 May 1975, the Stones drove down Fifth Avenue on a flatbed truck, playing 'Brown Sugar': leaflets were tossed to passers-by, giving details of the group's '1975 Tour of the Americas', due to open on 1 June in Baton Rouge, Louisiana, and end on 21 August in Caracas, the capital of Venezuela. It would be the longest set of dates ever performed by the group. There was a problem, however: Ron Wood needed to leave the Stones after their final date in the US, in Jacksonville, Florida, to join the Faces on tour. Who would play with the group for the South American shows?

The Stones were rehearsing at Andy Warhol's property in Montauk. On 18 May, Mick cut his hand badly on a restaurant window in the town: he had pushed against it, believing that it was the revolving glass door, and the subsequent wound needed twenty stitches. When Annie Liebovitz, the *Rolling Stone* photographer who was accompanying the rehearsals and tour, wanted to take pictures of the injury, Jagger initially demurred: but after he had decided to go along with Liebovitz's request, he was insistent that she use colour film and not merely black and white. (As the tour progressed, Annie Liebovitz was to become mired in the Stones' decadent lifestyle to such an extent that she felt she was fighting for her very soul.)

As announced, the dates began at the Louisiana State University in Baton Rouge on 1 June 1975; it was Ron Wood's twenty-eighth birthday, and before the show he was physically sick with nervousness. Much to the irritation of Keith, who felt the group should not have to rely on such frippery, a giant inflatable phallus formed the centrepiece of the stage set, which was designed in the shape of a lotus, five hydraulically raised petals jutting out into the audience. From then on, on subsequent tours, the Rolling Stones' stage sets would grow more and more costly, the group feeling a need always to outpace the visuals of the previous live outing. Mick's stage costume adopted a variety of guises, including that of a Cherokee Indian chief; Inca-style fabrics and Turkish pantaloons were included too. In terms of marketing it was surprising that the group did not have their new album in the stores; although here one might perhaps read a covert acknowledgement of the true source of the Stones' finances: although the group's records sold healthily, Led Zeppelin shifted five times as many 'units' as the Rolling Stones, the lion's share of whose income came from touring. As a last-minute gesture to the 'marketplace', a hastily assembled compilation of post-Decca songs, *Made in the Shade*, had been released on 13 June.

After the 25 June show at Madison Square Garden, the fourth of six concerts, Mick introduced the famously gay Billy Preston thus: 'He's staying at the St Moritz Hotel and he likes white boys.' Back at the Plaza hotel after the final Madison Square Garden concert, the film producer Julia Phillips found herself at a small party in Mick's suite (he had registered as Michael Phillips): 'Mick and Keith are between the beds on the floor of the bedroom, strumming guitars and not talking. They form a freaky little unit, right there on the floor, but there is something peaceful about the scene,' she thought. On 2 July, the Stones played their second show at the Capital Center, Washington DC. Along with Andy Warhol and fashion designer Guy Laroche, Bianca visited the White House at the invitation of Jack Ford, the son of President Gerald Ford, who had never heard of Mick Jagger. She was conducting an interview with Jack for Warhol's *Interview* magazine. Photographed reclining with him in the Lincoln bedroom, Bianca provoked considerable controversy, and the wrath of her husband; when Bianca and Jack Ford were pictured dancing together in New York the following week, the gossip only grew louder.

On 4 July, Independence Day, the Stones played to a crowd of 50,000 at the Memorial Stadium in Memphis. The following day Keith and Ron Wood decided they would take a pass on the *Starship*, the customised Boeing 720 jet liner in which the Rolling Stones were travelling, which Led Zeppelin and Elton John had also employed. Instead, they decided, they would drive across country to their next date, the Cotton Bowl in Dallas. In Fordyce, Arkansas, Keith – ever keen to be behind the wheel of a large, fast automobile – was pulled over by a police patrol. After being searched, he was charged with possession of an offensive weapon – his Swiss army knife: 'I bent down to change the waveband on the radio and the car swerved slightly. A police patrol vehicle then pulled out from a lay-by and stopped us. I was then questioned about having a "concealed weapon", a penknife complete with tin-opener and a device for removing stones from horses' hooves.' Luckily for Keith Richards and Ron Wood, the local cops' blend of naivety and reverent awe at their famous arrestees resulted in not the most assiduous of searches: both musicians had significant quantities of cocaine and heroin stashed about them. Only the cocaine was discovered, which Keith managed to persuade the arresting officers was tooth powder. Clearly feeling a need to immerse himself in the local customs, Ron Wood had emulated his guitar-playing predecessor in the Stones by almost instantly developing a heroin habit on joining the group; throughout this American tour and on subsequent European dates, Keith and Woody would smoke heroin-laced cigarettes while playing on-stage, presumably as some kind of narcotic respite from the heaps of cocaine and smack that before each show were piled carefully on top of their amplifiers, out of sight of the audience.

From 9 to 13 July, the Stones played five nights at the Forum in Los Angeles. At the first night's show, Ron Wood seemed rather to forget himself. 'They're a great rock 'n' roll band, aren't they? I wish I was playing with them,' he declared to the audience.

Bianca Jagger, who that morning had left the tap running in her bathroom and flooded her suite (something to which her husband was also frequently prone) at the Beverly Wilshire hotel, went to the concert with Raquel Welch; an unexploded cherry-bomb firework landed at her feet as she walked to her celebrity-area seat.

After that first LA show, a party was thrown for the group by Diana Ross at her home in Beverly Hills. This social occasion was rather tense: Ross had set up no fewer than four security checkpoints, through which each of the 500 guests had to pass, which meant there was a great deal of waiting around, pissing off the Stones. As Ms Ross' children were sleeping, the security guards then demanded that all guests leave the interior of the house and relocate in the garden – Bianca Jagger said she would only comply if 'Miss Ross' asked her personally. 'You should write something bitchy about her. She's very rude to people,' Mick suggested about his wife to the writer Lisa Robinson, who was accompanying the tour.

After the second night in LA, Keith commented on the new line-up: 'This band is less slick and sophisticated-sounding than the other one at its best, when everybody was in tune and could hear each other. This is a lot funkier, dirtier and rougher, and a lot more exciting. The problem for us when Mick Taylor left was whether to replace him or take the opportunity of a break to form a new band and make it different. Mick was a really nice player, but his interest was in melody and harmony and notes.' After the third night of the Forum dates, Ron Wood and Bill Wyman went to the Roxy on Sunset Strip to watch Bob Marley and the Wailers. On 19 July, Elton John joined the Stones on-stage at the Hughes Stadium in Denver: he rather outstayed his welcome, playing with the group for five numbers. 'People always want to know about your sex life,' said Mick that day. 'Because they've got nothing else to think about. Because they've got empty heads. Because stupid heads print it in newspapers. People like gossiping. Especially women. I am not down on women. I've got a song on the next album that's got a nice bit about them called "I Love Ladies".' We are still waiting to hear that song.

During the tour, en route to Milwaukee, Mick revealed his pragmatic attitude towards media coverage of himself: 'I don't read any of the analytical stuff. Those are the ones I skip. I only look at the front pages or the pictures, actually. Someone asked me if I minded bad reviews and I said no. As long as my picture is on the front page, I don't care what they say about me on page 96.' Of the addition of Ron Wood to the group, he declared, 'Ron Wood had to please both me and Keith. I can sort of tell a good guitar player, but probably Keith can tell better than me. Remember, he used to be lead guitarist for the Rolling Stones. Ron seems a natural in the respect that both he and Keith are brilliant rhythm guitarists. It allows a certain cross-trading of riffs not previously possible.'

Mick's thirty-second birthday took place in the inauspicious setting of Bloomington, Indiana, where the group played at the University Assembly Center; it was noticeable that Mick looked ten years younger than his birthdate would suggest. On 2 August, after what was originally intended to be the final show of the tour at the Gator Bowl in Jacksonville, Florida, Mick showed that he and the then prevalent mood of feminism did not necessarily see eye to eye: 'There is really no reason to have women on tour unless they've got a job to do. The only other reason is to screw. Otherwise they get bored, and they just sit around and moan.' No wonder the Coalition Against Macho-Sexist Music condemned the Stones for being 'perpetrators of sexist rock'. In Toronto Keith discovered that a blind girl had been following the group, hitchhiking to every show. He insisted that the road crew transport her to the concerts, making sure she had prime tickets every night. Later this simple act of kindness would be repaid. Keith had been accompanied throughout the tour of the United States by Uschi Obermeier: waking in Chicago, he found a 'goodbye' note from the sumptuous German model.

To maximise profits, the tour had been extended for another three dates, winding up in Buffalo in New York state at the appropriately named Rich Stadium; before that final show Mick, Keith and Ron Wood did acid, playing before an audience of 80,000 as they were tripping: the resultant set was somewhat sprawling. As a consequence of the extra shows, the Faces had to cancel the first three shows of their own tour. And with Ron Wood missing in action with the Faces, the South American dates were cancelled indefinitely.

After the tour ended, Mick went on holiday with Bianca and Jade to Ireland, where he was the guest of charming, amiable Desmond Guinness at Leixlip Castle. While there he announced that the Stones planned a pre-Christmas three-week European tour. Keith, meanwhile, had taken off for a sojourn in Thailand, the climate no doubt being the main attraction. Returning to the United States, he met up with Anita Pallenberg in Los Angeles. She fell pregnant again; it seemed that this awkward couple were unable to escape a destiny together.

In New York that summer Andy Warhol painted Mick Jagger's portrait. An established ritual of any of Warhol's fresh portraits was the 'unveiling' lunch, at which assorted invited celebrities would mingle. The Rolling Stones singer, however, broke with this tradition. 'Mick was wary of being used and said no,' said Bob Colacello, at the time the editor of Warhol's *Interview* magazine. As was his wont when working with a subject who might interest other collectors, Andy Warhol had painted several versions of the Jagger portrait. 'Mick, known for his frugality, restricted his choice to the three most flattering,' remembered Colacello. When Mick came to view the pictures, the writer observed a vignette that clearly indicated the apparent dysfunction in the Jagger marriage: 'He came down to look at it alone, and Bianca arrived a little later and left a little earlier in her own limo, their movements, like their marriage, increasingly out of synch.'

In December 1975 Mick tried to patch up the holes in his marriage. He took Bianca and Jade to Rio de Janeiro for Christmas. She responded to his generosity on the trip by displaying considerable passive aggression, a symptom of the deep depression welling within her over the state of her marriage. She was also consumed with a destructive mixture of guilt and secret joy over her own affairs: she had been seeing the actor Ryan O'Neal on and off since he had been in London in 1973, making Stanley Kubrick's *Barry Lyndon*. (During the time they were seeing each other, O'Neal also had relationships with Ursula Andress, Barbra Streisand and Joan Collins.) Her name was also linked with Jack Ford and the tennis champion Björn Borg, among others. But what could she do? She knew of Mick's endless parade of women (and sometimes men); although the motive of revenge had not been far from her mind when she first indulged in extramarital relationships, she also needed succour from the stresses of what was increasingly a dreadful partnership.

Mick's musical companionships seemed to be faring better, however. On 18 December Keith Richards turned thirty-two – and got his birthday present: after the completion of a British tour, Rod Stewart announced that day that he was leaving the Faces. His press spokesman declared, 'Rod feels he can no longer work in a situation where the group's lead guitarist, Ron Wood, seems to be permanently on loan to the Rolling Stones.' Woody was now free to join the group.

In January 1976, while the record that would be titled *Black and Blue* was mixed at Atlantic Studios in New York, Mick bought a house in Manhattan, on West 72nd Street. In February the group engaged Hiro, the Japanese fashion photographer, to shoot the sleeve for the new album: the shots were taken on a beach on Sanibel Island in Florida. Gossip columns carried scurrilous stories about Mick, Keith and Ron Wood all using the same stall in the restroom of a Miami restaurant, emerging with apparent bad head colds. On 28 February 1976 it was announced that the group would tour Europe in the spring, and that Ron Wood had now joined the group permanently as guitarist. A little under a month later, on 26 March, Anita

Pallenberg gave birth prematurely in Geneva to another son, Tara, his name a tribute to the late Tara Browne, whom she had first met through Brian Jones.

The twentieth of April 1976 saw the release of *Black and Blue*, the new album from the Rolling Stones. The fresh blood had clearly been good for the group: it was their best record since *Exile on Main Street*, and a demonstrably different sound from any of the records that had preceded it. Hinged around semi-funk, semi-reggae grooves it sounded fresh and vital from the moment the stylus hit the vinyl on track one, side one. 'Hot Stuff', the opening tune, set the tone, a number clearly influenced by the wildly sexual style of the new imperial guards of American black music, the Ohio Players; the more lyrical, melodic 'Hand Of Fate' continued the mood, followed by a superb rendition of a reggae tune, Eric Donaldson's huge Jamaican hit 'Cherry Oh Baby' ('Irie!' called out Keith, using a Rastafarian term of approbation, in the midst of the middle eight; he was plainly enjoying himself). The side sloped to a close with 'Memory Motel', a semi-ballad love song set in a motel in Montauk. Side two staggered in with 'Hey Negrita', another semi-reggae song, 'inspired' by Ronnie Wood (as with 'It's Only Rock And Roll', he surely would have preferred a compositional credit and the resulting royalties) whose title was a reference to Mick's pet name for Bianca (he would also refer to her, simply, as 'B'). 'Melody' was a slow blues, and 'Crazy Mama', a moody tune in a similar mould, rounded off the set; in between was 'Fool To Cry', the by now obligatory commercial Stones ballad that served as the single-as-trailer. There were only eight songs, but with a running time of almost forty minutes *Black and Blue* was a significant return to form.

On the European tour, which kicked off in Frankfurt, Germany, on 28 April, the group included four numbers off the new album: 'Fool To Cry', 'Hey Negrita', 'Hand Of Fate' and 'Hot Stuff'; also featured were 'Honky Tonk Women', 'All Down The Line' off *Exile*, 'Get Off Of My Cloud', 'You Can't Always Get What You Want', 'Happy', 'You Got To Move', 'Brown Sugar', 'Midnight Rambler', 'Jumpin' Jack Flash' and 'Street Fighting Man'. Mick wore a silver leather bum-freezer jacket, and climaxed the set by swinging on a rope over the audience, drenching the front rows of the audience with buckets of water. 'Messrs Wood and Richard flanked Jagger, looking for all the world like a pair of diseased crows,' wrote Charles Shaar Murray in his review of the first night's show for the *NME*.

On the American leg of the tour the group's set was preceded by the pseudo-portentous bombast of Aaron Copland's *Fanfare for the Common Man*, a piece of music once used for the same purpose by pomp-rockers Emerson, Lake and Palmer. In Europe, the sounds were considerably hipper: Robert Johnson, Earl Hooker, Bo Diddley's 'You Don't Love Me', and assorted scratchy 45s direct from Kingston; although reviewers made the understandable assumption that these songs were the choice of Keith Richards and possibly Mick Jagger, the tape had been put together by the latest addition to the Rolling Stones, Honest Ron Wood.

At that first Frankfurt show the tone of the tour had been set by Keith's falling flat on his back during the final number, continuing to play until he was pulled to his feet by Mick Jagger; during 'Fool To Cry' he had visibly nodded out, playing as though he were sleepwalking. On 1 May a *Daily Mirror* story indicated that Keith and Anita were planning to marry on stage during the British dates. 'I've been asked so often by the press and by both our families when we are going to get married that I thought we might as well,' said Keith. 'There are so many papers we have to produce, especially when we travel with the children, that it might just simplify things to have the same name on our passports.'

Keith might well have required some legal support in his life. At five in the morning on 19 May, returning to London with Anita and Marlon from the group's show the previous night in the vast cowshed that is the New Bingley Hall in Stafford, Keith nodded out while barrelling down the fast lane of the M1 motorway past the Newport Pagnell service station. Glancing against the central barrier, the rebuilt Bentley bounced off the road and down an embankment into a field, where it was discovered by a police squad car. Although Keith had immediately ditched his stash of assorted drugs, he had neglected to remove the solid-silver coke spoon and container he wore around his neck with naughty-schoolboy-like bravado. The investigating police officers saw it straight away, and the devices and contents were taken away for 'analysis'.

The show had to go on, of course. Back in London for their first dates with Ron Wood, the group played six nights at the 17,000-capacity Earl's Court exhibition hall, from 21 to 26 May. On the first day of the London shows, Princess Margaret – clearly ignoring the dictum of her sister, Queen Elizabeth II, that her friendship with Mick Jagger was not especially in accord with her royal position – was a backstage visitor. She did not show up, however, at the party the group threw after the first date at the Cockney Pride pub, a consciously arch venue, at Piccadilly Circus.

After one show Mick went to dinner with Bryan Ferry and his girlfriend Jerry Hall, a beautiful, leggy 19-year-old Texan who became one of the first supermodels. In the restaurant and later at Ferry's newly purchased elegant Holland Park house, Mick Jagger flirted with increasing outrageousness with the model, infuriating the fey Ferry, who stormed off to bed. Jerry Hall was so shocked by Mick Jagger's behaviour that she refused to lower herself (literally, as he was some four inches shorter than her) to kissing him goodnight. All the same, a connection had been made.

Marlon Richards went everywhere with his father on those dates, propping up barstools with him as his sidekick while Keith glugged down large measures of Jack Daniel's. Marlon, at the age of seven, was Keith's confidant and best friend, a typical and not necessarily healthy example of a child 'parenting' a dysfunctional father, a role reversal that inevitably made Marlon old before his time. Even then, signs of inchoate anger would surface in the boy; once, when Bianca Jagger put him to bed, she found that Marlon's socks were literally stuck to his feet: he had been wearing them for a month, the small boy told his glamorous carer. 'He took care of me while I was doing heroin on the road. He used to be my roadie when he was five, six, seven. He's seen everything. To him it's not a big deal. It's just something Dad did. But we keep together and we love each other,' said Keith later, with no sense of self-reproach.

Dandelion, however, found herself virtually ignored. She clearly could not cope with parents who seemed unable to cope with her; at the age of four she could hardly speak. 'On the road she used to go off by herself, pick up guys, bring them back: "Mummy, here!" Big guys. And I'd get really scared. And she'd go out of the hotel room and I'd find her sitting on the lap of somebody,' remembered Anita. Eventually, after much consultation within the family, Dandelion, who soon renamed herself Angela, went to live with Doris Richards in Dartford, and was never to live with Keith again.

Perhaps it was good for her to be out of the way: Keith Richards was having a terrible time. On 4, 5 and 6 June, the Stones played at Les Abattoirs in Paris. The shows were being recorded for a possible double live album. During the morning of the final concert, Anita, in Geneva with their baby son, found that ten-week-old Tara had suffocated in his cot – a 'cot death', as such mysterious incidents are defined. Anita flew straight to Paris and into the arms of Keith who, smacked out even more than usual, played an extraordinary show that night; the passion and intensity of his playing was preserved on the live album, *Love You Live*, three sides of which came from that final Paris show. Was Tara's death the wake-up call he had long needed? Nick Kent, the *NME* journalist who, to his own detriment had so often embarked on heroin binges with Keith Richards, certainly thought so: 'I really thought Keith and Anita were going to die. I'd seen him in bad states but they were crying and literally carrying each other out after the gig that night. Keith is a bright guy and a sensitive guy, but he was taking such large amounts of that drug that they killed his conscience. I think that Tara's death made him understand it morally. "We're going to shit. My family's falling apart. I'm going to jail." '

Keith's personal hell showed no sign of receding. On 9 June Newport Pagnell police confirmed the results of the analysis of the coke paraphernalia confiscated from him on the night of the car crash. He was to be charged with possession of LSD – a tab had allegedly been found in the car – as well as cocaine. The news of Tara's death was kept from the press until 18 June. When the house in Switzerland was cleared out by a mutual friend, he found over five hundred used syringes scattered about the property, as well as drugs worth more than £10,000, the equivalent in 1976 of an executive's annual salary.

On 2 August Keith was in court in Newport Pagnell on charges of cannabis and cocaine possession, to be remanded on bail until the following month. Nineteen days later the group appeared at Knebworth House in Hertfordshire at the by now annual one-day festival, widely rumoured to be the group's last appearance; on her way home alone Bianca's limousine broke down. 'A BBC-TV crew, returning from Knebworth, sighted Bianca Jagger, all in white, standing by her ditched limousine and trying to thumb a ride back to London,' wrote Philip Norman in his fine work *The Stones*. 'The BBC men offered her a place in their car. Travelling back, sharing the marijuana joint she offered round, they were surprised how friendly, warm and funny Bianca turned out to be.' On 6 September Keith again appeared before Aylesbury Magistrates Court, and was remanded on bail until 6 October. On that date he arrived two and a half hours late for the hearing, claiming his trousers had not been returned from the dry-cleaner's. 'It strikes me as extraordinary that any gentleman of his stature can only afford one pair of trousers,' said Mrs Mary Durbridge, the presiding magistrate, forfeiting Keith's bail of £100. He elected for jury trial on the charges of cocaine and LSD possession and was given further bail of £5,000.

As with many rock 'n' roll musicians, the emotional development of the Rolling Stones' key players had effectively ended with the beginnings of their success, when life became a glorified version of hotel room service, and anything – food, females, cars, expensive overseas holidays, houses, drugs – could be obtained with a phone call. They had little sense of the full extent of the sycophancy that surrounded them, an obsequiousness that meant their every whim would be granted unquestioningly because their employees' and associates' livelihoods were assured thereby.

The teenage male gang aspect of the group had been given a further lease of life with the addition of Ron Wood, an ideal partner-in-crime for Keith Richards, whose idea of fun could be satisfied in the finding of more and more arcane ways of wrecking hotels. Despite his grief at Tara's death, Keith had participated with gusto in the trashing of their Viennese hotel ('No: not the chandelier!' Mick's careful tones could be heard exhorting him above the general clamour of destruction) on 23 June, the last day of the European tour, for which the group were presented with a damages bill of £5,000. Despite their being men in their early thirties, Keith and Woody together turned into naughty schoolboys: Mick would be infuriated when, as he tried to discuss business with Prince Rupert, the duo, considerably chemically fortified, would burst into his hotel suite and bounce up and down on his kingsize bed as 'the Trampolini Twins'. For his part, Mick's leonine narcissism and adoration of the wealthy and famous irritated and angered Keith, almost as much as the singer's exaggerated campness and endless dramatics hit nerves in the first man in the group to have worn eye make-up.

It was not an easy time to be managing the Rolling Stones; rather than risk the rigour of potentially fractious studio sessions for a new album, Mick Jagger decided to press ahead with his plans for the group to release a live double album. There seemed to be a market for such records, especially in the United States where, that summer, Peter Frampton's *Frampton Comes Alive* soft-rock set had topped twenty million sales. The group, it was decided, would reconvene in Toronto, Canada, and play a number of shows that would be recorded in a small club, the El Macombo, to round off the material already in the can.

In the choice of location there was a practical consideration: it was highly likely that Keith would be found guilty of the drugs charges arising out of the M1 car-crash drugs bust; and that as a consequence he would not be permitted to enter the United States. Furthermore, as well as allowing Mick to commute to Manhattan to negotiate a new contract for Rolling Stones Records, which had run the course of its present deal with Atlantic and for which Mick was seeking an advance in the region of fifteen million dollars, Canada seemed a suitably out-of-the-way location for the group to weather the present storms of musical fashion. In Britain there had been a shift in critical consensus that had led to hip individuals re-evaluating the position of the Rolling Stones.

Like something that had been simmering so palpably below the surface of contemporary culture that it could almost be touched, punk rock had all of a sudden emerged as the populist mouthpiece in the late summer of 1976. Accompanied by a succession of contrived outrages, largely hinged around fights at gigs, the Sex Pistols had outclassed the Rolling Stones as *the* expression of grassroots angst. Nick Kent, the *NME* writer in whom had appeared to be imbued the spirit of the Rolling Stones, had been attacked with a bicycle chain at the 100 Club Punk Festival at the end of August 1976 by Sid Vicious, who was soon to be given the job of bass player with the Pistols; The Clash, who had also played at that event, had a song whose chorus line ran, 'No Elvis, Beatles or Rolling Stones/In 1977'. Yet soon, in clear emulation of 'Mr Rock 'n' Roll', Vicious would have as bad a heroin habit as Keith Richards; Pistols' guitarist Steve Jones and Clash founder Mick Jones hero-worshipped the Stones' guitarist. Most of the derision heaped upon the Rolling Stones was aimed at Mick Jagger and his socialite lifestyle: Keith Richards' 'outlaw' life was considered by even the most hardline punks as the epitome of cool, and he emerged scot-free from this trial by the next generation of British rockers.

How would he fare, however, when he came once again to face a British court over the small matter of the Newport Pagnell drugs bust?

In fact, yet again Keith managed to slip away from court without a prison sentence. At Aylesbury Crown Court on 13 January 1977 his legal counsel put forward a partial defence that the Rolling Stones were such an anarchic bunch of bohemians that after a show, individual members of the group would merely grab whatever item of clothing came to hand in the dressing room and depart wearing it: hence Keith could hardly be expected to know what was in his pockets. In the stuffy, backwater atmosphere of Buckinghamshire, such a line was not going to wash with the jury and judge; besides, the coke-snorter had been around his neck. Mick Jagger, who had arrived from Los Angeles to offer support, discreetly held his head in his hands as the case drew to a conclusion. Consequently after a three-day trial Keith was found guilty of possession of the cocaine-snorting paraphernalia and its residue; it was accepted, however, that the tab of acid in his car might have been the property of some other unknown individual. Keith Richards was fined £750 with £250 costs, a sentence of considerable leniency; but he was warned that if he was ever again before a court in Britain on drugs charges, there would be no question of him not being given a custodial sentence.

On 16 February it was announced that the Rolling Stones had signed a deal for Rolling Stones Records with EMI Records for rights in all the world territories except the United States and Canada. On 18 February Keith had another court judgement go against him, a relatively minor one this time: almost predictably he had omitted to purchase a road-tax disc for his Bentley and was fined £25 for using the car in that condition on the night of the Newport Pagnell bust. Two days later Mick, Bill Wyman, Charlie Watts and Ron Wood arrived in Toronto. Five nights of shows at the El Macombo were due to begin on 4 March and the group needed to be at their sharpest for the live recording; it was more than six months since they had last played live, and any hint of rustiness needed to be scraped off their playing.

Yet 'Mr Redlands', the name under which Keith Richards had been booked into the Harbour Castle Hilton Hotel in Toronto, was not yet in Canada; the sobriquet was the clue to his whereabouts. At Redlands, life was being lived in customary fashion, Keith too busy rolling joints and jacking up smack and snorting coke and swigging down Jack Daniel's even to think about taking the increasingly frantic phone calls from Toronto, let alone getting on a plane. In the midst of yet another pointless, demeaning argument with Anita an angry telegram arrived, signed by the other four Stones: WE WANT TO PLAY. YOU WANT TO PLAY. WHERE ARE YOU?

Five days after the rest of the group had arrived in Toronto, Keith, Anita and Marlon were splayed in their first-class plane seats, heading for Canada. In order to alleviate his almost overwhelming feelings of stress, Keith stumbled off to the bathroom, banged up the smidgen of smack he had brought with him for the purpose, stashed the works in a waste bin and drowsily edged his way back to his seat, dropping the spoon in which he'd cooked the heroin in a bag belonging to Anita. It was a strange thing to do: was this a subconscious attempt to sabotage his life and thereby be forced to come off heroin? Was it a way of trying to get Anita out of his life? Or was Keith simply so out of it that he didn't know what he was doing? Whatever the reason, there was a good chance the spoon would never have been discovered had Canadian customs officials, irritated by Anita's superstar arrogance, not decided to search every single one of her twenty-eight pieces of luggage. The spoon was discovered, coated in the residue of Keith's in-flight fix, along with a lump of hash that Anita had forgotten she had with her; along with these items a TicTac mint discovered in the bottom of her bag was also sent for analysis. Arrested but not yet charged, Anita was soon despatched on her way from the airport to the Harbour Castle Hilton. No charges were brought against Keith.

Two days later a posse of plain-clothes Royal Canadian Mounted Police came knocking on the door of their hotel suite. Thinking it was probably Marlon, Anita opened the door and the Mounties stepped through it, waving warrants to search the premises. Within no time at all, they had unearthed an ounce of heroin and five grams of white powder. Much more difficult than finding the drugs was the task of getting the sleeping Keith to wake up. By the time he came to, his cheeks had been slapped so many times they were red. Keith claimed afterwards to have been upset that the officers were in plain clothes and were not wearing the Mountie uniforms he had seen in children's comics, but this seems like characteristic after-the-event bravado; the reality was that Keith had not especially improved his position by asking the Mounties if he could have back a bit of the heroin until he managed to cop some more. The fact was, he was in a very serious situation indeed, initially with both himself and Anita facing charges not simply of heroin possession but of heroin trafficking. The charges against Anita were ultimately dropped; Keith, however, was looking at the likelihood of a lengthy prison term in a Canadian jail: the charge carried a sentence of seven years to life.

No sympathy came his way from the rest of the Rolling Stones. It was only ten weeks since he had been threatened with a prison term in Britain. The group were furious with him for so jeopardising their futures. They were also frightened: what if they were planted with drugs and busted themselves? Mick flew off to Manhattan for a couple of days, ostensibly for meetings about the new recording contract, which also had a shadow cast over it by Keith's latest and most serious bust. Unable to feed his habit, Keith now went into serious withdrawal; drug-free Bill Wyman, who had hardly spoken to him for the entire decade, was so moved by his plight after he found Keith rolling around in agony on his bathroom floor that he summoned the more streetwise Ron Wood, and the pair set off to score some smack for Keith to save him from such pain. Even so, Keith's level of denial about his personal problems was extraordinary. When Chet Flippo arrived to interview him for *Rolling Stone*, Keith's art-school outlaw persona raised its characteristic head in the interview he gave: 'They are out to make rock and roll illegal. That's the basic drive behind the whole thing. They are just scared of that rhythm. Every sound has an effect on the body, and the effects of a good backbeat makes those people shiver in their boots. So you are fighting some primeval fear that you can't rationalise.' That was it then: it had nothing to do with possession of an enormous amount of a deadly narcotic.

The shows at the El Macombo, which seemed likely to be Keith Richards' swansong, did benefit from this position; although they had been cut down to two dates, Flippo believed them to be the greatest gigs he had ever seen. For Mick the shows on 5 and 6 March were pretty much business as usual: the zip of his jumpsuit was pulled down to just above his pubic bone – like many Hollywood stars Mick was apparently devoid of bodily hair – and girls at the front of the stage in the small club spent much of the gig grabbing at his genitals. 'It was fun on stage last night,' said Mick the next day, 'but all these girls were grabbing my balls. Once they started they didn't stop. It was great up to a point, then it got very difficult to sing.' Asked what would happen to the Stones if Keith was sent to jail, Mick Jagger took up a habitual pragmatic position: 'If the Rolling Stones wanted to tour badly or to go on stage, I think they'd have to. Obviously we wouldn't if Keith were only in jail for a short period of time, but we can't wait five years.'

To add to the political nightmare of the group's situation, Margaret Trudeau, the twenty-eight-year-old somewhat estranged wife of self-styled hip-and-groovy Canadian prime minister Pierre Trudeau, insisted on hanging out with the group, ostentatiously smoking marijuana. The press couldn't believe its luck; she was allegedly deeply embroiled in an affair with Mick. There was not an ounce of truth in this. From Manhattan Mick issued a press statement: 'Margaret Trudeau is a very attractive and nice person, but we are not having an affair. I've never met her before, and haven't seen her since I got to New York. In fact I haven't seen her since Sunday. What can I say? I'm in New York to be with my wife and my daughter.' But Margaret Trudeau *was* having an affair with one member of the Rolling Stones – Ron Wood. The Canadian dollar had fallen one and a half cents against the pound, and this minor currency crisis was blamed on her relationship with the group.

On 7 March, the day after the second El Macombo show, Keith was in court, and was remanded for seven days until 14 March on the heroin possession charges. As he left the building his hair was grabbed by angry bystanders with screams of, 'Deport the limey!' and, 'Junkie bastard!' He had been ordered to return to court the next day, when he was also charged with possession of a fifth of an ounce of cocaine, further to the analysis of the white powder in the hotel suite. By now Keith's customary bravado in the face of the legal process had evaporated: his head bowed, he looked a broken man. On 14 March, at the Brampton courtroom in Toronto, he was further remanded on bail until 27 June. The same day Anita was fined $400 for importing hashish. By now the rest of the Stones had left Canada – fled, more like – leaving the odd couple on their own, overseen by poor Marlon. One old ally did remain behind, however; loyal, dependable Ian 'Stu' Stewart. On 12 March Keith went into Toronto's Interchange Studios with Stu, where he recorded a handful of sad, desperate blues songs that he had learned from Gram Parsons back in those deranged days in the South of France. Somewhere in the midst of it all Keith came to his senses, and decided to face his personal pain.

CHAPTER 22

A ROCK AND A HARD PLACE

For the rest of March 1977 the traumatised Keith Richards remained in his Toronto hotel suite, on bail. When he, Anita and Marlon visited Niagara Falls, Keith was only half joking when he asked, 'Shall I jump?' At the end of that month Keith Richards' lawyers managed to obtain permission for him to leave Canada to 'practise his profession'; his legal representatives furthered their argument with the information that he had been granted a US visa to attend heroin-addiction treatment at the Stevens Psychiatric Center in New York state: the visa carried the strictest of provisos, only permitting him to travel within a thirty-mile radius of the clinic. With Anita, he went through a cure based around the administering of mild electric shocks, like neuro-electric acupuncture; this was the 'black box' treatment developed by addictions specialist Meg Patterson, who had helped Eric Clapton to come off heroin. As part of the treatment, which Keith approached in a state of fear, he also underwent detoxification and therapy. When Mick Jagger was obliged to drive out to the clinic to let him hear a mix of the tapes of the new album *Love You Live*, the tension between them dissolved in a drinking session that concluded – in a reversal of their usual roles – with the singer passing out, dead drunk. (When it was released in September of that year, *Love You Live* proved to be a phenomenal warts-and-all representation of the Stones' live set, an absolutely fabulous, rough, raw record. Which was just as well, all things considered. 'Keith, of course, is completely straight,' Mick utters at one point between songs, with a clear double meaning, in a brief peroration about the sexuality of the various group members, during the El Macombo sequence; the rest of the live album had been recorded on that night in Paris that Keith's son Tara had died.)

The cure was successful. But Keith didn't stick to it; back in New York, he was hanging out and trying to record with John Phillips, former leading light of the Mamas and the Papas, who had made such wistful, innocent-sounding hits as 'California Dreamin' '. Phillips was now himself mired in heroin addiction, and very soon Keith was back on smack (Phillips had some stuff of his own to blot out with the drug: he had had a brief affair with Bianca Jagger, which Mick had discovered. Apparently unfazed by this revelation, Mick had continued his friendship with the American musician, until the moment for revenge came and Mick fucked his seventeen-year-old daughter.)

Toronto was a turning-point not only for Keith and Anita, but also for Mick and Bianca Jagger. Back in New York, Mick had once again run into the rangy Texan model, Jerry Hall, at Studio 54, the disco temple of decadence. Mick was especially impressed that Jerry was a self-made success, earning huge fees for her modelling: she even owned her own ranch in Texas. When her father suddenly died within days of this meeting, Bryan Ferry, her emotionally uptight boyfriend, claimed he was too busy making his new album to see her. Genuinely concerned, Mick put a symbolic protective arm around Jerry and helped her through it. Here was another foreign girlfriend – as his mother had been, his female archetype (even Marianne was only half English). Bryan Ferry, long established as Jerry's boyfriend, who was recording in Switzerland, was distraught: 'But I thought Mick was my friend,' he cried to Simon Puxley, his closest real friend. The self-styled lounge lizard subsequently immersed himself in his work and poured his emotions into *The Bride Stripped Bare*, thereby making one of his finest-ever albums.

Mick and Bianca separated. It was the usual way of things at the end of a Mick Jagger relationship: when his wife filed for divorce, Mick's response was to cancel immediately all Bianca's New York charge accounts. At 48 Cheyne Walk, even the furniture was removed, and Jade was told it was being taken away to be repaired. Mick offered Bianca a settlement of $100,000. Bianca responded by attempting to get the case heard in California, with its laws that were extremely favourable for 'wronged' women, hiring Marvin Mitchelson, a celebrated Los Angeles lawyer who had wrung an enormous 'palimony' settlement from Lee Marvin for his ex-mistress. Mitchelson shortly announced that he would be claiming twelve and a half million dollars from Mick Jagger, which amounted to half his estimated earnings since the marriage, as well as maintenance of over $13,000 a month. Ultimately Mick managed to get the case heard in a British court, and in 1980 Bianca received a final settlement of one million dollars and custody of Jade.

Marsha Hunt continued to refuse to comment publicly on her case against Mick. In September 1977 a mutual friend of Marsha and Mick Jagger brokered a meeting between them. Karis had an afternoon out with her father, who had arrived with Jerry Hall, his new girlfriend, and although she now had a code name and number for calling him, he didn't offer her any more money – even though Marsha felt it was clear that he could see how she had stretched herself to pay for Karis's education.

By now Anita was in a far worse physical state than Keith had ever been. Her teeth resembled an exaggerated version of Keith's, prior to the costly reconstruction job on which Keith had embarked in 1974. Her metabolism running awry from drug and alcohol consumption, this once stunningly beautiful woman was bloated and ungainly, her skin blotchy; with her unshaven legs she resembled an ancient Mediterranean peasant woman. She found herself effectively banished to Frog Hollow, a house Keith had bought in South Salem in New York State, from whence she would foray forth to New York nightclubs, manic and unrecognisable, allegedly on the prowl for teenage boys.

In March 1978 the group moved to Woodstock in upper New York State, ostensibly to begin rehearsals for that summer's US tour. The chief priority for Mick Jagger, however, was to get Keith off heroin; Keith concurred that this was absolutely paramount, and persuaded Meg Patterson to let him have one of her black boxes. Like many people, Mick lived on several levels at the same time; and although on one hand he was motivated by genuine concern, there was another very Mick Jagger purpose at work here. 'Millions of dollars depended on it,' wrote Jerry Hall in *Tall Tales*, her autobiography.

And the whole thing was going to fall through if Keith didn't get off heroin. Mick loves Keith, you know. They're like a married couple and they're dearest friends. And it gave Mick a very good feeling to be able to help Keith. He did it staying with us in Woodstock. He got off heroin right on our couch. I don't know if Keith even remembers this, but for a few weeks he was just lying there. Mick and I would feed him. And every time the clips fell off we'd hook them back on. And we'd cover him with a blanket at night. It must have been so painful. He just slept and slept all the time. And he lost a lot of weight, and when he got up he'd be so weak. And then he started getting better. You know the feeling you have when you have a child and you watch him grow? We were like, 'Look, he's having a bath!' and 'Oh, did you see what he was doing today? He's really much better.'

Then when he started getting more together you could see him getting more macho. His ego thing was coming back and he'd start going out and throwing knives at trees. He started getting his temper back and we didn't mind that because it was a good sign. And he started suntanning and exercising and Mick talked to him a lot and it was so sweet to see. For Mick, seeing his friend get himself together is what made him really never want to take strong drugs again.

What Keith really needed now, Mick and Ron Wood decided, both wary that Keith and Anita might resume their relationship, was some sexual healing. One early spring day Jo Carslake, Woody's girlfriend, arrived in Woodstock with a beautiful friend, Lilly Wenglass Green, a Swedish model with a strong character and a good sense of humour, with the specific intention of having her get off with Keith. Importantly, drugs held no great appeal for Lilly. For the next two years she was Keith's girlfriend, shielding him from individuals likely to offer him narcotic substances, and thereby incurring their wrath. One of those who found herself almost religiously kept away was Anita Pallenberg, who plunged even more deeply into a state of almost permanent self-anaesthesia.

Mick showed an unexpected side when he appeared in *The Rutles*, a hilarious spoof documentary produced by *Monty Python* star Eric Idle that parodied the career trajectory of the Beatles. First screened in the United States at the end of March 1978, Mick played himself, giving his memories of the golden era of Rutlemania: 'We were living in squalor. We didn't have any money, and there were the Rutles on TV with girls chasing them. And we thought, "This can't be that difficult." So we thought we'd have a go ourselves.' Describing the Stones as having been 'the south's answer to the Rutles', he recalled seeing them play at New York's Che stadium: 'About twenty minutes, and that was it – off! Helicopter. Back to the Warwick hotel. Two birds each.' His memories were vivid, he said, of his journey with the Rutles to see Arthur Sultan, the Surrey mystic and ouija-board guru, in Bognor Regis: 'The Bognor thing was really funny – the Bognor Express they called it in the newspapers. Someone was very late – one of the girls, they're always late! They thought we were trying to get on the Rutles' bandwagon – y'know, the Rutles' mystical bandwagon. This wasn't true at all: we were just as eager as anyone else to find out about this board-tapping business in Bognor.' Why did the Rutles break up? 'Women. Just women, getting in the way. *Cherchez la femme*, y'know.' Filmed before he and Bianca had split up, the sixty-minute programme featured a cameo part by Mick's now estranged wife, as Martini, a French actress who spoke 'no English and precious little French'. Both emerged well from this piece of state-of-the-art comedy, and you felt sorry that they had allegedly parted company.

As Keith emerged from purgatory into some approximation of normality, he and Mick headed to Jamaica for the One Love Peace Concert on 27 April 1978, the hippest cultural event anywhere on the planet that year, which was held when Bob Marley returned to Jamaica following an assassination attempt on him in December 1976. The concert was an attempt to bring to their senses the warring political factions in the island's undeclared civil war, and in a moment of intense symbolism Marley held aloft the hands of Prime Minister Michael Manley and opposition leader Edward Seaga and brought them together. Just before Bob's symbolic act the more militant Peter Tosh – the self-styled 'Minister of Herb' who was formerly one third of the Wailers with Bob Marley – had berated the leaders of the 'shitstem' and to their fury lit up a spliff on-stage, an offence for which he was soon soundly beaten by members of the Jamaican police force.

At the end of 1977 Keith had persuaded Mick that Rolling Stones Records should sign the superb Tosh, who had played in the Wailers for almost ten years prior to the release of the classic *Catch A Fire* and *Burnin'* albums and the subsequent break-up of the original trio. Tosh had a wealth of material, some of which by now had appeared on two milestone LPs on the Virgin label, *Legalise It* and *Equal Rights*.

For the first Peter Tosh single on the Stones' label, Tosh and Mick between them chose a version of the Temptations' classic '(You Gotta Walk And) Don't Look Back', which he had previously covered in 1966 with the Wailers for Jamaica's seminal Studio One label. On this new version he and Mick bouncily traded lyrics, and the record was a UK hit. A promotional film, a performance video, was shot at Strawberry Hill, an exquisitely beautiful location in the Blue Mountains ten miles above Kingston, somewhere secure and out of the way of the capital's volatile political scene. As a backdrop for the shoot a great many bed-sheets were painted red, gold and green by a sound man from Scratch Perry's Black Ark studio: they included the odd detail of Mick's Dunlop-tyre lips painted in Rastafarian colours. Adrian Boot was there to take photographs. 'Jagger was in a very good mood, enjoying it because Strawberry Hill is fun,' remembered Boot. 'He was poncing around the lawn, smoking spliffs, rapping with Sly and Robbie. He was dressed incongruously, as though he was going to a New York nightclub, in some creamy striped thing. He and Tosh were getting on well: in Tosh's eyes, Jagger was this super-duper megastar. And as far as Jagger was concerned, Tosh was this highly credible Jamaican musician who was going to transform his business life. So there was synergy there. I often think the later bitterness in Tosh came from that period and because he didn't become that superstar.'

In a rather typically piratical Jamaican manner, playback tapes of the single went missing from the shoot: 'A few days later the single was on the streets in a dub version, before Mick Jagger had even flown back to England.' On a *Saturday Night Live* performance of the song, Peter Tosh was horrified and furious when – in mid-song, and networked on US television – Mick, in an act of arch wilfulness, leaned forward and kissed the militant Minister of Herb full on the lips: such 'battyman' behaviour was anathema to the Jamaican, and he considered it the gravest of insults.

Still, Tosh performed as support act to the Stones on the group's next tour, along with the revered American R 'n' B singer Etta James.

Keith Richards had always been a true guitar freak, adoring the different feel and tone he would get from vintage instruments; hence his great distress after the theft of eleven of his guitars from Nellcôte. One of the first British rockers to play a Gibson Les Paul, on early American tours he would search out pawnbrokers with Brian Jones, buying up guitars they wouldn't have had a hope of finding in Britain. By the early 1970s he had started to concentrate on playing Fender Telcasters; he was also fond of the Dan Armstrong plexiglass guitar, and among the instruments stacked together on the sleeve of *Get Yer Ya-Yas Out*, the plexiglass belonged to Keith and the Les Paul was Mick Taylor's. In the studio, Keith favoured playing through very old Fender amps. After Keith ordered ten new reproductions of vintage Fender Telcasters, he sent them back when they arrived, claiming they looked too new – he wanted brand-new, vintage, battered guitars, looking as though they had been around since the 1950s: as a consequence, Fender had to invent ways of making them looked aged. As a consequence of this whim of Keith's, Fender developed a line of highly priced vintage replicas called 'Relics' – thoroughly beaten-up new guitars.

Over the years Keith's playing became increasingly idiosyncratic. In the first and third phases of the group's career, he went for a style derived from the Muddy Waters group of the 1950s in which the sound of the guitars would mesh together. During the Mick Taylor phase, however, there was a much clearer demarcation between the lead and rhythm guitars. This was the period during which Keith Richards first became regarded as a guitar hero: his idiosyncrasies included the open G tuning he had learned from Ry Cooder in the late 1960s, and his fondness for removing the bottom string from his instruments. What are the ingredients of your style? he was once asked. 'Five strings, two fingers, one arsehole,' came the reply.

From the moment he joined the group, Ron Wood did most of the slide work, and played a customised Zemaitis guitar with an engraved steel front, a workshop creation. As well as helping create the illusion that Keith had two faces and four hands, Ron Wood, one of nature's second bananas, was an easy guy to be in a band with, a nice bloke, who was fun to be around and didn't get in other people's faces. During those 1978 dates Honest Ron Wood healed the rift between Keith and Bill Wyman that had lasted for almost ten years, bringing them together in a hotel room: 'Keith insisted I had never liked him,' said Bill. 'It was like two kids making up after a fight. "I never disliked you, Keith," I answered. "Remember when you went to live in Switzerland for a drug cure – I wrote you letters, and you sent me a lovely letter back with pressed flowers in it? It was *you* who never made any attempt to keep a relationship going." "Oh well, let's be mates now then," he said. And we were. Woody is a great catalyst.'

The next US tour dates, confined to the United States (Canadian shows were not deemed appropriate, and the US tour was overshadowed by the knowledge that Keith might be going to jail straight after it), were designed to promote the new album, *Some Girls*, another exceptional piece of work that Mick had originally hoped would out-punk any of the new punk acts who were beginning to show that they were more than merely a fad – even though it was clearly as influenced by disco as it was by punk. In their darkest personal moments, the Rolling Stones had produced a trilogy of terrific major long-playing records – *Black and Blue*, *Love You Live* and now *Some Girls*, all of which have more than stood the test of time. Recorded in Paris, *Some Girls* sold eight million copies, the Rolling Stones' biggest-selling album ever.

Marvin Mitchelson seemed to have become the *bête noire* of Mick Jagger. Living in 1978 in Los Angeles, Marsha Hunt had been so broke she had had to go on social security. When she factored in the miserly nine pounds a week that Mick was paying her for Karis, she made a decision. She went to see Mitchelson at his office in Century City, a few weeks before the Stones were due to play in the southern Californian city on the *Some Girls* tour. She made it clear to the lawyer that she wanted support for her daughter, that she was not after Mick's fortune. Mitchelson asked her where the settlement deeds were of 9 December 1974. When Marsha told him they were in London, he called his secretary and asked her to book a seat on a plane to London the next afternoon. 'Marvin's speed and tenacity were unbelievable. He took instructions to represent me on 14 July, and by 22 July he had already been to England and back, served Mick with papers and had the courts withhold Mick's share of the gate receipts for the two Stones concerts in Anaheim, California, which reputedly grossed four million dollars . . . He knew that Mick's lawyers could avoid the issue again if we weren't in a dominant position.'

Mick offered to settle out of court. But Marsha had decided that Mick's contribution to Karis's upkeep wasn't the only issue: she wanted him to acknowledge paternity. In January 1979 the case was heard, Mick's paternity was declared and maintenance ordered, which Marsha was not permitted to reveal: it was not a huge amount, however, and there was no lump-sum payment.

Keith's own legal affairs proceeded at a pace of which Jarndyce and Jarndyce would have been proud: his lawyers managed to hold the Toronto drug bust in abeyance until October 1978, when he pleaded guilty to possession of heroin, the trafficking charge being dropped to one of simple possession. Judge Lloyd Graburn believed in Keith's efforts to cure himself for good. He was given a one-year suspended sentence and was ordered to make regular visits to a probation officer. He had to agree to have regular treatment for his smack addiction at New York's Stevens Institute, and he was also ordered to play a benefit concert for the Canadian Institute for the Blind within six months. The Rolling Stones played the date on 22 April 1979, a day before the end of the six-month period. The opening act was the New Barbarians, a between-Stones'-tours group formed by Ron Wood that 'Jah Keith', as Woody affectionately called Keith, had somewhat reluctantly agreed to join for its first tour. Later it transpired that the blind girl Keith had helped out on the 1975 US tour was the niece of Judge Graburn. She had told her uncle of Keith's charitable act, inspiring him to order Keith to play that charity concert in aid of the blind as part of his sentence.

Once the pressures of the Toronto court case were over, Keith was able to concentrate on removing heroin from his life altogether. Apart from the occasional lapse, Keith now began to live a heroin-free life. Assorted dependencies remained; he had effectively come off smack by shifting his addictions. Now he became a cocaine-addicted alcoholic, the edge of both those fiery substances softened by an endless supply of spliffs. On 3 December 1978 Keith released his first solo single, a Christmas record, a version of Chuck Berry's 'Run Rudolph Run', backed by his own interpretation of the Jimmy Cliff song he so adored, 'The Harder They Come'. Underpromoted, the record did not sell well. With a rather Jamaican sense of timing, the Christmas single did not come out in England until the following March when, again, it did not perform well on the sales charts.

On 20 July 1979 another terrible scandal blew up around Anita: during an alleged game of Russian roulette at Frog Hollow, Scott Cantrell, a seventeen-year-old boy, shot the top of his head off and died instantly. The newspapers were filled with stories of sex orgies and witchcraft – the location of Frog Hollow in South Salem only adding further fuel to the fire. Although Anita was arrested by the police, she was only charged with possession of a stolen firearm, the provenance of the .38 pistol that had lain around the house having always been unclear. While she faced a possible four years in prison for that offence alone, some of Keith's luck seemed to have rubbed off on Anita, and she got away with a fine of a thousand dollars. Having once again attracted the attention of the forces of law and order to herself and Keith, it was the final straw for him; Anita was an absolute liability, and there was no longer any possibility of a reconciliation. But that same year, relaxing with Lilly in a borrowed house on a hillside in Laurel Canyon in Los Angeles, Keith smelled smoke: more spontaneous combustion. They escaped out of a window before the entire wood-framed building went up in flames.

With scoring and shooting up heroin no longer a full-time job for Keith, his thought processes now had a surfeit of free time. For the first time in ten years he began to involve himself in the course of the career of the Rolling Stones. This was not necessarily appreciated by Mick, who, through a combination of necessity, natural inclination and flair had been obliged to run the group for that entire period. The extent to which this was and still is virtually unique among major recording artists should not be underestimated – Mick Fleetwood's captaincy of Fleetwood Mac being about the only other comparable example – and it had earned Mick Jagger a reputation, from which he did not shy, as 'the greatest businessman in rock 'n' roll'. Now Keith – never the best at economising – had come along, wanting to put his oar in and get a hearing at the same time. But Keith did know his music: not even Mick could deny that. All the same, there were fights over the content of *Emotional Rescue*, the new album they recorded in Paris in the autumn of 1979, a curious mixture of Chic and Bee Gees-style disco fused with rock and country and reggae and sub-punk tunes. There was even more controversy and anger when Mick despatched a telex to the group's New York office, declaring he was on his way with Jerry to Morocco for an extended period, and that he had no intention of going on the road that year to promote *Emotional Rescue*. Keith, who had still not completely recovered financially from the beating that the Toronto bust had given his bank account, was furious.

Twenty-two-year-old Patti Hansen, New York's top model, a working-class girl (her father had been a bus driver) with great spirit, had been recommended to Keith as a potential girlfriend; the relationship with Lilly had gradually fallen apart over the previous few months, and he was looking for a love he could call his own. At first, Keith had intensely disliked Jerry Hall almost as vehemently as he had Bianca: he thought her stupid and superficial. As he got to know her better, however, he discovered that she was almost the definition of the all-American 'swell girl', a woman with a big heart. It was Jerry who acted as cupid between Keith and Patti Hansen, inviting her to his thirty-sixth birthday party at the Roxy roller disco in Manhattan. Not that this was perhaps the best of occasions for the pair to meet: looking like the cat who had got the cream, Keith had just emerged from a private room where he had been enjoying one of his birthday gifts, a top-flight hooker who had been despatched to him in a limousine, naked with a ribbon tied around her, when Anita had arrived with Marlon, demanding to be with him.

When Patti Hansen did get to spend time with Keith, she discovered him to be a sincere, quiet person who seemed to need a friend more than a lover. Patti was known for being very funny, and she and Keith shared the same sense of humour. At first they simply hung out together, enjoying the usual Keith lifestyle of hip clubs and obscure Brooklyn reggae shops, and time spent at various, sometimes dubious, people's apartments. On New Year's Eve Patti returned from a visit to her family to find him sitting on her stairs, waiting for her to return. That was it: when she discovered that Keith was still dabbling with junk, personally going down to Manhattan's Alphabet City to score off street-corner dealers, always packing a piece in case he was rolled, she made it her personal mission to get him off heroin once and for all.

Now instead Keith simply drank even more alcohol as a substitute, two or three bottles a day of vodka or Jack Daniel's or Rebel Yell or Jamaican rum; he tried to turn his alcoholism into some sort of hip virtue, rarely being photographed without a bottle in his hand; he would conduct interviews over a couple of bottles and a table lined with finest snow, which he had refused even to consider giving up. Like Jerry Hall, Patti had wealth of her own, and she didn't need to rely on Keith for anything.

In a spare moment during 1981 Keith had recorded the Hoagy Carmichael standard 'The Nearness of You' with Bobby Keys, 'him on sax and me on piano'. Immediately afterwards, he had disappeared down to Barbados for songwriting sessions with Mick. While he was on the Caribbean island, he had one of those moments that made everything seem worthwhile: the eighty-six-year-old Hoagy Carmichael had learned of the recording, and phoned Keith Richards from his home in Palm Springs. To Keith's surprise, the call turned out to be something of a hustle: an effort by the great songwriter to turn Keith on to his other songs – he even offered all the relevant details about the publishers of the individual compositions he mentioned. Then Hoagy said that he knew Barbados: had Keith tried the local drink? he asked. All Keith had been drinking, he replied, was rum punch. No, the great songwriter passed his wisdom on to the Rolling Stone, Keith should ask for something called 'corn and oil' – 'corn', he explained, was a certain type of rum and the 'oil' was felernum, a liqueur made from sugar cane. Hoagy encouraged Keith to drink this, seeming to think it would be right up his street. Keith always found such paternal advice most touching.

Six months later, on 27 December 1981 Hoagy Carmichael passed away. Keith's version of 'The Nearness Of You' was never released.

*

The principal reason for Mick's reluctance to tour in support of *Emotional Rescue* was that he was attempting to revive another career, that of actor. He departed for South America to star in *Fitzcarraldo*, the new film being made by Werner Herzog, the visionary German director. The production was plagued by problems, not the least of which was when the film's Brazilian jungle base camp was attacked by headhunters. When work on the film began to extend into time that the Stones had set aside to record a follow-up to *Emotional Rescue*, Mick simply walked off the project and flew to Paris for the studio sessions. These took far less time than had previous recent albums by the group. *Tattoo You*, as the album was eventually called (Mick appended a last-minute 'You' to the original single-word title), was put together from out-takes and instrumentals from sessions for previous albums. It was a conscious effort at economy of time, but it was also a reflection of Mick and Keith's increasing inability to write together.

Among the tunes the group came up with was 'Start Me Up', arguably the best song and certainly the best single released by the group since 1980; it had first been recorded in 1978 as a reggae number. 'Waiting On A Friend' had first been tried out as long ago as the *Goat's Head Soup* recordings. A month of recording in Paris in November 1980 put the new album together. The record was a simultaneous number one in the UK and the US. After much persuasion from Keith, and a calculation of the fortune he could earn from Prince Rupert, Mick was persuaded to take the Stones back on the road, and in September 1981 the group began a world tour, kicking off with shows in twenty-six cities in the United States. It was an enormous success from the very start, when the Stones played a warm-up date before an audience of 300 in Worcester, Massachusetts: 11,000 people turned up, trying to get into the show.

Robert Fraser, soon to die from AIDs, always used to say that it was easy being a junkie if you had enough money always to be able to purchase the best drugs and aftercare: it was when you didn't have that financial backing, he added, that life became impossible and could even end. Certainly one of the reasons that Keith had survived his life as a junkie was that he had a ceaseless flow of ready cash, as well as a support system of employees. 'He'd be up for four or five days and fall asleep where he was, and someone would pick him up. From about sixty-six onwards, they had their blokes looking after them,' said a friend.

Gered Mankowitz, the photographer who had so cemented the group's early image, had almost no contact with the Stones at all during the seventies. In 1978 he had been watching a television interview with the haggard death mask that Keith had become, when his four-year-old daughter gripped his hand in fear. ' "Daddy, what's wrong with that man?" she said. I thought that was quite an upsetting experience,' he remembered.

In 1982, when the group's *Tattoo You* tour was about to hit London, the *Observer* magazine asked him to photograph the group once again, for a cover story to coincide with the Wembley dates. 'We went through this incredible farce of actually getting out to Shepperton where we had to meet in secret lay-bys and be picked up. It was really ridiculous. My assistant and I were sitting in my office, literally all day. We'd get a call at three o'clock from the Stones' office: "Hi, I'm just letting you know that Keith's got up, and he's really looking forward to seeing you later on tonight." And I'd get another call half an hour later, "Just wanted to let you know, Keith's in the shower . . . You will be picked up at this place at seven o'clock on the A12." Six o'clock I'd get another call. "We're going to have to push this back – Mick's had to take a meeting. Sends his best wishes, really looking forward to meeting you later, but they don't think they're really going to be starting until about eleven o'clock. Is that OK?"

'Eventually we got there, and it was wonderful: hugs and kisses, Keith gave me a huge embrace, as did Mick. They were on one of the stages rehearsing, and Ronnie Wood came up and said, "I'm the one you never photographed," and that was sweet, and Bobby Keys was there and Stu was there. It was wonderful, Rupert was already there. Bill Graham was in the background, running the tour. All his people were into major teams with huge infrastructures, and everybody had their own individual person – bully, chauffeur, masseur: they were amazed by this welcome.

'By this time, photographers were very controlled. Mick said, "You don't need flash, do you, Gered? You never used to, and I'm sure you don't now." So I did a load of available-light stuff, and it was very nice.

'But I wanted to do a cover, a group picture for a cover. Of course, when they were rehearsing, you couldn't do that. There was a sort of green room with old sofas. I set up a shot in there, and I kept on saying, "Could we do this?" "Yeah, yeah, yeah," they said. But they never actually got it together to do it. At five o'clock in the morning, they all went off. Mick said, "We'll do it: just come back." Kiss-kiss, goodbye.

'So we went off, happy, high, feeling great. Then I went back the following night to shoot my cover. Arrived at ten o'clock. Totally different atmosphere. Charlie was the only one who was there. He was always very friendly. Stu was there, also friendly. By one-thirty, the word came through that Bill wasn't well. About two o'clock, Mick and Keith turned up with Ronnie. And they were really angry and drunk. Keith was strange and mysterious, and looked at me and gave me hard looks. A bit of a snarl, so theatrical. So I kept on the periphery.

'When they started working I took a few pictures and no one minded.

So I thought I'd take the four of them for the cover – no Bill, but the magazine would have to live with it. I set it all up so it would only take them five minutes. But they were rehearsing and they were pissed and angry. Then there was a drink–sandwich break. Mick and Keith were with Charlie, and I wandered over, and they looked at me in a pretty unpleasant way. I said, "What's happened? What is going on?" And Keith turned to me and said, "Oh man, you really bring us down, man. You remind us of all the money we lost in the sixties." And that was it. I said, "How do you work that out?" "Well, you know, it was a bad time for us. And you remind us of this really bad vibe. You bring us down." So I said, "Are you going to do the cover?" And they said, "Oh, they'll have to make a cover out of what they've got." And basically, I was asked to leave. So I packed up and left. My assistant was really upset, but I was laughing. He asked why. I said, "Because my whole experience of the Stones has just repeated itself in two nights." '

Keith had become used to not seeing his father. Although he had written an explanatory, reassuring letter to Bert Richards after the 1967 Redlands bust, asking him not to judge him too harshly, he had never received a reply – which hurt him. All the same, he always meant to get in touch with him again but somehow another year, another five years would go by, another ten years, and he'd have put it off again. In the summer of 1982, however, when the *Tattoo You* tour reached London to play two nights at Wembley stadium on 25 and 26 June, he finally got around to making that essential phone call to Bert Richards. It was almost twenty years since he'd last seen his father; in contacting Bert he had been prompted partially by Patti's evident fondness for her own father, who was not in the best of health, which only served to remind Keith of the potential consequences of time. Bert, who was now in his seventy-seventh year, was totally matter-of-fact when his son phoned him: 'All right, son: meet me down the pub.'

His father's straightforward tone was not one necessarily shared by Keith: fearing an argument with Bert, he took Woody along with him as support. But Bert's first words dissolved the two decades since they had last laid eyes on each other: ' 'Allo, son, 'ow ya doin'?' Backstage at the Wembley shows, Bert Richards was in the dressing room, even drunker than Keith – at one point the entire set of musicians, including the support act, the J. Geils Band, joined in a communal performance of the old Irish tune 'Danny Boy'. Public consumption of drugs was now off-limits, Keith having to disappear to the bathroom for the occasional bolstering snort of coke; even the professional joint-roller who had loosely made his way onto the payroll was banished while Bert was around.

This was to the considerable chagrin of Ron Wood, now so immersed in the same kind of narcotic addictions that had once plagued Keith, that Keith, observing Ron's out-of-it state on-stage at one of the Wembley shows, kicked him in the arse. Some felt that this anger towards Woody was hypocritical, at least suggesting a measure of guilt on Keith's part about the condition to which the impressionable guitarist had been reduced. With Keith practically cured of his heroin addiction, Ron Wood had taken up the apparently obligatory mantle of Rolling Stones resident drug casualty that Brian Jones had first worn so disastrously. During sessions in Los Angeles in 1979 for Ian McLagan's solo album, that troublesome Bobby Keys had turned up one day with small rock-like pellets of cocaine, thereby introducing Woody and Mac to the perils and expense of a freebasing habit. As had been the case with Brian – and as it had never been with Keith – Woody's plight garnered no sympathy whatsoever from the rest of the group, and he was mercilessly bullied by Mick and Keith. Earning less than half what the other Stones made, Woody was soon broke.

Bert Richards approved of the backstage fare: as it is part of Keith's staple diet, the tour contract's backstage rider always insisted on the availability of substantial portions of shepherd's pie – ever since a member of the road crew accidentally ate Keith's supper and was threatened with having his legs cut off and put in a shepherd's pie. As Keith's main drug was now alcohol, he and his father would happily knock back bottles of Jamaican overproof rum together. Bert was intrigued by the flashy Jamaican style his son would adopt in the endless games of dominoes they would play together, a favourite pastime on the Caribbean island, one at which Keith had become an adept. The following year Keith installed his father in the Long Island house in which Anita and Marlon were still ensconced, to the teenage boy's benefit. The tour was the usual huge success, though those around the group could not help but notice that there was tension between Mick and Keith.

There were also tensions for Keith with other work partners. By 1982 the relationship between Peter Tosh and Rolling Stones Records had irrevocably fallen apart, the reggae star blaming the label for his never attaining Bob Marley-like heights of success. All the same, Keith had let Tosh and his entourage stay, seemingly indefinitely, at Point of View, his house above Ocho Rios. That year, however, Keith decided he needed some time in Jamaica, and called the house from the United States, asking Tosh if he could now move out. Tosh refused. Keith boarded a plane to Jamaica, once again telephoning Point of View when he arrived at Montego Bay airport. Peter Tosh was intractable: in a flurry of Jamaican epithets and curses, the 'Minister of Herb' told Keith that Tosh was now master of Point of View and that if *bumbacla'at* Keith came anywhere near his house, he would shoot him. 'You'd better make sure that your gun is loaded then,' screamed a furious Keith Richards, 'because mine is, and I'm coming over right now.' He slammed down the receiver and tore along the ninety-minute drive to Ochos Rios. He arrived at his Jamaican home, and strode up to the front door, with a machete – not a firearm – in his right hand. But Point of View was deserted: Peter Tosh had got the message, and had split.

On 1 September 1982, Keith experienced more spontaneous combustion: Redlands was ablaze yet again, sixty-five firemen being needed to put out a fire in which serious damage was done to the roof. Towards the end of the month Mick travelled by helicopter from Manhattan to JFK Stadium, accompanied by his daughter Jade, to watch the Who; Jade, however, was far more interested in seeing The Clash, the act who had sung 'No Elvis, Beatles, Or Rolling Stones/In 1977', whom the Who had asked to play support and who had a top-five album of their own at the time with *Combat Rock*; later Mick took Jade to see the Police at their show in Hartford, Connecticut. On 3 November it was the twelfth birthday of Karis, the daughter of Mick and Marsha Hunt. Marsha's friend Sting – she called him her 'little brother' – threw a celebration party for Karis at his home in Hampstead. When mother and daughter returned home, Karis found a trio of red-wrapped packages waiting for her from her father. As Marsha remembered, however, their contents meant nothing compared to the effect of the phone call from Mick in New York. At least his daughters had not deserted Mick – as Jerry Hall, tired of a combination of his repeated philandering and verbal bullying, had done: newspaper reports indicated that a marriage was imminent between her and Robert Sangster, the millionaire racehorse owner whom she had met that June at Royal Ascot.

For once in his life Keith was experiencing greater personal happiness than Mick. A report in the *Sun* newspaper, in the edition dated 12 November, declared that Keith was shortly to marry his 'beautiful model girlfriend Patti Hansen'. Later that week other newspaper reports spoke of an effort at reconciliation between Mick and Jerry Hall that had failed when he angrily berated her about her relationship with Sangster. By Christmas, however, they were flying off together to the exclusive Caribbean island of Mustique.

At the end of 1982 Keith moved with Patti Hansen to Baja California, the peninsula on the west coast of Mexico, setting up home for the following eighteen months in Cabo San Lucas, the luxury resort favoured by Hollywood movie stars of a bygone era. They intended to marry there, but in January 1983 Patti's father Alfred Hansen died, and the nuptials were postponed. After the funeral, at which Keith served as a pallbearer, and the wake in New York, he flew to Paris to work on the new Stones' album, to be titled *Undercover.*

At the end of February 1983, a press release from the Stones' office announced that John Ryle, the literary editor of the *Sunday Times*, had been taken on for the tedious task of doing the actual writing of Mick's autobiography, for which he was to receive £50,000 – Mick had secured a million pound deal for himself. Eventually, Ryle pulled out of the project, the book utterly stymied by Mick's legendary inability to remember anything. Was this a consequence of long-term marijuana consumption? Or a subconscious desire to deny the shocking truth of his past? (In 2002, it was announced that 'the group' had signed a deal with publishers Weidenfeld & Nicolson, for a collective autobiography to be published in the year 2003: we'll believe it when we see it, snorted cynics – or realists, as they preferred to view themselves.)

For a while, however, Ryle had rather a good time of it, accompanying Mick to conduct interviews with him on Mustique, where Mick was holidaying with Jerry Hall and checking on the progress of a house he was having built on the island, a favourite location of his friends Princess Margaret and David Bowie, the last word in exclusivity.

At the beginning of May 1983 Patti Hansen began work in San Francisco on *Hard to Hold*, a film in which she had a starring role; she was joined by Keith, who later flew to New York where, at the Hit Factory, Mick and Ron Wood had begun mixing songs the group had recorded in Paris. The next month Keith flew down to Jamaica, abandoning work on the new album and leaving Mick to continue with the rhythm section from the newly hip Sugarhill Records, the rap label from whom the world first heard of Grandmaster Flash. Talk suggested that Keith had left New York because he was fed up with working with Mick. Returning to Manhattan a little later, he bought four floors of an East Fourth Street apartment building for $750,000, which were then substantially renovated. (In July Keith – who never especially took to rap music – played with the great rock 'n' roller Jerry Lee Lewis, a man whose life mirrored that of Keith in terms of perpetual tragedy, at a concert in Los Angeles.)

The following month Mick gave a revealing interview in the British press: 'When you get to my age, you really have to work at staying young. You've got to be fit, because rock requires a tremendous amount of energy and I find that if your body is alive, your mind becomes alive. That's vital in a business that is as fast as this one. Once I led the typical dissipated life of a rock star, full of drugs, booze and chaos. But these days my health is my most treasured possession. When I'm on tour I never touch hard liquor, and I try to get as much sleep as I possibly can. I like to get as much as ten hours a night. I don't go to clubs or discos,' he added, in words that no doubt reassured Jerry Hall about the future of their relationship, 'except to pick up girls.'

All the same, Mick spent his fortieth birthday with Jerry in the north-eastern American state of Vermont. 'If anyone asks me about my birthday I'll punch them in the mouth,' he threatened. A few days later, on 10 August, Keith went to Marlon's fourteenth birthday party at Anita's house on Long Island. At the end of that month the Rolling Stones signed a deal with Columbia Records under which they were to be paid $6.5 million per album for four records. Tucked in among the information about this new contract was the revelation that Mick and Jerry were expecting their first child, to be born five months from then.

Keith was dismayed, however, to discover that Walter Yetnikoff, the controversial, bullish boss of Columbia, considered that what he was really buying for such a large amount of money was Mick Jagger, and that he was openly encouraging Mick to become a solo artist. (Yentikoff was also writing such an enormous cheque because included in the deal were the rights to the back catalogue of Rolling Stones Records: when he immediately repackaged the albums in the new form of compact discs, the advance was recouped in no time.) As *Undercover*, a new album released in November 1983, brimming with anger and misogyny, was the Stones' least successful record for years – it only scraped into the US Top Ten – it could seem that this was the time for Mick to make such a move. ('Undercover Of The Night', the album's sort-of title track, was a song about the Disappeared of Argentina, men and women who had been taken away, never to be seen again, during the years of dictatorship that had culminated in the invasion of the Falklands Islands in April of the previous year.) Not everyone was pleased about the Rolling Stones being back in business with a new album, however: assorted American chapters of the Hell's Angels seemed suddenly to remember the feud between themselves and the group over Altamont, and threatened dire consequences, a contract allegedly having been taken out on Mick. 'That festival happened fifteen years ago, so I was a bit surprised to hear about this supposed contract,' said Mick. 'But the guy who said that was just trying to make a name for himself. The Hell's Angels called a press conference and I met them in a bar in New York and they said that they truly wanted to be friends.' But did he have a few moments of nervousness? 'Well, yeah, anyone would.'

It was certainly the occasion for a change of life for Keith Richards. On 18 December 1983, on his fortieth birthday, he and Patti Hansen were married in Cabo San Lucas. Lotus-land was not to remain uncritically welcoming, however; by the end of the following year, Keith got word that it would be to his advantage not to return to his halcyon Mexican home: his lifestyle had attracted the attention of the local police, who were waiting for an opportunity to bust him. He never returned to Baja California.

In January 1984 Mick donated £32,000 to Britain's gymnastic team for their appearance at the Olympic games due to be held in Los Angeles that summer. Not forgetting his roots, nor his family, the gift was partially out of respect for his father, Joe Jagger. On 2 March Jerry Hall gave birth to Elizabeth Scarlett in New York; Mick attended the birth. Later that month, Bill declared that Mick seemed to have changed irrevocably: 'Mick is a very difficult person to know now. We are a band, you know, and Keith Richards runs the Rolling Stones, really.' By May 1984, after a week's holiday in Mustique with his family, Mick was at Compass Point studio in Nassau in the Bahamas, recording his first solo album, which was being produced by the then current studio wunderkind Trevor Horn. That year Karis went to stay with Mick, Jerry and their new baby Elizabeth, while Marsha Hunt went to Czechoslovakia to film *The Howling II*. Karis then went to Rio with Mick and his family for the Christmas holidays. The following Easter, Karis went to meet Mick in Paris, with Marsha also going along; together they all went to the Tour d'Argent.

By that time *She's the Boss*, Mick Jagger's first solo album, had been released, on 4 March 1985. The production credits had shifted, offering the names of Mick, Bill Laswell and Nile Rogers, the guitarist-half of the Chic production team. Made not only at Compass Point but also at the Power Station in New York, the record included one song co-written with Keith. Among the musicians playing with Mick on the record were the then ubiquitous Jamaican rhythm section of Sly Dunbar and Robbie Shake-speare, Herbie Hancock, Nile Rogers and his bass-playing partner Bernard Edwards, Pete Townshend and Jeff Beck. The album made number eight in the US and number six in Britain.

Fourteen days after the final arrival of Mick's album, Patti Richards, née Hansen, gave birth on 18 March to Theodora Dupree, in New York. Reflecting the contemporary fashion in parenting, Keith was there at the birth, as Mick had been at his daughter Elizabeth's. Two months later, Jerry confirmed that she was pregnant again. Meanwhile, Mick had been asked to return the advance for his uncompleted autobiography.

On 29 June Mick and David Bowie recorded the Martha and the Van-dellas' Motown classic 'Dancing In The Street', the profits to be given to Live Aid, the epoch-making concert that was the inspiration of Boomtown Rats' singer Bob Geldof, whose early career had marked him out as a Mick Jagger copyist. A number-one single in the UK, 'Dancing In The Street' was that year's fastest-selling record. When the spectacular concert was staged on 13 July, Mick performed his first-ever solo concert at JFK stadium in Philadelphia, backed by Hall and Oates and joined by Tina Turner for a pair of numbers, 'State Of Shock' and 'It's Only Rock And Roll'. Piqued by Mick's appearance – which he had at first told the other Stones would not happen – Keith Richards and Ron Wood played shambolically with Bob Dylan on the final set of the show. On 28 August 1985 James Leroy Augustine was born to Mick and Jerry at Lennox Hill Hospital in New York. James was Mick's first son.

Birth and death are seemingly inseparable: on 12 December 1985 the ever-loyal Ian 'Stu' Stewart suddenly collapsed and died. 'Who's gonna tell us off now, when we misbehave?' asked Keith at the funeral. Mick was in tears. Two months later the group played a tribute show to Ian at the 100 Club in Oxford Street. Perhaps his death had not been in vain: Mick and Keith left the club arm in arm. Gered Mankowitz was invited to the event: 'Keith was fantastic. Gave me a huge bearhug. Charlie was lovely. Bill was always very friendly. All Mick said was, "I saw your book" – by then I'd done a photo book about the Stones – "I suppose you made a lot of money out of it." I said, "No, virtually nothing." "Oh ... Oh, it was OK." I do have a tremendous fondness for Keith. I have a tremendous fondness for Mick also, but I feel you never know where you stand with him.'

At the end of March 1986, the Stones released the first of those $6.5 million albums, *Dirty Work*; 'Harlem Shuffle', a cover of the classic Bob and Earl R 'n' B song, was the first single off the new album; although weak and predictable, the single was a Top Five hit in the US, doing almost as well in the UK. The album, which was also extremely weak, made number three in America and number four in the UK. Two months later Keith declared that, 'If Mick tours without the band, I'll slit his throat.' On 6 June 1986 Keith, who in January had presented Chuck Berry with his Rock 'n' Roll Hall of Fame award, joined his great inspiration on-stage at a blues festival in Chicago. The following month he was in St Louis, where Berry lived, in discussion about a film project based on the life of the great man. As he always did when in crisis, Keith returned to what he knew best: the songbook of Chuck Berry, and he set about his task of musical director on *Hail! Hail! Rock 'n' Roll!*, in which he also performed. It was another partnership that had its elements of psychological sado-masochism, Chuck not always being the easiest person in the world with whom to get on. (No doubt Keith could have lightened things up with a joke or two about video cameras, had he known that by the end of the decade Berry would have been indicted in his home state for allegedly secretly filming women visiting the bathroom in his club in St Louis. Funnily enough, no one seemed to voice criticism of Chuck over this, as though it was simply confirming what we had suspected all along of someone with such a lascivious grin.) When Keith invited Chuck down to Jamaica to work with him, the American was like a fish out of water, experiencing extreme culture shock, which set in as soon as Keith drove him along the anarchic Jamaican roads from the airport.

Also in June that year, the Rastafarian film director Don Letts flew to Jamaica on holiday with former Clash founder Mick Jones, with whom he had joined up in the group Big Audio Dynamite; accompanied by their wives and young children, Letts and Jones were staying at Goldeneye, the former home of James Bond author Ian Fleming, in the small town of Oracabessa on the island's north coast, some twenty miles to the east of Ocho Rios. In the departure lounge at Heathrow airport Don had seen a man carrying a guitar case, who turned out to be Keith Richards' guitar roadie. 'Tell Keith to come and check us at Goldeneye,' said Letts, joking.

A couple of days later he was lying on Goldeneye's secluded private beach when a shadow loomed over him: a shirtless Keith was standing there, an enormous blade stuffed into his belt. He invited them to come up to Point of View. They went up there almost every other night, often after eating with Keith at Nuccio's, an Italian restaurant then in Ocho Rios; Don Letts noted that in all mentions of Mick, Keith would employ the sobriquet 'Nellie' (Keith and Ron would also often refer to him as 'Brenda').

At the 'quite rudimentary and spartan' Point of View, Mick Jones would indulge in guitar duelling sessions with 'Master Keet', as the Jamaican help referred to the Rolling Stone. 'Keith didn't want to hear any contemporary music – he was only playing Chuck Berry and reggae,' said Letts. 'We asked him if he knew what was going on in New York with rap music. But he wasn't interested at all. He looked incredibly healthy.

There weren't any heavy drugs around, just spliff and Jack Daniel's. He had a few Rasta friends up there, who seemed to spend every evening killing giant flying cockroaches that were so enormous it sounded as though a piece of metal was being smashed.'

A more introspective, deeper side of Keith emerged in his conversations with one of the women in their party. It transpired that, at this time when his spouse Patti was about to give birth to their second child in New York, Keith was living in Jamaica so that he wouldn't fall foul of the US taxation authorities, which would have endangered not only his own financial status but also the elaborate fiscal structure of the entire group: the band members were inextricably interwoven and interdependent; their fortunes and financial futures glued together by Prince Rupert's skilled international book-keeping.

On 28 July 1986, Patti Richards gave birth to Alexandra Nicole at the Lennox Hill Hospital in New York.

Mick still had a tendency to resort to fisticuffs if things were not going his way: eating in a restaurant in Los Angeles with Dave Stewart of the Eurythmics on 16 September 1986, he punched a photographer who attempted to take a snap of the two men; Stewart, who was apparently everybody's favourite collaborator at the time, worked on Mick's next solo album. On 16 October, with Anita Pallenberg and Marlon in the audience, a pair of concerts to celebrate the sixtieth birthday of Chuck Berry at the Fox Theater in St Louis were filmed, to form part of the *Hail! Hail! Rock 'n' Roll!* documentary tribute to the legendary rock 'n' roller.

In November 1986, Mick began recording his second solo album in Holland. At the end of that year, both Rolling Stones main men headed for the Caribbean, Keith and his family to Point of View in Jamaica, and Mick and Jerry to Mustique, where they were joined by David Bowie for the New Year. On 6 January 1987 Mick and Jerry flew on to Barbados, where he was to continue working on his new album at the studio owned by Eddie Grant. Two weeks later, when Jerry Hall went to Barbados airport to collect items that had been forwarded on from Mustique, she discovered that one of the packages waiting for her contained a colossal twenty pounds of marijuana; 'Is this some kind of sick joke?' were her reported words when presented with the 'evidence'. Arrested for smuggling the drug into the island, she was held overnight in prison before Mick was informed of the charge: he immediately coughed up the required $5,000 bail. Mick hardly smoked any more, and there was no way that he and his entourage were going to hammer through such an enormous amount of weed in a few weeks of recording. In a part of the world by no means immune to police corruption, the marijuana was an obvious set-up, a clear attempt to extract a substantial pay-off from the Rolling Stone (Ron Wood and Jo Howard had undergone a similar experience in 1980 on the island of St Marteen, when he was alleged to have been found in possession of 200 grams of cocaine – after four days the charges were dropped). Yet this made the consequences of the discovery no less frightening for Jerry Hall: ordered to surrender her passport, she was instructed to report to the appropriately named Holetown police station twice a week until her trial, which was due to begin on 13 February.

At the subsequent trial, undertaken with all the ponderous, bewigged solemnity of the English legal system as it is practised in former British colonies, the wafer-thin case against Jerry Hall was assiduously torn apart and exposed for the malicious nonsense it was by her expensive legal counsel. All the same, the presiding magistrate required a further adjournment to consider the 'complexity' of the legal arguments. When a verdict was finally arrived at on 20 February, the magistrate delivered a lengthy peroration before pronouncing Jerry not guilty. Mick and Jerry immediately caught a plane to New York, the supermodel furious about the $130,000 in cancelled modelling bookings she had lost.

In the 3 March 1987 edition of the *Sun*, it seemed that all was not at all well in the Rolling Stones' camp. Keith gave an interview in which he expressed his disquiet and his ire at the rumours of a solo tour by his schoolfriend from Dartford: 'I'm not sure when it all started to go wrong. Up until the beginning of the eighties you could have called me up at the North Pole and Mick at the South Pole and we would have said the same thing, we were that close. I didn't change but he did. He became obsessed with age – his own and others'. I don't see the point of pretending that you are twenty-five when you're not.' Later that same month, at a wedding reception in Manhattan, formally attired in a black suit, Keith stood very much on his own, glass in hand, his slight stature seemingly reduced even further by an almost visible cloud of depression that hung over him. 'Everyone knows what's going on from what they read in the papers,' he said, suffused by his downcast mood, 'but I don't know what's going on at all.' It seemed it was all over for the Rolling Stones. 'I don't know if we will ever go back on the road,' admitted Bill Wyman. 'That depends on the glamour twins, Mick and Keith Richards, becoming friendly again. They're the problem.'

What did this look like to outsiders? Caught up in their images, in the midst of a desperately selfish decade, Mick and Keith played out their mutual antagonism in public, in the media, internationally. There seemed no reason whatsoever why the group would play together again. And would anyone want them to? The galactic levels of narcissism and sulkiness on display seemed to render them both suitable cases for treatment. What was interesting was the full extent to which Keith seemed to be in thrall to Mick's wishes; guilty over having almost brought the group to an end so many times during the 1970s, Keith now appeared almost desperate in his efforts to hold the Rolling Stones together, and utterly dependent on the almost petulant whims of Mick Jagger. When he announced he was to make a solo record, you felt it was almost the action of a desperate man, backed into a corner. Wasn't this the man whom Alexis Korner had insisted was driven by belief whilst Mick was motivated by fear? Now it seemed almost like a case of role reversal.

Mick had made two solo albums, one of which had been released, the second whose release was imminent; Bill Wyman had had a solo hit with a single with the rather postmodern title of 'Je Suis Un Rock Star'; Charlie had his jazz group, the Charlie Watts Orchestra; Ron Wood, who many fans still thought of as a member of the Faces, was busy being Ron Wood. Now Keith had his own album to do; perhaps predictably, Keith continued to be apparently unable to evade some of the problems that had dogged him for almost the previous two decades. On 8 April 1987, the last day of recording his first solo record, he was obliged to retreat from Studio 900 on 19th Street in Manhattan, as fire blazed through the building.

In July Keith signed a deal to release the album with Virgin Records the following year. On 3 October *Hail! Hail! Rock 'n' Roll!* received its favourable première at the New York Film Festival, the same day that *Primitive Cool*, Mick's second solo album, entered the US charts at number 81; the record rose no higher than 41, and in Britain only made number eighteen: essentially the record was a flop. Did Mick's own personality have any bearing on this lack of success? Although the record contained songs aimed directly at Keith – 'Shoot Off Your Mouth' and 'Kow Tow' – by now he was having difficulties with another musician, Jeff Beck; a projected tour with Beck had been cancelled, claimed the guitar hero, following arguments over the amount of money Mick was willing to pay the established star. 'It was laughable, an insult,' said Beck. 'I wanted to teach him a lesson because I believe that if you want the best you have to pay for it. The kind of money he offered is what you pay an ordinary session musician. Mick's problem is that he's a meanie. He's no better than a glorified accountant. He counts every single penny. For someone with his money, I can't believe how tight he is.'

By early spring of 1988, Mick made a brief eight-date tour of Japan with a visually spectacular show, that included forty girls dancing during 'Sympathy for the Devil'. Clearly Mick had no problems with his own earnings on this outing, of a million pounds a night. Ron Wood was also in Japan, touring with Bo Diddley: Mick and Woody met up for one drunken night at a hotel. Back in the US, Keith continued work on *Talk is Cheap*, his first solo album.

In May 1988, all five members of the group held a meeting at the Savoy hotel in London. Mick announced that he had a further tour planned, of Australasia this time, that had been set up to support his solo album. Keith countered with the information that he would be touring the United States when his own solo album was released. There was a sense, however, that the group could get together again. 'Darling,' said Keith to Mick, 'this thing is bigger than both of us.' 'Keith pointed out,' said Bill, 'that people don't bother to sustain a fight with enemies. And that was the basis of his healing process with Mick that enabled us to return so successfully to the American stage.' They agreed in principle that in 1989 they would start to work together on a new album and a world tour.

Before this could happen, however, Mick undertook his tour of Australasia, in September and October; and on 4 October, Keith's first solo album, *Talk Is Cheap* was released. It made number twenty-four in the United States, a bigger hit than Mick's second solo album had been. With his group, the X-Pensive Winos, Keith began a US tour that ran through the last two months of that year, playing at venues ranging from small clubs to arenas: among the musicians a familiar figure was on saxophone in Bobby Keys, who had at one stage had been reduced to playing L.A. bars, billed as 'the sax sound of "Brown Sugar" '. In Jamaica, Point of View had suffered serious damage when Hurricane Gilbert rampaged across the island in October, and in London Keith played at the Smile Jamaica concert, organised to bring financial relief to victims of the devastating storm. In an interview in *Rolling Stone* magazine, part of a barrage of publicity to promote *Talk is Cheap*, he appeared to refute what he had said at the New York wedding party in March. Was this an effort at conciliation? 'Mick's and my battles are not exactly as perceived through the press or by other people. They're far more convoluted because we've known each other for most of our lives – I mean, since we were four or five. So they involve a lot more subtleties and ins and outs than can possibly be explained. But I think there is on Mick's part a bit of a Peter Pan complex. It's a hard job, being the frontman. In order to do it, you've got to think, in a way, that you're semi-divine. I love Mick. Most of my efforts with Mick go to trying to open his eyes: "You don't need to do this. You have no problem, all you need to do is just grow up with it".'

Less than four weeks from the end of the X-Pensive Winos tour, Mick and Keith met up in Barbados to endeavour to write songs for a new album. They then moved to Montserrat, to record the album at Air Studios. 'They seemed like a young band again,' said Bill, attributing this to the long period they had spent away from each other. Their task was to finish an album in five weeks, which would be the fastest since the early 1960s; if the record came out in time, they would tour the US that autumn. They succeeded, meeting the deadline of the end of April. The following month the group came together in Amsterdam, convenient for the purposes of avoiding having to pay tax. It would seem that although Mick had restored his relationship with Keith, all was not amicable with everyone in the group. In the middle of the month it was reported that Charlie Watts, outraged at being called in his hotel room by Mick with the words 'Is that my drummer boy? Why don't you get your arse down here?', had punched out the Stones' singer. 'I figured Mick and I would go out for a drink,' recalled Keith. 'We had a great time, and at five in the morning Mick came back to my room. Mick was drunk – and Mick drunk is a sight to behold. Charlie was fast asleep, and Mick shouted those words at him. Charlie shaved, put on a suit and tie, came down, grabbed him and went *boom*! Charlie dished him a walloping right hook. He landed in a plateful of smoked salmon, and slid along the table towards the window. I caught his leg and saved him from going into the canal below.' Perhaps Mick felt it best not to fall out with everyone in the group: at the wedding of fifty-two-year-old Bill Wyman to nineteen-year-old Mandy Smith the following month, he presented the bass player with a Picasso etching for which he had paid £200,000.

Four weeks later the group held a press conference on a flatcar in Grand Central Station, New York, to announce a tour to coincide with the release of their new album, which was to be titled *Steel Wheels*. The record, which was thoroughly undistinguished, was released on 29 August, and the tour began two days later in Philadelphia at the Veteran Stadium before a 55,000-strong audience. The following year the tour continued in Japan and Europe; in July, dates in Cardiff and London were rescheduled after Keith infected a finger after cutting it on a guitar string; the tour concluded on 25 August at Wembley stadium, after the group had played to over six million people.

Keith had bought Anita a flat in Tite Street in Chelsea, around the corner from 3 Cheyne Walk: 'absolutely gorgeous, not huge, but such a comfortable place you never want to leave it', said a regular visitor. 'That's what you get when you go out with Keith Richards and not Mick Jagger,' Marianne Faithfull wryly said to the conceptual record producer Hal Willner, when he commented on this. As long as her mother had been alive, Marianne had been wary of commenting in the press on her relationship with Mick Jagger; any time she had done so, she would receive phone calls suggesting that perhaps her mother might be evicted from the house near Reading in which Mick graciously had allowed her to be lodged. Although Marianne had hoped that her son Nicholas might be allowed to live there, she had no such luck: the moment her mother passed on, the place had to be handed back to Mick.

At the time of the *Steel Wheels* tour, Willner was working on a record in which assorted musicians interpreted the work of the late jazz great Charlie Mingus. One person who had to agree to participate was Keith Richards, who pulled Charlie Watts in to the project. The only mutually satisfactory point of rendezvous was in Spain, when the group played in Madrid on 15, 16 and 17 June 1990. On the afternoon of 17 June, Keith and Charlie joined Willner in a Madrid recording studio. The producer was astonished at the extent to which, while on the road, Keith and Mick lived completely separate lives. He noted that they stayed in separate parts of their luxury hotel, surrounded by their separate encampments: Keith had an entire floor, with all his posse; Mick also had an entire floor, in a different wing of the hotel: he always did this, wherever they stayed – he didn't want to be busted, ever again. This had the effect of separating the musicians – some of the horn section would be in one part of the hotel with Keith, others were with Mick; Charlie was in a somewhat difficult position, clearly being a floating voter who liked both individuals equally. When Keith worked on the Mingus tune, he told Hal Willner that this kind of music was his best work, what he was really good at, but that no one was interested in this side of him.

The tour over, the Stones went their separate ways. On 21 November 1990, on a beach in Bali, Mick married Jerry Hall in a Hindu ceremony: their children Elizabeth and James, a nanny and Alan Dunn, a Stones' employee of long-standing, were the only witnesses. Eighteen days later, the newly-weds shared a party in the unlikely location of Margate in Kent with Joe and Eva Jagger, who were celebrating their golden wedding anniversary.

From February to May 1991, Mick worked on his part in *Freejack*, starring Anthony Hopkins and Emilio Estevez; he performed a suitably dark role as efficiently as he could in what was essentially an unimpressive science-fiction film set in a dystopian United States. Returning to London from his work on the film Mick bought Downe House, an eighteenth-century Georgian mansion on Richmond Hill, for £2,500,000. Not that the palatial home was likely to be the scene of much rock 'n' roll bacchanalia: in London Jerry had complained to the *Sun* newspaper that her husband was no longer a 'party animal': 'Now he doesn't drink, doesn't smoke and wants to go to bed early. It's a real bore.' Mick's songwriting partner, however, had clearly not turned over any such new leaf, and in New York was working on material with the X-Pensive Winos. An X-Pensive Winos live album was released before Christmas on Virgin Records, with whom a few days before the Stones had signed a worldwide three-album deal worth $44 million.

On 12 January 1992 Jerry gave birth in London to Georgia May Ayeesha Jagger. Four days later Mick was at the première of *Freejack* at Grauman's Chinese Theater on Hollywood Boulevard. While on a promotional tour of the Far East, Mick was discovered to have spent time in Thailand with one Carla Bruni, a twenty-two-year-old model. Piers Morgan, then the show-business editor of the *Daily Mirror*, later the newspaper's editor, felt that there was more to this than met the eye. Mick, he believed, was concerned that his image as a rock 'n' roll rake might have been suffering from his recent marriage. Mick's London public relations adviser phoned Piers. 'He said, "Do you know where Mick is?" "I imagine he's with his wife, who's just had their third child." "No", I was told, "he's in a hotel in Thailand with Carla Bruni – spelled B-R-U-N-I." Mick's credibility as a bad boy was back, and suddenly Carla was a famous model – even though no one had ever heard of her before.'

Time seemed only to complicate Mick's multi-layered life; on the one hand he attended daughter Karis's graduation ceremony with Marsha Hunt and the wronged Jerry Hall at Yale University that May, and rushed from Jerry's thirty-sixth birthday party at Downe House to the hospital room of daughter Jade who had given birth to Assisi, a daughter fathered by her boyfriend, the artist Piers Jackson; yet he was still involved with Carla Bruni, who was almost exactly the same age as Karis. Should he have been surprised that Jerry was proclaiming publicly that she had decided to divorce the man with whom she had lived for fifteen years but to whom she had only been married for just over eighteen months? 'I honestly didn't know anything about it until it was in the newspapers. I don't think there's any hope for us any more,' she said, after learning of his latest affair. Soon, however, the estranged pair were back together.

Meanwhile, Mick and his occasional working partner Keith were making separate solo albums. As befitted the man who saw himself as the last of the rock 'n' roll gunslingers, Keith beat Mick to the draw: hoping to take advantage of the Christmas market, *Main Offender* came out in October 1992; but the record only scraped into the US Top 100, while in Britain it made it to number fifty. When Mick's *Wandering Spirit* was released in February 1993, it got to number eleven in the US. The previous month, Bill Wyman had announced his departure from the Rolling Stones, after more than thirty years with the group. (By now, Bill's marriage to his teenage bride Mandy had disintegrated, and he was about to wed again; his thirty-year-old son Stephen, however, declared that he was to marry Mandy's forty-six-year-old mother Patty, thereby making Bill his own ex-wife's step-grandfather.)

Both Mick and Keith turned fifty in 1993: 300 guests, including Keith and Bill, celebrated Mick's birthday with a fancy-dress party in Twickenham, close to Downe House. For his own celebration Keith hired out the Metropolis Restaurant in Manhattan and invited 150 close friends: Mick was not present.

The following year saw a new album, *Voodoo Lounge*, far stronger and more varied than *Steel Wheels*, and the beginning of another world tour, which ran until the summer of 1995. 'There were a few intense moments,' Mick told *Q* magazine about the making of *Voodoo Lounge*. 'I don't particularly enjoy intense moments. People get very wound up about their songs. I do. Very precious. Very proprietorial. Everyone's playing them wrong. Play it faster, Keith, for Christ's sake, we can't play it this slow, everyone is falling fucking asleep! That was the source of some interesting discussions with Keith. Because if it doesn't get me up on to my feet then I get bored. But Keith just likes things too slow and sometimes I have to give in and let him have his ... slow things.' In the autumn of 1996, Mick was seen out in Los Angeles with Czech model Jana Rajlich and the actress Uma Thurman, with whom he was seen necking at the Viper Room in West Hollywood. Jerry Hall hired Anthony Julius, the lawyer from the London firm of Mishcon de Reya who had negotiated the substantial divorce settlement of Diana, Princess of Wales, from her husband Prince Charles. The threat of a potential nuclear financial explosion in his life seemed to bring Mick to his senses: soon the couple were back together.

In 1997 it was back to Barbados for Mick and Keith for songwriting, then to L.A. for recording sessions, working this time with a number of producers – Don Was, the Dust Brothers and Babyface. Rather to the amazement of both Mick and Jerry, she discovered she was pregnant once again. Also in 1997 Mick portrayed drag-queen nightclub owner Greta/George in a film adaptation of Martin Sherman's *Bent*. It was not a mainstream hit.

The album, *Bridges to Babylon*, much of which sounded like a heinous racket, was released at the end of September 1997, six days after the *Bridges of Babylon* tour had opened in Chicago on 23 September. The planning of the European leg of the tour (sponsored rather oddly by Castrol, a company with no connections to Babylon whatsoever) in the summer of 1998 had taken into account the possible effect of that year's World Cup football matches. At the dramatic World Cup football game in St Etienne between England and Argentina in 1998, the television cameras cut repeatedly to Mick who was in the crowd, cheering on his side. '*In-gur-land-In-gur-land-In-gur-land*,' he passionately chanted with the rest of the English supporters, boyishly clapping his hands (as he had in those early performances of 'Not Fade Away') in time with the three syllables, absolutely caught up in the heartbreaking passion of the epic match, which England was fated to lose. These little vignettes provided a rather affecting public picture of the private Mick – just one of the crowd, a good bloke.

A year later, on Friday 11 June 1999, in another football stadium, the Rolling Stones played the last date of their *Bridges to Babylon* tour, a home game, at Wembley stadium in north-west London. (The original British *Bridges to Babylon* dates in 1998 had been cancelled following tax changes that year which would have exploded the elaborate tax structure created for the Stones, endangering their income for the decade of half a billion pounds.) Mick appeared to have the same body he had when the Stones appeared for the first time on *Thank Your Lucky Stars*, thirty-six years previously: thanks to his almost neurotic daily exercise regime, he still had a twenty-eight-inch waist. And there too were the identical twitchy little movements, and an apparently identical parallel-cut pair of trousers, in dark grey, worn with a long-sleeved, purple crew-neck top, exactly as Mick Jagger had always liked them. Except that the clothes seemed to change for every song: now he was dressed in a cropped silver jacket. 'I'm trying to catch my breath!' he uttered, after 'Paint It, Black', during which he had indulged in his habitual hurtling around the stage, as though he were warming up for an appearance in Joe Jagger's *Seeing Sport*. ('I do wish Mick would stop running around stage and showing us how fit he is,' opined the writer Charles Shaar Murray, 'and just get on with doing some great singing. Also – and this applies equally to Keith – I think that when men are past the age of fifty it is rather unseemly for them to be showing us their nipples and armpits.') 'I'm feeling fantastic: it's great to be 'ere – 'ome at last,' Mick whooped after 'Gimme Shelter'.

You could always identify where Ron Wood was on-stage by the cloud of cigarette smoke hanging over him: this was useful, as not once during the 150-minute show did a spotlight illuminate him. Although you felt Woody needed to sprint down the walkway that was situated above the audience as often as he could, probably to run off whatever stimulant was coursing through his veins, you thought it might be all Keith could do to anchor himself to the spot. Oh look: as Mick disappeared off the stage, probably for a cup of tea in Charlie's Winnebago, Keith stepped up to the mike. 'It's kinda sad they're going to demolish this place,' he declared regally, waving his arms about the hallowed, condemned stadium, in a voice so slurred and stretched out it was hard to comprehend. 'Gotta move it on before they make me run,' he muttered, sitting himself on a high stool to provide beautiful bottleneck at the beginning of 'You Got The Silver'. During 'Route 66', he ran – the inevitable cigarette lodged in the corner of his mouth – along the walkway above the audience to the smaller stage that had been assembled in the middle of the pitch. In the stands a film-business lawyer was observed surreptitiously lighting a joint, the only scent of hash to be smelled in the entire stadium, it seemed: there were probably more drugs residing in Keith's body than in the rest of the audience put together. It was a revival show, a museum piece of a concert, played to an extremely straight crowd, made up of what looked like a high percentage of geography teachers.

Despite those lessons from Eric Clapton so long ago, Mick's on-stage guitar playing had never looked convincing; it was as though he was trying hard to convince us that he was as serious a musician as Keith. Now, on 'Ruby Tuesday', he played the instrument and still looked terrible. Mostly, though, he played guitar on a lot of the rotten new songs. You knew one was coming every time he picked up the instrument; and each time a rotten new song was played, the crowd thinned as hordes disappeared to the bars or bathrooms. It was quite clear: this was a Golden Oldies show, exactly what the ageing, 80,000-strong audience required, a victory for the back catalogue of the Rolling Stones. It was also clear who was and who was not really a member of the group: at the end of the show, Mick, Keith and Charlie Watts came out to wave triumphantly at the crowd, but not Ron Wood, as though he was still depping from the Faces. Another day, another four million dollars.

CHAPTER 23

WHAT, ME WORRY?

Even before the final London *Bridges to Babylon* dates had been played, Mick was receiving intimations that the increase in his fortune that the tour had brought might not be permanently resident in his various bank accounts. In July 1999, press reports revealed that not only had Mick been having an eight-month-long affair with a London-based Brazilian model called Luciana Morad, but that she was now pregnant by him, and seeking a chunk of his fortune as a settlement – she had already refused the £300,000 Mick had offered as a once-and-for-all pay-off. Luciana, whose mother was a Brazilian soap-opera star, lived in south-west London, and described Mick as 'kind of handsome in his skinny little way'. She had first met him at the Stones' *Bridges to Babylon* concert in Rio de Janeiro. When she was eighteen, Luciana Morad had had an affair with the then forty-five-year-old Rod Stewart, one of Mick's long-standing rivals in the rock 'n' roll bedroom stakes. Her name had also been 'linked' with Jean-Claude Van Damme; she allegedly had an IQ of 165 and spoke five languages. She gave birth to an eight-pound boy, Lucas, who was Mick's seventh child. (At the Wembley dates, Mick Jagger added a new line to the chorus of the song 'Some Girls': '*Some girls give me babies I didn't ask for*' ...)

Hardly unexpectedly, Mick had mentioned nothing to Jerry Hall about Luciana, only telling her about the pregnancy when he learned that news of it would be breaking in the following morning's newspapers. Around the time of the revelations, Mick and Jerry both attended the sports day of James, their eldest son, a frosty atmosphere between them as Mick concentrated on joining in a game of cricket. That week, Mick had also been photographed leaving the Chelsea town house of Vanessa Neumann, a Venezuelan heiress, who owned a house in Mustique, where he had met her. In the wake of the news of his relationship with Luciana Morad, there were further revelations: model Nicole Kruk told papers how Mick had smeared her body with crème caramel before licking it off; Beverly Hills television sex therapist Natasha Terry spoke of her 'three-in-a-bed romp' with Mick; Hungarian porn star Orsolya Dessey said that Mick had kissed her 'all over' on a hotel sofa ('He's a deliciously sensitive man. He made sure I had a wonderful time, although deep down he seemed extremely lonely.')

Jerry also discovered that a few days before one of his visits with Luciana Morad, Mick had had a 'date' with Carla Bruni, his old Italian flame. Jerry was seen glaring at her husband at a dinner party thrown by Elton John; all evening Mick proceeded to become more and more drunk, and was reduced to performing backing vocals when Elton sang. Jerry called up Mishcon de Reya once again, and was said to be seeking a £50-million settlement package. Mick, meanwhile, was angry and unhappy about the reported modelling ambitions of his daughter Elizabeth. News of the pending divorce led to assessments of his wealth; there were all the properties: as well as the house in Richmond, he owned La Fourchette, a chateau in the Loire valley near Amboise with its own recording studio, valued at £1.2 m; a brownstone house in New York's Upper West Side, valued at £2.5 m; and Stargroves, the multi-million-pound Japanese-style house on Mustique, one of only eighty-six properties on the island, that he had named after the Berkshire mansion he had sold long before. He was also rumoured to own another property in London, a house behind Barnes Common, that was on the way back to Richmond from the West End, and that he kept for discreet liaisons.

When Mick first suggested he would fight a ruthless battle over the divorce, Jerry sent a copy to his lawyers of what she might write in another autobiography unless a just settlement was arrived at. Jerry's final payout included £10 million in cash, £105,000 per annum maintenance, the ownership of their house in Richmond and financial arrangements for their four children, still leaving Mick with a considerable amount of his estimated £200-million fortune. Mick tried successfully to contest that their marriage was unlawful, employing a pair of experts in Indonesian matrimonial law, managing to persuade the court that the wedding on the Bali beach was invalid. 'Over that he behaved quite badly – no doubt about it – but I think he does regret it,' said Jerry considerately. 'They never told me it wasn't a proper marriage. As far as my family, my friends and I am concerned, Mick and I got married.' (The divorce from Jerry was not good for Mick's image: 'The Nijinsky of the rock stage metamorphosed into a randy old skinflint vainly seeking to renew his youth with girls young enough to be his daughter; pathetically unable to commit himself even to a woman who had borne him four children, and willing to resort to any stratagem that might stop her getting her hooks into his cash,' wrote Philip Norman in the *Sunday Times* magazine.)

'I should have put my foot down a lot earlier,' said Jerry, a year after the initial revelation. 'If I'd done that, we might not have divorced. I always hoped that one day he'd outgrow it, but it's humiliating loving someone so much that you forgive the infidelities. I should have been very firm. I should just have said: "Look, I'm not putting up with this", and been strong enough to walk out.' In the end, Mick moved into his own apartment in their Richmond home, and he and Jerry appeared to be frequent and close companions; there was a general feeling that Jerry had turned the tables and got the better of him.

On 7 February 2001, Mick Jagger was ordered by a New York court to pay $10,000 a month to Luciana Morad for the upkeep of their twenty-month-old son Lucas. Initially, Mick had attempted to deny being Lucas's father, demanding a DNA test before admitting paternity. As the result of her new fame, Luciana was given her own television show in Brazil.

At the end of March 2000 Mick returned for the first time since he had left the establishment to Dartford Grammar School, to open the £2.25 million lottery-funded Mick Jagger Performing Arts Centre. Memories of school-friends of Mick were dredged up. 'He wasn't a rebel in any way,' said Dick Taylor, of this famous member of the MCC. 'He worked well, was quite bright and did a lot of sports. He was a nice guy to have around, he wasn't disruptive. He never got into real trouble, as far as I can remember. His accent at school was quite fine. He was one of the best-spoken people there.'

At the end of November 2000 Mick Jagger presented the Literary Review's Bad Sex Award to the writer Sean Thomas at the Naval and Military Club. 'I assume I was chosen for this because I'm a musician,' suggested Mick, 'and there's no such thing as bad sex with a musician. Bad sex is no sex. It's quantity really, not quality.' The audience applauded his candour.

Always anxious to keep his career moving, Mick embarked on a major project, something he had been threatening for many years: with Victoria Pearman, a Los Angeles-based American producer, he formed Jagged Films, with several movies in development. The one on which most progress had been made was *Enigma*, a film of Robert Harris's novel about the cracking of the Enigma code used by German U-boats during the Second World War. The script was to be written by the playwright and screenwriter Tom Stoppard, whose work Mick Jagger had long admired and with whom he was friends.

Three months after Robert Harris had a meeting with Stoppard at his Chelsea apartment, the prospective scriptwriter asked Harris to show him around Bletchley Park, where the Enigma code had been deciphered. Michael White, the British film and theatre producer, was there; so was Mick Jagger, his 'arrival, complete with bodyguard, in the busy public bar provoking one of those stunned silences that usually only happen in westerns. He was not at all what I had expected. My vague prejudice that he was just a rock star indulging himself in a new hobby was dispelled almost from the moment he opened that famous mouth. For one thing, he seemed to have read every important book that had been published about Enigma. And he was serious. When we arrived at the Park – to the astonishment of a visiting busload of pensioners – he produced a video camera and filmed everything he was shown: the huts, the wireless sets, the replica of Colossus (the first computer), an Enigma machine.' (When Mick Jagger introduced Harris to Charlie Watts, at a party at the house on Richmond Hill, the Rolling Stones drummer's humorous truculence reassured Harris about Mick's seriousness. 'So you're the fucker who's responsible,' he said. 'I'm sick of hearing about fucking *Enigma*. It's all he ever talks about – who says what to who in what scene and when.')

Once the script was completed, the film could not progress until a director was found. After Ridley Scott and Peter Weir both passed on the film, they found a more suitable candidate: Michael Apted, the British director who had made *Coal Miner's Daughter*, *Gorky Park* and *Gorillas in the Mist*, among other films in an impressive body of work. The budget was set at £13.5 million. However, Apted was now slated to direct the next James Bond film, *The World is Not Enough*. Although this would occupy him for the following year, it had the consequence of considerably upping his bankability. In February 2000, Mick learned that Kate Winslet, also hugely bankable after the enormous success of *Titanic*, suddenly had a 'window' in her career; having recently learned she was pregnant (nothing to do with Mick), Winslet had pulled out of a long-term project and was free to film immediately, provided she had finished work by May, when the pregnancy would begin to show.

Although extremely hands-on on the set of *Enigma*, Mick found himself obliged to work within the democratic parameters of film-making, something that apparently did not come easily after over thirty years of autocratic rule with the Rolling Stones. 'It's like being in a very large rock band in which everyone's got an opinion, and those opinions aren't always valid 'cos they're from people who are not, sort of, in it. They're only saying it as an extension of their own ego,' he said, clearly not perceiving the irony in his words. Mick admitted that the length of time required to make the film taxed his short attention span: 'Quite often when I record a song, writing it and making a demo is the big thing and, after that, I think, how do I actually translate this into real life? A lot of the time I think I can't be bothered. It would be so much easier if I just had it and played it to myself. Because the rest of it is very time-consuming.'

In April 2000, Eva Jagger, the only person who still addressed her son as 'Michael', was admitted to hospital in Wimbledon in south-west London, suffering from heart abnormalities. She never fully recovered, and on 25 May Eva passed away. Mick flew back from Cannes, where he had been publicising *Enigma*. At the funeral service at St Andrew's church in Ham, near Richmond in Surrey, all Mick's family was in attendance. Fighting back his tears, accompanied by his brother Chris on guitar, Mick led the congregation in an emotional performance of the traditional gospel song 'Will The Circle Be Unbroken', and his mother's two favourite hymns, 'Morning Is Broken' and 'Abide With Me'. Jade, his daughter by Bianca, sobbed uncontrollably. Mick was red-eyed, and was reunited more closely with Jerry at the funeral, where she visibly comforted him. Charlie Watts, Ron Wood and Keith, who flew in from the United States, were there to support their friend. Four months later, in September, ninety-year-old Bert Richards also died, of old age, at Keith's house in Connecticut, his son at his bedside. Bert was cremated after a small private funeral.

When *Enigma* hit British cinemas in the Spring of 2001, it received good reviews, which frequently concentrated on its abiding vein of rather old-fashioned Englishness, one of warm beer and Harris tweed jackets and open-topped roadsters. Speaking of the limitations of such a specifically 'English' film, Mick explained, 'I didn't want to make teenage comedies, and I didn't want to make really trashy films. I wanted to make films that were a bit challenging, to be honest. I thought this was a good example of that. That doesn't mean to say I don't want to see trashy teenage movies every now and then. Or lots of movies with what my small children call "splosions" in them. But I don't want to work on them.'

Mick gave junketsful of interviews to promote the picture. 'He moves in his seat like a man registering small electric shocks, and talks off the top of his head in long, mad sentences that just keep unravelling,' Emma Brockes described one of the interviews in the *Guardian*: ' "I think movies in the country, it's very complicated, and we could bang on about it for ever, but because English movies are made in English, it's a very strange animal, and the French movie industry is very different because it's very obviously French." He beams.' Jagged Films was to be an ongoing entity. Mick was said to have written a script himself, a potential Jagged Films production, an 'autobiopic' that dealt with the rise of a rock phenomenon and his relationships with his parents and later his own family. The production company was also developing a script, entitled *The Map of Love*, about the relationship between the poet Dylan Thomas and his wife Caitlin.

When Neil Norman asked Mick in the *Evening Standard* what advice he would give his sons and daughters, he replied thoughtfully: 'At the risk of sounding boring, I would say that if you can, you should follow the things you really love to do. You should not be sidetracked because you have to pay the mortgage. I know that's easy for me to say, but I think you should follow your desires, especially in creative fields. It would be difficult for a more prosaic career. You know, "Follow your love of accounting". I gave a talk at a school careers lecture recently. It all seemed so boring and dull. It didn't excite you. Life is very, very exciting.'

What was exciting Mick now was the prospect of another solo album. The amount of energy Mick put into the pre-publicity for this record, *Goddess in the Doorway*, was unprecedented, almost as though he was making such an effort because it was shockingly frightening to step outside of the Rolling Stones. His enormous insecurity – this, after all, is the man whom Alexis Korner had decided was driven by fear – led to his seeming never to be out of the British press for a single day for the two years before the release of *Goddess*. It was overkill, far too much Mick, thank you, until the only response his image drew was a stifled yawn.

The final shot in this round of self-promotion was a self-produced television documentary, *Being Mick*, directed by Kevin Macdonald, who had won an Oscar for Best Documentary at the 2000 Academy Awards. Even accepting the vanity-publishing nature of the project, discriminating audiences still accepted the good-bloke image of Mick that was cleverly presented: you could see just how much he really liked the idea of being Mick Jagger.

But life is much harder outside of the gang: the record flopped badly, publicly; slightly to his surprise, it seemed, he had found that the name 'Mick Jagger' still carried far less brand loyalty than the still clumsy-sounding 'Rolling Stones'. In a readers' poll in *Q* magazine of the 100 greatest music stars of the twentieth century, Keith Richards, of whom you almost never heard, came in at number 11, Mick at 22 – Keith, the cool muso who loves his guitar more than his bank balance versus Mick Jagger, the hard businessman and friend of the paparazzi.

The difference in their choice of Caribbean residences defines Mick and Keith. Keith adores the shabby, frayed-at-the-edges charm of wild, dystopian Jamaica; Mick loves neat, opulent, safe Mustique, which he may well feel is a more appropriate location for holidays with his children. Having spent much of the 1960s deriding the idea of the family unit, he is – paradoxically, considering his unmarried status – now very much the family man (and ever keen on expanding that family, it seems). He seems genuinely to like all the women with whom he has had affairs, and – as he always has done – often falls in love with them quite easily. Mick hyped himself up as the great stud, until he became what he wished to be; the old adage of being careful what you wish for, for it might come true, seems to have been borne out in ways to which Mick doesn't really seem to object. All the same, he seems happiest when talking about his children. Holidaying in Mustique with his daughter, he takes a suitcase containing only the suit of armour his daughters like him to don, when they address him as Sir Omeletto. As well as loving music and making records, which he prefers to performing on-stage, he has an incredible fondness for business. And, courtesy of assiduous, almost obsessive exercising, he still has that twenty-eight-inch waist.

Keith tucked himself away in Jamaica following the *Bridges to Babylon* tour, emerging for the 1999 *Q* Awards to receive a lifetime achievement gong (little did he know it, but Keith was the second choice, after former Clash singer Joe Strummer, who, on tour in the United States, was obliged to send his regrets). Keith seemed disapproving of Mick's favourite hobby: 'He's intent on being Casanova or Don Juan. He's always looking for it, which is a little cruel on his loved ones. I don't talk to Mick about his love life because it's like: "Whoops! You've skidded on another banana skin." '

Mick 'n' Keith: does Keith Richards, the man who is always mentioned as the second of the pair, feel forever in the shadow of Mick Jagger? Would Keith have lived a different life within the Rolling Stones if their double-act had been billed 'Keith 'n' Mick'? In their modes of speech can be heard the separate life-courses taken by the two Dartford boys. Social chameleon Mick can have any variety of accents, whatever the moment requires: 'Mockney' whine, thoughtful received English (useful for interviews with broadsheet newspapers, or school prize-giving ceremonies), mid-Atlantic rock-star prattle ('Awright? Awright-awright-awright! Whoo!'). For Keith, long gone are the fey, elfin-prince hushed tones of the mid-1970s; now he speaks in a gruff, seemingly permanently slurred semi-Jamaican accent, falling into patois at the oddest of moments: there are those who run into him frequently who claim not to be able to understand a word he says. With time Keith's nose seems to have grown broader, more defined, until you might wonder if he hasn't had some expensive nasal reconstruction job; his hair, hung with totems and tie-ons, has the patched greyness of a storm-cloud.

During the *Bridges to Babylon* tour there had been reports that Keith was back on smack. Describing himself as 'an amateur chemist, a drug-ologist' to *GQ*, Keith admitted that he had had 'a little taste' of heroin on the group's most recent tour. But he claimed he hadn't seriously fallen back into his old ways. 'In the old days, I really didn't want to deal with being a star every day, and you could kind of hide inside heroin. It was like a cocoon, a soft wall between you and everything else.'

It has become increasingly clear to what extent the Keef badman image is simply an art-school version of showbiz, with all the talk of guns and knives, all the macho outlaw bullshit. But then, that's his construct, that's his existence, that's how it works for him. And he really seems to be happy. At various times everyone loves it, Keith living out his task as an archetype. The fact is that Keith has a job many men would adore: all he has to do most of the time is stay at home, lie on his couch and listen to very loud music and take drugs. 'The sainted Keith Richards that every man secretly wants to go to bed with,' as David Gates, the author of *Preston Falls*, has a female character remark in the cult novel.

At a dinner party in London, the novelist Fay Weldon found herself seated next to Mick Jagger. 'He talked about the merits of different brands of washing machines and the rules of life, which are the rules of laundry: take care, take time, take lots of water and get it right,' she told the *Sunday Times*. In the diary section of the edition of the *Evening Standard* dated 6 December 2001, the following item was tucked away: 'An unlikely rapport has sprung up between Chelsea Clinton and Bianca Jagger, ex-wife of Mick. The daughter of the former President, who is studying for a Masters in International Relations at Oxford, was invited by Bianca to hear her lecture on human rights at Westminster Cathedral last night. Bianca's subject, "Justice and Revenge", was, she joked, one her marriage to Mick had well prepared her for, before she turned her attention to the abuses of human rights worldwide.' Seemingly a changed – or, perhaps, misjudged – woman, Bianca had altered her life irrevocably and impressively. No longer the superbabe riding into Studio 54 on a white charger, by the 1990s she had revealed the depth of her commitment to radical change, using her position in society to point out its radical ills, writing newspaper articles about massacres of Bosnian Muslims and sitting on committees for Amnesty International, speaking out against globalisation. In April 2002, she was in Jenin, seeking the truth about the massacre of Palestinians in the town.

The edition of the London *Evening Standard* magazine dated 23 March 2001 contained a picture of a suitably dissolute-looking individual captioned 'Keith Richards'. Except that it was Ron Wood.

In the summer of 2001, a ten-year-old boy at Emanuel school in south-west London went looking around the buildings for a friend called Turner. In the music room who should he walk into but Mick Jagger, checking out the establishment as a possibility for his daughter Georgia.

At a fashionable dinner party that same summer, in the inevitable ultra-hip and moneyed location of London's Notting Hill, Peter Mandelson, the controversial close friend of Prime Minister Tony Blair and *enfant terrible* of the ruling Labour Party, was heard to voice his thoughts: 'Oh, we'd love to give Mick a knighthood. But we can't give a knighthood to Mick and not to Keith. And we can't possibly give one to Keith.' Mandelson and Jagger might not have seemed the most likely pairing, but they did have a number of friends in common. Both men had been guests of the Marquis of Cholmondeley at Houghton Hall in Norfolk, where Mandelson reputedly impressed Mick with his brisk daily jogs in the grounds of the eighteenth-century mansion. The late Princess Margaret, Mick's old friend, was said to have been a campaigner for his being knighted; her nephew Prince Charles, the Prince of Wales, had expressed surprise when Mick told him there never had been any hint that he might receive an honour. Peter Mandelson, who in his role of 'Prince of Darkness' enjoyed unofficial royal connections, continued to push along the idea of a 'gong' for Mick Jagger. Clearly a Cabinet-level decision was reached. On 9 June 2002, the *Sunday Times* trumpeted its lead front-page story: 'At last, His Satanic Majesty is called to the Palace'. No more Sir Omeletto; arise, Sir Mick.

It was all useful publicity for the Rolling Stones tour that Mick had announced would begin in the United States in September ('Either we stay home and become pillars of the community or we go out and tour. We could not find too many communities that still needed pillars,' said Mick, always ready with a quote), two months after his fifty-ninth birthday and three months before that of Keith. Advertisements for the concerts would carry the tagline: 'THE TOUR THAT ONLY 1 BAND WOULD DARE TO ATTEMPT!' For this tour in their fortieth anniversary year, the Stones announced, they would play not only stadiums but also arenas and small theatres in the same towns.

Before this could take place, however, Mick travelled down to Jamaica, the actress and model Sophie Dahl in tow, to stay at Goldeneye in Ora-cabessa. As this day-sleeper does everywhere he goes, Mick immediately covered the slatted window shutters with black plastic bags. The staff at Goldeneye addressed him as 'Mr Jaguar'. 'That's an old joke,' Mick would riposte, slightly irritably, not appreciating that they genuinely believed this to be his name – to her face, they had called his friend Princess Margaret 'Mrs Queen'. Every day he'd go up to Keith's place where it was said the pair were writing songs.

How did Keith greet Mick when he drove over to Ocho Rios to Point of View? Was Mick aware of his Dartford schoolfriend's response on hearing the news of his imminent arrival in Jamaica? When he learned that Mick was flying down to the island, the Human Riff was in the Toscanini Italian restaurant at Harmony Hall, looking suitably timeless, like his waxwork, as he has done now for many years. 'Oh fuckin' hell!' groaned Keith. 'Wha's 'e comin' down 'ere for? Wha's 'e want?'

ACKNOWLEDGEMENTS

Many, many people have assisted in this book. Particular thanks are due for their indefatigable help and support to: Julian Alexander, Dave Ambrose, Adrian Boot, Mick Brown, Alan Card, Roy Carr, Lucinda Cook, Glen Colson, Trevor Dolby, Pam Esterson, Marianne Faithfull, Oliver Foot, Lynne Franks, Vivien Goldman, Barney Hoskyns, Dickie Jobson, Nick Kent, Don Letts, Nick Logan, Gered Mankowitz, Versa Manos, Sherif Mehmet, Charles Shaar Murray, Ian Preece, Robert Sandall, Alex Manos Salewicz, Cole Salewicz, Jon Savage, Neil Spencer, Julian Temple, Steve Thorpe, Andrew Tyler, Pandora White, Timothy White, Hal Willner. To those who have been omitted, my most sincere apologies.

NOTES

Among the countless articles and books consulted for this tome, special respect should go to the following (apologies to anyone excluded – it is not a conscious act!):

Chapter 1

Page 9
Mick Jagger: Primitive Cool by Christopher Sandford, Victor Gollancz, London 1993, p. 19.

Page 10
Stone Alone by Bill Wyman with Ray Coleman, Viking, London 1990, pp. 93, 325.

Mick Jagger: Primitive Cool, p. 20.

Page 11
Mick Jagger: Primitive Cool, p. 17.

Page 12
Mick Jagger: Primitive Cool, pp. 16, 18, 20.

Page 13
Mick Jagger: Primitive Cool, pp. 20, 21.

The Rolling Stones: A Life On the Road, eds Jools Holland and Dora Loewenstein, Virgin Books, London 1998, p. 10.

Stone Alone, p. 93.

Chapter 2

Page 14
Stone Alone,

Page 15
Stone Alone, p. 95.

Page 16
Stone Alone, p. 96.

The Rolling Stones: A Life On the Road, p. 10.

Keith: Standing in the Shadows by Stanley Booth and Bob Gruen, St Martin's Press, New York 1995, p. 13.

Chapter 3

Page 18
Mick Jagger: Primitive Cool, pp. 23, 24, 26.

Page 19
Stone Alone, pp. 93, 94.

Page 20
Mick Jagger: Primitive Cool, pp. 25, 26.

Page 21
Mick Jagger by Anthony Scaduto, W. H. Allen, London 1974,

Stone Alone, p. 94.

Page 22
Stone Alone, p. 95.

Page 23
Mick Jagger: Primitive Cool, p. 30.

Page 24
Mick Jagger: Primitive Cool, pp. 28, 32, 33.

Page 25
Mick Jagger: Primitive Cool, pp. 36, 37.

Page 26
Mick Jagger: Primitive Cool, p. 41.

Chapter 4

Page 28
Stone Alone, p. 96.

Page 29
Stone Alone, p. 97.

Page 30
Stone Alone, p. 97.

The Rolling Stones: A Life On the Road, p. 11.

Page 31
Stone Alone, p. 98.

The Stones by Philip Norman, Elm Tree Books, London 1984, p. 40.

Chapter 5

Page 32
Stone Alone, p. 98.

Page 33

Alexis Korner by Harry Shapiro, Bloomsbury, London 1996.

Mick Jagger: Primitive Cool, p. 44.

Page 34

Stone Alone, p. 93.

Page 36

Keith: Standing in the Shadows, pp. 29, 34, 35.

Stone Alone, p. 99.

Page 37

The Stones, p. 53.

Keith: Standing in the Shadows, p. 14.

Phelge's Stones: the Untold History of the Rolling Stones by James Phelge, Buncha Asshole Books, London 1999, pp. 115, 116, 151, 152.

Stone Alone, p. 125.

Page 52

Phelge's Stones: the Untold History of the Rolling Stones, pp. 98, 100, 107, 110, 112, 113.

Page 53

Phelge's Stones: the Untold History of the Rolling Stones, p. 28.

Page 55

Phelge's Stones: the Untold History of the Rolling Stones, p. 64.

Chapter 6

Page 56

Stone Alone, p. 129.

Mick Jagger, pp. 79, 80.

Page 57

Stoned by Andrew Loog Oldham, Secker & Warburg, London 2000, p. 186.

Page 59

Stone Alone, pp. 133, 135.

Stone Alone, p. 104.

Robert Greenfield *Rolling Stone* interview.

Page 45

Keith: Standing in the Shadows, pp. 39, 40.

Page 46

Stand Alone, p. 109.

Page 47

Stone Alone, pp. 75,108, 112, 113.

Page 48

Stone Alone, p. 116.

Phelge's Stones: the Untold History of the Rolling Stones, p. 54.

Page 49
Phelge's Stones: the Untold History of the Rolling Stones, p. 58.

Keith: Standing in the Shadows, p. 41.

Stone Alone, p. 106.

Page 50
Phelge's Stones: the Untold History of the Rolling Stones, p. 79.

Page 60
The Rolling Stones: A Life On the Road, p. 23.

Page 61
Phelge's Stones: the Untold History of the Rolling Stones, p. 198.

Page 62
Stone Alone, p. 149.

Stoned, p. 344.

Page 64
Stoned, p. 247.
Phelge's Stones: the Untold History of the Rolling Stones, p. 158.

Page 65
Phelge's Stones: the Untold History of the Rolling Stones, pp. 160–4, 265.

Chapter 7

Page 66
The Rolling Stones: A Life On the Road, p. 26.

Page 67
The Rolling Stones: A Life On the Road, pp. 23, 26.

Stone Alone, pp. 153, 155.

Page 68
Stone Alone, pp. 158, 172.

Page 69
Stone Alone, pp. 151, 156.

Phelge's Stones: the Untold History of the Rolling Stones, p. 217.

Page 70
Keith: Standing in the Shadows, p. 52.

The Stones, p. 89.

Page 71
Mick Jagger, p. 128.

Page 72
Stone Alone, pp. 167, 169, 182.

Page 75
The Rolling Stones: A Life On the Road, p. 26.

Stoned, pp. 267, 275.

Page 76
Faithfull: An Autobiography with David Dalton, Michael Joseph, London 1994, pp. 1–10.

Page 77
Faithfull, pp. 19–21.

Page 79
Phelge's Stones: the Untold History of the Rolling Stones, p. 295.

Stand Alone, p. 204.

Page 80
Phelge's Stones: the Untold History of the Rolling Stones, pp. 276, 281, 290.

Page 82
Phelge's Stones: the Untold History of the Rolling Stones,

Mick Jagger: Primitive Cool, p. 70.

Page 83
Be My Baby by Ronnie Spector with Vince Waldron, Macmillan, London 1991.

Page 84
The Stones, p. 124.

Mick Jagger, p. 132.

Page 85
Be My Baby,

Page 86
Phelge's Stones: the Untold History of the Rolling Stones, p. 357.

Chapter 8

Page 91
Keith: Standing in the Shadows, p. 61.

Chapter 9

Page 101
Groovy Bob, The Life and Times of Robert Fraser by Harriet Vyner, Faber and Faber, London 1999, p. 103.

Page 103
Mick Jagger, p. 142.

Page 141
Mick Jagger, p. 141.

Chapter 10
Page 106
Mick Jagger, p. 143.

Chapter 11
Page 112
Faithfull,

Mick Jagger,

Page 114
Mick Jagger,

The Stones,

Groovy Bob, The Life and Times of Robert Fraser, p. 138.

Page 115
The Stones,

Stone Alone,

Chapter 12
Page 117
The Stones,

Stone Alone,

Page 118
The Stones,

Stone Alone,

Faithfull,

Pages 119–22
Up and Down with the Rolling Stones by Tony Sanchez, William Morrow & Co. Inc., New York 1979.

The Stones,

Stone Alone,

Faithfull,

Page 123
Groovy Bob, The Life and Times of Robert Fraser, pp. 141, 142.

Keith: Standing in the Shadows, p. 75.

Page 125
The Stones, p. 187.

Page 127
Faithfull,

Jagger Unauthorised by Christopher Andersen, Simon & Schuster, New York 1993.

Page 128
Stone Alone,

Chapter 13
Page 129
Up and Down with the Rolling Stones,

The Stones,

Stone Alone,

Faithfull,

Page 130
The Rolling Stones: A Life On the Road,

Pages 131–4
Up and Down with the Rolling Stones,

The Stones,

Stone Alone,

Faithfull,

Page 135
Up and Down with the Rolling Stones, p. 82.

Groovy Bob, The Life and Times of Robert Fraser,

Page 136
Groovy Bob, The Life and Times of Robert Fraser, p. 175.

Page 137
Faithfull,

Page 138
Groovy Bob, The Life and Times of Robert Fraser, p. 197.

Up and Down with the Rolling Stones, p. 83.

Page 139
The Stones,

Page 140
Stone Alone, p. 493.

Page 141
Stone Alone, p. 469.

Page 143
Faithfull,

Page 144
Up and Down with the Rolling Stones, p. 108.

Stone Alone, p. 483.

Chapter 14

Page 152
Up and Down with the Rolling Stones,

Page 154
Stone Alone, p. 507.

Page 156
Faithfull,

Page 157
Faithfull,

Page 158
Keith: Standing in the Shadows,

Page 159
Keith: Standing in the Shadows,

Alexis Korner,

Page 160
Faithfull,

Chapter 15

Page 163
Stone Alone, p. 534.

Page 164
Faithfull,

Real Life: the Story of a Survivor by Marsha Hunt.

Chapter 16

Page 166
The Stones, p. 279.

Page 167
Faithfull,

Performance by Mick Brown, Bloomsbury, London 1999.

Page 168
Faithfull, p. 194.

Page 170
The Family by Ed Sanders, Hart-Davis, 1972.

Page 173
Keith: Standing in the Shadows, p. 108.

Page 174
Mick Jagger,

The Stones,

Pages 176–8

Bill Graham Presents by Bill Graham and Robert Greenfield, Doubleday, New
York 1992, p. 294.

Keith: Standing in the Shadows, p. 120.

The Stones,

Stone Alone,

Chapter 17

Page 179

Keith: Standing in the Shadows, p. 172.

The Stones, p. 306.

Page 180

Robert Greenfield *Rolling Stone* interview.

Page 181

Real Life: the Story of a Survivor, p. 134.

Page 182

Real Life: the Story of a Survivor, pp. 134, 135.

Page 184

Real Life: the Story of a Survivor, p. 138.

Keith: Standing in the Shadows, p. 128.

Page 185

Keith: Standing in the Shadows, p. 125.

Page 186

Faithfull,

Performance,

Page 187

Real Life: the Story of a Survivor,

The Stones,

Mick Jagger,

Page 189

The Stones,

Mick Jagger,

Up and Down with the Rolling Stones,

Page 190

Real Life: the Story of a Survivor, p. 143.

Page 191

Real Life: the Story of a Survivor, p. 146.

Page 192

Up and Down with the Rolling Stones, pp. 207, 208.

Page 194
Keith Richards by Victor Bockris, Da Capo Press, 1998, p. 186.
Up and Down with the Rolling Stones, p. 219.

Chapter 18
Page 196
The Stones, p. 318.

Page 199
Up and Down with the Rolling Stones, p. 272.

Page 200
Exile by Dominique Tarle, Genesis Publications, Guildford 2001.

Up and Down with the Rolling Stones,

Page 201
Exile,

Page 202
Exile,

Real Life: the Story of a Survivor,

Page 203
Exile,

Page 204
Exile,

Page 207
Stone Alone, p. 12.

Page 208
A Journey Through America with the Rolling Stones by Robert Greenfield,
    Panther, 1975.

Page 209
A Journey Through America with the Rolling Stones,

Page 210
A Journey Through America with the Rolling Stones,

Chapter 19
Page 215
Keith Richards,

Up and Down with the Rolling Stones,

Page 216
Up and Down with the Rolling Stones, p. 264.

Page 218
Up and Down with the Rolling Stones,

Keith Richards,

Page 220
Keith Richards,

Up and Down with the Rolling Stones,

Page 222
Keith Richards,

Up and Down with the Rolling Stones,

The Stones,

Page 223
Real Life: the Story of a Survivor, pp. 161, 162.

Page 226
Keith Richards,

Up and Down with the Rolling Stones,

The Stones,

Stone Alone, p. 14.

Page 228
Jagger Unauthorised,

Page 233
The Stones,

Holy Terror: Andy Warhol Close Up by Bob Colacello, HarperCollins, 1990.

Rebel Heart, an American Rock'n'roll Journey by Bebe Buell with Victor Bockris, St Martin's Press, New York 2002.

Page 234
Rebel Heart, an American Rock'n'roll Journey, pp. 100–2.

Page 235
Rebel Heart, an American Rock'n'roll Journey,

Jagger Unauthorised,

Chapter 20

Page 238
Alexis Korner,

Page 240
Keith Richards,

Up and Down with the Rolling Stones,

The Stones,

Page 242
You'll Never Eat Lunch In This Town Again by Julia Phillips, Heinemann, London 1991.

Page 245
Holy Terror: Andy Warhol Close Up,

Page 248
Keith Richards, p. 250.

Page 249
The Stones,

Page 252
The Stones,

Stone Alone,

Up and Down with the Rolling Stones,

Keith Richards,

Chapter 21

Page 255
The Stones,

Stone Alone,

Up and Down with the Rolling Stones,

Keith Richards,

Page 257
Real Life: the Story of a Survivor,

Page 261
Real Life: the Story of a Survivor,

Page 262
Keith Richards,

Page 263
Keith Richards,

Page 267
Keith Richards,

Page 269
Real Life: the Story of a Survivor,

Keith Richards,

Page 271
Keith Richards,

In addition, Massimo Bonanno's *The Rolling Stones Chronicles* (Plexus, 1997) has been of great assistance as a compilation of news stories; as has James Karnback and Carol Bernson's *The Complete Recording Guide to the Rolling Stones*. Innumerable newspaper and magazine articles and television and radio interviews have also been consulted.

BIBLIOGRAPHY

A Journey Through America with the Rolling Stones by Robert Greenfield, Helter Skelter Publishing, London 1997

Alexis Korner by Harry Shapiro, Bloomsbury, London 1996

Be My Baby by Ronnie Spector with Vince Waldron, Macmillan, London 1991

Bill Graham Presents by Bill Graham and Robert Greenfield, Doubleday, New York 1992

Exile by Dominique Tarle, Genesis Publications, Guildford 2001

Faithfull by Marianne Faithfull with David Dalton, Michael Joseph, London 1994

Groovy Bob, The Life and Times of Robert Fraser by Harriet Vyner, Faber & Faber, London 1999

Holy Terror: Andy Warhol Close Up by Bob Colacello, HarperCollins, 1990

Jagger Unauthorised by Christopher Andersen, Simon & Schuster, New York 1993

Keith Richards by Victor Bokris, Da Capo Press, 1998

Keith: Standing in the Shadows by Stanley Booth and Bob Gruen, St Martins Press, New York 1995

Mick Jagger by Anthony Scaduto, W. H. Allen, London 1974

Mick Jagger: Primitive Cool by Christopher Sandford, Victor Gollancz, London 1993

Performance by Mick Brown, Bloomsbury, London 1999

Phelge's Stones: the Untold History of the Rolling Stones by James Phelge, Buncha Asshole Books, London 1999

Real Life: the Story of a Survivor by Marsha Hunt

Rebel Heart, an American Rock'n'Roll Journey by Bebe Buell with Victor Bokris, St Martin's Press, New York 2002

Stone Alone by Bill Wyman with Ray Coleman, Viking, London 1990

Stoned by Andrew Loog Oldham, Secker & Warburg, London 2000

The Family by Ed Sanders, Hart-Davis, 1972

The Rolling Stones: a Life on the Road, eds Jools Holland and Dora Loewenstein, Virgin Books, London 1998

The Rolling Stones: Rip This Joint, The Stories Behind Every Song by Steve Appleford, Thunder's Mouth Press, New York 2000

The Stones by Philip Norman, Elm Tree Books, London 1984

Up and Down with the Rolling Stones by Tony Sanchez, William Morrow & Co., New York 1979

You'll Never Eat Lunch in This Town Again by Julia Phillips, Heinemann, London 1991

INDEX

Compiled by INDEXING SPECIALISTS (UK) Ltd., 202 Church Road, Hove, East Sussex BN3 2DJ. Tel: 01273 738299. E-mail: *richardr@indexing.co.uk* Website: *www.indexing.co.uk*